HELPING PARENTS SOLVE THEIR CHILDREN'S BEHAVIOR PROBLEMS

HELPING PARENTS SOLVE THEIR CHILDREN'S BEHAVIOR PROBLEMS

Edited by
Charles E. Schaefer
Andrew R. Eisen

JASON ARONSON INC.
Northvale, New Jersey
London

Copyright © 1998 by Jason Aronson Inc.

10 9 8 7 6 5 4 3 2 1

Library of Congress Cataloging-in-Publication Data

Helping parents solve their children's behavior problems / edited by
    Charles E. Schaefer, Andrew R. Eisen.
        p.   cm.
    Includes bibliographical references and index.
    ISBN 0-7657-0148-0 (alk. paper)
    1. Child psychotherapy—Parent participation. 2. Mental health
consultation. I. Schaefer, Charles E. II. Eisen, Andrew R.
RJ505.P38H45 1998
618.92'89—dc21   97-38469

Printed in the United States of America on acid-free paper. Jason Aronson offers books and cassettes. For information and catalog write to Jason Aronson Inc., 230 Livingston Street, Northvale, New Jersey 07647-1731. Or visit our website: http://www.aronson.com

To Anne,

C. E. S.

To Linda and Zachary,

A. R. E.

Contents

Preface

During the past thirty years, there have been numerous reports in the literature by behavior modifiers who have helped parents manage their children's behavior more effectively. Since parents are the most important persons in the lives of their children, they tend to have an enormous influence on their children's behavior. This influence is generally much greater than that which a mental health professional can have through an hour a week of individual therapy. Many experts believe that the potential of parents as behavior change agents has barely been tapped.

"Behavioral counseling" is the term usually applied to the approach in which therapists use strategies based on learning principles to help individual parents resolve specific behavior problems of their children. Parent involvement ranges from carrying out detailed instructions to participating as co-therapists in behavioral analysis and implementation of the treatment plan. In light of the available evidence, there is little doubt that parents can be trained in an individual way to apply behavioral techniques to resolve their children's behavior problems.

Behavioral counseling has been found to be an effective way for clinicians to resolve the perpetual "minimax" conflict of bringing about maximal behavioral change with minimal expenditure of professional time and energy. Behavioral counseling is a short-term, problem-focused, cost-effective treatment approach.

The purpose of this volume is to help mental health professionals help parents cope with specific behavior problems of childhood. Accordingly, the reader will find both contemporary and classical articles (that still ring true) from the professional literature which have a highly applied focus. Thus, this book contains articles of a practical nature which enable mental health professionals to give parents specific "how to" advice on resolving common behavior problems of childhood (infancy to age 13). Comprehensive in scope, the book deals with such problems as anxiety, nightmares, disruptive behaviors, bedwetting, thumbsucking, crying, dawdling, sibling rivalry, and noncompliance.

With the rapid approach of the twenty-first century comes the realization that to be a successful child therapist one must be able to work with the constraints of the managed-care revolution. To avoid being faced with clients whose insurance has "run out" before substantial therapeutic gains have been made, efficient, well-structured, and empirically supported approaches to therapy must be sought and put to use. Behavioral counseling represents one such approach.

Charles E. Schaefer, Ph.D.
Hackensack, New Jersey

Andrew R. Eisen, Ph.D.
Teaneck, New Jersey

Contributors

Christina D. Adams, Ph.D.
  Department of Clinical and Health Psychology
  University of Florida Health Science Center
  Gainesville, FL

Kenneth W. Allen, Ph.D.
  SA HealthPlus Care Plan Training Unit
  Flinders Medical Center
  Bedford Park
  South Australia

K. Eileen Allen, Ph.D.
  Department of Psychology
  University of Washington
  Seattle, WA

Teodoro Ayllon, Ph.D.
  Department of Psychology
  Georgia State University
  University Plaza
  Atlanta, GA

Nathan H. Azrin, Ph.D.
  Department of Psychology
  Nova Southeastern University
  Ft. Lauderdale, FL

Roger Bach, Ph.D.
  private practice
  Westwood, CA

Wesley C. Becker, Ph.D.
  Department of Psychology
  University of Illinois
  Champaign, IL

Karen L. Beckstrand, Psy.D.
  Forest Outpatient Clinic
  Forest Health System, Inc.
  Des Plaines, IL

David J. Biemer
  Program Review and Evaluation Division
  Texas Department of Human Resources
  Austin, TX

Michael L. Bloomquist, Ph.D.
  Division of Child and Adolescent Psychiatry
  University of Minnesota Hospital and Clinic
  Minneapolis, MN

T. Berry Brazelton, M.D.
  Department of Medicine
  Boston Children's Hospital
  Boston, MA

Joan S. Buell, Ph.D.
  Department of Psychology
  University of Washington
  Seattle, WA

Carole E. Calladine, ACSW
  private practice
  Cleveland, OH

Esther L. Cava, Ph.D.
  c/o Michael P. Cava
  15 Northshore Drive
  Tuscaloosa, AL

Debra L. Creedon, Ph.D.
  University of Mississippi Medical Center
  Jackson, MS

Patricia Dalton, Ph.D.
  private practice
  Washington, DC

Peter J. D'Amico, Ph.D.
  Bradley Hospital
  Riverside, RI

Ronald S. Drabman, Ph.D.
  Department of Psychiatry and Human Behavior
  University of Mississippi Medical Center
  Jackson, MS

V. Mark Durand, Ph.D.
  Department of Psychology
  SUNY at Albany
  Albany, NY

Andrew R. Eisen, Ph.D.
  Department of Psychology
  Fairleigh Dickinson University
  Teaneck, NJ

M. Jerome Fialkov, Ph.D.
  Western Psychiatric Institute and Clinic
  University of Pittsburgh School of Medicine
  Pittsburgh, PA

Joel Fischer, Ph.D.
  University of Hawaii School of Social Work
  Honolulu, HI

Wayne W. Fisher, Ph.D.
  The Kennedy-Krieger Institute
  Baltimore, MD

Richard M. Foxx, Ph.D.
  Penn State University, Harrisburg
  Behavioral Science Department
  Middletown, PA

Cynthia Frame, Ph.D.
  Department of Psychology
  University of Georgia
  Athens, GA

S. Frantz-Renshaw, Ph.D.
  Department of Psychology
  Nova Southeastern University
  Ft. Lauderdale, FL

Alice G. Friedman, Ph.D.
  Department of Psychology
  Binghamton University
  Binghamton, NY

Karl E. Goeke, Ph.D.
  Penn State University
  University Park, PA

Beatrice Hamilton, Ed.D.
  professional practice
  Delmar, MD

Rachel T. Hare-Mustin, Ph.D.
  private practice
  Haverford, PA

Florence R. Harris, Ph.D.
  Department of Psychology
  University of Washington
  Seattle, WA

Kelley A. Harrison, Ph.D.
  The Kennedy-Krieger Institute
  Baltimore, MD

Betty M. Hart, Ph.D.
  Department of Human Development
  University of Kansas
  Lawrence, KS

Cornelius J. Holland, Ph.D.
Department of Psychology
University of Windsor
Windsor, Ontario, Canada

Alan E. Kazdin, Ph.D.
Department of Psychology
Yale University
New Haven, CT

Jonathan Kellerman, Ph.D.
Children's Hospital of Los Angeles
Los Angeles, CA

Wallace A. Kennedy, Ph.D.
Department of Psychology
Florida State University
Tallahassee, FL

Bryan Lask, M.D.
Consultant Psychiatrist
The Hospitals for Sick Children
London, England

Ronald A. Madle, Ph.D.
Psychological Services
Sunbury, PA

Johnny L. Matson, Ph.D.
Department of Psychology
Louisiana State University
Baton Rouge, LA

Jodi A. Mindell, Ph.D.
Department of Psychology
St. Joseph's University
Philadelphia, PA

Sam B. Morgan, Ph.D.
Department of Psychology
Memphis State University
Memphis, TN

Joseph J. Moylan, Ph.D.
professional practice
Clayton, NC

Laura A. Nabors, Ph.D.
Department of Pediatrics
Division of Behavioral and Developmental Pediatrics
University of Maryland School of Medicine
Baltimore, MD

Robert Nehs, Ph.D.
professional practice
Detroit, MI

John Neisworth, Ph.D.
Penn State University
University Park, PA

Robert G. Nunn, Ph.D.
professional practice
San Diego, CA

K. Daniel O'Leary, Ph.D.
Department of Psychology
SUNY at Stony Brook
Stony Brook, NY

Susan O'Leary, Ph.D.
Department of Psychology
SUNY at Stony Brook
Stony Brook, NY

Thomas H. Ollendick, Ph.D.
Department of Psychology
Child Study Center
Virginia Polytechnic Institute and State University
Blacksburg, VA

Cathleen C. Piazza, Ph.D.
Severe Behavior Disorders Unit
The Kennedy-Krieger Institute
Baltimore, MD

Gina S. Richman, Ph.D.
Child and Family Therapy Clinic
Department of Psychology
The Kennedy-Krieger Institute
Baltimore, MD

Michael S. Rosenbaum, Ph.D.
Center for Cognitive-Behavioral Therapy
Mobile, AL

Joel A. Ross, Ph.D.
professional practice
Levittown, NY

Charles E. Schaefer, Ph.D.
Department of Psychology
Fairleigh Dickinson University
Teaneck, NJ

T. J. Sneed, Ph.D.
Anna State Hospital
Anna, IL

William A. Sonis, Ph.D.
National Institute of Child Health and Human Development
Bethesda, MD

Chris E. Stout, Psy.D.
Department of Clinical Research and Evaluation
Forest Health System, Inc.
Des Plaines, IL

Jane A. Summers, Ph.D.
The Kennedy-Krieger Institute
Baltimore, MD

Ralph Wetzel, Ph.D.
Consulting Psychologist,
private practice
Tucson, AZ

Montrose M. Wolf, Ph.D.
Department of Human Development
University of Kansas
Lawrence, KS

PART I
Assessment

1

An Interview Guide for Counseling Parents

CORNELIUS J. HOLLAND

This chapter outlines a procedure found helpful by the author as an interview guide when counseling parents for behavior problems of their children. A modified form of the present procedure based on "The Analysis of Human Operant Behaviour" by Reese (1966) and *Child Development 1* by Bijou and Baer (1961) was found to be readily understood by parents with secondary school educations who attended a clinical group led by the author to teach parents to apply behavioral principles, generally operant in nature, to a wide range of problems the parents were experiencing with their children.

The guide serves not only as a method for the interviewer to assemble the necessary data but simultaneously as a training aid for parents, especially when used in conjunction with such a book as *Living with Children* by Patterson and Gullion (1968). When the interview guide has been completed, most of the information necessary for behavioral analysis will have been gathered, as well as a selection of the procedures required by the parents to bring about change.

The points for analysis should be carried out as exhaustively as possible before the actual reinforcement program is introduced by the parents. It is better to have too much information than too little, and only with patient and repeated observation of the behavior and the environmental conditions within which the behavior occurs will the necessary clarity of the determinants emerge. For example, behavior such as tantrums may be a function of either positive reinforcement or avoidance. Although the topography of the behavior is similar, it is important to locate and specify the major controlling stimuli, that is, whether they occur antecedent or consequent to the behavior in question, and whether they have positive reinforcing or aversive properties.

Not every point covered will be equally appropriate for every behavior problem. With some cases such as tantrums, simple extinction procedures may be sufficient; with others, such as attempting to shift behavior from competition to cooperation, extinction, punishment, and positive reinforcement may be indicated and subsequently used in the total program. Nevertheless, it is well to cover every point. Often a complete coverage introduces the possibility of using simultaneously two or three techniques for behavior modification and, as such, enhances the possibility of success.

Readers will recognize the outline to be focused on the single child. However, other children in the environment present no need for additional principles. If parents experience some difficulty in modifying a child's behavior because of the intrusions or interferences of a second child, they merely must see these intrusions as behaviors on the part of the second child and apply the same principles to them accordingly. An example of this would occur when one sibling teases another and the teasing behavior is maintained by the reactions of the second child. In addition to reinforcing either positively or negatively nonteasing behavior of the first child, the parents may reinforce positively the second child whenever he does not react to the teasing in his usual manner, thus indirectly instituting an extinction procedure for the unwanted behavior.

A final point should be kept in mind. Although the author believes the outline follows the principles of reinforcement theory closely, the points covered are in a sequence which the author finds helpful to himself. Counselors who wish to use the outline may find other sequences more appropriate. It is also to be understood that the guide does not suggest the use of a mechanical gathering of information devoid of the rhythm and pace found in the counseling experience. The points covered in this guide are logical in nature and are not intended to place artificial constraints on the counselor or the parents. Neither are they intended as substitutes for the more traditional skills of a sensitive ear or a judicious tongue.

1. Have the parents establish general goals and complaints.

This step usually presents no problem for the parents or the psychologist since most of what the parents say concerning their child implicitly contains the present complaints (symptomatology) and goals (what the parents want the child to do or become). Usually much of this is revealed in the first interview. Subsequent interviews may serve to clarify, but it is the author's experience that general complaints and goals are readily isolated even though not explicitly stated by the parents.

The above does not imply that the interviewer is merely a passive recipient of information. It is surprising how often parents voice complaints about their children without being able to state clearly what they want the child to do, even in the general way discussed here. It is the job of the interviewer to make this vagueness on the part of the parents known to them so that they may become more definite about it themselves. Some problems with children probably find their inception just in this area, where demands are made by parents without any clear notion of what they want the child to do. Consider the frequent exhortation from parents for their child to be "good" without clarifying the terminal behavior which defines "goodness" for the parents. An interesting result of this clarification is that behavior often changes to some extent spontaneously in the desired direction before the parents put into operation any of the specific procedures for behavior change.

2. Have the parents reduce the general goals and complaints to a list of discrete behaviors which require an increase or decrease in frequency.

A procedure commonly used and found by the author to be helpful is to have the parents make a list of five or ten behaviors they wish to increase and five or ten they wish to decrease, and then have the parents rank order them in terms of severity or nuisance value. It has been the experience of the author that a generalized change in the child's behavior usually takes place after three or four behaviors have been systematically altered so that going through the entire list is unnecessary.

3. Have the parents select from the ranked list a single problem behavior on which to concentrate their efforts.

The behavior that is selected is often the one causing the most difficulty or the one most dangerous to the child's welfare. This suggestion of focusing on a single problem while ignoring the others is one of the most important ways of bringing about some kind of manageable order into the entire attempt at behavior modification. Often parents who make contact with child guidance centers feel overwhelmed and confused by the difficulties their children are having or causing. By suggesting a focus on one problem behavior, the parents can be relieved by dealing with the many other problems for the present. Also, by reducing the immediate requirements of the parents to more manageable proportions, it is more likely that any efforts at behavior change will meet with success. This in turn helps develop confidence in the methods used, and more importantly gives the parents some sense of control over what they formerly considered an almost hopeless situation.

4. Have the parents specify in behavioral terms the precise behavior that is presently occurring and which they desire to change.

This will require on the part of the parents a detailed observation of the behavior in concrete terms. By doing so the parents get closer to the actual behavior they want changed so that it becomes salient for them. Also, when they focus on the actual behavior, and not on inferences from the behavior, they are able to get a better idea of the frequency with which the behavior occurs. It is the change in frequency, consistent with operant psychology, which is the criterion of success or failure of the program.

5. Have the parents specify in behavioral terms the precise behavior which they desire.

This rule is very similar to the requirements of Number 4, but here the parents must articulate in behavioral terms the terminal behavior, or goal, for any problem which they wish to modify. The task for the interviewer is to help make the goals as clear and precise as possible. Not only is this rule important in terms of measuring the success of the program, but it often reveals the first step toward the goal.

6. Have the parents discuss how they may proceed to the terminal behavior in a step-by-step manner.

It is important for the parents to realize that it is often self-defeating to insist upon the terminal behavior immediately. For various reasons the child may not be capable of it either because the final behavior necessarily requires the foundation of prior learning, or the final behavior desired is of an aversive nature to the child.

Also important is the implication that, in proceeding in such a step-by-step fashion, the parents are required to make clear to themselves what is the first step toward the final goal. Often the first step or steps are already present in the child's repertoire but are ignored by the parents and thus remain at an operant level.

It is well, therefore, as an exercise for the parents to have them rehearse the steps required by the child in moving from his present behavior to the terminal behavior. By doing so, the parents are less likely to insist upon too much too soon, and will also better appreciate approximations already being made by the child toward the terminal behavior.

7. Have the parents list positive and negative reinforcers which they think will be effective in bringing about behavior changes.

Although the assumption being made throughout this interview guide is that behavior is maintained by environmental consequences of the behavior, it is not always easy for parents to isolate the reinforcers effective in controlling their child's behavior. Some of course are quite common, such as candy, but others (and probably the more important ones) are or may be quite specific to the child, such as being given the opportunity to make an independent choice. But it must be emphasized that discovering a reinforcer as being either positive or negative is an empirical matter for the most part which usually must be tested in a trial and error fashion. One complaint by parents heard by counselors in a guidance clinic is that what they consider rewarding for their children often has the opposite effect. As an extreme example, certain forms of praise or attention, if applied following behavior, may act as an aversive stimulus and thus be functionally punishing if the reinforcement history of the child were appropriate. More commonly, what are considered rewards by the parents are neutral for the children. There are, however, good guesses that can be made based on the fact that the child shares a common culture in which certain stimuli take on positive values for most of the children in it.

The task of the interviewer is to determine as completely as possible the total resources which are accessible to the parents or anyone else dispensing the reinforcers. It is helpful to explore systematically the social resources available to the parents, such as praise, attention, affection, or recognition; the physical resources available in the home, such as radio, TV, and games; and the activity resources available to the child, such as riding a bicycle or making a phone call. A list of these made by the parents is helpful in fitting the reinforcer to the desired behavior in as natural a manner as possible, as well as helping the parents realize the many reinforcers available to them which may be used when any unexpected situation occurs which makes immediate reinforcement desirable.

8. Have the parents discuss what deprivations are possible.

The value of a reinforcer fluctuates with the child's being either deprived or satiated with it. Withholding toys, for example, will enhance the value of a toy when it is given following a behavior which is desired. If toys are given haphazardly, they should not be expected to be effective in behavioral control. The same can be said for affection or praise or any other stimulus serving as a reinforcer.

Many parents are reluctant to deprive their children of praise or affection for obvious reasons even though an indiscriminate use of these reinforcers may actually be doing harm to the child. It has been the experience of the author, however, that children whose behavior is being modified by these procedures do not suffer a loss of positive reinforcers in the long run; in fact, there is usually a gain when the problem behavior begins to diminish and the parents are more comfortable with the child. It has also been the experience of the author that deprivation of such activities as watching TV or using the phone are often the only deprivation necessary to bring about desired change. More importantly, the child is usually in some deprived state already. Some piece of sports equipment that the child greatly desired but cannot have at present is a deprived state for these purposes; also such things as a pet, a watch, or a toy which the child values but does not have can be considered instances of deprived states. Therefore it is helpful to discuss with the parents the usually many things the child greatly desires but does not have, or is not obtaining as often as he desires.

9. Have the parents clearly establish what they want to do, either to increase or decrease a behavior or to do both.

This information has already been determined from the ranked list of behaviors which the parents wish to change. It is introduced again because in many instances parents do not merely wish to decrease a behavior but also to increase an incompatible behavior. It is helpful if they have clear what is required for the total modification desired. Much of the success of this method depends on the readiness on the part of the parents to act immediately, either by reinforcing or withholding a reinforcer, and a clear notion of what they desire helps them to do so.

10. Have the parents discuss the situation in which the desired behavior should occur.

The requirements for this step are to determine the discriminative stimuli for the desired behavior. If, for example, the parents desire to change their child's behavior from a withdrawn, isolated social style to one of more social participation with peers, the presence of the child's peers would be the discriminative stimuli, at which time any increase in social participation would be reinforced. If the parents desire an increase in obedience on the part of their child, the situation or discriminative stimulus would be the verbal statement of the request or demand made by the parents. The behavior that is desired need not occur all the time but only under certain specifiable stimulus conditions, and isolating these stimulus conditions allows the parents to become aware of the precise circumstances in which reinforcement is to take place.

11. Have the parents discuss the situation in which the undesired behavior should not occur.

The behavior that is unwanted and should be decreased occurs under specifiable stimulus conditions. These also have to be made known, for they constitute discriminative conditions for some positive reinforcer which they must become aware of and withhold if possible. A not uncommon occurrence is found when children throw tantrums in stores but do not do so at home. The child has learned that tantrum behavior does not yield to positive reinforcers except under the discriminative conditions in which the mother will give in to the child in order to terminate the aversive tantrum which for the mother occasions social embarrassment.

12. Have the parents determine a situation which increases the likelihood that some form or portion of the desired behavior occurs.

If, for example, the parents desire to increase their child's obedience, it is likely that sometimes the child is obedient. It is also likely that the obedience often goes unrewarded. It is precisely at these times that the program should focus its initial efforts, for strengthening the

behavior under a structured situation will usually increase the likelihood of its occurrence under those conditions in which it is not now
occurring.

Another example would be the attempt to increase cooperative
behavior between sibs who show too much hostile competition. It is
unlikely that competition occurs every time the children are together.
Those times in which the children are together and are either cooperative or at least noncompetitive can be used by the parents as a situation in which they introduce some structure for the desired behavior.
If the parents know, for example, that a certain toy or activity usually
results in some cooperative behavior on the part of the sibs, at least
for a while, this could be used by the parents as the structured situation to begin the reinforcing of the desired behavior. If it were decided
that the first step toward the final terminal behavior of prolonged cooperation was to have one minute of cooperative or noncompetitive
play, the parents would reinforce after that period.

13. Have the parents discuss how they may increase desired behavior by immediately giving a positive reinforcer following the behavior.

This of course is a basic principle of reinforcement theory. The
crucial requirement is the immediate application of the reinforcer. The
efficiency of this program depends on the availability to the parents of
effective primary or secondary reinforcers which can be given immediately. Parents with whom the author has worked are usually quite able
to develop star systems or other token economies, a certain number of
which could be exchanged for backup reinforcers.

A most effective reinforcer of course is the verbal stimuli of the
parents, which constitute praise or recognition. It has sometimes been
found, however, that the parents' verbal behavior must first be paired
with backup reinforcers for it to become effective as a viable acquired
reinforcer in a program such as this.

It has also been found necessary at times to work out a system
whereby any token reinforcer is at first able to translate almost immediately into a backup reinforcer which the child can enjoy. It is often
too much to expect a child to accumulate fifteen or twenty tokens in
order to obtain a backup reinforcer when one of the problems the child
is having is an intolerance for delay of gratification.

In any event, the parents should be instructed to give some form
of praise whenever they give another reinforcer. Social reinforcers are

ultimately more relevant because they are less arbitrary and less artificial reinforcers in the child's broader social world.

14. Have the parents discuss how they may increase desired behavior by immediately terminating a negative reinforcer following the behavior.

Both positive and negative reinforcement strengthen preceding behavior, and both can be employed effectively in the program, although usually the positive reinforcement method is the chief instrument for change. However, if parents insist on certain activities on the part of their children, such as doing the dishes, and the child finds this to be aversive, a relief from this chore can be an important source of negative reinforcement and could be effectively used.

15. Have the parents discuss how they may decrease undesired behavior by withholding the reinforcers which follow it.

The requirements here on the part of the parents are to discover what stimuli are at present maintaining the undesired behavior, and to institute an extinction procedure. This often runs into several difficulties. The parents themselves may be providing the maintaining reinforcer. For example, a child of 9 who was a chronic complainer apparently was being reinforced by his mother's concern and her getting upset. Since she had developed a habit of responding to him in this way, it was especially difficult to have her withhold this reinforcer. Again, children are often systematically taught by their parents that positive reinforcers will occur only under forms of tantrum behavior which are so shrill and upsetting to the parents that they cannot tolerate them for any length of time. It is important for the interviewer to show the parents that "giving in" after prolonged or especially shrill tantrums is a learning experience for the child, leading to a prolonging or intensification of the undesired behavior.

Another difficulty is that extinction procedures often increase the undesired behavior initially. In the example cited above with the 9-year-old boy, when the mother began to ignore him, his first reaction was to increase the complaining both in frequency and intensity.

A third difficulty is that extinction is a vastly different procedure from intermittent reinforcement. Unless the parents are made to see the differential effects of each, withholding of the maintaining reinforcer may not be complete and may lead to a resistance to extinction. It is for the above reasons that the author has found extinction to be most

effective when there exists the possibility of combining it with positive
or negative reinforcement of incompatible behavior.

The fourth difficulty, and perhaps the most serious, is the fact that
often the parents do not have control over the maintaining reinforcer.
Another way of saying that parents have lost control over their child's
behavior is to say that the undesired behavior is being effectively controlled by other people, agencies, or circumstances. Although this situation introduces real difficulties, some of which may never be overcome,
a solution can often be achieved by the reinforcement of incompatible
behavior if the reinforcer used for the incompatible behavior is of greater
value to the child than the reinforcer presently controlling the undesired behavior.

**16. Have the parents discuss how they may decrease undesired
behavior by removing a positive reinforcer.**

This is a punishment-by-loss technique which may prove effective
in suppressing behavior long enough for the desired behavior to occur. Although many children who come to guidance clinics have been
punished often enough already, the author believes such a procedure
may at times be the only technique effective in suppressing a behavior
whose necessity to change is obvious. Behaviors such as running out
into the street between parked cars, firesetting, and physically abusive
behavior toward another child readily come to mind as behaviors in
which the parents cannot wait for the reinforcement of incompatible
behavior to occur, or for extinction to take place.

The threat of punishment-by-loss can also be used, the threat being
seen as a conditioned aversive stimulus. It must be discovered, however, whether or not threats from the parents have actually acquired
aversive properties, as often threats have not been followed up by the
parents in the past and are therefore looked on by the child not as a
discriminative stimulus for punishment but as neutral stimuli.

**17. Have the parents discuss how they may decrease undesired
behavior by time-out.**

Time-out is any procedure in which the child is removed from the
source of positive reinforcers. Putting the child in his room for a certain period of time or in the familiar corner is a common time-out
procedure. It must be carried out in such a way, however, that the child
does experience a loss of reinforcers; putting a child in his room where

many of his toys are available to him could not be considered a time-out procedure.

Often when a child has been given a time-out period, at least if this has not been a common punishing procedure in the family, the child will react very strongly in a negative manner. It is well to establish at the beginning the time-out procedure as a punishment by making the relief from the room or corner contingent upon a set period of time in which none of the negative behavior has occurred. If it does occur, relief from the time-out period should be made contingent upon the absence, for a specified period of time, of the undesired negative behavior.

18. Discuss with the parents how they may pattern the reinforcers they give to the child.

The parents should give reinforcers every time the desired behavior occurs until it becomes strongly established, then they should give them randomly. This is the familiar shift from a continuous reinforcement schedule to a variable interval or variable ratio. There are no ready rules with which the author is familiar to move from a continuous to an intermittent schedule. It seems desirable, however, to tell the child that he shouldn't expect a reward every time the desired behavior occurs, even when the child is still being reinforced continuously. It also seems desirable to move from a continuous through a fixed schedule before establishing a random one.

19. Have the parents discuss how they may vary the reinforcers they give to the child.

The parents will have available to them a list of reinforcers which they are reasonably sure are positive for the child. The parents have options of giving different amounts of the same reinforcers or different reinforcers. Varying the reinforcers enhances the probability that desired behavior, when it occurs, will be maintained for long periods of time.

20. Have the parents discuss how they may apply two or more procedures simultaneously.

Success is enhanced by the parents having at their disposal as many procedures as can be applied to the behavior in question. The most obvious situation is an extinction procedure coupled with positive reinforcement of incompatible behavior, but other combinations are also possible and should be explored depending on the nature of the behavior the parents wish to change.

21. Have the parents rehearse verbally the entire program.

This will require that they are able to specify clearly each step covered by the program. Such rehearsal enhances the success of the program by making salient to them such crucial issues as the terminal behavior stated in behavioral terms, any incipient behavior present, the initial steps toward the goal, the discriminative stimuli involved, and the reinforcers which must be withheld or supplied.

References

Bijou, S., and Baer, D. (1961). *Child Development 1: A Systematic and Empirical Theory.* New York: Appleton Century Crofts.

Patterson, G. R., and Gullion, M. E. (1968). *Living with Children: New Methods for Parents and Teachers.* Champaign, IL: Research Press.

Reese, E. (1966). The analysis of human operant behaviour. In *Introduction to Psychology: A Self-Selection Test,* ed. J. Vernon. Dubuque, IA: William C. Brown.

2

A Single Interview

ESTHER L. CAVA

The effectiveness of training parents to modify their child's problem behavior has been well established. Karoly and Rosenthal (1977) found that after training parents in consistency, time-out, positive reinforcement, and so on, the child's deviant behaviors had been reduced. In addition, the general home atmosphere improved. Forehand and King (1977) found that not only had the child become more compliant after parent training but parent attitudes toward the child's behavior had changed. Hobbs and Forehand (1977) demonstrated the effectiveness of parental use of time-out for oppositional behavior. Webster-Stratton and colleagues (1988) found that children whose parents watched a videotape modeling treatment of child behavior problems improved; behavior problems were significantly reduced. Numerous other studies report essentially similar findings: parents can be trained to effect changes in their child's behavior.

This should not seem remarkable. After all, parents use behavior modification, whatever their child rearing practices are, even if they are often not aware of the fact and even if their approach is frequently random (Bandura 1969). And despite the popularity of day care, parents still appear to be the earliest and most important authority figures who can influence a child's behavior, particularly during the child's early and, what many believe, critical preschool years.

O'Dell (1974) outlines a number of reasons why teaching parents behavior modification techniques can be effective: the techniques are relatively easy for lay individuals to learn and to carry out; they can be learned relatively quickly, parents seem to prefer treatment that does not imply that the child is "mentally ill," and many of the child's behavior problems correspond to specific concrete behaviors which tend to be amenable to a behavior modification approach.

This chapter describes the training of parents in behavior modification techniques during a single interview. The format was in response to a long waiting list and was devised as a palliative treatment. Follow-up telephone calls revealed that the treatment was, in most cases, effective. The sole purpose of the single training session was to outline for the parents behavior modification techniques which might, at least, reduce the severity of the problem. The hope was that, if nothing else was accomplished, by being seen the parents' tension and anxiety, generated by waiting for help, might be reduced.

The possibility that parents could be trained to modify their child's behavior during a single interview was derived from the author's experience in advising parents of noncompliant nursery school children. The parents of these children preferred not to apply to the mental health clinic but were amenable to attending a single didactic parenting session. According to an informal follow-up with nursery school teachers and the parents, the intervention, in most cases, was effective.

It is suggested that with few exceptions, only children under the age of 10 be seen. Behavior of children over that age might be less amenable to change where the impetus for that change depends solely on a single behavior modification training session directed at the parents.

If both natural parents are in the home or if one natural parent and one stepparent are in the home, both parents are asked to come in with the child. It may be appropriate to ask a live-in boy or girl friend to attend.

Problems for which this technique seems to be most effective are those involving noncompliance, impulse control, lying, stealing, and poor academic performance. Some anxious children seem to also benefit from the implementation of the recommendations, probably because the recommendations require that the parents provide a more structured environment.

Typical Interview

The author began the interview by explaining the therapeutic plan to the parents. They were told that they would be seen only one time for one and one-half to two hours and that they would be called first after one week, then after two weeks from the first follow-up call, and finally three weeks from the second follow-up call. It was made clear at the time and again at the end of the session that if the parents continued to have problems, further parenting sessions as well as alternative treatment modes would be available to them.

To make certain that the child would be aware of the purpose of the visit, he was asked if he knew why he was there. If he indicated ignorance, he was asked if he had problems at home and/or at school. Whether he admitted or denied having problems, he was told that others were concerned about some of his behavior.

The parents were then asked to describe the problem behaviors. If they described the behavior in general terms, they were asked to give specific examples. To minimize the tendency of many parents to assume that the child's behavior is entirely willful, an assumption which can depress the child's self-esteem and damage the parent–child relationship, the child was asked why he engaged in the undesirable behavior. He usually indicated that he did not know why, and upon questioning, usually admitted that he would prefer to behave in a more acceptable manner. He was then told that his parents would help him with this.

Parents were then asked to describe how they have been handling the problems and if, as is often the case, they have been using physical punishment, inconsistent nonphysical punishment, or negative reinforcement without reward for acceptable behavior, they were told why these techniques have probably not been effective. The importance of consistency was explained before the actual training began.

Parents were given concrete, specific suggestions for handling each of the previously enumerated problem behaviors. Suggestions included time-out periods to be increased if similar behaviors recur within a relatively short period of time, the initial period and subsequent increases varying according to the child's age. Other logical consequences such as deprivation of relevant privileges were suggested and, where possible, unacceptable behavior was to be ignored. Throughout this portion of the interview, parents were frequently asked if they understood the recommendations and if the suggestions made sense to them. Also, the child's opinion was frequently solicited.

The importance of a single warning for teaching the child to take responsibility for his behavior was illustrated by asking the child who is responsible for the consequences if he is warned that they will ensue. In almost every case, the child pointed to himself.

The parents were then given suggestions for rewarding acceptable behavior. They were advised that, unlike negative consequences, rewards should be intermittent and should not be used as a bribe—promise of reward for behavior not yet implemented by the child. Rather the reward should be given only after the behavior has actually occurred.

Finally, parents were given the author's telephone number both at home and at the office and were encouraged to call if they encountered problems they could not handle. They were then given a form letter outlining, in general, the recommendations made to them. It should be noted that, rather than abusing the privilege, most parents were reluctant to call the author at home.

Where the intervention is limited to one session, emphasis is on the child's behavior and not on underlying psychodynamics. Emphasis, therefore, is on changing the environment and training the parents in behavior modification techniques rather than on trying to help the parents and/or the child gain insight into the reasons for the behavior. What frequently does occur as a result of the effectiveness of the training is that, as noted previously by other authors, parents' attitudes toward the child and toward the behaviors tend to change. In addition, the relationship between parents and child appears, anecdotally at least, to improve.

Like Partridge (1976), this author has found it necessary to recommend a mixture of negative and positive interventions. For many of these children, the response to positive reinforcement without some negative consequences appears to be minimal, perhaps because by the time they are referred to the clinic, there are few acceptable behaviors to reward.

This author advises the parents that explanations to the child concerning the negative consequences he has incurred be postponed until some time following the consequence since many children appear to perceive the discussion as implying negotiability. In addition, they may enjoy the attention which they may perceive as a reward for the unacceptable behavior. Alevizos and Alevizos (1975) found no differences in effectiveness between time-out plus explanation and time-out without explanation.

This technique, behavior modification training for parents in a single interview, helps to reduce the often prolonged delays before the child and/or family can be seen. In addition, if this approach works, the economic advantage to the parents is, in some cases, considerable. Although a single-session intervention may not always be the treatment of choice, it can be a viable alternative in situations where a waiting list precludes early attention.

Although in single interviews, marital problems and/or parental interpsychic problems are not investigated or treated, a competent clinician should, during the interview, be aware of cues that these problems exist and should see that they are addressed in subsequent interviews when simple parenting advice is not effective.

References

Alevizos, K. J., and Alevizos, P. N. (1975). The effects of verbalizing contingencies in timeout procedures. *Journal of Behavior Therapy and Experimental Psychiatry* 6:253–255.

Bandura, A. (1969). *Principles of Behavior Modification.* New York: Holt, Rinehart & Winston.

Forehand, R., and King, H. E. (1977). Noncompliant children: effects of parent training on behavior and attitude change. *Behavior Modification* 1(1):93–107.

Hobbs, S. A., and Forehand, R. (1977). Important parameters in the use of time-out with children: a re-examination. *Journal of Behavior Therapy and Experimental Psychiatry* 8:365–370.

Karoly, P., and Rosenthal, M. (1977). Training parents in behavior modification: effects on perceptions of family interaction and deviant child behavior. *Behavior Therapy* 8:406–410.

O'Dell, S. (1974). Training parents in behavior modification: a review. *Psychological Bulletin* 81(7):418–433.

Partridge, C. R. (1976). Immature character development: a new look at etiology and remediation of character disorders.

Webster-Stratton, C., Kolpacoff, M., and Hollinsworth, T. (1988). Self-administered videotape therapy for families with conduct-problem children: comparison with two cost-effective treatments and a control group. *Journal of Consulting and Clinical Psychology* 56(4):558–566.

PART II
Insecure Behaviors

3

Night Terrors

BRYAN LASK

Introduction

Night terrors (pavor nocturnus) have been known since ancient times, and according to Kottek (1981) were, like epilepsy, ascribed to demons. One of the more detailed early descriptions was that of Rhazes, in the fifteenth century, quoted by Still (1931) and Kottek (1981). Rhazes described "a certain affliction that happens to children. . . . The sign of it is a great wailing or much fear during sleep." Still (1931) also quoted a German physician, Wittich, who described "night screaming or fearful dreams and terrors in children." Wittich believed this condition to have "a great affinity to the falling sickness" (i.e., epilepsy) (p. 169).

From the earliest times, there has been dispute as to exactly what are night terrors. Rhazes explained the condition as being due to "the taking of more milk than the child can digest. The child therefore is given the sixth part of a dram of dyapliris and diasmuscum with the milk daily" (Radbils 1971, p. 373). (This might actually be one of the earliest descriptions of milk intolerance!) Other popular explanations have included epilepsy and hysteria. Although we now know that neither of these conditions accounts for pavor nocturnus, the actual cause remains unclear.

Definition and Presentation

Night terrors are nocturnal episodes of extreme dread and distress, intense vocalization including screaming, increased body movements, and marked autonomic arousal (Driver and Shapiro 1993, Fenwick

1986, Keener and Anders 1991, Lask 1988, Matthews and Oakey 1986, Schulz and Reynolds 1991). The body movements may be purposeless and uncoordinated, or complex, coordinated, and purposeful, including sleepwalking in up to 70 percent of sufferers (Lowe and Scott 1991). There is marked autonomic arousal as manifested by tachycardia, palpitations, tachypnoea, dilated pupils, sweating, and piloerection.

The episodes tend to occur during the first few hours of sleep, and are of relatively short duration (one to twenty minutes). The first signs are those of autonomic arousal, such as restlessness, sweating, and tachycardia, but the parents usually do not become aware of the episode until the child suddenly starts screaming or becomes extremely restless. Children with night terrors are not readily awakened although often they seem to be awake, and it is not possible to console them. They appear to be confused and disoriented. They are unresponsive to their surroundings and seem rather to be responding to frightening mental images (Keener and Anders 1991). The episode usually remits with the child returning to normal sleep, and it is unusual for there to be more than one per night. There is no recall of the incident the next morning.

Onset of night terrors is usually between the ages of 4 and 12 (Lowe and Scott 1991), with an incidence of between 1 and 4 percent of children in this age group (Fenwick 1986, Schulz and Reynolds 1991). Boys are more commonly affected than girls and the problem usually resolves itself by early adolescence (Lowe and Scott 1991).

The frequency of episodes may vary from nightly to once every few months. There is divergence of opinion regarding regularity. Keener and Anders (1991) consider episodes to occur irregularly, whereas Lask (1988) has noted that in many cases parents report that the episodes are absolutely predictable, often occurring at the same time almost or even every night. With regard to triggering factors, Driver and Shapiro (1993) state that night terrors may occur in response to stress and anxiety and may be more common when sleep schedules are irregular. Lask (1988), in contrast, reports that stress seems not to be relevant and that change in routine diminishes or eliminates the episodes.

Assessment and Differential Diagnosis

Developmental, medical, and family history are usually unremarkable, although Schulz and Reynolds (1991) have reported a greater incidence of night terrors than might be expected in the family history. Very rarely is there any evidence of psychiatric disorder in children with night terrors. Mental state examination is usually quite normal, and physical examination rarely reveals any abnormality.

Similarly, neurological investigations such as EEG (electroencephalogram) and CT (computerized tomography) scanning are within normal limits. Interestingly, there is general consensus that late-onset night terrors (i.e., above the age of 12) are much more commonly associated with major life stress and more serious psychopathology than is reported in childhood (Crisp et al. 1990, Kales and Scharf 1973, Keener and Anders 1991, Lowe and Scott 1991, Schulz and Reynolds 1991). Rarely will adults commit violent acts during a night terror (Fenwick 1986, Oswald and Evans 1985, Schatzman 1986).

The differential diagnosis includes nightmares and epileptiform disorders. Night terrors are easily distinguished from nightmares in that they occur in Stage 3 to 4 non-REM sleep, usually between one and three hours after falling asleep. In contrast, nightmares occur in REM sleep between three and six hours after falling asleep. With night terrors there are usually loud vocalizations, including screaming, and vigorous movements, often of a defensive or evasive nature, and very marked autonomic arousal. With nightmares, vocalizations are less common and less intense; there is little movement, and less autonomic arousal. It is difficult and sometimes impossible to wake a child from a night terror, whereas a child having a nightmare is easily awakened. Children having night terrors cannot be consoled, while children having nightmares are usually fairly easily soothed. The next morning children who have had a night terror have no recall of the episode, but children with nightmares often have a vivid recall of the dream.

There should be no difficulty in distinguishing night terrors from epileptiform disturbances, given the characteristic features of the former. Convulsions are not normally accompanied by the intense and often piercing vocalizations associated with night terrors, while epileptiform movements are likely to be of a tonic and clonic type. When there is any doubt about the diagnosis an EEG should be performed.

Pathogenesis

The cause of night terrors is not known. Given the frequency of a family history of either sleepwalking or night terrors, it is reasonable to assume a common genetically determined predisposition to these disorders (Kales et al. 1980). It has also been suggested that both these disorders represent an immaturity of the central nervous system in children (Driver and Shapiro 1993). Some such patients are reported to have a generalized, hypersynchronous symmetrical delta pattern on EEG before and during the episode (Driver and Shapiro 1993), while Kales and colleagues (1966) identified subsequent persistence of slow waves for a short while, which they suggested might also reflect cerebral immaturity. Broughton (1968) found the episodes to be associated with high-amplitude alpha rhythm, similar to that prompted in normal subjects wakened from deep sleep. He concluded that the patients were suffering from an arousal disorder.

It would appear, therefore, that night terrors occur at least to some extent in the context of cerebral immaturity, with some genetic contribution. It remains to be shown whether there is a different pathophysiology between childhood-onset and later-onset night terrors, given that the incidence of psychopathology differs. It is of course possible, however, that the psychopathology found in adults is primarily a secondary phenomenon.

Management

Although night terrors are benign and usually resolve themselves with time, treatment is often necessary because of the distress and disruption that the episodes cause, and because of the potential dangers associated with the violent movements and any associated sleepwalking.

A wide range of approaches to management has been proposed, although few approaches have been tested empirically. It may also be that the treatment needs of children differ from those of adults. For example, Lowe and Scott (1991) have suggested that psychotherapy may be of value for later-onset night terrors, but not in childhood. Suggested treatments in childhood may be categorized as pharmacological, psychotherapeutic, and behavioral.

Pharmacological Treatments

There is much controversy over the use of medication for childhood-onset night terrors. A number of reports have claimed the effectiveness of a variety of drugs including the benzodiazepines (Fisher et al. 1973, Kales and Scharf 1973, Keener and Anders 1991, Popoviciu and Corforiu 1986, Reimao and Lefevre 1982, Vela et al. 1982), the tricyclic antidepressants (Beitman and Carlin 1979, Keener and Anders 1991, Logan 1979, Persikoff and Davies 1971), and phenobarbitone (Cornfield et al. 1979). Their suggested mode of action is the reduction of Stage 3 and 4 slow-wave sleep.

There is no convincing evidence to indicate that these medications are more satisfactory than nonpharmacological treatment methods and they can have unpleasant side effects (Weisbluth 1984). It is probably wise to follow the recommendations of Lowe and Scott (1991) that medication should only be used in severe cases when other treatments have failed, and of Keener and Anders (1991) that medication should only be used if the symptoms are particularly hazardous or disruptive to the family.

Psychotherapeutic Treatments

The only authors to recommend the use of psychotherapy for night terrors in children are Driver and Shapiro (1993) who firmly state that psychotherapy and hypnosis are the treatments of choice, although they offer no rationale or evidence for their view. Maskey (1993) has pointed out that psychotherapy is expensive and often unavailable, while Lask (1993) has argued that both psychotherapy and hypnosis for young children are expensive, irrational, impractical, and of no obvious value.

Behavioral Treatments

These are the least toxic and probably most effective techniques for the treatment of childhood night terrors. Lask (1988) has reported the value of what has become known as *the waking treatment*. Parents are asked to note on five successive nights at what time the episodes occur, and whether there are signs of autonomic arousal. They are then advised to fully wake their child ten to fifteen minutes before the night terror usually occurs, and to keep him or her awake for five minutes. If the terrors occur at different times, the parents are advised to observe for signs of autonomic arousal and then to immediately wake their child. This process should be repeated on five to seven successive nights.

This technique was used for over fifty children with night terrors. In about 80 percent, the episodes stopped within one week. A small proportion of children relapsed within six months; all but one of these children made a complete recovery after a repeat course of waking. It does seem that if the instructions are carried out correctly this treatment is usually effective.

The reason this treatment works is not clear but probably relates to interruption of faulty slow-wave sleep patterns, with reversion to a normal sleep pattern and resolution of the disorder (Lask 1988). It is of interest that there have been anecdotal reports of resolution of night terrors following other less structured and intrusive changes to sleep patterns, such as going on holiday, moving home, changing bedrooms, or changing bedtimes. This treatment, and others for which claims of effectiveness are made, needs to be tested empirically against control and comparison interventions. A comparison of the waking treatment with relaxation is currently being conducted in Australia (James 1994).

Parental Counseling

This should be a sine qua non of the management of any childhood disorder. Parents need to have as full an understanding as possible of the etiology, course, treatment, and outcome of their child's problem. They should be encouraged to ask as many questions as they need, and, where possible, be given written and even diagrammatic explanations and instructions. Such advice and support are not only usually reassuring, but in many conditions have a beneficial effect upon symptoms. With mild night terrors, counseling may be sufficient for the parents to cope without the need for more complex treatments. When the terrors are more dramatic, parents are very much in need of the support and advice that should accompany any other treatment.

Case Illustration

John, whose developmental and medical history had been unremarkable, developed night terrors at age 5. These occurred five to six times per week, usually within two hours of his falling asleep, and were characterized by his appearing to wake with a start, after which he would scream very loudly, thrash around in his bed, and then take what appeared to be evasive action, covering his head and cowering. He could not be awakened or consoled. The episodes lasted for about five minutes, after which he would seem to return to normal sleep. He never had any recall of the incident the next morning. Occasionally his parents would be in his room immediately prior to an episode and note restlessness and sweating.

There was no family history of similar episodes, but intermittently there had been considerable marital disharmony. Physical examination revealed no abnormality.

Treatment with diazepam reduced the frequency of the episodes for about three weeks but then seemed to lose any effect. Tricyclic antidepressants made no difference. John was referred for weekly play therapy, which was stopped after three months because of lack of any effect.

The episodes continued in a similar pattern for two years, at which point John was referred to a specialist center where he was admitted for two days for further investigations. The only abnormality was in the sleep electroencephalogram, which was reported as showing minor, nonspecific changes. No terrors occurred during the admission, but John did complain of sleeping poorly because of noise on the ward. When he returned home the episodes recurred. It was decided to readmit him to see if once again the episodes remitted, and this proved to be the case.

It was hypothesized that the remission in hospital could be due either to being away from home, and therefore away from the associated stresses, or to the alteration in the sleep pattern imposed by the noise on the ward. A decision was made to test the latter hypothesis, by waking him frequently in the early hours of his sleep at home. This was done at hourly intervals between 8:00 and 11:00 P.M. every night for one week, after which he had no more night terrors. Annual follow-up for five years revealed no relapse and no other significant problems.

John was the first child to be treated by waking. While it might be hypothesized that his recovery was a natural process, this seems unlikely, and would be a remarkable coincidence, in that it coincided with the institution of a new and previously untested treatment. The fact that so many other children seem to respond well to this approach suggests that there is something beneficial in artificially altering the sleep pattern.

Summary

Night terrors are a relatively benign but distressing condition affecting 1 to 4 percent of children between the ages of 4 and 12. The cause is unknown, but seems to be linked to an abnormality of slow-wave sleep, which resolves with time in the majority of instances. There is rarely any evidence of individual psychopathology, and family pathology does not seem to occur any more commonly than in the general population. There are no abnormalities on physical examination or investigation. The most helpful treatment appears to be a combination of parental counseling and artificial waking in the early hours of sleep, and this is recommended when the terrors are particularly disruptive or distressing or threaten the child's safety.

References

Beitman, B., and Carlin, A. (1979). Night terrors treated with Imipramine. *American Journal of Psychiatry* 136:1087–1088.

Broughton, R. (1968). Sleep disorders: disorders of arousal. *Science* 159:1070–1078.

Cornfield, C., Chaplin, S., Doyle, A., et al. (1979). Side effects of phenobarbital in toddlers: behavioral and cognitive aspects. *Journal of Paediatrics* 95:361–365.

Crisp, A., Matthews, B., Oakey, M., and Crutchfield, C. R. T. M. (1990). Sleep walking, night terrors and consciousness. *British Medical Journal* 300:360–362.

Driver, H., and Shapiro, C. (1993). Parasomnias. *British Medical Journal* 306:921–924.

Fenwick, P. (1986). Murdering while asleep. *British Medical Journal* 293:574–575.

Fisher, C., Khan, E., Edwards, A., et al. (1973). A psycho-physiological study of nightmares and night terrors. *Archives of General Psychiatry* 28:250–252.

James, L. (1994). Personal communication.

Kales, A., Jacobson A., Paulson, N., et al. (1966). Somnambulism: psychophysiological correlates: 1. All night EEG studies. *Archives of General Psychiatry* 14:586–594.

Kales, J., Kales, A., Soldatos, C., et al. (1980). Night terrors: clinical characteristics and personality patterns. *Archives of General Psychiatry* 37:1413–1417.

Kales, A., and Sharf, M. (1973). Sleep laboratory and clinical studies of the effects of benzodiazapine on sleep. In *The Benzodiazapines*, ed. S. Garattini, E. Mussini, and L. Randall, pp. 577–598. New York: Roden Press.

Keener, M., and Anders, T. (1991). New frontiers of sleep disorders: medicine in infants, children and adolescents. In *Psychiatry*, vol. 2, ed. R. Mitchels. Philadelphia: J. Lippincott.

Kottek, S. (1981). "Matter Pueroum": a medieval naming for an enigmatic children's disease. *European Journal of Paediatrics* 137:75–79.

Lask, B. (1988). Novel and non toxic treatment for night terrors. *British Medical Journal* 297:592.

——— (1993). "Waking treatment" best for night terrors [correspondence]. *British Medical Journal* 306:1477.

Logan, D. (1979). Antidepressant treatment of recurrent anxiety attacks and night terrors. *Ohio State Medical Journal* 75:653–655.

Lowe, T., and Scott, C. (1991). Elimination disorders and parasomnias in childhood. In *Psychiatry*, vol. 2, ed. R. Mitchels, pp. 1–12. Philadelphia: J. Lippincott.

Maskey, S. (1993). Simple treatment for night terrors [correspondence]. *British Medical Journal* 306:1477.

Matthews, B., and Oakey, M. (1986). Triumph over terror [correspondence]. *British Medical Journal* 292:203.

Oswald, E., and Evans, J. (1985). On serious violence during sleepwalking. *British Journal of Psychiatry* 147:688–689.

Persikoff, R., and Davies, P. (1971). Treatment of pavor nocturnus and somnambulism in children. *American Journal of Psychiatry* 128:134–137.

Popoviciu, L., and Corforiu, O. (1986). Efficacy and safety of midazolam in the treatment of night terrors in children. *British Journal of Clinical Pharmacology* 16(suppl. 1):975–1025.

Radbils, J. (1971). The first treatise of paediatrics. *American Journal of Diseases of Children* 122:369–376.

Reimao, R., and Lefevre, A. (1982). Evaluation of flurazepan and placebo in sleep disorders in childhood. *Arquivos de Neuro-Psiquiatria* 40:1–13.

Schatzman, M. (1986). To sleep, perchance to kill. *New Scientist* 110:60–62.

Schulz, S., and Reynolds, C. (1991). Sleep disorders. In *Psychiatry*, vol. 2, ed. R. Mitchels, pp. 1–18. Philadelphia: J. Lippincott.

Still, G. (1931). *The History of Paediatrics*. Oxford: Oxford University Press.

Vela, A., Dobidez, B., Rubio, M., et al. (1982). Action of bormazepam on sleep in children with night terrors: 1. Sleep organisation and heart rate. *Pharmatherapuetica* 3:247–258.

Weisbluth, M. (1984). Is drug treatment of night terrors warranted? [correspondence]. *American Journal of Diseases of Childhood* 138:1086.

4

Night Fears

JONATHAN KELLERMAN

Fear of sleeping alone and nightmares are common problems in children. The relationship between conditioned anxiety and disturbances of sleep has been discussed by several authors (Cellucci and Lawrence 1978, Christozov and Dascalov 1970, Handler 1972, Kellerman 1979, Persikoff and Davis 1971, Taboada 1975) and behavioral approaches aimed at reducing anxiety have proved effective.

In the current report, a combined behavioral approach was effective in rapidly eliminating nocturnal anxiety in three children of different age levels. Behavioral analysis was used to specify stimuli that elicited, maintained and followed anxiety, and incompatible response training was used to achieve anxiety reduction. Operant reinforcement of appropriate nighttime behavior was used to overcome the deviant nocturnal behavior.

Case History

D., a 5-year-old boy, presented with a seven-month history of nightmares accompanied by nocturnal anxiety. These episodes were behaviorally similar to those common in classical night terrors (sudden waking, motility, screaming, no memory of the event [Kellerman 1979]. D.'s parents reported that their child had viewed a frightening Dracula movie on television and had experienced a nightmare that same evening. This did not recur, however, until two weeks later, when, while experiencing a fever due to chicken pox, D. spontaneously reported "seeing Dracula." From that time on, nightmares occurred from two to seven times a week, and the child's anxiety had generalized to his refusing to visit his maternal grandmother because it was in her house that he had seen the Dracula movie.

For several months before referral, D.'s parents had allowed him to sleep in their bed. Interestingly, several weeks after the chronic nightmares began, the child had requested to purchase a toy Dracula cape. His parents, adopting a protective stance, had refused, and had assiduously screened potentially anxiety-provoking television material from his view.

Methods

The assumption was made that the nightmares represented an anxiety reaction to a frightening film. In addition, inappropriate sleep behavior had been positively reinforced by allowing the child to sleep with his parents and the child's verbalized fear was followed by a great deal of parental attention. Consequently, the treatment plan devised had several facets.

1. D. was told that he could not be afraid and angry at the same time and that being angry at Dracula could make him feel better. During one individual session, he practiced repeatedly drawing Dracula and displaying anger, including tearing up the drawing and throwing it away. Angry verbal responses were displayed by the author and D. was encouraged to imitate them. By the end of the session D. was clearly enjoying this and was told that he could practice at home when he felt afraid.

2. D.'s parents were instructed not to protect him from what they felt were fearful stimuli as this tended to confirm to the child that characters on television or in the movies were to be feared. D.'s verbalized fear regarding Dracula was to be followed by the statement, "You can handle it" and the suggestion that he get angry at Dracula.

3. D. was instructed that he would no longer be able to sleep in his parents' room and that if he slept in the proper place he would be rewarded. With D.'s participation it was agreed that during the first week he could sleep anywhere in the house except his parents' room; after that he would be required to sleep in his room. Through discussion with D., several counter-anxious behaviors, in addition to anger, were obtained (turning on a night-light, going to the refrigerator for a snack, turning on the radio next to his bed, looking through a favorite picture book) and D.

was instructed to use these if he began to feel frightened. He was told to engage in these incompatible responses the minute he felt just a little afraid and not to wait until the anxiety intensified. Going into his parents' room was specifically excluded as an acceptable anxiety-reducing activity. Appropriate sleep behavior was to be recorded and positively reinforced with money (5 cents). Reinforcement was given on the morning following a full night of appropriate sleep. D. asked if he could use his money to buy a Dracula cape and was told that he could.

4. D.'s parents were given examples of assertive behaviors, particularly those related to mastery over fearful stimuli, and were instructed to look out for these and verbally praise them.

Results

The night following the initial session D. tried to gain entry to his parents' room and upon being refused permission to do so had a tantrum. His parents successfully extinguished this behavior by ignoring it. D. then curled up outside their door and slept, with no subsequent nightmares. Throughout the remainder of the first week he slept on a couch in the living room and was monetarily and verbally reinforced. Two nightmares occurred during the first week. During the second week D. slept in his own room and experienced no nightmares. He eventually earned enough money to purchase a Dracula costume. After four weeks, during which nightmares did not occur, monetary reinforcement for appropriate sleep behavior was faded out. Follow-up eighteen months later revealed maintenance of therapeutic gains, as did a second follow-up at twenty-four months. D.'s mother reported that he occasionally talked about Dracula but that it didn't seem to bother him. An increase in general assertiveness was noted. Total treatment occurred over three hourly sessions.

Two other cases were successfully treated using similar methods. An 8-year-old girl with a four-year history of separation anxiety, school phobia, fear of the dark, and anxiety about going to sleep was found to have fears focusing upon kidnappers breaking into her house at night. She drew a picture of a kidnapper, was given an explanation regarding the incompatibility of anger and fear, and was encouraged to practice getting angry at the intruder the moment she felt anxious. Appropriate nocturnal behavior was positively reinforced with money. During the first week she reported feeling less frightened at night and slept in her room uneventfully. After two weeks complete cessation of nocturnal anxiety was reported. Monetary reinforcement was faded out. Follow-up at sixteen months revealed maintenance of therapeutic gains.

A 13-year-old girl was referred due to a five-year history of anxiety associated with being alone at night or in the dark. She spent the night in her younger brother's room and experienced intermittent nightmares. Anxiety centered around being molested by a cat burglar or rapist and was reported to have increased following several stranglings that occurred near her neighborhood. A pattern of escape behavior had been learned in which she tried to stay in her room at night, experienced anxiety, waited until the level of discomfort rose to an intolerable level, and then left for an alternative sleeping place. Steps were taken to deal with reality issues that contributed to the anxiety (e.g., purchasing opaque drapes for bedroom windows, making sure that the family house was adequately secure). Several counter-anxious behaviors (watching television, reading, turning on a night-light, and getting a snack) were used contingent upon threshold anxiety. Appropriate nighttime behavior was monetarily reinforced. Within two weeks she was sleeping comfortably in her room and reporting no anxiety, and monetary reinforcement was faded out. Follow-up at nine months revealed stability of relaxed pre-sleep and sleep behavior.

Discussion

Three cases of successful rapid treatment of nocturnal anxiety and related problems in children of varying ages have been presented. All three of these cases had in common realistic occurrences that led to subsequent learning of disruptive, anxious associations. Treatment elements included careful behavioral analysis aimed at specifying the stimuli with which anxiety was associated, handling of reality factors that contributed toward maintenance of anxious behavior, instruction in practice of counter-anxious behaviors, and reversal of familial patterns of positive reinforcement of anxious behavior.

Speculation is offered here that, while most children are exposed to numerous fearful stimuli throughout their childhood, pediatric phobias are not ubiquitous because children naturally engage in self-curative behavior, mainly self-paced repeated exposure to fearful stimuli. Parental protectiveness may serve to intensify rather than reduce the child's anxiety by restricting the opportunity to engage in counter-anxious behavior. In addition, parental attention offered contingent upon fearfulness may very well contribute toward chronicity of problematic anxiety. It is possible that the implementation of a reward system may, in itself, have anxiety-reducing properties in that it offers the child a cognition (thinking about earning a reward) that is relaxing and therefore incompatible with anxiety. In the three cases cited, fearful stimuli could be avoided or escaped. Where a fearful response follows a repeated aversive stimulus that cannot be avoided, treatment may be more prolonged. An example of this is the case of a chronically ill child who is confronted with repeated, uncomfortable medical procedures. There is evidence, however, that similar behavioral methods may be used in reducing conditioned anxiety in such instances (Kellerman 1979).

It is not useful to conceptualize pediatric anxiety reactions in terms of syndromes or disease states in which the essential organizing criterion is the setting or time in which the fearful behavior occurs. Thus, thinking of all instances of nocturnal anxiety or nightmares as equivalent is not helpful in terms of developing treatment plans. Rather, a careful behavioral analysis aimed at eliciting the stimulus antecedents and consequences specific to individual cases paves the way to developing ways of helping patients develop counter-anxious strategies. It is precisely this need for individualized functional analysis, as opposed to standardized, packaged treatment, that has been so eloquently addressed by Phillips (1978). The rapidity and durability of therapeutic gains reported in the present study lend further credence to this notion.

References

Cellucci, A. J., and Lawrence, P. S. (1978). The efficacy of systematic desensitization in reducing nightmares. *Journal of Behavioral Therapy and Experimental Psychiatry* 9:109–144.

Christozov, C., and Dascalov, D. (1970). Correlation between clinical and EEG findings in children with night terrors and somnambulism. *Acta Paedopsychiatrica* 37:61.

Handler, L. (1972). The amelioration of nightmares in children. *Psychotherapy: Theory, Research and Practice* 9:54.

Kellerman, J. (1979). Single case study: behavioral treatment of night terrors in a child with acute leukemia, *Journal of Nervous and Mental Disease* 167:182–185.

Persikoff, R. B., and Davis, P. C. (1971). Treatment of pavor nocturnus and somnambulism in childhood. *American Journal of Psychiatry* 128:778.

Phillips, L. W. (1978). The soft underbelly of behavior therapy: pop behavior mod. *Journal of Behavioral Therapy and Experimental Psychiatry* 9:139–140.

Taboada, E. L. (1975). Night terrors in a child treated with hypnosis. *American Journal of Clinical Hypnosis* 17:270.

5

General Fears

PETER J. D'AMICO AND ALICE G. FRIEDMAN

Introduction

The purpose of this chapter is to provide practical methods for therapists who are treating children with excessive fears and the families of those children. The approach toward treatment is to help parents be the major agent of change for their fearful child. The therapist's role, therefore, is to teach parents how to best help their children overcome the fears.

Inclusion of parents (meaning the child's primary caretakers, including grandparents, other relatives, foster parents, or others) as co-therapists in the treatment of childhood problems is consistent with the theoretical underpinnings of behavior therapy and has been accumulating increasing empirical support. Evidence for its efficacy has been derived from research on parent behavioral training efforts, especially in the areas of noncompliance and conduct disorder (Graziano and Diament 1992). Early training programs focused on teaching parents specific techniques (such as "time-out"), which were of limited success. Parents often applied the techniques incorrectly and could not use them for new, emerging problems. More recent programs stress teaching parents principles of behavior change that serve as the rationale for the specific strategies. Once parents understand key concepts, they can apply them to a range of problematic situations and can alter them when they appear ineffective.

Training parents to be effective agents of change can be accomplished individually or in groups, using a variety of methods (e.g., lectures, written materials, films, modeling, coaching, etc.). Goals typically

include helping parents identify the major contributors to the problems and altering the home, school, or day-care environment or their
own behavior in a way to best facilitate positive behavior change.

Early reviews of the parent training literature (Berkowitz and
Graziano 1972, Graziano 1977, Johnson and Katz 1973) suggested that
using parents as behavior change agents could be effective across a wide
range of difficulties. Successful use of parents as co-therapists has occurred with some of the more discrete child behavior problems such as
pacifier reliance (Schloss and Johann 1982), firesetting (Kolko 1983),
obesity (Epstein et al. 1987, Israel et al. 1984), enuresis (Bollard et al.
1982), stuttering (Budd et al. 1986, Ladoceur and Martineau 1982), and
bedtime fears (Graziano and Mooney 1980, 1982).

Although the extension of parent training to the treatment of
children's fears has not been a major focus of research efforts, there
are a few studies of childhood phobias that have involved parents to
various degrees. For example, Blagg and Yule (1984) utilized parental
reinforcement as a component in the behavioral treatment of school
phobia, while Barlow and Seidner (1983) suggested that inclusion of
the parent in the treatment of adolescent agoraphobia (n = 3) was
needed for insuring attempts at exposure. The most parent-inclusive
treatment approaches have been described by those studies involving
both child and parent training to reduce severe bedtime fears (Graziano
et al. 1979, Graziano and Mooney 1982, McMenamy and Katz 1989).
Typically, although children are taught a variety of skills including
relaxation, pleasant imagery, and self-instruction to encourage bravery/
reduce anxiety, parents are instructed on how to effectively reinforce
compliance, recognize and reward incremental treatment gains, monitor target behaviors, and facilitate graduated exposure. These efforts
have paved the way for clinicians to consider educating and training
parents in more complex behavioral strategies such as those involving
counter-conditioning, as well as various combinations of operant and
classical conditioning techniques. Giebenhain and O'Dell (1984) have
created and tested the effectiveness of a training manual that provides
parental instruction in the use of several of these techniques, including behavioral monitoring, positive reinforcement, desensitization, and
verbal control strategies. In an earlier study, Friedman and Campbell
(1992) discussed the critical role of parents in the successful implementation of these various treatment components to reduce children's fear
of the dark. In this chapter, we discuss those factors associated with
successful parent involvement in the reduction of childhood phobias.

The scope of this contribution is limited to a discussion of clinical considerations that are indicated in the effective use of parents as change agents in the management of children's excessive fears. We focus on those assessment and treatment issues that appear to have the greatest impact on facilitation of the therapeutic process with parents and their child's subsequent behavior change. In addition, we offer some practical suggestions for the implementation of specific intervention strategies. A broader overview of the parent training paradigm is given in a recent literature review by Graziano and Diament (1992). For additional reading on the application of parent training to various childhood problems, we recommend a publication by Schaefer and Briesmeister (1989) entitled *Handbook of Parent Training*. This work covers a broad range of specific childhood disorders from sleep problems and enuresis to children who have a developmental delay or have been abused. The majority of the invited authors address parent involvement in terms of skill training and employment based on behavioral principles. Others suggest alternative approaches with interesting research ideas. The text is well written and practical. Finally, an excellent resource for parents is a recent publication, *Monsters Under the Bed and Other Childhood Fears*, by Garber and colleagues (1993). It is a valuable resource written in clear language that is informative, comprehensive, and well organized. Parents are introduced to a general understanding of the nature of fear, how to respond to their child, and how to help their child cope with and overcome fear. Concrete suggestions are then offered for a number of specific childhood fears, with various helpful activities for engaging the parent and child together.

Before proceeding, it is important to address one issue. There is a huge body of literature demonstrating that behavior modification can produce behavior change. However, it is also the case that misuse of these strategies, based largely on ignorance about the principles underlying their efficacy, can make problems worse. We therefore stress the need to ensure that parents are competent to use the principles effectively and that they understand the rationale behind specific strategies.

Rationale for Parents as Co-therapists

Although common sense dictates including parents in the design and implementation of intervention strategies, it is not uncommon for parents to have a limited role in their child's treatment. The goal of teaching parents behavioral principles is to assist their ability to alter the contingencies in the natural environment that maintain behavioral avoidance, thereby permitting the child the opportunity to learn adaptive coping skills and employ self-control strategies.

Training parents to be successfully involved in reducing their child's fear(s) can have many positive collateral effects in child and family functioning. First, research suggests that brief therapy is sufficient to effectively treat most simple phobias of childhood, obviating the need for long-term treatment (Friedman and Ollendick 1989). In light of the brevity of treatment, maintenance and generalization of treatment effects can be enhanced after brief intervention by assuring that parents have requisite skills to implement strategies in the home environment and extend them to new problem areas when they arise. Further, the most efficacious approach to treatment requires actual exposure to the fear-provoking stimuli (Menzies and Clarke 1993). Depending upon the source of the child's fear, it may not be possible to implement in vivo exposure in the clinic. The therapist cannot construct an environment similar to the bedroom situation for a child with phobia of the dark, for example. Parents, on the other hand, are often present while the child is exposed to fear-provoking stimuli in the natural environment. Thus, using parents as "therapist extenders" makes practical and theoretical sense. We believe that the argument can seldom be made not to include the parent in the child's treatment, because parents have the greatest influence over what is sustained in the child's environment.

Clinical Issues Pertinent to Parental Involvement

Several conceptual issues warrant attention as a prelude to discussing more practical considerations of assessment and treatment.

Transient Nature of Fears

Parents seeking treatment for their child's fear are sometimes not aware that certain fears are likely to accompany new developmental tasks for children and that these fears are generally common and transient (Bauer 1976). Parents must be educated about normal developmental changes. The emergence and resolution of fears follows a predictable developmental sequence, although the intensity and duration of fear may vary considerably. Infants and toddlers typically display fears when separated from their caretakers and in the presence of strangers. This is most common among children nearing the end of their first year and may persist, on and off, well into the twos. Parents who do not anticipate these changes may ridicule their child or otherwise project negative feelings about their child's clinginess. These fears must be considered by parents planning changes in the home, entering their child into a new day-care situation, or contemplating vacations. Fears of the dark are common among preschoolers and are also age-appropriate. Nighttime "lovies" and other sources of attachment can go a long way to helping children learn to comfort themselves. Professional intervention is rarely warranted for such distress. Fears of animals, not entirely irrational, tend to emerge a bit later. Simple strategies such as modeling safe but effective interactions with familiar animals teach children the difference between safe and unsafe animals. Obviously, distress related to such fears is not necessarily a sign that the fear is excessive. There is mounting evidence that temperamental factors may predispose a child to fears and that this tendency may persist throughout life. That does not mean, however, that timidity should be treated as a disorder. Rather, it more typically reflects natural variation in how individuals approach life's challenges.

Parents provided with understanding about developmental progression of fears can greatly influence the manner in which they respond to their child. Parents inquiring about fears should first be provided with anticipatory guidance which may lead them to conclude that formal treatment is not warranted. On the other hand, parents who are uneducated about developmental changes may overreact to an otherwise "normal" developmental challenge. Alternatively, they may fail to recognize fears that are indicative of problems and do warrant treatment. Thus, important roles of the therapist are to (a) educate parents about the changing nature of childhood fears, (b) delineate the relevance of fear to developmental progress, (c) provide parents with methods to identify fears indicative of problems, (d) teach parents strategies to help their child overcome fears, (e) be willing to advise parents when treatment is not warranted, (f) help parents accept the notion that their child may tend to be more timid than others, and (g) advise parents when treatment is warranted.

Child Characteristics

Child variables such as temperament, gender, age, and cognitive development can impact on a parent's perception of the seriousness of their child's fear. In comparing one sibling to another, parents may note appreciable differences in fearful responding among their children. Although the majority of parents seem to attribute these differences to acceptable variations in temperament or personality style, some parents may become unnecessarily alarmed at the relative intensity or duration of a fear that appears excessive. The therapist should talk with parents about their expectations of their child's behavior and the meaning timidity and fear have for them. Some parents may insist upon bravery for their sons while accepting some fearful behavior from their daughters. In fact, very young boys (toddlers) appear more apt to exhibit fearful behavior than their female peers.

Parents should also take into account differences in children's styles of reporting fear. For example, although school-aged boys may experience many of the same fears as similar-aged girls, girls may be more likely to report them (Ollendick et al. 1985). Thus, parents may view their daughter as more fearful, or they may underestimate their son's experience of fear.

Age-dependent cognitive/emotional influences are also relevant to how parents intervene with their child. Patterns of helping their child overcome fear may become outmoded, requiring a shift in approach. For example, a 4-year-old child who has acquired a fear of thunder and lightning may respond to parental reassurance/affection for bravery and a bedtime story about "the great rain maker in the sky." A child of 9 may not benefit at all from such an approach but instead benefit from exposure to thunder while in a safe environment and from accurate information about the process of thunder, the actual danger involved, and how to independently improve his or her own measure of safety.

Parent Characteristics

Effective reliance upon parents to implement behavioral strategies at home is dependent upon the parents' competency to understand behavioral principles and to use strategies correctly. Parents who are experiencing levels of distress themselves may be poor candidates for this approach. Parents with marital problems or strong disagreements about disciplinary practices and methods of dealing with their child's fears, or who are depressed, would benefit from more comprehensive treatment.

Even parents without coexisting difficulties may vary in their readiness to implement specific strategies. It is important to recognize that attempts to enlist a parent as an agent of change for their child without sufficient guidance could have a negative impact on the therapeutic process. Gauging the parents' level of general distress—as well as their distress associated with the child's fear—is an important barometer for decision making about the extent to which the therapist can rely on the parents to implement treatment.

Parental problems can be of sufficient magnitude to render this approach contraindicated. And efforts aimed at reducing parental distress may prove to be greater than expected. In this case, as well as in cases where parents are themselves excessively fearful, anxious, depressed, or otherwise psychologically distressed, individual therapy for the adult should be recommended.

Fear Specificity, Intensity, Duration, and Avoidance Behavior

The nature of a child's fear and the complexity of his or her avoidance behavior play an important role in determining the pace of parent involvement and eventually the length of treatment. Theoretically, a fear (which qualifies as a phobia) that is specific and recently acquired would be expected to extinguish more rapidly than one that is generalized or has already persisted for some time. As the complexity of the fear increases, so does the need for more intensive assessment, parent preparation, and intervention efforts. Thus, a child who has recently acquired a phobia of the next-door neighbor's dog is in all likelihood going to require significantly less parent preparation and time in treatment than a child who has developed a rather severe social phobia that has progressed over two years.

Some types of phobias seem to be more or less amenable to parent involvement, thus limiting the parents' capacity to aid in exposure. A young male adolescent's excessive fear of the opposite sex would set some rather delicate boundaries around the parents' role in therapy. The nature of fear may also impact on the clinician's decision to train parents individually or within a group format. Several children who fear various animals may benefit from their parents' involvement in a group with other parents. Parent groups are likely to be more successful if the nature of their children's fears share some commonalities. As mentioned previously, much success has been reported in the use of parent training groups with children's fear of the dark.

Assessment and Intervention

Preliminary Considerations

Conditions of Referral

Upon initial referral, a number of issues need to be considered prior to developing a treatment plan. The first is the decision about whether the child's fears warrant treatment at all. We typically will not treat children with age-appropriate levels or types of fear. Our rationale is that overcoming age-appropriate fear may have adaptive value. Additionally, coming to a clinic can be associated with stigma and may encourage the family to view the child as having a problem. When parents do inquire about treatment for their child's age-related fear, we typically educate the parent (providing anticipatory guidance for the future) rather than treat the child.

Phobias may co-occur in the presence of other childhood disorders or medical conditions, or may be part of complex multiple fear patterns (American Psychiatric Association 1994). The presenting complaint of excessive childhood fear is commonly associated with other, often primary, principle diagnoses (Strauss et al. 1988). Establishing the presence of a phobia and the absence of more significant difficulties is accomplished via a comprehensive initial assessment. Discovery of comorbidity obviously requires decisions about how to best structure treatment and which problems to deal with first.

Preparation

Many early parent-training programs failed to fully appreciate the importance of the parents' levels of knowledge and skill as determinants of treatment success (Blechman et al. 1989). Parents who lack formal education or have multiple problems (financial, marital, or psychological) of their own may find it difficult to apply what they learn to help their children. Parents vary significantly in ability to understand and implement strategies based on learning principles. It is therefore important to gauge parents' baseline knowledge and assess whether there are significant obstacles to successful treatment. Parents not well versed in effective behavior management skills may benefit from extended education sessions prior to their attempts to implement treatment in the home environment. This "training of skills phase" should not only focus on teaching parents behavioral principles but also provide opportunities to role-play relevant situations and to generate solutions to potential obstacles to effective treatment. More specific suggestions related to parent acquisition of knowledge are offered in the intervention section later in this chapter.

First Impressions

Parents and children are often relieved to learn that fears can be modified and that they both can have a primary role in overcoming them. However, they may have some initial reservations about actually implementing changes at home. Reservations may be related to claims that they have tried the approach already (to no avail) or to uncertainties about their own parenting abilities. Building upon the parents' preexisting strengths and their previous successes at helping their child overcome other difficulties can pave the way for acceptance of increasing responsibility for their child's treatment.

Assessment

Comprehensive assessment of childhood phobia should be sufficient to rule out the presence of more extensive difficulties, provide specific information about the phobic behavior to conduct a functional analysis, and formulate a treatment plan. When parents are responsible for implementing treatment, more emphasis must be placed on the feasibility of the approach for a particular family.

Parent Knowledge of Child Assessment Procedures

Care should be taken to fully inform parents of all assessment procedures so they may assist in a valid assessment of their child. The parents may be responsible for home monitoring or conducting a behavioral avoidance test in the home environment. Further, some of the strategies used by the therapist may involve exposure to the feared stimuli. It is important to determine if parents expect the child to have significant difficulty with a particular assessment procedure (such as a behavioral approach task) and how comfortable they are in eliciting successful cooperation from their child.

The Home Environment and Family Factors

There are several factors that appear to be associated with poor outcome in parent training and involvement. In addition to parent stress and psychopathology, Moreland and associates (1982) cite other variables such as lack of financial resources, low levels of formal education, certain parent discipline styles (authoritarian), family disorganization, family insularity (degree and quality of extrafamiliar contact), and a high number of child siblings. Graziano and Diament (1992) propose that altering the general approach to parent training is indicated in these cases.

We have found that consideration of all these variables is crucial to successful treatment planning, but that none should preclude treatment. Greater family instability warrants more extensive therapeutic involvement beyond the child's fear. The Family Environment Scale (FES) (R. Moos and B. Moos 1986) measures the social environment of the family along several dimensions including the domains of relationships, personal growth, and system maintenance. Subscales of these dimensions look more closely at family functioning variables (e.g., conflict, expressiveness, cohesion, organization, control, organization, etc.) and may be helpful in planning the parents' role in treatment. The following factors are likely to dictate significant modifications in approach and should be thoroughly assessed prior to treatment: (a) level of marital tensions/family discord, (b) usual discipline strategies, (c) impact of other caregivers, (d) reactions of siblings to the child's fear and their general level of adjustment, (e) family resources, (f) level of parent motivation and commitment to make changes, (g) overall climate of the home environment, and (h) existence of obstacles that may interfere with treatment.

Parent Assessment

We recommend the inclusion of both parents (if in the home) and suggest a general screening for parent pathology, parenting distress, and a self-report measure of fear. This is often a sensitive issue for parents intent on getting help for their child. Explaining that understanding the entire family is necessary for determining the most efficacious approach can help alleviate parental concerns. Parents may fill out the Symptom Checklist-90-R (SCL-90-R) (Derogatis 1992) or a similar measure, the Parenting Stress Index (PSI) (Abidin 1990), and the Fear Survey Schedule-II (FSS-II) (Geer 1965). This information can be helpful for the training phase of treatment, enabling discussion of the impact of distress on family parenting. It is also useful for gathering more specific information about parent fears, particularly because parents will be involved in exposure techniques requiring them to approach potentially feared objects. Severe scores on any of these measures should alert the clinician to the need for additional assessment and/or a possible psychological referral for one or both parents.

Importance of Relevant History

An important part of assessment involves determination of the history of parental attempts at helping their child overcome fear. A thorough analysis of parent–child interactions and reactions to fear is indicated. This information is central for understanding variables maintaining the child's fear and for suggesting targets for change in parent behavior. Once child behaviors have been identified, it is useful to specify the degree of knowledge and skill acquisition that parents will need. Important historical information to gather includes: (a) early parenting practices pertaining to dealing with previous developmental fears, (b) current stimulus situations where coping is successful and where it is unsuccessful, (c) parent attitudes toward and expectations about the child, (d) parents' understanding of fear and avoidance behavior, (e) parents' usual response to their own fears, (f) level of parent tolerance for their child's fear response and their subsequent behavior toward the child, (g) reinforcement of the child's avoidance behavior, and (h) reinforcement contingencies influencing parent behavior.

Parent Interview of Child Behavior

If there are questions about the extent of additional difficulties, or about a differential diagnosis, a structured interview may be appropriate. These tend to be time-consuming, and evidence that they improve upon a more traditional interview for treatment planning has yet to be gathered. However, gathering information in a systematic fashion may facilitate future efforts at evaluating which approach works for which child. The parent version of the Anxiety Disorders Interview Schedule for Children-Revised (ADIS-C-R) (Silverman and Nelles 1988) provides a thorough diagnostic evaluation of both internalizing and externalizing problems of childhood. It allows the parents to rate severity of fear, avoidance behavior, and interference in functioning. This information is valuable in comparing the child's report on these same indices in order to begin formulating a fear hierarchy.

Standardized Assessment of Child Behavior

As part of a detailed child assessment, we recommend assessing children's general level of adjustment in school and at home, overall level of fear (Fear Survey Schedule for Children-Revised [FSSC-R], Ollendick 1983), anxiety (Revised Children's Manifest Anxiety Scale [RCMAS], Reynolds and Richmond 1978), depression (Children's Depression Inventory [CDI], Kovacs 1980), and self-concept (Piers-Harris Children's Self-Concept Scale, Piers and Harris 1969). We limit our discussion here to the parent's contribution to child assessment. Descriptions of the other recommended child self-report instruments can be found in Friedman and Campbell 1992. A global measure of psychological adjustment such as the Child Behavior Checklist (CBCL)

(Achenbach and Edelbrock 1986) is useful in obtaining convergent information with parent interview data. The CBCL has been the most popular behavior rating scale used as an indicator of general behavior problems. Well-established norms are provided for each gender from ages 4 to 16, enabling a relatively confident judgment as to degree of deviance. In addition, post-treatment measures can be taken as an index of collateral behavior change; however, the instrument is limited in this regard.

Intervention Strategies

As with any intervention, the goal of treatment should include altering the existing environment to reduce the likelihood of the problem behavior; changing existing immediate contingencies; facilitating the development of more positive, adaptive strategies/behavior; and remediating deficits for long-term prevention (Evans 1989). Involvement of parents as agents of change provides an immediate vehicle for altering the environment and the existing contingencies. Parents are also encouraged to play a significant role in assisting the therapist in teaching more adaptive behaviors to the child. A thorough treatment plan that has been successfully implemented should provide the parent and child with a mode of communication and interaction that is preventive of future similar difficulties. Here we discuss several important pretreatment considerations in addition to the implementation of a treatment plan.

Pretreatment Considerations

Setting the Conditions for Therapeutic Efficacy

By allowing parents the opportunity to share past experiences and express their concerns openly, the therapist can set the foundation for a successful transition to the notion of "parent as co-therapist." A good starting point is to find out what the parents are already doing well and to reinforce their efforts and build upon them. This will build a positive, trusting relationship while encouraging them to learn additional ideas. Initial efforts can focus on the importance of the parents and home environment for creating the optimum therapeutic conditions. Parents often respond well to the idea that therapy will be time limited and that reduction of the child's fear will be targeted along with strategies for handling future problems.

Behavioral strategies are often misused by individuals who have been taught techniques but not the principles underlying them. Examples of such misuse include the wide acceptance of naively implemented "behavior modification" strategies sometimes seen in the school system. Providing a clear rationale for each component of treatment, delineating specific goals, and outlining the requirements for successful completion are important for ensuring correct implementation of each aspect of treatment, preventing such misuse (Mikulas and Coffman 1989).

Prior to a focus on any exposure-related tasks, it is important to set up the necessary conditions for successful parent-and-child interactions at home. In preparation for later sessions and exposure-related exercises, the parents and child are instructed to set aside a time for spending some positive time together. This time should be consistent each day, even if quite brief—to promote positive togetherness independent of phobic behavior. This may also help encourage a positive home environment in which to later introduce fear-related stimuli. Parents are often challenged by this relatively simple task as they come to recognize that making "special time" usually entails altering patterns in their daily schedule.

Parents and Children as Partners in Fear

The manner in which treatment is introduced to the parents and child is critical to reducing premature termination, enhancing compliance, and fostering successful completion of therapy. We have found that children and parents are quite receptive to the notion that they will learn "how to control fear" together and will complete relevant homework. This approach is also successful with adolescents, as they seem to enjoy the idea that their parents also have assignments. Children are much more likely to take steps toward fear reduction if the parent is both a model and a coach. Having parents implement the desired strategies shows the child that the parent is committed to helping and that treatment is important enough to engage in it themselves.

The final step prior to skill training is to set up a reward structure for the parent and the child. Both short- and long-term rewards facilitate treatment compliance and the achievement of goals. In the long run, the goal is that these artificial rewards will be replaced by the naturally occurring ones such as increased feelings of self-competency and enhanced freedom to pursue a wider range of activities. Early on, however, the choice of reinforcements for child compliance should be made thoughtfully. We have found the use of star charts and token economies (for later exchange for a desired but reasonable tangible reward) quite effective in this regard because they allow for visual inspection of specific goal attainment. But the need for consistency and fairness must be stressed. Once a child earns a token, poor behavior in another arena cannot result in withdrawal of the reward. Parent efforts can be reinforced with the use of therapy fee reduction, individual consultation, experimenter praise, group praise, or self-earned instrumental/material rewards (Schaefer and Briesmeister 1989).

Treatment Approach

Careful assessment may reveal deficits in the child that have increased the child's vulnerability to fear and anxiety. These may include depression, low self-esteem, and the like, which should be dealt with in therapy. Although a thorough discussion of the etiology and maintenance of fears is beyond the scope of this contribution, there is consensus that avoidance of fear-evoking stimuli appears to maintain phobic behavior. Treatments designed to promote exposure to phobic stimuli (ensuring that the feared outcome does not occur) appear to be most effective (Menzies and Clarke 1993). Because contact with the phobic stimuli is usually avoided, a number of steps may be necessary before the child is willing to attempt exposure. These usually include altering the contingencies at home to promote "brave" behavior, parent education, and teaching the child skills to cope (remain in the feared situations). The skill training may take the form of relaxation training, cognitive self-instruction, emotive imagery, or modeling via film or direct observation of others (including the parent).

Altering Contingencies

Assessment generally reveals aspects of the environment that are inadvertently reinforcing fear behavior. Depending upon the nature of the fears, this may include parental attention, affection, reassurance; substitution of other activities for a feared one (e.g., snack time being substituted for swimming for a water-phobic child); or decrease in responsibility contingent upon fear behavior (a child with a dog phobia may be excused from helping with yard work, for example). Altering these, by removing positive consequences of fear and implementing positive consequences of brave behavior, is the desired goal. This should be made explicit, in the form of rules that are always followed. Both parents, if involved, should agree on a "plan of action" that includes clearly delineated goals for change in their own behavior. Once the plan is established, parents should monitor their progress during the week and bring the home-monitoring forms to treatment for discussion. In addition, the use of tangible reinforcements, in the form of tokens, may be used temporarily to encourage the child to approach the phobic stimuli. These should be phased out, hopefully to be replaced with naturally occurring positive reinforcements such as parental praise or a sense of accomplishment. Both short- and long-term goals are constructed in clear, measurable terms.

Acquisition of Knowledge

Our focus here continues with the parents as participants in a shared treatment partnership with their child. Although the approach is offered with a single family case in mind, we believe the following is easily applicable to training parents in groups.

In order for parents to accept their role as co-therapists, they require a sufficient level of operating knowledge about the nature of fear and how this information applies to their child. We recommend a structured curriculum approach toward educating the parent, as this allows for the establishment of a criterion prior to learning behavioral skills. A combination of didactic presentation, general discussion, reading material, role-playing, and in-session exercises is tailored to the parents' base level of knowledge. We recommend five important topic areas, including information on fear in the course of normal development, child characteristics, components of fear, the nature of fear acquisition and maintenance, and general guidelines for parental response to their child's phobic behavior.

We have found success in presenting reading material and general discussion on the normal course of fear in development. Parents are receptive to the notion of "appropriate" fear as related to age-specific developmental tasks that the child attempts to master, and "inappropriate" fear as excessive (interfering with daily functioning) or age inappropriate. Most parents can easily enough come up with examples of how their child or they themselves have overcome developmentally appropriate fears. Following this line of discussion, the therapist can utilize the developmental context to discuss the individual child's age-related cognitive maturity and how this relates to the child's understanding of fear. In addition, child characteristics such as temperament and approach/avoidance tendencies add to a fuller appreciation of the child's predisposition to fear and his or her manner of coping with it.

In explaining the nature of fear, we engage the parents in identification of their child's fear in three domains: physiological arousal, cognitive aspects of fear (fearful thoughts and negative self-statements), and avoidance behavior. Here, tying in specific information gathered in assessment becomes useful in focusing the parents' attention toward fear behavior and in individualizing the child's treatment. Distinguishing a phobia as stimulus-specific fear is helpful in validating later intervention efforts. Parents seem to respond well to the story of "Little Albert" in discussing fear acquisition, the principle of classical conditioning, and stimulus generalization. In addition, we often talk to parents about other modes that contribute to fear behavior, such as modeling and family member fear behavior. Both parents and children respond to recent successful case examples that are similar in nature to the type of fear that the child is experiencing. This further contributes to parent understanding of the construct of fear. It also helps establish expectations for focused intervention, which include reducing avoidance behavior and promoting exposure to the feared stimulus (the principle of extinction). Fear maintenance is discussed in a few ways. The first is how fears fail to extinguish due to avoidance behaviors. The second is how avoidance leads to a positive feeling of relief which can reinforce the initial fear. Lastly, we discuss the related process of how fearful behavior may be reinforced by secondary gains. With a basic understanding of fear acquisition and maintenance, the parents become significantly more confident with treatment involving gradual exposure to the feared object or event and subsequent extinction of the fear.

Many times, parents are unaware that they often inadvertently contribute to the acquisition, enhancement, and maintenance of their child's fear. We discuss how this is part of being caring parents and wanting to do everything possible to help their child. However, we also note that this can cause difficulty for both the parents and the child. The clinician should encourage awareness of the parents' role in their child's fear by reviewing how their children's response to parental behavior is predicted by conditioning principles. Parents are usually receptive to this idea and ask for some general guidelines to better respond when their child is fearful. We suggest that parents acknowledge the child's feelings but also encourage them to use strategies (described below) to help them cope with and approach the feared object rather than avoid it. Parents can let their child know that it's okay to be afraid but that the fear is unfounded (assuming it is). Parents should take care to approach the situation in a matter-of-fact way and not to overreact. Parents should avoid forcing confrontation with the fear as well as avoid punishment or ridicule for fear behavior. By having appropriate expectations for gradual exposure in a supportive partnership, children are more likely to respond to parent directives. Other helpful strategies include having the parent model bravery, being patient and displaying confidence in the child, and attempting to utilize humor with the child.

Skills Training

Utilizing parents' knowledge about the principle of extinction, the goal of therapy is discussed as a gradual approach to fear exposure and mastery. The parents' first fear-related treatment assignment is to talk to their child in a supportive manner with the goal of sharing knowledge and educating the child about fear. It is explained to the parents that all opportunities to discuss or encounter fear-relevant information are potential "exposure" for the child. When parents use this framework of gradual approach, they can gauge the pace with which they can help their child to overcome fear. The therapist can help parents explain to their child about fear, including how it develops and how it can be overcome. Information is tailored to the child's level of understanding, with an emphasis on action-oriented learning. Parents and children are offered reading materials, coloring books, and hands-on exercises to aid in the communication process. The goal is for the parents to teach the child about fear and to help them identify and label feelings, thoughts, and behavior. We have found the use of a fear thermometer (Walk 1956), in addition to pictures of fearful facial expressions, quite helpful in helping parents measure their child's fear.

Over the course of the treatment sessions, the therapist guides the parents through a training module of modification skills designed to expose the child gradually to the feared object, beginning with stimuli that are associated with low levels of fear (simple discussions about the feared object, relevant pictures, brief encounters with stimuli related to the feared objects). Once children have some experience coping with stimuli associated with low levels of fear, they typically begin to develop an increasing sense of mastery and success. The general approach in teaching each skill is for the therapist to model the skill first, then to get the parents to model the same skill, either with the child or prior to the child's demonstration within session. For example, to begin the process, the clinician and parent explain what they are afraid of, how they feel, and how they cope with it prior to probing answers from the child. Homework is then assigned for the practice of each skill. The following skills aid in the process of parent–child involvement while allowing for gradual desensitization and mastery of fear. Designing a "best fit" between parent, child, and family circumstances requires a flexible approach with a variable time-frame.

Emotive imagery, relaxation, and cognitive self-instruction are three approaches that may facilitate the child's successful interaction with feared stimuli. Emotive imagery involves teaching the child to use images associated with "bravery" during exposure to phobic situations (Lazarus and Abramovitz 1962). Emotive imagery provides a nice means of getting the child and parent involved in approaching the fear as a team. The parent can help the child summon up images associated with current hero figures embarked on a special mission. Relaxation skills involve teaching the child to recognize bodily signals, to use breathing as a way to control their own body, and to learn muscle relaxation. The use of exercise may be helpful in attempting to introduce the child to changes in physiological arousal and implementing breathing and muscle control. When relaxation skills are paired with gradual exposure to feared stimuli, this is referred to as systematic desensitization—a preferred fear-reduction strategy in work with children (King and Gullone 1990). Cognitive self-instruction includes creating with the child specific self-talk strategies such as the selection of bravery statements ("I am brave") or positive self-statements ("I can do it"). Some children may also be receptive to cognitive strategies such as recognizing safety signals in the environment or by attending to the reality of the situation (stating the facts about a situation).

Constructing and Implementing a Fear Hierarchy

As an extension of the initial assessment, an important treatment-related task is the creation of a fear hierarchy to plan for gradual exposure. Identifying multiple specific fearful situations on a continuum from not very fearful to very, very fearful aids in charting the path for the progression of systematic extinction. Here, the fear thermometer can be used to rank-order the fears. Although attempts should be made to sequence the fear-evoking situations at small obtainable intervals, it is difficult to tell ahead of time how the pace of fear exposure will develop. Many factors contribute to the child's actual progress in approaching sequential items on the hierarchy, and, depending on initial successes, treatment can involve both multiple-exposure trials to the same or similar situation and sometimes skipping over an item that no longer evokes fear. Reconstruction or modification of the fear hierarchy is often necessary after beginning exposure trials. The optimal strategy typically involves creating tenable and realistic situations that are within the parameters of successful implementation of the parent–child dyad. Monitoring the child's fear reactions in each of the three domains discussed earlier helps in deciding whether it is time to move on from one fear item to the next on the hierarchy.

We believe it is helpful to approach exposure utilizing a variety of modalities. Children vary significantly in their ability to comply with exposure-related tasks, and it is helpful to consider flexibility in approaching each successive hierarchy item. Parents may consider starting out with tasks less threatening, like reading stories, making up imaginary tales, drawing pictures related to the fear, weaving the fearful topic into everyday discussion, and discussing others' similar fears before other more threatening tasks like looking at pictures/movies relating to the fear, talking directly about the fear, learning factual information about the feared object, having the child observe the parent or others approach and cope with the fear, and, finally, independent approach to the feared object.

Other strategies that have aided in successful exposure treatment include having the parent and child continue to role-play coping skills in pretend exposure situations prior to real exposure, setting up positive experiences associated with the feared object, allowing the child to have a security object or preferential play object with him or her upon exposure, or first approaching the feared item together. In addition, parents will likely find it quite beneficial to reinforce approach responses including the child's increased attention and proximity to the feared object.

Measuring Success

Home monitoring should include tracking the child's fear responses (e.g., fear thermometer, list of avoidant responses) in addition to charting the frequency and duration of approach responses toward fearful situations. With encouragement and in-session assistance, parents have been able to successfully develop a visible chart that serves as both a map of ongoing/future progress and a token economy system. Children seem to respond positively to a chart with successive hierarchy items on ascending steps or a hill that they eventually climb. This helps to set up expectations for success and reminds the child of previous achievements. Children can accumulate stars/stickers on the actual chart or collect points in exchange for desirable rewards later on.

Termination coincides with successful implementation of the exposure-related tasks with measurable reduction of fear behavior. The therapist should keep in mind that successful treatment involves training for generalization with an eye toward the prevention of future difficulties. Thus, in addition to discussing the general application of exposure to handling other potential fears, the therapist should spend time upon termination conferring with the parents about the general problem-solving approach they implemented to enlist their child in learning adaptive behavior. It is also important throughout treatment to be sure that parents are highlighting the positive aspects of their child, providing lots of praise not only for approaching feared objects and overcoming obstacles but also for all the wonderful things they value about their child. A positive focus, reinforced by the therapist, may go a long way toward preventing future problems and helping the child develop a healthy self-concept early in life.

Case Illustration

The following is a case description designed to illustrate how treatment components may be combined utilizing parents as effective mediators of change. To ensure confidentiality, aspects of the family characteristics have been altered.

Michael was a 10-year-old boy who was referred by his mother for persistent phobia of driving in automobiles following a car accident approximately four months earlier. In addition, Michael had begun to show various excessive fear reactions and social withdrawal at school. Mother (divorced) and child lived alone together, with maternal grandparents living nearby. At the time of referral, Michael would not take the school bus or drive with anyone other than his grandfather, following an elaborate ritual of safety checks and emotional reassurances.

Assessment

During the initial meeting, Michael and his mother were interviewed to determine further assessment needs. Consent was obtained for discussion with Michael's school teacher. Informal interview data suggested multiple fears and/or a possible anxiety disorder. Both child and parent versions of the Anxiety Disorders

Interview Schedule for Children-Revised (ADIS-C-R) were then administered. Mother completed the Child Behavior Checklist (CBCL), Parenting Stress Index (PSI), and the Symptom Check-list-90-Revised (SCL-90-R). Michael was administered self-report instruments relating to fear (Fear Survey Schedule for Children-Revised [FSSC-R]), anxiety (Revised Children's Manifest Anxiety Scale [RCMAS]), depression (Children's Depression Inventory [CDI]), and self-concept (Piers-Harris Children's Self-Concept Scale).

Information from Michael's mother and teacher suggested progressive difficulties with avoidance of certain school situations (gym, recess activities, after-school activities, and riding on the bus) and increased fear/anxiety concerning perceived danger (escalators, playing "rough" sports, field trips, and busy intersections). In addition, Michael had recently quit going to Boy Scout meetings following two years of enrollment and was disinterested in riding his bicycle. Parent interview with the ADIS-C-R indicated that Michael met criteria for phobia related to stimuli associated with the original car accident as well as generalized perceived danger. Mother's responses on the CBCL yielded a clinically significant elevation on the Anxious/Depressed subscale, along with a low Social Competence score. On a measure of general psychological distress (SCL-90-R), Michael's mother obtained an overall score within the normal range, while scoring high on the anxiety subscale compared to female norms. Her score on the Parenting Stress Index was significantly high.

The diagnostic interview with Michael revealed clinically significant levels of multiple fears, with mild to moderate depressive symptoms. His scores on self-report measures indicated high levels of fear of the unknown, fear of danger, and negative self-concept. His score on the CDI fell slightly below the clinical cutoff.

In the course of assessment, critical information was obtained regarding the family environment and history regarding Michael's phobias. Foremost, Michael and his mother had been adjusting to a new residence, away from the house where they had lived eight years previously. Michael's mother reported that she displayed increased fearfulness and worry at the time about starting a new job, moving, and selling the house. Both felt safe and relieved to have the support of Michael's grandparents nearby. At the time of the accident, Michael and his mother were driving near

Michael's prospective new school when they were hit broadside by another vehicle which Michael had seen and warned his mother about. Both Michael and his mother had to be hospitalized overnight for observation. Both received minor abrasions and were driven home the following day by the grandparents after significant protest from Michael, who asked to be taken home in the ambulance.

Further assessment information relating to mother's readiness for parent training revealed that she was herself reticent to get back behind the wheel and appeared to be maintaining Michael's fear by responding to his emotional protests with apologies and by giving in to his demands. Attempts at getting Michael to ride in the car with her or to ride on the bus were typically offered in all-or-nothing fashion, with rewards for cooperation. During the first three weeks of school, Michael had not been able to go beyond driving alone with his grandfather, while narrating a sequence of safety checks (double seat belts, stopping at the white line, speedometer check) and routine demands (drive in the right lane, window closed, let cars go ahead).

Intervention

Initial sessions focused on establishing firm and hopeful expectations about successful gradual exposure to driving with mother and eventually on the school bus. Because the primary fear stimulus was the original accident, it was predicted that with successful exposure to Michael and his mother driving in the car together, compliance with riding on the bus would be rather easily accomplished. It was decided that the grandfather would be useful in providing some assistance during treatment as a safety signal.

In order to enlist Michael's mother as an effective exposure agent, it was determined that she would need to both learn the principles of gradual exposure and perform them herself prior to instructing Michael. Mom grasped the concepts well, but needed much assistance in implementing the procedures and following through with her own emotional resolve. She recognized how she had been inadvertently maintaining Michael's fear behavior. After our third session together, mother was quite relieved to conceptualize the solution in terms of gradual extinction and expressed confidence in implementing the procedures. While the therapist and Michael's mother discussed homework assignments for mother's display of brave behavior with respect to driving, in addition to instruction on learning principles, Michael was asked to engage in low-level exposure tasks such as drawing pictures of cars/ school buses and talking about the accident. In addition, Michael was taught to use positive self-talk plus breathing to cope with his fear response and asked to practice it at home.

Parent and child were also asked to have a special time together each evening not relating to the problem situation and to set up a reward structure for each of ten steps (hierarchy items) they would eventually accomplish. By Session 4, Michael and his mother were given joint homework assignments and had developed a partnership in accomplishing the task together. We had been able to create a hierarchy ranging from lower-level fear-provocation tasks such as washing the car together, sitting in the car without the ignition on and listening to music, turning on and off the ignition, to higher-level exposure tasks such as going on a train/bus ride together, grandfather driving with mother in the back seat, driving by the original accident site, and mother driving with Michael and grandparents in the car first around the block, then later to school. Mother was instructed to perform at least two exposure trials per day. A visual chart was sent home for display of progress with rewards written in under each of ten steps. By Session 6, Michael had been able to tolerate mother being in the car while driving with grandfather, and they had also improvised on their own by boarding a school bus with Michael's new classmate friend. At the time of the seventh session, progress had accelerated quite nicely and Michael had taken the school bus home and had also driven with his mother for the first time in the driveway. Within the next two weeks, Michael had achieved the highest-level exposure item as both he and his mother drove to the accident site on the way to school. Upon termination, Michael and his mother had become quite impressed with their teamwork in approaching fear and were receptive to the model with respect to general problem solving as well as combating other fears/anxieties. Michael vowed to take mother to the pet store to acquaint her with various reptiles in order to help her overcome her reported fear of snakes. Follow-up two months later indicated maintenance of treatment gains and improved adjustment to their new home environment.

Conclusion

Successful involvement of parents as co-therapists or exposure agents in the treatment of children's fears is often the most preferred mode of fear reduction. Beyond the immediate access to in vivo exposure material, the therapist is in a position to teach parents new skills and adaptive ways of relating to their child in solving problems. Careful assessment of parental level of knowledge impacts directly on the degree of preexposure training and the subsequent pace of carrying out gradual exposure trials with fearful children. Frequently, parents contribute to the maintenance of their child's fear behavior and become frustrated at failed attempts to overcome the fear. Promoting a treatment model that guides their proactive efforts by offering incremental doses of success, parents gain an appreciation of their own competence, a tempered approach to their child's emotional distress, and a positive view of mental health professionals.

References

Abidin, R. R. (1990). *Parenting Stress Index: Manual*, 3rd ed. Charlottesville, VA: University of Virginia, Pediatric Psychology Press.

Achenbach, T. M., and Edelbrock, C. S. (1986). *Manual for the Child Behavior Checklist and Revised Child Behavior Profile*. Burlington, VT: University of Vermont, Department of Psychiatry.

American Psychiatric Association. (1994). *Diagnostic and Statistical Manual of Mental Disorders*, 4th ed. Washington, DC: American Psychiatric Association.

Barlow, D. H., and Seidner, A. L. (1983). Treatment of adolescent agoraphobia: effects on parent–adolescent relations. *Behaviour Research and Therapy* 21:519–526.

Bauer, D. H. (1976). An exploratory study of developmental changes in children's fears. *Journal of Child Psychology and Psychiatry* 17:69–74.

Berkowitz, B. P., and Graziano, A. M. (1972). Training parents as behavior therapists: a review. *Behaviour Research and Therapy* 10:297–317.

Blagg, N. R., and Yule, W. (1984). The behavioral treatment of school-refusal: a comparative study. *Behaviour Research and Therapy* 22:119–127.

Blechman, E. A., Tryon, A. S., Russ, M. H., and McEnrowe, M. J. (1989). Family skills training and childhood depression. In *Handbook of Parent Training: Parents as Co-Therapists for Children's Behavior Problems*, ed. C. E. Schaefer and J. M. Briesmeister, pp. 203–222. New York: Wiley.

Bollard, J., Nettlebeck, T., and Roxbee, L. (1982). Dry-bed training for childhood bedwetting: a comparison group with individually administered parent instruction. *Behaviour Research and Therapy* 20:209–217.

Budd, K. S., Madison, L. S., Itzkowitz, J. S., et al. (1986). Parents and therapists as allies in behavioral treatment of children's stuttering. *Behavior Therapy* 17:538–553.

Derogatis, L. R. (1992). *SCL-90-R; The Administration, Scoring and Procedures Manual-II for the Revised Version.* Towson, MD: Clinical Psychometric Research.

Epstein, L. H., Wing, R. R., Koeske, R., and Valoski, A. (1987). Long-term effects of family-based treatment of childhood obesity. *Journal of Consulting and Clinical Psychology* 55:91–95.

Evans, I. M. (1989). A multi-dimensional model for conceptualizing the design of child behavior therapy. *Behavioural Psychotherapy* 17:237–251.

Friedman, A. G., and Campbell, T. A. (1992). Children's nighttime fears: a behavioral approach to assessment and treatment. In *Innovations in Clinical Practice: A Source Book*, vol. 11, ed. L. VandeCreek, S. Knapp, and T. L. Jackson, pp. 139–155. Sarasota, FL: Professional Resource Press.

Friedman, A. G., and Ollendick, T. H. (1989). Treatment programs for severe night-time fears: a methodological note. *Journal of Behavior Therapy and Experimental Psychiatry* 20:171–178.

Garber, S. W., Daniels-Garber, M., and Freedman-Spizman, R. (1993). *Monsters Under the Bed and Other Childhood Fears: Helping Your Child Overcome Anxieties, Fears, and Phobias.* New York: Villard.

Geer, J. H. (1965). The development of a scale to measure fear. *Behaviour Research and Therapy* 3:45–53.

Giebenhain, J. E., and O'Dell, S. L. (1984). Evaluation of a parent-training manual for reducing children's fears of the dark. *Journal of Applied Behavior Analysis* 17:121–125.

Graziano, A. M. (1977). Parents as behavior therapists. In *Progress in Behavior Modification*, vol. 4, ed. M. Hersen, R. M. Eisler, and P. M. Miller, pp. 251–299. New York: Academic Press.

Graziano, A. M., and Diament, D. M. (1992). Parent behavioral training: an examination of the paradigm. *Behavior Modification* 16:3–38.

Graziano, A. M., and Mooney, K. C. (1980). Family self-control instruction for children's nighttime fear reduction. *Journal of Consulting and Clinical Psychology* 48:206–213.

——— (1982). Behavioral treatment of "night fears" in children: maintenance of improvement at 2½ to 3 years follow up. *Journal of Consulting and Clinical Psychology* 50:398–399.

Graziano, A. M., Mooney, K. C., Huber, C., and Ignasiak, D. (1979). Self-control instruction for children's fear education. *Journal of Behavior Therapy and Experimental Psychiatry* 10:221–227.

Israel, A. C., Stolmaker, L., Sharp, J. P., et al. (1984). An evaluation of two methods of parental involvement in treating obese children. *Behavior Therapy* 15: 266–272.

Johnson, C. A., and Katz, R. C. (1973). Using parents as change agents for their children: a review. *Journal of Child Psychology and Psychiatry* 14:181–200.

King, N. J., and Gullone, E. (1990). Acceptability of fear reduction procedures with children. *Journal of Behavior Therapy and Experimental Psychiatry* 21:1–8.

Kolko, D. J. (1983). Multicomponent parental treatment of firesetting in a 6-year-old boy. *Journal of Behavior Therapy and Experimental Psychiatry* 14:349–353.

Kovacs, M. (1980). Rating scales to assess depression on school-aged children. *Acta Paedopsychiatrica* 46:305–315.

Ladoceur, R., and Martineau, G. (1982). Evaluation of regulated-breathing method with and without parental assistance in the treatment of child stutterers. *Journal of Behavior Therapy and Experimental Psychiatry* 13:301–306.

Lazarus, A. A., and Abramovitz, A. (1962). The use of "emotive imagery" in the treatment of children's phobias. *Journal of Mental Science* 108:227–277.

McMenamy, C., and Katz, R. C. (1989). Brief parent-assisted treatment for children's nighttime fears. *Journal of Developmental and Behavioral Pediatrics* 10:145–148.

Menzies, R. G., and Clarke, J. C. (1993). A comparison of in vivo and vicarious exposure in the treatment of childhood water phobia. *Behaviour Research and Therapy* 31:9–15.

Mikulas, W. L., and Coffman, M. F. (1989). Home-based treatment of children's fear of the dark. In *Handbook of Parent Training: Parents as Co-Therapists for Children's Behavior Problems*, ed. C. E. Schaefer and J. M. Briesmeister, pp. 179–202. New York: Wiley.

Moos, R. H., and Moos. B. (1986). *Family Environment Scale: Manual*, 2nd ed. Palo Alto, CA: Consulting Psychologists Press.

Moreland, J. R., Schwebel, A. I., Beck, S., and Wells, R. (1982). Parents as therapists: a review of the behavior therapy literature—1975–1981. *Behavior Modification* 6:250–276.

Ollendick, T. H. (1983). Reliability and validity of the Revised-Fear Survey Schedule for Children (FSSC-R), *Behaviour Research and Therapy* 21:685–692.

Ollendick, T. H., Matson, J. L., and Helsel, W. J. (1985). Fears in children and adolescents: normative data. *Behaviour Research and Therapy* 23:465–467.

Piers, E. V., and Harris, D. B. (1969). *The Piers-Harris Children's Self-Concept Scale: The Way I Feel about Myself*. Nashville, TN: Counselor Recordings and Tests.

Reynolds, C. R., and Richmond, B. O. (1978). What I think and feel: a revised measure of children's manifest anxiety. *Journal of Abnormal Child Psychology* 6:271–280.

Schaefer, C. E., and Briesmeister, J. M. (1989). *Handbook of Parent Training: Parents as Co-Therapists for Children's Behavior Problems.* New York: Wiley.

Schloss, P. J., and Johann, M. (1982). A modeling and contingency management approach to pacifier withdrawal. *Behavior Therapy* 13:254–257.

Silverman, W. K., and Nelles, W. B. (1988). The anxiety disorders interview schedule for children. *Journal of the American Academy of Child and Adolescent Psychiatry* 27:772–778.

Strauss, C. C., Lease, C. A., Last, C. G., and Francis, G. (1988). Overanxious disorder: an examination of developmental differences. *Journal of Abnormal Child Psychology* 16:433–443.

Walk, R. D. (1956). Self-ratings of fear in a fear invoking situation. *Journal of Abnormal and Social Psychology* 52:171–178.

6

A Systematic Approach to
Separation Anxiety Disorder

BEATRICE HAMILTON

Children presenting with fears of leaving for school in the morning are invariably having problems at home, which may include domestic violence, parental psychopathology, or prolonged illness of the parent (Baldwin et al. 1982, Barkley 1981, Bloom-Feshbach and Blatt 1981, Buchsbaum 1987, Emery and O'Leary 1982, Field 1984, Patterson et al. 1989, Reite et al. 1981). In turn, a child's separation anxiety may aggravate familiar dysfunction as the parents focus on the child and away from their own conflicts, thereby reinforcing the child's maladaptive behavior (Brown and Christensen 1986). It is apparent that therapists need to be cognizant of these dynamics and work with school-related problems from a systematic approach. They should be aware of the roles of learning institutions, and utilize the skills of co-professionals where appropriate. Teachers can be an invaluable resource for the therapist by providing helpful information on the child's social, cognitive, psychomotor, and emotional functioning. The therapist can make recommendations to the teacher which would aid in developing positive coping skills.

A Case Study

This case demonstrates a family–school problem addressed from a systematic perspective. The case concerns Sue, a 4-year-old child entering kindergarten who has an intense fear of leaving her mother to attend school.

Sue's teacher referred her to a family therapist for help after two weeks of listening to her cry all day and call out, "I want my mommy." The teacher reported that Sue showed no interest in interacting with other children. She appeared sad and unable to concentrate on class activities. Additionally, both teacher and principal suggested that Sue not attend school for another year because her behavior indicated that she was too immature. However, according to state laws and placement tests given before entering kindergarten, she was ready for school.

An appointment was arranged with the family for an evaluation of the nuclear family system where school problems and an assessment of the family's interaction patterns were observed and discussed. During the assessment interview it was revealed that the parents had considered taking Sue out of school until the next school term. Two older children in the household, ages 15 and 17, had not presented any symptomatic complaints of school-related problems. Sue appeared to have a normal sibling relationship with both brother and sister. The father experienced no problem leaving the child, nor did the sister or brother. Throughout the interview Sue talked only when asked and did so with little verbal expression. She clung to her mother throughout the interview. The father emphasized that Sue complained of pains in her stomach, cried, stomped on the floor, and refused to dress for school. An examination by the family doctor revealed no physical ailment consistent with Sue's complaints.

During the interview process, the mother indicated that she was seeking counseling because she felt frightened and guilty about letting her child go anywhere without her. Also, there was stress in the marital relationship. When Sue was 3 years old the parents separated for four months. During that time Sue was allowed to sleep with her mother. Since the return of her father, on many occasions she had refused to sleep alone and would awaken during the night from nightmares about her mother abandoning her.

Results of the interviews confirmed a diagnosis of separation anxiety disorder. According to *DSM-III-R* (1987), this disorder is characterized by excessive anxiety concerning separation from major attachment figures or from home or other familiar surroundings. There are nine criteria for a diagnosis of separation anxiety, of which the child must manifest at least three of the following signs or symptoms:

1. Unrealistic worry that possible harm will befall major attachment figures or fear that they will leave and not return;

2. Unrealistic worry that an untoward calamitous event will separate the child from a major attachment figure (e.g., the child will be lost, kidnapped, killed, or the victim of an accident);
3. Persistent reluctance or refusal to go to school in order to stay with major attachment figures or at home;
4. Persistent reluctance or refusal to go to sleep without being next to a major attachment figure or to sleep away from home;
5. Persistent avoidance of being alone in the home, or emotional upset if unable to follow the major attachment figure around the home;
6. Repeated nightmares involving the theme of separation;
7. Complaints of physical symptoms on school days (e.g., stomachache, headache, nausea, and vomiting);
8. Signs of excessive distress on separation or when anticipating separation from major attachment figures (e.g., temper tantrums or crying, pleading with parents not to leave);
9. Social withdrawal, apathy, sadness, or difficulty in concentrating on work or play when not with a major attachment figure.

In addition to the presence of three symptoms, each disturbance must have been of at least two weeks' duration.

Sue exhibited five of the symptoms of separation anxiety disorder, specifically Criteria 3, 6, 7, 8, and 9.

Treatment focused on eliminating Sue's separation anxiety disorder. A family–school behavioral treatment model was designed which created a triadic relationship between child, parent, and school. The therapist met with all parties and everyone agreed upon a selected treatment plan.

The therapist designed a schedule of Sue's daily activities and behavior charts which were used to denote behavioral progress throughout the treatment. For rewards Sue's mother would pick her up from school each day. The teacher gave positive reinforcers (stickers) when she interacted appropriately with groups and when she completed assignments on time. A combination of behavioral modification techniques was utilized to minimize Sue's stress level; these included instruction, modeling, relaxation, and in vivo exposure. Several authors have found the latter to be effective in the treatment of anxiety-related disorders (Emmelkamp 1982, Goldstein and Chambless 1978).

It was explained to Sue and her parents that the only way to overcome her fear was to repeatedly confront the very situations she feared and avoided. It was further explained that her fears would be handled through a gradual approach, in a stepwise manner, increasing to more difficult tasks. For the treatment to work, Sue would need to complete each attempted task; however, in vivo exposures were regulated based upon Sue's readiness.

At the beginning of Week 1 of the treatment, the therapist picked Sue up from home and rode the school bus with her pointing out landmarks and places the bus would stop to pick up other children; this continued for four consecutive days. On the fifth day, the father or a sibling would put Sue on the school bus each morning. The teacher agreed to give Sue assignments which would make her mornings more enjoyable and reinforce participation in groups. The teacher was given specific assignments which included using behavioral charts to record Sue's progress while at school. A daily report of Sue's behavior was given to the therapist. The mother was provided with instructions and modeling techniques to assist Sue in a relaxation activity, used when Sue experienced nightmares. On Monday, after school, Sue would meet with the therapist for counseling.

After five weeks of treatment, Sue regularly rode the school bus with no problem. Weekends and holidays were setbacks for her. However, with reinforcement from both therapist and teacher, Sue was able to continue to work toward attending school. Sue not only completed kindergarten, she enjoyed it. Her mother continued to pick her up from school. On her first reporting period, she had all "A's" on her report card.

This case illustrates an effective approach for working with separation anxiety from a systematic perspective. Assessments and interventions by both family and school minimized the child's problems and also reduced stress within the family and family-school relationships.

References

American Psychiatric Association. (1987). *Diagnostic and Statistical Manual of Mental Disorders*. 3rd ed., rev. Washington, DC: American Psychiatric Association.

Baldwin, A. L., Cole, R. E., and Baldwin, C. P. (1982). Parental pathology, family interaction, and the competence of the child in school. *Monographs of the Society for Research in Child Development* 47(5), Serial No. 197.

Barkley, R. A. (1981). Hyperactivity. In *Behavioral Assessment of Childhood Disorders*, ed. E. J. Mash and L. G. Terdal. Ann Arbor, MI: Family Development Project.

Bloom-Feschbach, S., and Blatt, S. J. (1981). Separation response and nursery school adaptation. *Journal of the American Academy of Child Psychiatry* 21:58-64.

Brown, J. H., and Christensen, D. N. (1986). *Family Therapy Theory and Practice*. Monterey, CA: Brooks/Cole.

Buchsbaum, B. C. (1987). Remembering a parent who has died: a developmental perspective. In *The Annual of Psychoanalysis*, vol. 15. Madison, CT: International Universities Press.

Emery, R. E., and O'Leary, K. D. (1982). Children's perspective of marital discord and behavior problems of boys and girls. *Journal of Abnormal Child Psychology* 10:11-24.

Emmelkamp, P. M. G. (1982). In vivo exposure treatment of agoraphobia. In *Agoraphobia: Multiple Perspectives on Theory and Treatment*, ed. D. Chambless and A. J. Goldstein, pp. 43-75. New York: Wiley.

Field, T. (1984). Separation stress of young children transferring to new schools. *Developmental Psychology* 20:786-792.

Goldstein, A. J., and Chambless, D. L. (1978). Habituation of subjective anxiety during flooding in imagery. *Behaviour Research and Therapy* 16:391-399.

Patterson, G. R., DeBarsyshe, D. B., and Ramsey, E. (1989). A developmental perspective on antisocial behavior. *American Psychologist* 44:329-335.

Reite, M., Harbeck, R., and Hoffman, A. (1981). Altered cellular immune response following peer separation. *Life Sciences* 29:1133-1136.

7

"Errorless" Elimination of Separation Anxiety

JOHN T. NEISWORTH, RONALD A. MADLE, AND
KARL E. GOEKE

Typically, behavior modifiers have treated separation anxiety using techniques involving reciprocal inhibition. For example, Lazarus
and Abramovitz (1962) reported the successful use of emotive imagery
in treating several types of phobia in children. Patterson (1965) was able
to eliminate a separation anxiety problem in a 7-year-old child using a
combination of desensitization and reinforcement, both at school and
in the home. Reinforcement was used in two ways: (a) to
countercondition anxiety in the school situation and (b) to strengthen
nonanxious statements about the mother's absence. Successful elimination of separation anxiety in two preschool children using in vivo
desensitization, paralleling the work of Jones (1924) with phobics, was
reported by Montenegro (1968).

Numerous children's problems, including separation anxiety
(Kennedy 1965), have also been dealt with using operant techniques
such as time-out and extinction (Ross 1972). One of the persisting problems with these techniques, however, is their delayed effect and the
production of heightened responding during early stages of intervention (Sulzer and Mayer 1972). These effects particularly present problems where parents and teachers experience difficulty tolerating a child
in distress and where intermittent reinforcement of the problem becomes
likely in the less than optimal natural setting. The present study attempted to deal with these considerations by developing a technique
which produced minimal distress in child, parent, and teachers during
intervention.

Case History

A 4-year-old girl was enrolled in the University Preschool Laboratory. She and her family were natives of Argentina and the child was bilingual, speaking only Spanish in the home. She had one sibling, a 3-year-old sister, who was adjusting to another preschool without difficulty. The parents were separated, with the father in Argentina and the mother employed as a research assistant at the University. Due to the mother's circumstances the children were attended by a baby-sitter in the afternoons. Both children were physically healthy and displayed normal to advanced performance relative to other children their ages.

During the preceding year the child was enrolled in another preschool program at the same University. During this time her chronic crying, screaming, sobbing, and withdrawal became an increasing problem. According to anecdotal records, the child gained little from her experiences in the program. Her tantrum behaviors began when the mother left and continued until her return. The same reports identified the preschool as the primary site of the problem, although it occasionally occurred in other situations when the mother left the child. Not only did the child refuse to participate in program activities, but she did not engage in sustained social interaction with other children. The teachers and aides repeatedly attempted a variety of traditional techniques (e.g., rechanneling interest, cuddling, etc.) to involve the child in the program. Well-intentioned but unsystematic efforts to ignore the behavior were, understandably, ineffective. Despite all attempts the problem became an intense, maladaptive routine. On several occasions, when the problem reached proportions the teachers could not tolerate or deal with, the mother was contacted to take the child home. Numerous explanations were advanced for the problem, ranging from the child's "immaturity" to a possible "bilinguality barrier."

For the following year the child was assigned to a behavioral preschool program. Administrative personnel felt, however, that if the child continued to exhibit the problem, with the consequent agony to the mother, the child would be withdrawn from preschool entirely.

Intervention Plan

The objective of the proposed intervention strategy was to eliminate the maladaptive cluster of behaviors (i.e., crying, sobbing, screaming, and withdrawal) with as little distress as possible to the child. This was necessitated by the fact that the mother, as well as some of the preschool staff, found it difficult to endure the child's distress without attending to her. Records and observations indicated this probably played an important role in the maintenance and, perhaps, development of the problem. Because of this, a procedure based on the principle of stimulus fading (Terrace 1963) was developed. Essentially, the use of this principle entails engineering the situation to set the occasion for the desired response, that is, nonanxious behavior, at full strength and then gradually to return the situation to its original state without losing control of the response. Although relatively unexplored, this technique has been used successfully with behaviors ranging from oral reading (Corey and Shamow 1972) to heterosexual responsiveness (Barlow and Agras 1973).

Plans were made to have the mother remain in the vicinity of the preschool for several sessions. She would then be used as a reinforcer for the child's nonanxious behaviors. However, in an attempt to preempt the occurrence of the problem behaviors, the length of time the child had to exhibit nonanxious behavior would gradually be extended. That is, rather than fade the mother spatially as Patterson (1965) did, the mother would be temporally removed. Technically, the plan involved the use of differential reinforcement of other behavior with a progressively increasing criterion.

Use of the mother as a reinforcer was based on two considerations. First, none of the usual events in the preschool appeared to serve as a reinforcer for the child, while the mother did. Secondly, since the inconsistent pattern of parental attention to the problem behaviors probably played a significant role in the problem's maintenance, the use of the mother as a reinforcer also contributed to the restructuring of her contact with the child. This, hopefully, would increase the likelihood of generalization and maintenance of the intervention results. Since the mother's presence could not be manipulated in the manner which is optimal for reinforcer delivery, a method was developed for signaling the child that the mother was about to appear and for cueing the mother to enter the room. The bell of a standard kitchen timer was selected for this purpose since it could also be used to time the delay interval between the mother's leaving and reappearing.

Finally, the plan involved a brief discussion with the mother. In this session, the basic principle of positive reinforcement was explained as well as the rationale for the intervention plan. This session was conducted several days prior to the first day of baseline, which made possible the assessment that the discussion with the mother, itself, was insufficient to change the child's behavior. The mother fully agreed to participate in the program.

Procedure and Results

For ten preschool sessions, each about three hours in length, baseline data were collected on the duration of anxious behaviors (crying, screaming, and sobbing, without being injured). For the first two days of baseline, two observers recorded the duration of anxious behavior and obtained interrater agreements of 94 percent and 96 percent, respectively. Due to the high agreement on response occurrence, only one observer recorded in later sessions, except for a reliability check on Day 13, which yielded 92 percent agreement. During baseline, anxious behavior occurred with a mean duration of 152 minutes. There was no detectable trend toward increasing or decreasing duration.

On the first day of intervention (Day 11), the procedure of reinforcing nonanxious behavior was initiated. Starting with delay intervals from a few seconds' duration and gradually increasing them over the next several days, as shown in Figure 7-1, the child was reinforced for progressively longer periods of nonanxious behavior during which time she was encouraged and increasingly consented to become involved in program activities. In addition, the length of time the mother remained to reinforce the child was gradually decreased from seven minutes. As shown in Figure 7-1, introduction of the intervention plan resulted in almost immediate cessation of anxious behavior. In fact, only ten minutes of anxious behavior were exhibited during the course of intervention. This is considerably less than would have been expected with time-out or extinction. On the seventeenth day the timer was removed from the preschool. This resulted in the immediate emission of anxious behavior, which corroborates the timer's potency in the plan. Because of this it became necessary to remove the timer gradually throughout the seventeenth day by increasing the distance between the timer and child. In addition, the child was reinforced for increasing involvement in program activities. This was accomplished without incident or recurrence of anxious behavior. One session of follow-up data collected each month showed no signs of problem recurrence. In addition, the mother reported a decrease of the problem in other settings.

Discussion

It appears significant that the intervention strategy used in the present study was successful in eliminating separation anxiety with a

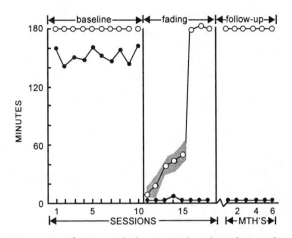

Figure 7-1. Duration of anxious behaviors (closed circles) and mean length of the delay interval (open circles) during baseline, fading, and follow-up. The shading indicates the range of the delay intervals on days with more than one interval.

total of only ten minutes of anxious behavior during intervention. Typically, operant strategies for eliminating behavior, such as time-out and extinction, result in continued or pronounced responding in the early stages of intervention (Sulzer and Mayer 1972). A second aspect of the study, restructuring the mother–child contact contingencies, appeared to be facilitated by the absence of anxious behavior in the child during intervention. While not formally evaluated, it also appeared that this facilitated the maintenance and generalization of the intervention outcomes.

References

Barlow, D. H., and Agras, W. S. (1973). Fading to increase heterosexual responsiveness in homosexuals. *Journal of Applied Behavior Analysis* 6:355–366.

Corey, J. R., and Shamow, J. C. (1972). The effects of fading on the acquisition and retention of oral reading. *Journal of Applied Behavior Analysis* 5:311–316.

Jones, M. C. (1924). Elimination of children's fears. *Journal of Experimental Psychology* 7:282–290.

Kennedy, W. A. (1965). School phobia: rapid treatment of fifty cases. *Journal of Abnormal Psychology* 70:285–289.

Lazarus, A. A., and Abramovitz, A. (1962). The use of "emotive imagery" in treatment of children's phobias. *Journal of Mental Science* 108:191–195.

Montenegro, H. (1968). Severe separation anxiety in two preschool children successfully treated by reciprocal inhibition. *Journal of Child Psychology and Psychiatry* 9:93–103.

Patterson, G. R. (1965). Learning theory approach to the treatment of a school phobic child. In *Case Studies in Behavior Modification*, ed. L. P. Ullman and L. Krasner. New York: Holt, Rinehart & Winston.

Ross, A. O. (1972). Behavior therapy. In *Psychopathological Disorders in Childhood*, ed. H. C. Quay and J. S. Werry. New York: Wiley.

Sulzer, B., and Mayer, G. R. (1972). *Behavior Modification Procedures for School Personnel.* Hinsdale, IL: Dryden Press.

Terrace, H. S. (1963). Discrimination learning with and without "errors." *Journal of the Experimental Analysis of Behavior* 6:1–27.

8

Shyness

DAVID J. BIEMER

Shyness: The Social Anxiety Epidemic

In a Stanford University survey of over 5,000 individuals (Zimbardo 1977), over 40 percent said that shyness was a personal problem for them. When applied to the general population, this proportion translates into 84 million people with varying degrees of difficulty in social situations. The problem is so widespread that most experts consider shyness a social epidemic (Buss 1980, Trower et al. 1978, Zimbardo 1977).

Despite the extensiveness of the problem of social anxiety and the serious consequences of it, relatively little has been written on the subject. Only recently have researchers begun to systematically study the problem. The research that has been done has focused almost exclusively on shyness in adulthood. This is especially surprising when it is considered that the highest prevalence of shyness is found among school children in the seventh and eighth grades. Six out of ten children in this age group reported problems with shyness (Zimbardo 1977). Yet, one of the only extensive works on social anxiety in children is *The Shy Child*, by Stanford University social psychologists Zimbardo and Radl (1981).

The Shyness Control Program

There is a systematic approach that has been successfully employed with adults and children in group and individual formats. The program has been structured for groups of children in at least three formats: (1)

two-hour sessions, once a week for six consecutive weeks; (2) a more abbreviated program of two-hour sessions, once a week for four consecutive weeks; and (3) a marathon four-hour session. Group size in the two extended formats range from three to twenty-five participants. The marathon session has accommodated up to eighty youngsters. Participants have mostly been 11- to 15-year-olds.

For youngsters in this age range, the sessions should be light, upbeat, and positive. It helps to bring humor into the meetings whenever possible. Laughter is an excellent way of getting inhibited youngsters to loosen up and view shyness with less apprehension.

A flow chart serves as the framework for the system and represents a wide range of tested and proven clinical methods employed by practitioners in the field of anxiety management. In presenting the program, ample use is made of newsprint, graphics, and handouts. The flow chart is prominently displayed and referred to throughout the program. This keeps participants aware of the stage of problem solving under consideration.

What Is Shyness?

Shyness is the habit of being afraid of people or social situations. When a shy child is exposed to a fear-producing social stimulus, a strong reaction occurs. This emotional reaction has three basic components: subjective feelings of fear and distress, heightened physiological arousal, and motor responses consisting of either withdrawn, frozen behavior or frenzied, "flight" behavior (Hersen 1973, Marks 1969, Rachman and Costello 1961). Shyness is a three-dimensional fear.

Cognitive Fear

Shy people think differently from nonshy people. They bombard themselves with a steady stream of absolute and negative self-statements. The content of the shy person's private world is predominantly self-critical, leading to lowered self-esteem.

Physiological Fear

The physiological dimension of shyness is characterized by activation of automatic defenses manifested in increased pulse rate, perspiration, elevated blood pressure, and blushing. The shy person reacts subjectively to an objectively harmless social situation as though it were an actual physical threat. The results are that shy persons exhibit more hand tremors, perspire more, get drier in the mouth, and generally are more nervous in public than nonshy people.

Behavioral Fear

Shy persons perform less in social situations. They are less proficient in initiating conversations, in small talk, and in giving and receiving compliments. In addition to these deficits, shy persons can be seen exhibiting behavioral excesses, such as rowdiness and other forms of disruptive behavior that serve to compensate for the shy person's lack of more appropriate social competencies.

In general, shyness is a fear of things in public. The fear manifests itself in three ways: (1) shy thoughts, (2) shy feelings, and (3) shy behavior.

Shyness Consequences

The effects of being shy can be devastating. Shyness makes it difficult to meet new people, make and maintain friendships, or enjoy social experiences. Possibly worst of all, shyness is self-perpetuating and self-intensifying. The heightened emotionality that shyness causes in novel social situations is stressing, uncomfortable, and noxious.

Consequently, new social experiences are avoided. Because these situations are avoided, they tend to remain novel. The result is a cycle of increasing social uneasiness toward an expanding array of social experiences. Left unchecked, this cycle can culminate in total withdrawal and isolation of the individual.

What Causes Shyness?

Experts do not agree on what causes shyness. Professionals with a strong psychoanalytic orientation feel that shyness is a reaction to the unfulfilled primal wishes of the id. Other specialists feel that certain people are born with a predisposition to social anxiety. Developmental psychologists take the view that intense and frequent social anxiety among young children has its roots in early parent–child relationships (Mussen et al. 1963).

Behaviorists maintain that shyness is best explained as learned habits of responding with anxiety and impaired performance to social situations. These habits are learned primarily through one's own negative personal experiences in interacting with others or through vicarious experiences, that is, through observation of what is perceived to be aversive in the interpersonal experiences of others.

The Shyness Control Program views shyness as a complex of normally developed behavioral, cognitive, and emotional habits. To replace the normally developed (but maladaptive) shy habits with more adaptive response patterns entails the same principles of learning that led to the shyness condition.

A carefully structured stepwise process is employed in the Shyness Control Program to accomplish this relearning. This process is shown in Figure 8–1.

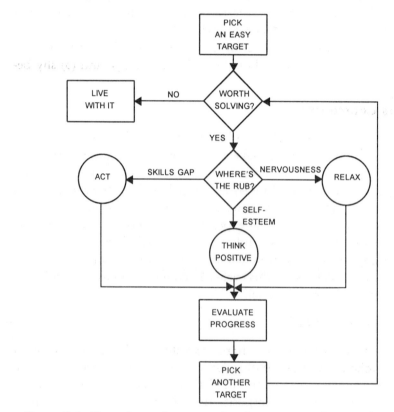

Figure 8–1. Flow chart of steps in the shyness control process.

Pick an Easy Target

The program begins with a comprehensive personal inventory of the events and persons that precipitate the shyness reaction. There are a number of checklists and inventories that might be used to facilitate identifying situations that or individuals whom the shy person finds problematic.

The Stanford Survey on Shyness that is reproduced in the appendix of Zimbardo and Radl's (1981) *The Shy Child* includes a two-part checklist. The first part is a listing of situations and activities that elicit shyness. The second part is a list of the types of people who elicit shyness.

The present author has also used a brainstorm technique that is labeled STP (a takeoff on the famous oil additive familiar to most young people). The acronym stands for "socially terrific person." Participants are asked to list all the things that constitute a socially terrific person. The question is: Which of these are the STP born with and which did he or she learn? The implication here is that shy people can also learn to be socially skilled. This brainstorm technique is a competency model against which participants can compare their own proficiency. This in turn leads to identifying targets of change.

Worth Solving?

At this stage in the program, participants are asked to make a two-column list. In one column, they list the consequences of overcoming the targeted shyness situations. In other words, what is there to gain in acting nonshy in a particular situation? The second column lists the advantages of not changing—of continuing to respond in a shy way to a situation. The imbalance of the two columns is a graphic way of showing younger people that overcoming shyness is worth the effort.

Where's the Rub?

Specifying the particular form of impairment involved in shyness is of critical importance to successfully changing shy habits. Early research on methods of overcoming social anxiety focused on helping the shy person learn the social skills that he or she was presumably lacking. This approach has had a significant impact on some individuals but has failed to improve the condition in other persons.

It was later determined that some socially anxious people were as skillful in verbal and nonverbal behaviors as nonshy persons. For these individuals, shyness was found to be a problem of inhibition. In effect, the shy person knew what to do, but either performed with a high level of self-consciousness and reluctance or failed to perform because of his or her inhibiting anxiety.

The difference in working with adults and children is that shyness for adults is more a problem of inhibition than of skills deficiency. They are troubled primarily with negative appraisals of themselves and their performance. Young people, on the other hand, simply have not yet developed an adequate repertoire of skills. When teaching problem-solving skills to youngsters, it is important that they understand how a change strategy relates to the assumed problem source.

The following list shows the alternative sources of the shyness problem and how strategies of change differ depending on the problem source:

1. If the trainee does not know how to perform the verbal and nonverbal skills, the training goal is to acquire the necessary verbal and nonverbal skills.
2. If the trainee has the skills but excess nervousness interferes with performance, the training goal is to acquire skills in relaxation for remaining calm in social situations.
3. If the trainee has the skills but excessive self-consciousness and negative self-talk interfere with performance, the training goal is to replace habits of negative thinking with more positive, rational habits.

Skills Gap/Act

Skill acquisition is the goal for the trainees whose social anxiety is related to not knowing requisite verbal and nonverbal skills. This is the area of the program that young participants find most useful. It is practical, provides for immediate application, and meets what most participants feel is their most pressing need.

With the help of fellow participants, trainees identify alternative ways of responding to their targeted situations. The approach with which each is comfortable is selected, and the role-play situation is set up. A small segment of the role-play scenario is performed, with the group leader modeling appropriate social behaviors. Participants are then asked to practice the same small segment. This is followed by a critique of the performance.

The behaviors that are typically monitored for critique are divided into three categories: verbal, nonverbal, and content. Verbal behaviors include voice quality elements such as firmness of voice, absence of stammering, calmness, and steadiness of voice tone. Nonverbal behaviors include eye contact, posture, gesture, and fidgeting of hands or other parts of the body. Content elements include open- and closed-ended questioning, minimal encouragements, and paraphrasing and feedback comments.

These three types of behavior are monitored and critiqued as they occur at three stages of a conversation: (1) the initiation of the contact, (2) the maintenance of the conversation, and (3) the bringing of the transaction to a suitable conclusion. The power of these behavioral practice techniques in modifying behaviors and in developing new ones has been thoroughly documented under laboratory conditions (McFall and Lillesand 1971, O'Connor 1973, Zimmerman and Pike 1972).

Nervousness/Relax

Relaxation is the goal for participants whose social anxiety is related to inhibition from physiological arousal. The purpose of the relaxation training sequence is to teach the participants responses that are incompatible with anxiety reactions. This is done by assisting them to gradually learn to respond with more productive, nonanxious feelings toward previous fear-provoking situations.

Several case histories detailing the successful use of relaxation approaches with phobic children have been reported (Eysenck and Rachman 1965, Lazarus 1960, Wolpe 1958, 1969). Tasto (1969) reported a successful application of muscle relaxation in treating a 4-year-old boy with a phobia of loud noises.

The first exposure to the relaxation training sequence is typically met with a substantial amount of amusement. This is not discouraged since the participants' laughter is itself relaxing and therefore consistent with the objectives of this phase of the program. A secondary gain from the relaxation training sequence is that young participants become less self-conscious as they do "silly things" in public, such as furrowing their brows, gritting their teeth, pulling their heads into their shoulders, and so on.

This process teaches participants to perceive when parts of their body are tense and how to relax away the tension. Using the checklist items from the "Pick an Easy Target" segment of the program, participants are shown how they can apply this powerful relaxation skill to situations that make them nervous.

Self-Esteem/Think Positive

To many experts, self-esteem is defined in the internal dialogues we have with ourselves. Positive self-esteem is equivalent to approving and rewarding self-statements. Negative self-esteem amounts to covertly criticizing one's self.

One theoretical framework for the relationship of self-statement to maladaptive behavior stems from the rational emotive therapy model developed by Ellis (1962). Ellis (1977) took the position that inappropriate behavior is less a function of a particular event than it is of what one says to him- or herself about the event.

Other researchers have supported the view that maladaptive thoughts can impair performance in social situations (Knaus 1974, Meichenbaum 1977). Developing more adaptive habits of thinking is the goal for participants who know how to behave but avoid or are reluctant in social situations because of self-consciousness and a feeling of inadequacy. To overcome this type of shyness, the goal of the positive thinking training sequence is to assist the trainee in overcoming the following and similar forms of maladaptive thinking:

1. Overgeneralization—"I messed up one time at a party and therefore I will make a fool of myself at all subsequent parties."
2. Absolutism—"I slipped up on part of the speech and therefore the whole speech was a total flop."
3. Misattribution—"I said hello and he did not respond. I must have done something to make him mad at me."
4. Catastrophizing—"I got an 'F' on my homework. What an awful development. What will I do now?"

One of the most successful approaches for teaching young people to think more rationally is a writing exercise. Participants are given a form with instructions to fill in the following areas:

1. Describe a situation from your "Pick an Easy Target" inventory that makes you shy.
2. What put-downs are you thinking to yourself?
3. How do these thoughts make you feel and behave?
4. What "up" thoughts could you think of to replace the put-downs?
5. How would these positive, more realistic thoughts make you feel?

The effectiveness of the positive thinking sequence with young participants is limited by the relative brevity of the program. Even in this short period, however, participants become more aware of what they are saying to themselves and how this can affect what they feel and do.

Evaluate Progress

The next stage in the Shyness Control Program is the planned carrying out of specific tasks outside the group session. Basically, this stage amounts to "homework." The goal is to ensure that what the participants were successful in performing in the training group, they can also successfully perform in those very situations that caused them to seek out assistance. A record-keeping form, written as a contract, is used to document completion of the homework assignment.

With the assistance of other group members, the trainees plan for performance of the specific target behaviors that are identified in the first step of the Shyness Control Program. Participants have already determined the nature of the shyness problem (skills gap, nervousness, or poor self-esteem) and have practiced to master the specific responses necessary to overcome the problem. What remains is performance in the external environment.

Research on self-monitoring and self-reward indicated that self-monitoring is one of the most promising means by which behaviors can be maintained over time. Bandura (1977) regards self-monitoring as a "generalizable skill in self-regulation that can be used continually" (p. 144). That children can be taught the social skill to self-monitor has been demonstrated in the review of literature by Masters and Mokros (1974).

Shy youngsters seem to enjoy the "show and tell" of discussing their homework. This is done at the beginning of each meeting. The concluding time in each session is spent identifying new homework. This is entered on the contract form and signed by the group leader.

Pick Another Target

The final step in the Shyness Control Program is the first step in a brand new cycle. Depending on an individual's success with the first target behavior, the new goal may be a less ambitious version of the previous goal or a more challenging situation from his or her inventory of fear-provoking situations. The remainder of the steps with respect to the new target proceed as previously described.

Conclusion

Shyness is an unpleasant experience for the majority of people who have learned to be shy. Over time, many people unlearn shy responses and come to enjoy social interactions. Others remain shy throughout their lives.

The Shyness Control Program is a comprehensive approach to a complex problem. It can be tailored to a variety of time frames and to group or individual formats. Depending on the homogeneity of a group in terms of their shyness source, the *act*, *relax*, and *think positive* parts of the training sequences can be emphasized. Each sequence, however, should be touched on to some extent, since shyness impairs each of the response domains to some degree.

Young participants who conscientiously follow each of the program steps can gain in three ways:

1. They become more relaxed, confident, and skillful in social contacts and therefore initiate more contacts.
2. They become less preoccupied with and worried about their shyness.
3. They acquire problem-solving skills that can be applied to other maladaptive habits.

References

Bandura, A. (1977). *Social Learning Theory*. Englewood Cliffs, NJ: Prentice-Hall.

Buss, A. A. (1980). *Self-Consciousness and Social Anxiety*. San Francisco: Freeman.

Ellis, A. (1962). *Reason and Emotion in Psychotherapy*. New York: Lyle Stuart.
———— (1977). The basic clinical theory of rational-emotive therapy. In *Handbook of Rational-Emotive Therapy*, ed. A. Ellis and R. Grieger. New York: Springer.

Eysenck, H. J., and Rachman, S. (1965). *The Causes and Cures of Neurosis*. San Diego, CA: Knapp.

Hersen, M. (1973). Self-assessment of fear. *Behavior Therapy* 4:241–257.

Knaus, W. J. (1974). *Rational Emotive Education*. New York: Institute for Rational Living.

Lazarus, A. A. (1960). The elimination of children's phobias by deconditioning. In *Behavior Therapy and the Neuroses*, ed. H. J. Eysenck. New York: Pergamon.

Marks, I. M. (1969). *Fears and Phobias*. New York: Academic Press.

Masters, J. C., and Mokros, J. R. (1974). Self-reinforcement processes in children. In *Advances in Child Development and Behavior*, vol. 9, ed. H. Reese. New York: Academic Press.

McFall, R. M., and Lillesand, D. B. (1971). Behavior rehearsal with modeling and coaching in assertion training. *Journal of Abnormal Psychology* 77:313–323.

Meichenbaum, D. (1977). *Cognitive Behavior Modification: An Integrative Approach*. New York: Plenum.

Mussen, P. H., Conger, J. J., and Kagan, J. (1963). *Child Development and Personality*. New York: Harper & Row.

O'Connor, R. D. (1973). Relative efficacy of modeling, shaping, and combined procedures for modification of social withdrawal. In *Behaviour Therapy and Practice*, ed. C. M. Franks and G. T. Wilson. New York: Brunner/Mazel.

Rachman, S., and Costello, C. G. (1961). The etiology and treatment of children's phobias: a review. *American Journal of Psychiatry* 118(2):97–105.

Tasto, D. L. (1969). Systematic desensitization, muscle relaxation and visual imagery in the counterconditioning of a four-year-old phobic child. *Behaviour Research and Therapy* 7:409–411.

Trower, P., Bryant, B., and Argyle, M. (1978). *Social Skills and Mental Health*. London: Methuen.

Wolpe, J. (1958). *Psycho-Therapy by Reciprocal Inhibition*. Stanford, CA: Stanford University Press.

———— (1969). *The Practice of Behavior Therapy*. New York: Pergamon.

Zimbardo, P. G. (1977). *Shyness*. Reading, MA: Addison-Wesley.

Zimbardo, P. G., and Radl, S. (1981). *The Shy Child*. New York: McGraw-Hill.

Zimmerman, B. J., and Pike, E. O. (1972). Effects of modeling and reinforcement on the acquisition and generalization of question-asking behavior. *Child Development* 42:892–907.

9

School Phobia

WALLACE A. KENNEDY

School phobia, a dramatic and puzzling emotional crisis, has attracted considerable attention for a number of years. Phobias in general are the subjects of widely differing theories of dynamics and treatment. The controversy regarding the treatment of children's phobias dates from the earliest case studies presented by Freud (1909), continues through the laboratory demonstrations of Watson and Jones (Jones 1924) to the later experimental treatment of Wolpe (1954). To date (1965), there have been five broad reviews since the earliest paper presented by Johnson and colleagues in 1941: Klein (1945), Waldfogel and colleagues (1957), Kahn (1958), Glasser (1959), and Sperling (1961). These reviews in the main support the contention that the major weight of evidence thus far leans toward the psychoanalytic interpretation of phobias, while the work of Wolpe is more consistent with the approach presented herein.

The psychoanalytic theory stresses the role of the mother in the development of school phobia. A close symbiotic relationship, which displays itself in an overdependency, is present between the mother and child. Stemming from an unsatisfactory relationship with her own mother, the mother finds it difficult to cope with her own emotional needs. The father often is in a competing role with the mother, and seems to try to outdo her in little tasks around the home: in trying to strengthen his own image, he depreciates that of the mother. He too overidentifies with the child. Thus, the emotional climate of his family prevents the child from ever finding out whether or not he, of his own volition, can solve problems. Possessive, domineering parents tend to make the child's growth toward independence difficult. His guilt regarding his own impulses is transformed into depression: the anxiety can reach extreme proportions.

On the other hand, Wolpe (1954) sees the phobia as a learned reaction, which he treats through direct symptom attack with what he calls reciprocal inhibition, or desensitization.

Interest in the school phobia problem, which occurs at the rate of seventeen cases per thousand school-age children per year, has been greatly intensified in the past few years. An extremely significant advance was made by Cooledge and the Judge Baker group in 1957, when they presented evidence that there were not one, but two types of school phobia, which, although sharing a common group of symptoms, differed widely in others. These are referred to as Type 1 school phobia, or the neurotic crisis, and Type 2 school phobia, or the way-of-life phobia. The common symptoms are: (a) morbid fears associated with school attendance; a vague dread of disaster; (b) frequent somatic complaints: headaches, nausea, drowsiness; (c) symbiotic relationship with mother, fear of separation; anxiety about many things: darkness, crowds, noises; and (d) conflict between parents and the school administration.

At the Human Development Clinic of Florida State University, ten differential symptoms between Type 1 and Type 2 school phobia have been determined (see Table 9–1 below). A differential diagnosis can be made logically and empirically on the basis of any seven of the ten.

Type 1	Type 2
1. The present illness is the first episode.	1. Second, third, or fourth episode.
2. Monday onset, following an illness the previous Thursday or Friday.	2. Monday onset following minor illness not a prevalent antecedent.
3. An acute onset.	3. Incipient onset.
4. Lower grades most prevalent.	4. Upper grades most prevalent.
5. Expressed concern about death.	5. Death theme not present.
6. Mother's physical health in question: actually ill or child thinks so.	6. Health of mother not an issue.
7. Good communication between parents.	7. Poor communication between parents.

8. Mother and father well adjusted in most areas.	8. Mother shows neurotic behavior; father, a character disorder.
9. Father competitive with mother in household management.	9. Father shows little interest in household or children.
10. Parents achieve understanding of dynamics easily.	10. Parents very difficult to work with.

Table 9-1. Ten differential school phobia symptoms.

Problem

In the fall of 1957 the Clinic embarked upon an experimental procedure for the treatment of Type 1 school phobia—a procedure similar to that of Rodriguez and colleagues (1959) with one major exception: whereas Rodriguez made no distinction between types of school phobia and treated in the same manner all cases which came to the clinic, the fifty cases reported herein were selected on the basis of the criteria mentioned above. The Florida State University Human Development Clinic, as a teaching and research clinic, does not generally see deeply disturbed children, but refers them to other agencies.

In the eight-year period covered by the report, there have been six cases which would meet the criteria of Type 2 school phobia. These six cases were treated by supportive therapy for the children and parents. None of the six Type 2 cases had more than three of the ten Type 1 criteria, and the results were completely dissimilar to those reported for the fifty Type 1 cases. All of the Type 2 cases were chronic in nature. All had family histories of one or more parents seriously disturbed. Two of the cases were diagnosed as having schizophrenia; two were diagnosed as having character disorders with the school phobia being a minor aspect of the case. One of the six was hospitalized; one was sent to a training school. Of the four remaining, two were able to go to college, although their records were poor and their symptoms continued. These six cases were in treatment for an average of ten months. In no circumstances was a school phobia case changed from Type 1 to Type 2, or vice versa.

This experimental procedure with Type 1 school phobia was begun with considerable caution, with only one case in 1957 and two the following spring. The treatment involved the application of broad learning theory concepts by blocking the escape of the child and preventing secondary gains from occurring. In addition, the child was reinforced for going to school without complaint. This rapid treatment procedure has now been followed with fifty cases.

Subject Population

Subjects for the fifty cases over an eight-year period were school-age children, all suffering from the first evidence of a phobic attack, from the geographical area served by the Human Development Clinic of Florida State University. The subject distribution by year and sex is illustrated in Table 9-2, by symptom and sex in Table 9-3, by age and sex in Table 9-4, and by grade and sex in Table 9-5.

Year	Male	Female	Total
1957	1	0	1
1958	1	1	2
1959	4	2	6
1960	4	8	12
1961	6	3	9
1962	5	4	9
1963	4	5	9
1964	0	2	2
Total	25	25	50

Table 9-2. Year of treatment and sex of fifty Type 1 school phobia cases.

	Symptom	Male	Female	Total
1.	First attack	25	25	50
2.	Monday onset—Thursday illness	24	25	49
3.	Acute onset	25	23	48
4.	Lower grades	22	18	40
5.	Death theme	22	22	44
6.	Mother's health an issue	23	21	44
7.	Good parental marital harmony	24	23	47
8.	Good parental mental health	23	24	47
9.	Father helper in the house	21	21	42
10.	Parents achieve insight quickly	24	25	49

Table 9-3. Symptom checklist and sex of fifty Type 1 school phobia cases.

Age	Male	Female	Total
4	0	1	1
5	3	1	4
6	2	3	5
7	3	2	5
8	3	1	4
9	3	5	8
10	4	3	7
11	1	2	3
12	3	0	3
13	2	4	6
14	1	2	3
15	0	0	0
16	0	1	1
Total	25	25	50

Table 9-4. Age and sex of fifty Type 1 school phobia cases.

Grade	Male	Female	Total
Nursery school	0	2	2
Kindergarten	4	0	4
First	4	4	8
Second	0	1	1
Third	6	4	10
Fourth	3	4	7
Fifth	2	2	4
Sixth	3	1	4
Seventh	2	2	4
Eighth	0	2	2
Ninth	1	2	3
Tenth	0	1	1
Total	25	25	50

Table 9-5. Grade and sex of fifty Type 1 school phobia cases.

The fathers' mean age for the male subjects was 36; the mothers', 35. For the female subjects the fathers' mean age was 38; the mothers', 36. The boys' mean age was 9; that of the girls', 10. There was no definite pattern in birth order of the subjects, or in number of siblings.

Method and Results

During the course of the past eight years, fifty cases of Type 1 school phobia have been treated. Five of these cases might be considered semicontrols because they were untreated Type 1 cases of some duration, or they were Type 1 cases unsuccessfully treated elsewhere before they were seen at the Clinic. One of these semicontrol cases had been out of school for one year, and the other four had been out for over three months.

All fifty of the cases responded to the treatment program with a complete remission of the school phobia symptoms, and follow-up study indicates no evidence of any outbreaks of substitute symptoms or recurrence of the phobia.

In the follow-up schedule the parents were phoned in about two weeks, and again in six weeks, to see if the progress had continued. They were then phoned on a yearly basis, except in 1961, when follow-up interviews were conducted reaching nineteen of the twenty-one cases completed at that time. During the course of the eight years, six families were lost because of moving with no forwarding address. Of these lost cases, none had been followed less than two years, two were followed three years, and one for four years.

Rapid Treatment Procedure

The rapid treatment program for Type 1 school phobia involves six essential components: good professional public relations, avoidance of emphasis on somatic complaints, forced school attendance, structured interview with parents, brief interview with the child, and follow-up.

Good Professional Public Relations

It is necessary to establish good communication with schools, physicians, and parent groups, such that the cases are likely referred on the second or third day of the phobic attack. This groundwork involves the typical mental health consultation and case-by-case follow-up with the referring source.

Avoidance of Emphasis on Somatic Complaints

If phobic qualities predominate, that is, if the child conforms to seven of the differential symptoms of Type 1 school phobia, emphasis on somatic complaints should be avoided. For instance, the child's somatic complaints should be handled matter-of-factly, with an appointment to see the pediatrician after school hours. Abdominal pains will probably require the pediatrician to make a prompt physical examination, but this can probably be done on the way to school.

Forced School Attendance

It is essential to be able to require the child to go to school. In all of the present cases, simply convincing the parents of this necessity and having them come to a firm decision has generally been enough. The ability to be decisive when necessary has been essential.

Have the father take the child to school. These fathers are not unkind, and they can show authority when necessary.

Have the principal or attendance officer take an active part in keeping the child in the room.

Allow the mother to stand in the hall, if she must, or to visit the school during the morning, but not to stay.

Structured Interview with the Parents

Stressing the following points, conduct with the parents a structured interview designed to give them sufficient confidence to carry out the therapeutic program even in the face of considerable resistance from the child.

Lead the Interview.

The confidence of the parents is greatly increased by the interviewer's verifying the history rather than taking it. Correctly anticipating seven out of ten variables within a family structure is well calculated to induce full cooperation.

Be Optimistic.

Stressing the transient nature, the dependable sequence of a difficult Monday, a somewhat better Tuesday, and a symptom-free Wednesday, tends to lighten the depression of the parents regarding their child's unwillingness to go to school.

Emphasize Success.

Type 1 cases always recover. Ninety percent of the Type 1 phobics stay at school most of the first day. Along with optimism comes a slight mobilization of hostility which helps the parents to follow the plan.

Present the Formula.

Simply but directly, with repetition for emphasis, outline a plan for the parents to follow, assuming that it is the end of the school week by the time of the referral and that the interview with the parents is conducted on Thursday or Friday.

Parent Formula

Do not discuss, in any way, school attendance over the weekend. There is nothing a phobic child does better than talk about going to school. Don't discuss going to school. Don't discuss phobic symptoms. Simply tell the child Sunday evening, "Well, son, tomorrow you go back to school."

On Monday morning get the child up, dressed, and ready for school. Give the child a light breakfast to reduce the nausea problem. Have the father take the child matter-of-factly off to school. Don't ask him how he feels, or why he is afraid to go to school, or why he doesn't like school. Simply take him to school, turn him over to the school authorities, and go home.

If the child therapist has not seen the child the previous week, he may see him after school on the first day.

On Monday evening, compliment the child on going to school and staying there, no matter how resistant he has been, no matter how many times he has vomited, cried, or started to leave. If he has been at school for thirty minutes on Monday, progress is being made. Tell the child Monday evening that Tuesday will be much better, and make no further mention of the symptom.

Tuesday can be expected to be a repetition of Monday, but with everything toned down considerably. On Tuesday evening, encourage and compliment the child strongly for doing so much better.

Wednesday should be virtually symptom free. Wednesday evening, with considerable fanfare, give a party for the child in honor of his having overcome his problem.

Brief Interview with the Child

The child himself should be seen only briefly by the child therapist and only after school hours. The content of the interview should be stories which stress the advantage of going on in the face of fear: how student pilots need to get back into the air quickly after an accident, and how important it is to get right back on the horse after a fall. In addition the therapist can describe real or imaginary events in his own childhood when he was frightened for a while but everything turned out all right—all to stress to the child the transitory nature of the phobia.

Follow-Up

Followup by phone, being chatty and encouraging and not over-solicitous. In the long-range follow-up, chat with the parents about further school phobia symptoms, incidence of other phobias, school attendance records, academic progress, and the occurrence of other emotional problems in the child.

Discussion

Two legitimate concerns have been expressed regarding prelimi-nary reports at local meetings. The first is a concern about the claim of complete remission for all fifty cases—a claim inconsistent with the usual child guidance clinic success rate—and the consequent belief that the criterion for success is simply too narrow. Only self-report data and reports from school administrations are available regarding the symp-tom-free nature of these children once this phobic episode has passed. It is true that no diagnostic evaluation has been undertaken with any of these children during follow-up. It must be remembered, however, that the definition of symptom remission is restricted to those obvious symptoms which might conceivably lead the parents or school officials to re-refer the children to the clinic. In this regard, these fifty children in the Type 1 school phobia group are symptom free.

Because of the nature of the Human Development Clinic and the nature of this project, careful selection has been exercised in accepting cases, as mentioned above. Due to the relationship between the schools and the clinic, and the clear definition of cases suitable for the project, there is reason to believe that the majority of Type 1 school phobia cases in the five-county area the clinic serves have come to our atten-tion, whereas the local county mental health clinic has received a high percentage of the Type 2 cases. The success of the Type 2 cases of school phobia accepted by the Human Development Clinic for teaching pur-poses has not been remarkable.

The second concern is that perhaps what is called Type 1 school phobia is not really a severe phobic attack at all, but borders on ma-lingering of a transient nature which would spontaneously remit in a few days anyway. In fact, because of the apparent sound mental health of the family as a group, its middle-class values which stress school, and the family's good premorbid history, including the academic record of the child, there is little reason to doubt that the majority of the cases would eventually return to school whatever treatment was undertaken. However, our five semicontrol cases and evidence seen from other clinics of Type 1 cases that have been out of school for prolonged periods suggest that this method of treatment may accelerate or facilitate the remission. Recommendation for the use of this technique is restricted, then, to those cases showing Type 1 symptoms which, in spite of their possible transient nature, present a rather serious problem to teachers, parents, and counselors.

References

Cooledge, J. C., Hahn, P. B., and Peck, A. L. (1957). School phobia: neurotic crisis or way of life. *American Journal of Orthopsychiatry* 27:296–306.

Freud, S. (1909). Analysis of a phobia in a five-year-old boy. *Standard Edition*.

Glasser, K. (1959). Problems in school attendance: school phobia and related conditions [Abstract]. *Pediatrics* 55:758.

Johnson, A. M., et al. (1941). School phobia: a study of five cases [Abstract]. *American Journal of Orthopsychiatry* 11:702.

Jones, M. C. (1924). A laboratory study of fear: the case of Peter. *Journal of Genetic Psychology* 31:308–315.

Kahn, J. H. (1958). School refusal—some clinical and cultural aspects [Abstract]. *Medical Officer* 100:337.

Klein, E. (1945). The reluctance to go to school. In *Psychoanalytic Study of the Child* 1:263. New York: International Universities Press.

Rodriguez, A., Rodriguez, M., and Eisenberg, L. (1959). The outcome of school phobia: a follow-up study based on forty-one cases. *American Journal of Psychiatry* 116:540–544.

Sperling, M. (1961). Analytic first aid in school phobias [Abstract]. *Psychoanalytic Quarterly* 30:504.

Waldfogel, S., Cooledge, J. C., and Hahn, P. B. (1957). Development, meaning and management of school phobia [Abstract]. *American Journal of Orthopsychiatry* 27:754.

Wolpe, J. (1954). Reciprocal inhibition as the main basis of psychotherapeutic effects. *A.M.A. Archive of Neurology and Psychiatry* 72:204–226.

10

Obsessive-Compulsive Behaviors

PATRICIA DALTON

Obsessive-compulsive behavior in a child presents serious problems for both the child and for those in his immediate environment; it is both internally and interpersonally disruptive. It also presents a challenge to the therapist, who is unlikely to have previous experience with such children. A review of the literature suggests that obsessive-compulsive disorders are rare in children and in adults, an estimated 1 to 3 percent of the clinical population (Judd 1965). The obsessive-compulsive symptom complex in children is a well-defined psychological syndrome, with high interdisciplinary consensus on identifying factors. It consists of a constellation of trivial motor acts that are experienced as aversive by the child and resisted unsuccessfully. Typical examples are counting, touching, and washing compulsions.

The varied etiological conceptualizations regarding obsessive-compulsive disorder stand in sharp contrast to the agreement regarding its description. The first such formulations emphasized early childhood learning and trauma. Freud (1913) theorized that the origin of this problem was the individual's anxiety in connection with the Oedipus complex. Later, neo-Freudians such as Adler (1956) and Sullivan (1956) placed more emphasis on the family's primacy in the development of various neurotic disorders. It was posited that obsessive-compulsive symptoms are generated in interpersonal relations, particularly in the mother–child relationship (Rado 1959). Individual play therapy, however, has been the standard psychodynamic treatment for young children with this problem. Obsessive-compulsive disorder has historically been considered resistant to treatment in adults (Kringlen 1965) and in children (Hollingsworth et al. 1980, Judd 1965). In addition, long treatment duration has been expected. The average length for psychodynamic treatment is one and one-half to two years, with thrice-weekly sessions with the child and additional meetings with the parents with another therapist (Adams 1973).

Behavioral theories regarding this disorder focus on detailed behavioral analyses of the obsessive-compulsive symptoms as they occur in the present, and include formulations regarding maintenance of the symptomatology as well as causation. They are similar to psychodynamic approaches in their emphasis on the individual. Behavioral therapy reports have indicated that direct treatment of the compulsions can be successfully utilized in cases of both long-standing and recent onset obsessive-compulsive behavior. Techniques such as systematic desensitization (Walton and Mather 1963), thought stopping (Stern 1970), and implosion (Meyer 1966) have been used with obsessive-compulsive adults. Behavioral interventions have also been reported as successful with obsessive-compulsive adolescents and children (Fine 1973, Weiner 1967).

Family therapists view the etiology of childhood dysfunction in yet another way. While acknowledging the power of early life events, they view the family dysfunction as also occurring in the present and maintaining the symptoms. The original Oedipal triangle is seen as continuing over time, with the child inappropriately involved in the lives of his parents as well as inviting such involvement in his life (Napier and Whitaker 1978). The symptomatic child is viewed as a member of a coalition with one parent against the other or as providing a problem situation for conflicting parents to fight over, rather than dealing directly with their difficulties (Harbin 1979). Another view (Madanes 1980) is that the child's disturbed behavior is protective of his parents in that it provides them with a respite from their own problems and a reason to hold themselves together in order to care for their problem child. Madanes has emphasized that the child's symptomatic behavior becomes the basis for inappropriate power over his parents and that it is the parents who must solve the child's problem. The therapist's role is to arrange the therapy so that the parents no longer need the child's protection and are able to convey this to the child.

Family therapy approaches utilizing behavioral techniques appear promising in the treatment of obsessive-compulsive disorder in children (Fine 1973, Harbin 1979, Scott 1966). Several methods for dealing with the obsessive-compulsive symptoms have been described: to eliminate them directly by interruption (Fine 1973) or by ordeal (Harbin 1979) or to modify them (Weiner 1967). The present chapter proposes a third alternative, that of ignoring the obsessive-compulsive symptoms and concentrating on more functional behavior. Many of the theoretical ideas and techniques have been described previously by Haley (1977), Madanes (1980), and Selvini Palazzoli et al. (1974). The case was discussed in weekly supervisory conferences; live supervision using a one-way mirror or video equipment was precluded because of lack of facilities.

Case Report

Phillip A., a 9-year-old fourth-grade boy, was referred for therapy by the school psychologist for compulsive, ritualistic behaviors including frequent handwashing and checking behind doors when entering a room, daydreaming and disorganization academically, and poor academic progress despite an above-average IQ and abstract reasoning ability in the genius range. The family consisted of Mrs. A., a 40-year-old homemaker; Mr. A., a 54-year-old white-collar government worker; Susan A., age 17, a high school junior; and Phillip A., the identified patient.

Session 1

An inquiry into the present problem yielded varied opinions. Mrs. A. described her concern regarding her son's compulsive behaviors and daydreaming and also regarding the ominous findings of the psychological testing. Mr. A. indicated that he was not as worried as his wife, adding that he had also daydreamed as a boy and hoped his son would grow out of it. Susan's comment was that she wished that she and Phillip had a normal brother–sister relationship, playing and kidding around. Phillip said that he didn't like it when the kids in school clapped when he had to leave early, as had happened that day, and were mean to him. The parents said they had attempted to solve the problem in the past by reminding P. of his compulsive behavior and daydreaming when he was doing them, in the hopes that he would stop.

During the session, Mrs. A. was talkative and animated, Mr. A. was quiet and impassive, Susan was somewhat impatient, and Phillip spent most of the session looking out of the window, occasionally talking in a sing-song way while others were speaking. He had little eye contact with anyone but his mother, she and he played "footsie" during the session, and she told him at one point to "tie our shoes." She also complained about the lack of morals and ethics of many parents and children in their community. Mrs. A. frequently scanned the therapist, seemingly concerned about how she was being evaluated as a mother. I ended the session remarking on the parent's concern for their son and willingness to act on his behalf, and expressing confidence that the problem could be solved.

Comments

The first task was to join the family in a casual and accepting manner (Minuchin 1974). The next was to gather detailed information on the problem, including each family member's perspective, and to inquire into previously attempted solutions. The therapist discerned a fairly standard sequence of interactions (Haley 1977): mother focuses intensely on the child; father withdraws; child exhibits symptomatic behavior; mother worries, urges father to take action; father says it's not so serious and that mother is overreacting; mother assumes father doesn't understand, becomes anxious, and focuses on the child; father withdraws; child exhibits symptomatic behavior, and so on. (This example began arbitrarily with the mother's behavior; the behavior chain is thought to be a circular one that can be initiated at any point.)

The goal of the therapy was to reinstate a normal family hierarchy, in which parental and spouse roles are clearly delineated from those of the children. The working strategy at this point was to use directives designed to increase the father's involvement with his son, to decrease the mother's involvement with the boy, and to encourage normal behavior in Phillip while ignoring compulsive behavior. Because the boy's compulsiveness was assumed to mirror his mother's obsessive concerns about him, functional mothering behaviors were to be encouraged, whereas obsessive concerns were not. An important background strategy was to work toward each family member's goals: to get Phillip to behave more normally (mother's); not to label him as a problem child or crazy (father's); to work toward a normal sibling relationship (Susan's); and to assist P. in making friends (Phillip's). Mrs. A.'s disdainful remark about people in their community cued the therapist to work toward a rapprochement between the family unit and the wider world.

Session 2

Mr. and Mrs. A. agreed on an initial goal that Phillip become more self-sufficient in the morning. The directive for Mr. A. was to help P. each night with his homework for one-half hour and to help his son in picking out clothing for the next day. Mrs. A. identified goals of brushing his teeth, getting himself dressed, combing his hair, and remembering his lunch money and books each morning. At this point I expressed doubt to Phillip that he could change all these things at once. He protested that he was sure he could. I then helped him to make a chart listing each responsibility. His mother was given the job of observing whether or not he had done these things, but was told not to remind him to do them. I expressed sympathy for how frustrated she must feel having to help her son each morning and encouraged her instead to take time to prepare the family a nice breakfast and to relax with a cup of coffee. Susan was told that it was not necessary for her to attend the sessions unless she wished to, since she was a busy teenager.

Comments

In this session, a critical component was persuading the parents and Phillip to follow the directives. The father was told that he was needed by his son in a unique way, as a male with expertise regarding homework and men's clothing. I empathized with Mrs. A. as a woman and a mother, pointing out the frustrations of being ever available to children and the joys of solitude. Finally, by "insulting" Phillip and appealing to his pride, a situation was constructed in which he could be expected to resist, thereby saving face and, not unimportantly, following the directive.

Another important component in this therapy was the relative absence of interpretation of family patterns and dynamics. An important practical consideration is that it would serve to encourage further intellectualization in a family whose modus operandi is obsessive to begin with. Another potential problem is the discourtesy to the parents implied by pointing out the mother's involvement with her son and the father's withdrawal. As Haley (1977) points out, they understand this perfectly well; what they don't know is how to change it gracefully. It is also assumed that they have come for therapy ambivalently,

both desiring change and fearing it. The goal was to head off therapeutic resistance by allying with the parents and disarming them. The
parents were not viewed as pathogenic but as doing the best they could
at the time for their son. This conceptualization of their behavior as
normal and understandable given its context is conveyed on explicit,
verbal levels but more importantly on implicit, nonverbal ones, and
appears very important to the successful outcome of this case. One of
the most serious potential dangers of child-focused therapeutic work is
the subtle and at times overt disparagement of the parents that can be
conveyed by child therapists advocating for one member of a dysfunctional system.

Additional interventions were the disruption of dysfunctional interactions between family members by redirecting and shifting interactions, interrupting, questioning, and expressing puzzlement about them.
Finally, I spent time each session interacting with the boy playfully and
seriously about normal 9-year-old pursuits; this activity was designed
to take the focus off the parents as well as to model new ways of behaving with their child without stating this. It was very important to
avoid seducing the child as a "better mother" or to compete with the
parents in any way.

Session 3

Mrs. A. brought the chart and reported that Phillip had done
pretty well, although she explained that she had had to remind
him to check his chart. The first week she gave him credit even if
he was reminded; the second, only if he was reminded once. I
praised her for her resourcefulness and told her to continue to use
her judgment about this the next week. Mr. A. reported that since
Phillip didn't want help with his homework, he hadn't forced it.
I urged the father to be persistent, emphasizing that growing boys
need their fathers. Mrs. A. asked if she was too helpful in inter-
vening when the neighborhood kids were picking on her son. I
shrugged and said that it was hard to tell, adding that kids have
their own world and seem to fight their own battles.

Phillip had been listening intently and had not been looking
out the window. He then volunteered the information that he had
stopped checking behind doors. When asked how he had accomplished this, he said he "just decided to." I replied that there was
no point in talking about that anymore, adding that he struck
me as a boy who could do almost anything once he decided to.

Comments

It is assumed that Mrs. A. improvised on the directive because the task required more rapid disengagement from her son than she could accomplish. Rather than criticize her for not following through on the original directive, I praised her for her ingenuity. I also avoided joining in her self-critical comment about being too helpful to her son. Rather than seize upon this as an important insight, the subject was shifted to Phillip's need to learn to navigate in a child's world. Her question about whether his rambling was normal was one of many skirting the issue of mental illness, with the inevitable implications of defectiveness, intractability, and permanence. All such questions were sidestepped and put into a positive and normal framework. Mr. A.'s reluctance to approach his son is typical of fathers who are out of the mainstream of the family. It was important to convey respect for and affirmation of the vital importance of a father to his child.

This session marked a turning point. The therapy was having an effect on symptoms, the mother had tested out her fears with the therapist, and the father had been pulled in as an active participant.

Sessions 4 and 5 (School Conference)

Phillip's behavior was much improved, and his mother had only reminded him once not to forget his charts. Mr. A. had helped Phillip with his homework every evening but one, and Phillip reported that he had checked behind doors twice that week. I wondered aloud how it had happened, told him that he would probably decide whether or not to continue it in the future, and changed the subject.

Mrs. A. expressed concern about Phillip playing elaborate imaginary games of football and bowling and asked me if this was normal. She was encouraged to talk to her husband about it. The discussion ended with me talking to Phillip about his (one) friend. I explored with the parents the possibility of inviting his friend over, using the rationale that "kids need other kids." They agreed to this, although Mrs. A. expressed some subtle reluctance. The plan was to continue the original task of charting the next week, adding a gold star if he did his tasks without needing to be reminded.

A conference was held at his school later that week. The teachers indicated three areas for improvement: paying attention in class, participating in class, and being better organized in his school assignments. A chart was devised for the teacher to fill out each day and sign and give to Phillip to bring home for his parents' signatures. The parents decided on a consequence of allowance reduction for not bringing them home.

Comments

Mrs. A.'s gradual relinquishment of her son by reminding him to look at his chart and her reluctance to have his friend over were cues to the therapist to slow down in the therapy. The client seems to understand best that a system cannot go from abnormal to normal in one step. By design, much time was spent in this session discussing Mr. A. and Phillip's homework hour, less time for the mother's concerns, and almost no time for Phillip's comment that he had been checking behind doors again. I also deliberately encouraged the parents to discuss problems together in the session rather than with me, in order to emphasize their own ability to solve them. Finally, it was important to redefine Phillip's imaginary game-playing as normal, as indeed it was for a bright boy without friends.

Sessions 6, 7, and 8

Phillip brought a near-perfect chart to the sixth session. When I told him that it was time to start charting all by himself, his mother announced with pride that he had already done this for three days. Phillip suggested the additions of making his bed and hanging up his clothes to his chart. Mrs. A. said that his schoolwork was improving, and Mr. A. reported that he and his son were continuing their homework hour.

Phillip brought another excellent chart to the seventh session. He later complained that the kids were still teasing him at school. At one point, Mrs. A. told Phillip to quit playing "footsie" with her. At the beginning of Session 8, Mrs. A. told me that she was going back to work full time, adding that she could not have gone back if Phillip had not improved as much as he had. This was discussed as a major change for the whole family.

Comments

Progress was indicated by Phillip's desire to chart independently, his improved schoolwork, and Mr. A.'s increasing involvement with his son. Most important was Mrs. A.'s independent decision to return to work. Other nodal points were that for the first time Phillip addressed a problem bothering him (friendships), and his mother moved to put an end to their foot play. I had the feeling of being peripheral; the family was instigating change on its own.

Sessions 9, 10, and 11

At Session 9, Mr. and Mrs. A. reported that Phillip was getting ready for school in the morning without the benefit of his chart, was playing with the neighborhood kids, and had joined a baseball team. Mr. A. said that as a baseball player his son had trouble paying attention and with losing his temper when he struck out. At my encouragement, Mr. A. offered some man-to-man suggestions to his son for solving these problems. I introduced the idea of meeting every other week.

By Session 10, Phillip was growing careless. He did not do his homework on two occasions, was haphazard about bringing his reports home, and was leaving clothes and toys all over the house. Phillip told me that he did not want to stop coming each week, and we discussed this. Since he had a baseball game scheduled for the evening of the next appointment, I told him that it was more important that he play baseball than come to talk about problems.

At Session 11, Mr. and Mrs. A. reported that Phillip had done a complete about-face. He was late getting ready in the morning, was not bringing home school reports and papers, and was daydreaming again. Mrs. A. stated that his problem must be a serious emotional one and that treating problem behaviors alone was not good enough; Mr. A. said that all Phillip needed was good discipline. I listened, feeling dismayed and puzzled myself, while aware that the parents had also reverted to their former pattern exactly. I gave the directive to chart morning as well as bedtime behavior for the week.

Comments

In retrospect, it is apparent that the relapse was likely. Its effects could have been softened or nullified by going more slowly with the move toward disengagement and termination, encouraging the relapse when he began to backslide or prescribing a relapse when he was still doing well (Haley 1977). Unfortunately, in this case the mother's comments about the therapy being "only" symptom treatment resurrected my worst fears as a trainee new to family treatment; I was well aware of this criticism of behavioral and strategic approaches by more traditionally trained professionals. This anxious response was a tactical error that was redressed in the next therapy session.

Sessions 12 through 15

By Session 12, Phillip was back on track, getting himself dressed and bringing his papers home. He had even had a line drive in a baseball game. Phillip said that he wanted to have a friend overnight. He also said that he had gotten beaten up by one of the older boys for kissing his younger sister. Everyone laughed. I asked his mother who she thought was the expert on handling women in their family, and Mrs. A. teasingly replied that her husband was. I asked him to help his son with his timing. The parents then mentioned a problem they were having concerning disrespect on Susan's part. Phillip asked to leave the room if they were going to discuss her instead of him. I said yes, telling him that I had something important to tell him first. I then referred to his previous relapse as an experiment to see how many different ways he could be in order to compare them. He was told to finish up the experiment by washing his hands and checking behind doors even more the next week.

By Session 13, to which I invited Susan, Phillip had accomplished his directive. Again Mrs. A. expressed worry ("He is neurotic, doesn't seem happy, has these tics"), and Mr. A. was quiet. This time I met their anxiety with aplomb. I said that the therapy may seem like symptom treatment but that it is much more, that it gets rid of things you can see but also things you cannot see. I predicted calmly that Phillip would give up his symptoms when he was ready. Susan's perspective on her brother's behavior was that Phillip was acting older, that now they horse around and have fun, and that Phillip acts older when their parents aren't around. The directive given was for Phillip to have a handwashing time each morning for ten minutes so he would not forget how to do it.

Mrs. A. called to cancel the next session, saying that she felt that there was no need for it since things were going well. She laughed about the handwashing exercise, saying that he had got-

ten bored with it. She reported that Phillip had gone to a neigh-
boring state to visit his grandparents with his father, since she had
had to work. He also had camped out all night with his day camp
group. I congratulated her on his success and asked what it was
like for her to send him off camping. She said that it was hard for
her, thinking of him out in the dark all alone. I shared some of
my feelings about my own baby daughter, remarking on the
changes that parents must go through having a trusting and dependent child with parents the center of her universe at one time,
then having to let go of the child to make her way in the world.
Mrs. A. said that she never had so much trouble letting go of
Susan. I replied that sometimes it is tougher with a son and with
the youngest but that she was probably doing the right thing for
her son by fighting the urge to hang on.

The final two sessions were uneventful. Phillip enthusiasti-
cally reported on all kinds of activities and friends in his day camp.
He also reported with pride that he had ridden a roller coaster. I
commented on how grown-up he had become. Mr. and Mrs. A.
seemed relaxed and pleased, although Mrs. A. reiterated concern
about certain behaviors that continued to annoy her. I commented
that life would be very boring indeed if all their problems were
solved and added that they had a boy who had come a long way
and looked pretty normal to me.

Comments

The second "relapse" gave me a chance to rectify my previous mistake, with the desired results. All behavioral indices
(friends, activities, absence of compulsive behaviors) as well as
Phillip's alertness and attention level in the sessions indicated that
the therapy was completed. In addition, Mr. A. and Phillip were
comfortable enough together to enjoy a week's vacation without
Mrs. A., and she could let them go. For the first time, Mrs. A.
could speak to me about the painfulness of letting go of her son.
I referred to my own experiences as a mother in order to share
with her and to equalize their relationship. This step is important
at the end of therapy, because it lowers the therapist's hierarchi-
cal position from that of an expert and symbolizes the family's
readiness to solve their own problems. Finally, taking it for granted
that some problems remain is in keeping with the hypnotherapeu-
tic rule of the "unresolved remnant": therapy should never aim at

complete resolution but only at improvement (Watzlawick 1978). It conveys a non-utopian ideal that is difficult for clients (especially obsessive ones) to accept, and allows the family to go, on their own, well beyond the limits of change that the therapist may consider possible for them.

Follow-Up

I received a call from Phillip's school principal seven months after treatment was completed. She expressed concern that he had recently begun to backslide; after being more well-organized and attentive, he was losing interest in class and making lists of pro football players and friends when he was supposed to be working. However, he was not handwashing or checking behind doors. She wondered if it might be because his sister was leaving for college soon. She said that Mrs. A. had raised the possibility of returning to therapy. I suggested that she advise Mr. and Mrs. A. to wait a while to see if the problem persisted, and the principal agreed. During the following weeks Phillip's behavior became more normal, and additional sessions were not needed.

At a one-year follow-up call, Mrs. A. said that Phillip was symptom free in terms of handwashing and compulsive checking. This information was corroborated by the school principal. He was busy with friends and activities, which included piano lessons, kickball, and overnight visits and camping with friends and cousins. Mrs. A. said she and her husband were quite proud of him. When Phillip got on the phone, he told the therapist that he had learned to swim and could go off the low and high boards, frontwards and backwards. When asked how he had done all this, he replied, "I just jumped in." He said later, "And I don't look behind doors, and washing my hands—I got over that one. Today I got all dirty. I forgot to wash them [his hands] doing Army crawls all over the place."

Discussion

Fagan (1970) has suggested three major outcome criteria for psychotherapy: (a) how rapidly the symptom has been removed; (b) what positive behavior has replaced it; and (c) how little disturbance has been created in interlocking systems. Data obtained at the end of this therapy and at follow-up yield a positive outcome on each of these criteria. In regard to the first, the therapy was relatively brief, with fifteen sessions over a seven-month period. The importance of rapid symptom alleviation for obsessive-compulsive children must be underscored. For one reason, long-term therapy is expensive for the family in terms of money and time. A hidden cost of therapy without emphasis on symptomatic relief is the time lost developmentally by the child in critical areas of self-esteem, peer relationships, and educational progress while waiting for change in the preoccupying symptoms that keep him out of the mainstream. The longer the dysfunctional process goes on, the more damage may accumulate to repair. Regarding the second criterion, positive behaviors that replaced the symptoms in this case included new friendships, participation in activities outside the home, improvement in schoolwork, and more time spent with the father and sister. In terms of the third criterion, there appeared to be very little disturbance of interlocking systems. The family as a whole did not suffer adverse repercussions as a result of the therapy. On the contrary, they were involved in each step of a change process that was calibrated to their needs. It is significant that the mother, who might have felt the most bereft by changes in her son, found a new job to challenge and occupy her.

This condensed case report with my rationale and comments is not presented as comprising all aspects of this therapy, nor is it intended to be a definitive statement on the reasons change occurred in this family. It is important to recognize and take seriously the extraordinary complexity of the therapeutic process. At the same time, the scientific utility of attempting to specify the so-called "active ingredients" of psychotherapy (Bergin and Lambert 1978, Strupp 1973) is acknowledged. It has been observed that diverse methods of therapy share factors that contribute to successful outcome. The relationship ingredients in this therapy are considered to be examples of such nonspecific factors. The therapeutic alliance between therapist and parents as well as that between therapist and child was an affirmative and respectful one. Such an alliance is considered to have been a necessary but not sufficient condition for change in this family and child. It can be viewed as providing the substrate on which the technical aspects acted. In contrast, the technical aspects of this particular therapy are viewed as vital to the rapidity of symptom reduction and overall systemic change.

Several technical interventions will be highlighted. First, my positive connotation (Selvini Palazzoli et al. 1974) of the parents' efforts on their son's behalf helped head off resistance and paved the way for the sense of mastery they achieved in helping their son to help himself. It was important not to reinforce the mother's self-critical comments and to give the parents credit for the success of the therapy rather than the therapist. The other important instance of positive connotation was the refusal to define the child as pathological and defective, which could have served as a self-fulfilling prophecy and further crystallized the problem. The somewhat bizarre quality of obsessive-compulsive symptoms makes this atmosphere of affirmation all the more important.

Second, the gradual decrease in the mother's intrusiveness and gentle increase in the father's involvement in the boy's life through the use of various directives and therapeutic suggestions appear to be another crucial aspect of the therapy. These interventions realigned the family relationships and facilitated later emphasis on his involvement with the wider world. One retrospective study (Hollingsworth et al. 1980) of obsessive-compulsive adults who were treated in childhood found a striking impairment of interpersonal relationships in their adult lives. Facilitation of such relationships in these children during childhood is too important to be left to chance and can be tackled directly as illustrated in this therapy. The therapist encouraged the boy's involvement with peers and activities, suggesting risk taking as an antidote to obsessiveness. It is significant that at follow-up he described an impulsive act—"I just jumped in" (when learning to swim)—the opposite of a compulsive one.

Finally, a major technical aspect of this treatment was the recording of functional behaviors and ignoring of obsessive-compulsive ones. Charting appears to be an ideal vehicle for change in these families, since it paradoxically allows both parent and child their obsessiveness but rechannels it to more constructive ends.

Mediating the relationship and technical aspects of this therapy were the fit of the therapeutic orientation and approaches used to my way of thinking and therapeutic style. An atmosphere of confidence and optimism was conveyed to the family, which helped them to make changes they otherwise might not have made.

References

Adams, P. (1973). *Obsessive Children*. New York: Brunner/Mazel.
Adler, A. (1956). *The Individual Psychology of Alfred Adler*, ed. H. Ansbacher and R. Ansbacher. New York: Basic Books.

Bergin, A., and Lambert, M. (1978). The evaluation of therapeutic outcomes. In *Handbook of Psychotherapy and Behavior Change: An Empirical Analysis*, 2d ed., ed. S. Garfield and A. Bergin. New York, Wiley.

Fagan, J. (1970). The tasks of the therapist. In *Gestalt Therapy Now: Theory, Techniques, Applications*, ed. J. Fagan and I. Shepherd. New York: Harper & Row.

Fine, S. (1973). Family therapy and a behavioral approach to childhood obsessive-compulsive disorder. *Archives of General Psychiatry* 28:695–697.

Freud, S. (1913). The predisposition to obsessional neurosis. In *Collected Papers II*. New York, Basic Books, 1959.

Haley, J. (1977). *Problem-Solving Therapy*. San Francisco: Jossey-Bass.

Harbin, H. (1979). Cure by ordeal: treatment of an obsessive-compulsive neurotic. *International Journal of Family Therapy* 1:324–332.

Hollingsworth, C., Tanguay, P., Grossman, L., and Pabst, P. (1980). Long-term outcome of obsessive-compulsive disorder in childhood. *Journal of Child Psychiatry* 1:134–144.

Judd, L. (1965). Obsessive compulsive neurosis in children. *Archives of General Psychiatry* 12:135–143.

Kringlen, E. (1965). Obsessional neurotics. *British Journal of Psychiatry* 111:709–722.

Madanes, C. (1980). Protection, paradox, and pretending. *Family Process* 19:73–85.

Meyer, V. (1966). Modification of expectations in cases with obsessional rituals. *Behaviour Research and Therapy* 4:273–280.

Minuchin, S. (1974). *Families and Family Therapy*. Cambridge, MA: Harvard University Press.

Napier, A., and Whitaker, C. (1978). *The Family Crucible*. New York: Harper & Row.

Rado, S. (1959). Obsessive behavior: so-called obsessive-compulsive neurosis. In *American Handbook of Psychiatry*, vol. I, ed. S. Arieti. New York: Basic Books.

Scott, M. (1966). Treatment of obsessive behavior in a child. *Southern Medical Journal* 59:1087–1089.

Selvini Palazzoli, M., Boscolo, L., Cecchin, G., and Prata, G. (1974). The treatment of children through brief therapy of their parents. *Family Process* 13:429–442.

Stern, R. (1970). Treatment of a case of obsessional neurosis using thought-stopping technique. *British Journal of Psychiatry* 117:441–442.

Strupp, H. (1973). Toward a reformulation of the psychotherapeutic influence. *International Journal of Psychiatry* 11:263–327.

Sullivan, H. S. (1956). Obsessionalism. In *Clinical Studies in Psychiatry*, ed. H. Perry, M. Gawel, and M. Gibbon. New York: Norton.

Walton, D., and Mather, M. (1963). The application of learning principles to the treatment of obsessive-compulsive states in the acute and chronic phases of illness. *Behaviour Research and Therapy* 1:163–174.

Watzlawick, P. (1978). *The Language of Change: Elements of Therapeutic Communication.* New York: Basic Books.

Weiner, I. (1967). Behavior therapy in obsessive-compulsive neurosis: treatment of an adolescent boy. *Psychotherapy: Theory, Research and Practice* 4:27–29.

11

Depression

CYNTHIA FRAME, JOHNNY L. MATSON,
WILLIAM A. SONIS, M. JEROME FIALKOV,
AND ALAN E. KAZDIN

Childhood depression has been an active source of controversy and empirical investigation in recent years (Cantwell and Carlson 1979, Puig-Antich 1980, Schulterbrandt and Raskin 1977). Evidence has emerged that depression in children can be reliably diagnosed using Research Diagnostic Criteria (RDC) or *DSM-III* (e.g., Carlson and Cantwell 1979, Kashani et al. 1981, Puig-Antich et al. 1979). In addition, several techniques have been developed to diagnose depression and to measure its severity (Kazdin 1981, Kovacs 1981, Petti 1978).

A growing body of literature for adults has suggested that behavior therapy may be useful to treat depressive disorders, particularly non-psychotic, unipolar depression (Rehm 1981). However, treatment of depressed children has yet to be evaluated systematically with psychosocial or behavioral techniques. The present investigation reports the case of a 10-year-old child diagnosed as meeting criteria for a major depressive disorder. Behavioral treatment was conducted on symptoms of depression the child manifested in daily living.

Method

Subject

Dale was a 10-year-old male inpatient of borderline mental retardation (full scale WISC-R IQ = 79) on a children's psychiatric intensive care unit. The inpatient facility houses eighteen children who are admitted on a short-term basis for their acute psychopathology. Dale was admitted because of his recent history of suicidal thoughts and gestures, violent temper outbursts, and poor school performance. He was not on medication at any time during his hospitalization.

Assessment

The subject was assessed with several different measures of depression. First, a psychiatric interview revealed that Dale met *DSM-III* criteria for a major depressive episode. Second, upon admission, Dale's mother completed several measures including the Children's Depression Inventory (CDI) (parent-rated) (Kovacs and Beck 1978), the Child Behavior Problem Checklist (CBP) (Achenbach 1978), and the Bellevue Index of Depression (BID) (Petti 1978). On each measure, Dale met criteria considered significant for depression. Specifically, Dale received a score of 27 on the CDI rated by his mother; scored one and one-half standard deviations above the mean for depression on the CBP; and met the Weinberg criteria (Brumback et al. 1977) for depression on the BID.

The diagnosis was corroborated further by a rater who was naive to Dale's diagnosis and admitting problems. The rater viewed a videotaped interview of Dale and completed the CDI and Depression Adjective Checklist (DACL) (Lubin 1967) for the child. The rater's judgments placed Dale in the clinically depressed range on the CDI with a score of 21, and at the 71st percentile for depression according to the DACL. Finally, reports by hospital staff revealed that Dale was frequently uncommunicative in interpersonal situations, with poor eye contact, inaudible speech or one-word answers, bland facial expression, and body positions indicative of social withdrawal, such as turning his head away from a speaker or placing his hands over his face. These last four areas were targeted for behavioral intervention.

Assessment was conducted daily while the subject responded to different situations in simulated role-play. The sessions were held on the inpatient unit in a treatment room with an observation booth separated by a one-way mirror through which the sessions were videotaped for later coding.

Target Behaviors

The following behaviors were identified for assessment and treatment:

1. *Inappropriate body position*

The subject assuming any body position which indicated lack of interest or participation in the conversation during a response to a question. Examples included turning the head away, placing his hands over his face, bending forward or away from the interviewer, or standing with his back to the interviewer.

2. Lack of eye contact

The patient failing to look the interviewer in the eye at any time while delivering a verbal response.

3. Poor speech quality

This category was scored for occurrence if the subject: (a) uttered one or more words which were too soft or garbled to hear clearly, (b) spoke two or fewer words in response to a question or replied: "I don't know," or (c) responded to a question with a latency of three seconds or longer.

4. Bland affect

Bland affect was defined as lack of emotional tone and inflection in the voice, and failure to employ facial, hand, or arm gestures, while speaking.

Each behavior was rated as occurrence or nonoccurrence during the child's response to each of the twelve role-play situations presented, one at a time, within a daily session. Thus, for each behavior, the child's score could range from 0 to 12 per day, where zero represented nonoccurrence of the target behavior. Scenes involved typical everyday situations from home or hospital life, such as: "You are in the lunch line. A new girl is right behind you. A staff member says, 'Dale, tell the new girl how to earn dessert.'"

Assessment periods were identical for baseline, treatment, and follow-up, and occurred immediately after training during the treatment conditions.

Reliability of Assessment

Ratings were made by a doctoral-level psychology intern and an undergraduate psychology student who were trained by a third person to a criterion of 80 to 90 percent agreement on all target behaviors. The student was "blind" to the experimental conditions and observed the videotaped sessions in random order.

Reliability was assessed by computing a Pearson product-moment correlation coefficient between the raters' session scores for each behavior. Eighty-six percent of the sessions were rated by both observers, divided equally among baseline and treatment conditions. Agreement was high for each behavior: $r = 0.99$ for inappropriate body position, $r = 0.94$ for poor eye contact, $r = 0.83$ for poor speech, and $r = 0.95$ for bland affect.

Experimental Conditions

The treatment was evaluated in a multiple-baseline design across each of three phases. The intervention consisted of a behavioral training package designed to alter the specific responses which characterized Dale's social interactions. The experimental design included three assessment periods: namely, baseline, treatment, and follow-up.

Baseline

During baseline sessions, behavior was assessed in the manner described above. However, no attempt was made to intervene to alter performance. The durations of the baseline phase differed for each behavior to meet the requirements of a multiple-baseline design.

Treatment

Treatment was administered individually to the child by a psychology intern who served as the therapist. Twenty-minute sessions were held each weekday in the same room as described for assessment. Treatment consisted of a skills-training package involving instructions, modeling, role-play, and performance feedback. Both assessment and novel role-play scenes were used for training. The child was told at the beginning of each session what constituted the inappropriate behavior to be trained that day, and a more appropriate response was modeled for him by the therapist. The child was then asked to perform a role-play scene. Appropriate responses were praised and followed by the presentation of a new scene. Inappropriate behaviors were immediately identified, and the child was required to repeat the role-play scene until his response was altered and acceptable, at which time the next scene was introduced. This procedure was repeated for the duration of the twenty-minute session.

After an eight-day baseline for all behaviors, the subject was trained simultaneously on the first two behaviors, body position and eye contact, for six sessions. This was followed by five sessions for the treatment of speech quality, and ended with nine sessions teaching the child to express affect appropriately. The subject was given a small reward (candy or chewing gum) at the end of each daily session, contingent upon cooperation during the session rather than quality of response.

Follow-up

At the end of treatment the child was discharged from the hospital. Twelve weeks after treatment, the child returned to the hospital for reassessment. The conditions of assessment were identical to those described in the baseline phase.

Results

The mean occurrence of each of the target behaviors across baseline, treatment, and follow-up phases for the twelve role-play situations are presented in Table 11-1. Daily performance is illustrated in Figure 11-1, which shows that treatment produced marked changes in behavior. The first two behaviors treated were inappropriate body position and poor eye contact. Although considerable variability was evident during baseline, these behaviors were high rate and either stable or increasing in the opposite direction of the desired changes. Both of the behaviors were rapidly modified in the appropriate direction with the introduction of treatment. Inappropriate body position and poor eye contact were consistently near zero at the conclusion of the treatment phase.

	Baseline	Treatment	Follow-Up
Inappropriate body position	9.3	0.9	4.0
Poor eye contact	10.3	2.4	4.0
Poor speech quality	6.9	0.7	2.0
Bland affect	7.0	0.3	0.0

Table 11-1. Mean frequency of each of the four target behaviors by experimental condition.

The third behavior treated was speech quality. During baseline, which extended well into the treatment phase for the first two behaviors treated, no appreciable change of the target behaviors was noted.

However, when treatment began, rapid reductions to near zero responding were noted. Response rates were maintained at this level throughout the remainder of the treatment condition. The most variable behavior in baseline was bland affect, which was the final behavior treated.
Despite this variability, the inappropriate behavior at its lowest rate
during baseline was much higher than at any point following the inception of treatment.

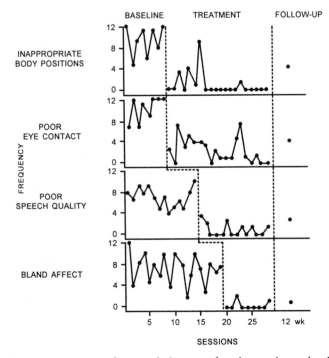

Figure 11–1. Frequency of target behaviors for the twelve role-played
scenes during baseline, treatment, and follow-up.

In general the pattern of the data is relatively clear. Each behavior systematically improved when treatment was introduced, thus meeting the criteria of the multiple-baseline design. The effects achieved with
treatment continued to be evident twelve weeks later when the child
returned to the hospital for follow-up assessment. At follow-up some
increases were evident, especially for inappropriate body positions, but
all behaviors remained well below the baseline rates (see Table 11–1
and Figure 11–1).

Discussion

The present study suggests that behaviors characteristic of depression can be identified, reliably assessed, and treated successfully in children. The present use of multiple measures and the reliance upon several sources of information greatly enhanced confidence in the general diagnosis of depression given to the child. There was consensual validation that depressive behaviors were present and problematic and that these behaviors formed a symptom cluster typical of a depressive disorder. This suggests that the diagnosis did not result from artifacts of particular assessment devices or bias of a particular observer. The demonstration also is consistent with the growing body of evidence that depression in childhood is an identifiable psychiatric entity.

The treatment of selected depressive behaviors was quite successful in this study. Changes in undesirable behaviors were immediate, marked, and durable. Demonstration of treatment effects in a multiple-baseline design ensured that improvement was not attributed to extraneous factors, since each target behavior failed to decrease until it was subjected to treatment. These results are consistent with those of Matson (1982), who successfully reduced the frequency of depressive behaviors in four mentally retarded adults. To the authors' knowledge, the present study is one of the first demonstrations of the efficacy of behavior therapy with a child for behaviors characteristic of depression. Therapeutic changes were achieved without the use of medication. Because of the undetermined efficacy and side effects of antidepressants in children, an effective behavioral approach for depressive behaviors would provide an especially valuable treatment alternative.

The present study represents an encouraging first step toward the investigation of behavioral treatment of depression in children. However, much additional research is needed. One concern is the inability of the present study to permit analysis of the effectiveness of the individual treatment components.

This issue may be minor in light of the demonstrated efficacy of the package, as well as findings by other investigators that the combined treatment package is generally superior to isolated techniques in the training of social behaviors (Bellack and Hersen 1979). A second issue pertains to the generalization of therapeutic change. Although it is valuable to know that depressive behaviors can be controlled within the treatment setting, evidence for generalization of appropriate behaviors to daily life situations would be highly desirable.

The most important limitation of the present study is the inability to demonstrate elimination of a depressive disorder. The target symptoms chosen for treatment were an important part of this child's depressive symptom picture, but were neither pathognomonic for, nor unique to, depression. There is no evidence that the other facets of the depressive disorder (vegetative signs, for example) were altered by the treatment. Although multiple symptoms of the child's depression were successfully treated, the extent to which treatment eliminated the disorder remains unclear.

References

Achenbach, T. M. (1978). The child behavior profile: I. Boys aged 6–11. *Journal of Consulting and Clinical Psychology* 46:478–488.

Bellack A. S., and Hersen, M., eds. (1979). *Research and Practice in Social Skills Training*. New York: Plenum.

Brumback, R. A., Dietz-Schmidt, S. G., and Weinberg, W. A. (1977). Depression in children referred to an educational diagnostic center: diagnosis and treatment and analysis of criteria and literature review. *Disorders of the Nervous System* 38:529–535.

Cantwell, D. P., and Carlson, G. (1979). Problems and prospects in the study of childhood depression. *Journal of Nervous and Mental Disease* 167:522–529.

Carlson, G. A., and Cantwell, D. P. (1979). A survey of depressive symptoms in a child and adolescent psychiatric population. *Journal of the American Academy of Child and Adolescent Psychiatry* 18:587–599.

Kashani, J. H., Barbero, G. J., and Bolander, F. D. (1981). Depression in hospitalized pediatric patients. *Journal of the American Academy of Child and Adolescent Psychiatry* 20:123–134.

Kazdin, A. E. (1981). Assessment techniques for childhood depression: a critical appraisal. *Journal of the American Academy of Child and Adolescent Psychiatry* 20:358–375.

Kovacs, M. (1981). Rating scales to assess depression in school aged children. *Acta Paedopsychiatrica* 46:305–315.

Kovacs, M., and Beck, A. T. (1978). Maladaptive cognitive structures in depression. *American Journal of Psychiatry* 135:525–533.

Lubin, B. (1967). *The Depression Adjective Checklist, Form A*. San Diego, CA: Educational and Industrial Testing Service.

Matson, J. L. (1982). The treatment of behavioral characteristics of depression in the mentally retarded. *Behavior Therapy* 13:209–218.

Petti, T. A. (1978). Depression in hospitalized child psychiatric patients: approaches to measuring depression. *Journal of the American Academy of Child and Adolescent Psychiatry* 17:49–59.

Puig-Antich, J. (1980). Affective disorders in childhood: a review and perspective. *Psychiatric Clinics of North America* 3:403–424.

Puig-Antich, J., Chambers, W., Halpern, F., et al. (1979). Cortisol hypersecretion in pre-pubertal depressive illness: a preliminary report. *Psychoneuroendocrinology* 4:191–197.

Rehm, L. P., ed. (1981). *Behavior Therapy for Depression: Present Status and Future Directions.* New York: Academic Press.

Schulterbrandt, J. G., and Raskin, A., eds. (1977). *Depression in Children: Diagnosis, Treatment and Conceptual Models.* New York: Raven.

PART III
Habit Disorders

12

Toilet Training

RICHARD M. FOXX AND NATHAN H. AZRIN

Until a child has learned to toilet himself properly and without a reminder, the parent and the child must suffer problems of hygiene, skin irritations, excessive dependence on the parent, inconvenience, expense, and, as the child matures, also social embarrassment. Although all normal children seem to learn eventually to toilet themselves, parental "common sense" procedures have resulted in no more benefit than has occurred without training. For example, Madsen and colleagues (1969) found that parental training for one month reduced accidents by only 5 percent, which is about the same insignificant decrease that they obtained without any toilet training. In view of this failure of training efforts, the common attitude of permissiveness regarding toileting (Spock 1968) is understandable and justified. One can understand why this permissive view of toilet training as an exercise in futility has recurred about every decade for the past sixty years (Wolfenstein 1965). Some success in reducing training time has been indicated by special reinforcement procedures (Madsen 1965, Madsen et al. 1969, Mahoney et al. 1971, Pumroy and Pumroy 1965). Unfortunately, all of these procedures have required at least one month of training, all but one (Madsen et al. 1969) have been tested with only one, two or three children, and all but one (Mahoney et al. 1971) still required continuous reminders to toilet at the end of training. In spite of these limitations, these results indicate that intensive training can reduce somewhat the age at which a child will toilet himself.

Recently, a method has been developed for rapidly training the retarded to toilet themselves without prompting (Azrin and Foxx 1971, Azrin, Sneed, and Foxx 1973, Foxx and Azrin 1973a). The success of those efforts indicated that similar and even more rapid training might be achieved with normal children by use of that general method. The present study evaluated a modification of that method with a group of nonretarded children.

Method

Children

Thirty-four children were selected for training, twenty-two boys and twelve girls. Children were recruited by a newspaper ad, by a word-of-mouth request by the authors, and by referral from mothers whose children had been trained by the procedure. Since the training procedure required the child to be capable of responding to verbal instructions, a screening test was devised for ascertaining a potential trainee's instructional responsiveness. The child was asked successively to point to his (1) nose, (2) eyes, (3) mouth, (4) hair, (5) to sit down, (6) to stand up, (7) to walk with the mother to another room, (8) to look at the mother, (9) to imitate the mother in a simple task, (10) to bring the mother a toy. Of the forty-three children referred, nine could not satisfy the test for instructional responsiveness. All but two of the nine children were under 20 months of age. The mean age for the final sample of thirty-four children was 25 months with a range of 20 to 36 months. Virtually all of the parents mentioned difficulties in toilet training their child that led them to seek outside assistance and several mentioned the use of spankings and rewards. Several children, especially the younger ones, did not speak more than a few words and did not dress themselves.

General Rationale

The present method was based on the same rationale used previously to devise a rapid toilet training procedure for the retarded (Azrin and Foxx 1971, Foxx and Azrin 1973a). Normal testing was viewed as a governed reaction that included dressing skills, independence of action, and awareness of one's appearance, as well as sensitivity to bladder and bowel pressures. The general method was to provide an intensive learning experience that maximized the factors known to be important for learning, and then to fade out these factors once learning had occurred. The learning factors maximized were a distraction-free environment, a large number of trials, consideration of the component responses, operant reinforcement for correct responses, a variety of reinforcers, quality of the reinforcers, frequency of reinforcement, manual guidance, verbal instruction, immediacy of reinforcement, immediacy of detection of incorrect responses, and negative reinforcement for the incorrect response. For the present application to nonretarded children, the previous reliance on manual guidance was deemphasized and greater reliance placed on verbal instructions. An imitation procedure was added as well as a procedure for verbal and symbolic rehearsal of the benefits of toileting correctly. Since children are typically more active than adults, the adult procedure (Azrin and Foxx 1971) was changed to require more activity. A description follows of the specific procedure used to emphasize each of these learning factors.

Setting (Distraction-Free Environment)

Distractions and competing activities could be expected to interfere with the child's performance of the required toileting. Accordingly, all toys were removed and only the trainer was present. Although training was conducted in the home of the child or in the home of the trainer, the parents and family members were asked to leave for the day. The trainers were two adult female assistants. Only one assistant was used for each child.

Increased Number of Trials: Increased Urinations

In order to provide many opportunities to reinforce correct toiletings and to negatively reinforce incorrect toiletings, a high frequency of urinations would be desirable. An increased frequency was achieved by giving the child fluids to drink about every five minutes, such that about two cups were consumed per hour. The drinks were selected on the basis of the mother's statement of what the child preferred and usually consisted of soft drinks, juices, punches, and milk.

Operant Reinforcement for Correct Toileting

Reinforcement for a response is known to increase the strength of that response. Consequently, reinforcers were given for the act of urinating in the "potty-chair" that was provided, and also for each of the component skills preceding and following the urination. Reinforcement was withheld at other times and for non-toileting acts.

Component Skills

Common sense application of reinforcement procedures is often interpreted to mean reinforcing the child after he has completed a correct urination. The present procedure considered each of the component skills such as approaching the potty-chair, grasping the pants, lowering the pants, sitting on the potty-chair, wiping oneself, arising after urination, raising the pants, removing the urine-filled pot from the chair, bringing the pot to the toilet, emptying the pot, flushing the toilet, and returning the pot to the chair. Reinforcers and instructions were given for each of these component acts.

Quality of Reinforcers

Tasty edibles were used as reinforcers. In addition, an effort was made to identify for use as reinforcers many other events that were of central importance to the child's happiness by questioning the mother and child beforehand. Thus, for a given child a specific type of sweets (such as chocolates) or food (such as potato chips) was used. In addition, the reinforcement consisted of effusive verbal praise, a hug, kisses, caresses, smiles, and applause. Symbolic types of reinforcers were also included (see "Verbal and symbolic rehearsal" below) by telling the child how pleased his important friends, relatives, and "heroes" would be.

Variety of Reinforcers

Since any single reinforcer might lose its effectiveness through constant and exclusive use, the large variety of reinforcers described above were used successively and in various simultaneous combinations.

Immediacy of Reinforcement

The more immediate the reinforcement, the greater is the strength of the reinforced response. Since the major response act was urinating while seated on the potty-chair, immediate detection and reinforcement at this moment was critical. Although close visual observation of the seated child would usually be sufficient for immediate detection and was used for five children, a special signaling potty-chair assisted in this detection. The special chair sounded a musical signal when urination activated a device located in the bowl of the chair. The trainer was then alerted and immediately reinforced the child. For the component skills, such as lowering the pants and sitting on the chair, the trainer relied solely on visual observation, and gave immediate reinforcement for each component.

Frequency of Reinforcement

The greater the frequency of reinforcement, the greater the strength of the reinforced response. This principle dictated that the reinforcement be given for every instance of correct urination and every instance of the component skills. Only when the habit and skills were firmly established was the reinforcement frequency decreased (see "Fading of prompts and reinforcers" below).

Graduated Guidance

For each of the component skills, the trainer instructed the child as to what to do, then manually guided the child through the proper movements if the child did not initiate the movement himself. The manual guidance was graduated at any given moment such that no more guidance was used than was necessary for the movement to be carried out. This Graduated Guidance technique, described in detail (Azrin and Foxx 1971, Foxx and Azrin 1972, 1973a,b), served the purpose of teaching the child the correct movements as well as motivating him to respond quickly to instructions.

Verbal Instruction

The child was instructed to carry out the correct toileting in a detailed manner that specified each movement, such as putting the fingers beneath the briefs and toward the back of the hips rather than simply instructing him to go to the toilet or to lower his pants. The Graduated Guidance ensured immediate completion of the skill in the rare event that the instructions were not understood or were ignored. The reinforcers at the completion of the act encouraged the child to carry out the act at the next opportunity whether that act had been carried out as a result of instructions or of the Graduated Guidance.

Imitation

Imitation is a proven method of teaching details of a skill and was used in addition to verbal description. Directed imitation was used to teach the child how to toilet and to learn the positive benefits of doing so. The child was given a hollow doll that could be filled with water through the mouth and would release the water through a hole between its legs. The trainer taught the child to perform all of the toileting skills and procedures with the doll that were being used with the child, such as praising and feeding the doll, lowering and raising its pants, and allowing it to urinate in the potty-chair. This directed imitation was conducted continuously between the child's own practice trials at the start of training until the child had learned the component toileting skills.

Dry Pants Check

The objective of the training was not to educate the child to urinate frequently and correctly but to do so at whatever frequency was necessary to insure dry pants. To teach this awareness of his appearance the trainer inspected the child's pants about every five minutes, having the child himself touch his pants, and reinforcing the child if the pants were dry. The fluids were given as part of this reinforcement and thereby fulfilled the double function of increasing the frequency of urination as well as being a reinforcer.

Negative Reinforcement for Accidents

To discourage accidents, the trainer reprimanded the child when he wet his pants. The trainer also omitted the reinforcers at the next dry-pants check, and omitted any social interaction with the child for about five minutes (time-out from positive reinforcement). Also serving as a negative reinforcer was the requirement that the child himself change into dry pants, which was done at the end of the time-out period so that wet pants would be associated with loss of social interaction. The final element of the negative reinforcement was a required period of practicing rapidly the complete act of toileting (described below under "Positive practice"). The trainer closely observed the child's pants, expression, and posture so as to detect an accident immediately and to impose the negative reinforcers immediately.

Prompted Practice Trials

To provide practice in toileting and to associate urination in the potty-chair with reinforcement, the child was instructed to toilet himself about every ten minutes. He was allowed to sit on the potty-chair for about five minutes during each trial until one or two urinations occurred during the first minute after seating himself. This short latency urination was interpreted to mean that the child was bladder trained. Thereafter, he was required to be seated for only about one minute during each trial.

Positive Practice

A period of required practice in toileting was used as an educational tool as well as a negative reinforcer. After the verbal reprimand had been given for an accident, the trainer required the child to practice going to the potty-chair from various locations in the house for a total of ten rapidly conducted trials. During each trial, the child went to the chair, lowered his pants, seated himself for about two seconds, stood up, raised his pants and then moved to another location. As described in detail elsewhere (Azrin, Kaplan, and Foxx 1973, Foxx and Azrin, 1972, 1973a,b), this period of positive practice was educative but also negatively reinforcing because of the effort required.

Verbal and Symbolic Rehearsal

An objective of the procedure was to create a desire by the child to remain dry in order to please his parents, family, and friends. Yet the limitations of the training situation precluded the possibility of having these "significant others" actually present and participating. As a substitute, this social reinforcement was arranged symbolically by telling the child, as part of the reinforcement, that each of these persons would be delighted at his success. A list of these significant individuals was obtained prior to the training and included favored television or story-book characters as well as real persons. To insure the child's involvement, the child was asked to reply to questions about this symbolic reinforcement such as "What will Santa Claus (or Mickey Mouse, or Daddy, or Mommy, or your brother Bobby) say about your dry pants?"

Fading of Prompts and Reinforcers

The detailed instructions and continuous reinforcement for each component skill were given at the start of training but then withdrawn as the child progressed. The instructions on the practice trials were successively omitted for each component act that was conducted at least once without instructions. The instruction to initiate a practice trial was omitted entirely once the child initiated and carried out one entire practice trial without any prompts having been given. Also, after this unprompted toileting, reinforcers for correct toileting were given only intermittently, and then discontinued entirely as were also the dry-pants inspections. The critical point in training was the first occasion of toileting with no need for instructions. Typically, only an additional half-hour or hour was needed thereafter with no instructions during that time and with the reinforcement for dry pants given only once or twice. Thus, the trainer was functioning primarily as an observer after the first unprompted toileting.

Post-Training Attention

The primary motivation desired for maintaining the toileting habit was the pleasure of the child's parents and family. To insure this motivation after training, the parent inspected the child's pants before each meal or snack and at naptimes and bedtime and praised the child for having dry pants. If an accident occurred, the parent reprimanded the child, made him change his pants, and required him to practice going to the toilet (positive practice). No reminders to toilet were given. This scheduled attention to the child's appearance was conducted only for a few days after training and then discontinued once the child had no accidents.

Results

Reduction of Accidents

Figure 12-1 shows the number of accidents before and after training for the thirty-four children. The mothers had recorded the number of accidents by counting the number of times the child had to be changed each day during the week preceding and following training. Following training, the parents were contacted every month for four months by telephone or by a personal visit from one of the trainers. Prior to training, the children averaged about six accidents per day per child. Within the first post-training week, accidents had decreased by 97 percent to 0.2 accidents per day per child, or about one per week. This near-zero level of accidents endured during the entire four-month follow-up period and applied to bowel movements as well as urinations. A within-subject comparison of the children's pre- and post-training accidents by the Wilcoxin Matched-Pairs Signed Ranks Test (Siegel 1956) showed a significant (p < 0.01) reduction of accidents for the very first day after training and for each month of the post-training period.

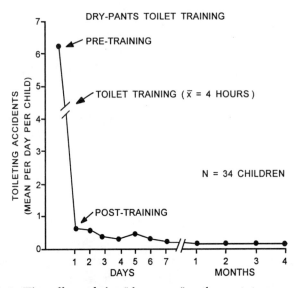

Figure 12-1. The effect of the "dry-pants" toilet training procedure on the frequency of toileting accidents, both bladder and bowel, of thirty-four normal children. The toilet training period is shown as an interruption in the curve and required an average of four hours per child. The "pre-training" data point represents the children's accident rate per day during the week prior to training. Data points are given for the first seven days after training and monthly thereafter. Each datum point is the average number of accidents per day per child.

Training Time

The mean training time was 3.9 hours; the median time was 3.5 hours and the range was a half-hour to 14 hours. Training was considered complete when the child toileted himself completely and with no prompts. The older children, aged 26 to 36 months, were trained in a training time of about 2.25 hours. The 20- to 25-month-old group had a mean training time of about 5 hours.

Parent Reaction

Most of the parents, although hopeful, were somewhat skeptical about the favorable outcome of a training program, possibly because of their own unsuccessful experiences in attempting to train their children. Upon seeing their child independently toilet himself, raise and lower his own pants, carry the plastic pot into the toilet and empty the contents into the toilet, flush the toilet, and replace the plastic pot, the parents characteristically expressed disbelieving pleasure. These parents were eager to suggest friends and relatives whose children might also benefit from the training procedure. It was found that the only parent who did not express pleasure over the rapidity which his child was trained had bet a friend $100 that his child would not be trained in one day. Ironically, this child was trained in about half an hour. Although the child did not have an accident for two months after training, we discovered on the three-month follow-up that the child had been returned to diapers for no apparent reason other than the economic consideration of the wager.

Reaction of the Children

Most of the children reacted to the training program as if it were a very pleasant experience, hugging and kissing the trainer. The high density of positive reinforcement in the form of hugs, praise, candies, applause, smiles, treats, and the undivided attention of the trainer undoubtedly contributed to the children's pleasant attitude during the training program. Several features of the program seemed especially pleasurable to the children, including playing with the doll, emptying the potty, and flushing the toilet.

A few of the children initially reacted negatively to the attempts to toilet train them. These children were generally "problem children" who resisted most efforts by the parents and also actively resisted the toilet-training attempts by their parents despite being physiologically and psychologically ready for training. Typically, these few children engaged in a temper tantrum at the start of training but cooperated thereafter when this initial reluctance was overcome by providing them with immediate Graduated Guidance whenever they failed to respond to a request. The typical comment by the mothers of these problem children was that the child had become more cooperative and pleasant in his general conduct after the toilet training.

Bedwetting

None of the children were given specific training for bedwetting (enuresis). Yet the mothers of ten children (about 30 percent) reported that their child stopped wetting at night during the entire first week immediately following the daytime training. Follow-up checks showed that all ten of these children continued to stay dry at night during the four-month follow-up period.

Discussion

The results showed that the training program was an effective method of training normal children to toilet themselves without any prompting. All thirty-four children were trained. Training was accomplished rapidly, requiring an average of only four hours per child and only about two hours for children older than 26 months. The accidents quickly decreased to a near-zero level and remained near zero during the four-month follow-up. Bowel training and bladder training were accomplished concurrently with no need for a differential training procedure. An incidental benefit was that bedwetting (enuresis) was also eliminated for about one-third of the children. Successful training was achieved even for children as young as 20 months, for problem children who resisted any type of training, and for children who did not speak. The training program appeared to be a pleasant experience for the children.

The present results demonstrate that toilet training is not a futile exercise; training can be achieved by intensive learning procedures, as was also indicated by other reinforcement studies (Madsen et al. 1969, Mahoney et al. 1971). Consequently, one can no longer defend an attitude of fatalistic permissiveness on the grounds that bladder and bowel control cannot be hastened. A permissive attitude would still be justified if the training effort produced an enduring negative emotional attitude. The results showed the converse: the children who were negative prior to training were described as more pleasant and cooperative after training. Permissiveness does seem justified for the average child under 19 months of age. The present results showed that all normally responsive children over 19 months of age could be trained in a few hours, but greater difficulty should be expected with younger children as indicated by the present finding that the younger children required more training time. Since normal toileting requires locomotive skills, manual dexterity, and maturation of the bladder and bowel muscles, little gain would occur from training prior to the emergence of these skills. Also, the present method relies heavily on verbal, instructional, and symbolic procedures and should not be so rapidly effective with children who are not verbally and socially responsive. Overall, we suggest that training be deferred until a child is 20 months of age since the training effort for the average child below that age might counterbalance the convenience of having him trained.

References

Azrin, N. H., and Foxx, R. M. (1971). Autism reversal: eliminating stereotyped self-stimulation of the retarded. *Journal of Applied Behavior Analysis* 4:89–99.

Azrin, N. H., Kaplan, S. J., and Foxx, R. M. (1973). Autism reversal: a procedure for eliminating the self-stimulatory behaviors of institutionalized retardates. *American Journal of Mental Deficiency.*

Azrin, N. H., Sneed, T. J., and Foxx, R. M. (1973). Dry bed: a rapid method of eliminating bedwetting (enuresis) of the retarded. *Behaviour Research and Therapy* 11:427–434.

Foxx, R. M., and Azrin, N. H. (1972). Restitution: a method of eliminating aggressive-disruptive behavior of retarded and brain damaged patients. *Behaviour Research and Therapy* 10:15–27.

——— (1973a). *Toilet Training the Retarded: A Rapid Program for Day and Nighttime Independent Toileting.* Champaign, IL: Research Press.

——— (1973b). The elimination of autistic, self-stimulatory behavior by overcorrection. *Journal of Applied Behavior Analysis.*

Madsen, C. H. (1965). Positive reinforcement in the toilet training of a normal child. In *Case Studies in Behavior Modification*, ed. L. P. Ullmann and L. Krasner, pp. 305–307. New York: Holt, Rinehart & Winston.

Madsen, C. H., Hoffman, M., Thomas, D. R., et al. (1969). Comparisons of toilet training techniques. In *Social Learning in Childhood*, ed. D. M. Gelfand, pp. 124–132. Belmont, CA: Brooks/Cole.

Mahoney, K., Van Wagenen, R. K., and Meyerson, L. (1971). Toilet training of normal and retarded children. *Journal of Applied Behavior Analysis* 4:173–181.

Pumroy, D. K., and Pumroy, S. S. (1965). Systematic observation and reinforcement technique in toilet training. *Psychological Reports* 16:467–471.

Siegel. (1956). *Non Parametric Statistics for the Behavioral Sciences.* New York: McGraw-Hill.

Spock, B. (1968). *Baby and Child Care*, rev. ed. New York: Pocket Books.

Wolfenstein, M. (1965). Trends in infant care. In *Marriage, Family and Society*, ed. H. Rodman, pp. 116–127. New York: Random House.

13

Bedwetting

NATHAN H. AZRIN, T. J. SNEED, AND
RICHARD M. FOXX

About 10 percent of all children are enuretic at the age of 6 years, and some are still enuretic as teenagers. When enuresis is eliminated, the child's emotional adjustment has been found to be improved (Lovibond 1964). The most effective treatment for enuresis is the urine-alarm technique which was first used extensively by Mowrer and Mowrer (1938) based on their Pavlovian conditioning analysis. A loud buzzer (UCS) sounds as soon as a specially constructed bed pad is moistened by urine. The procedure requires several weeks or months, has a relatively high relapse rate, but is initially effective for as many as 80 to 90 percent of enuretics (see reviews by Jones 1960, Lovibond 1964, Yates 1970). A new procedure, the "dry-bed" procedure, has been developed from an operant model rather than a respondent model and has been used with profoundly retarded adult enuretics who were institutionalized (Azrin, Sneed, and Foxx 1973). This dry-bed procedure required only one night of intensive training followed by use of the urine-alarm apparatus for as little as one week. Some of the major features of the intensive training procedure were (1) large fluid intake to increase the desire to urinate, (2) hourly awakenings, (3) teaching the client to awaken to mild prompts, (4) practice in going to the toilet, (5) reinforcement for urinating in the toilet at night, (6) use of the urine-alarm apparatus to signal a bedwetting, and (7) training in awareness of the dry versus wet condition of the bed. When an accident occurred, the client received verbal disapproval, he was required to change the bedsheets, and he was required to practice arising from the bed to walk to the toilet. After one night of intensive training, the urine-alarm apparatus remained on the bed until one week elapsed without an accident. During that time, accidents received the same treatment, but the other procedures were omitted. Bedwetting virtually ceased within only two or three days after the intensive training.

The surprisingly rapid success of the dry-bed procedure with the retarded adults led the authors to believe that even greater success might be achieved with nonretarded enuretic children (Azrin, Sneed, and Foxx 1973). Surprisingly, preliminary results indicated greater difficulty with the normal children. One plausible reason was that the adults had already achieved some degree of control as evidenced by their wetting their beds only 50 percent of the time rather than the typical 100 percent for the normal enuretic child. A second apparent reason was that the sleeping parent did not react to a signaled bedwetting as reliably as did the night-duty attendants for the retarded residents in the institution. The procedure was, therefore, modified. To ensure the awakening of the parent, a buzzer was located in the parent's bedroom in addition to the usual buzzer in the enuretic's bedroom. Other procedural changes were made to capitalize on the greater understanding and cooperation of the nonretarded child. The child was given lengthy verbal instruction and explanations regarding the procedure, he was required to answer questions about the procedure, he was taught to engage in the required practice trials with a minimum of supervision, and he was given training in deliberately delaying his urination similar to that used by Kimmel and Kimmel (1970). A second change that was natural to the home, rather than the institutional situation, was for the parent to require the child to toilet himself at the time that the parent went to sleep for the night, thereby easing the child's problem of inhibiting his urine throughout the remainder of the night.

The dry-bed procedure and its present modifications were devised with the view that the elimination of bedwetting was an operant process rather than Pavlovian conditioning. To evaluate this view, the present study included a procedure in which the unconditioned stimulus, the buzzer, was not present in the child's room, but only in the parent's bedroom. If the treatment process depended on Pavlovian conditioning, this omission of the UCS buzzer for the child should not result in conditioning, since the remoteness of the parent's bedroom rendered the sound of the buzzer faint, if audible at all, to the sleeping child. Conversely, if bedwetting did cease when the UCS buzzer was omitted, Pavlovian conditioning could not be responsible for the decrease.

Method

Subjects

Twenty-six children were obtained as clients in response to a newspaper advertisement that offered free treatment for bedwetters 3 years of age or older. The only two children excluded were one who had a suspected medical problem, and one whose father did not desire a training effort. The average age was 8 years, including three children under 6 years of age. Nineteen were boys and seven were girls. All but one child, IQ of 70, had apparently normal intelligence. All but two had been wetting every night since infancy. Even these two exceptions had been fairly consistent bedwetters during the previous year, and prior to that time they had never remained dry for more than two months. Virtually all of the parents had sought medical assistance, and two had enrolled their children in a commercial training program with limited success.

Experimental Design

The experimental design, as outlined in Table 13-1, provided a within-subject as well as a between-subjects comparison between the standard urine-alarm method and the new dry-bed procedure. The twenty-six children were divided into thirteen pairs matched for age, sex, and frequency of bedwetting. Within each pair, the children were randomly assigned by a coin flip to the Control Group (Standard Urine-Alarm Procedure) or the Experimental Group (Dry-Bed Procedure). The first seven pairs were in Experiment I, whereas the subsequent six pairs were in Experiment II. The two experimental groups and the two control groups were very comparable to each other with respect to age (7.5 ± 0.5 years), to sex (about a 2:1 ratio of boys to girls), and to mean frequency of bedwetting (95 ± 5 percent of the time). The dry-bed procedure was used in both Experiments I and II. In Experiment I, the urine-alarm sounded in the parents' bedroom as well as in the child's room, thereby providing the additional likelihood of awakening the parent (see Table 13-1). In the dry-bed procedure of Experiment II, the urine-alarm sounded only in the parents' room and not in the child's room, thereby providing an evaluation of the Pavlovian interpretation which requires the use of the alarm to condition the child. The within-subjects comparison was provided (see Table 13-1) by instituting the dry-bed procedure for the children in the control group after two weeks of training by the standard urine-alarm procedure.

		First two weeks	After first two weeks
Exp. I	Experimental group:	Dry-bed procedure (parent-and-child alarm)	Dry-bed procedure (parent-and-child alarm)
	Control group:	Standard conditioning procedure (child-only alarm)	Dry-bed procedure (parent-and-child alarm)
Exp. II	Experimental group:	Dry-bed procedure (parent-only alarm)	Dry-bed procedure (parent-only alarm)
	Control group:	Standard conditioning procedure (child-only alarm)	Dry-bed procedure (parent-only alarm)

Table 13–1. Experimental design for the dry-bed procedure.

Apparatus

The urine-alarm apparatus was a commonly used and commercially available bed pad. It consisted of two aluminum-foil sheets connected to a battery and separated by a sheet of absorbent cloth. When the child urinated, the urine passed through the perforations of the upper sheet of aluminum foil and was absorbed by the cloth, thereby causing a small electrical current to flow between the metal sheets and triggering the buzzer in the circuit box that was connected by wires to the metal sheets. In its usual application, the buzzer was located within 6 feet of the child's bed (child-only alarm procedure). For the dry-bed procedure of Experiment I, a second buzzer was added that was located in the parents' bedroom such that bedwetting caused both buzzers to sound simultaneously (parent-and-child alarm procedure). For the dry-bed procedure of Experiment II, the buzzer sounded only in the parents' bedroom and not in the child's room (parent-only alarm procedure).

Control Group (Standard Urine-Alarm Procedure)

The children in the control group received training as described in the written instructions of the commercially available urine-alarm apparatus. The procedure incorporated the principal features of the standard urine-alarm conditioning method used in previously reported applications. Before the enuretic child went to bed, he was told by his parents that they were displeased with his bedwetting. The urine-alarm was placed in the bed such that when the child wet his bed, a loud alarm sounded in the circuit box located near the child's bed. The parent awakened the child, if he had not already been awakened by the alarm, and sent him to the toilet to finish urination. The parent then required the child to wash his face to assure complete awakening. The parent reset the alarm, changed the wet sheets, and returned the child to bed. During the next two weeks, the parent reacted to bedwettings in this same manner, the urine-alarm remaining on the bed during the two-week period. On the first night, a trainer was present throughout the night (just as he was for the children in the dry-bed group), to explain the procedure to the parents and to assure that they followed the standard procedure in the event of a bedwetting.

Dry-Bed Procedure

Table 13–2 outlines the sequence of procedural steps in the dry-bed procedure.

I. **Intensive Training (One Night)**
   (A) *One hour before bedtime*
      1. Child informed of all phases of training procedure
      2. Alarm placed on bed
      3. Positive practice in toileting (20 practice trials)
         (a) Child lies down in bed
         (b) Child counts to 50
         (c) Child arises and attempts to urinate in toilet
         (d) Child returns to bed
         (e) Steps (a), (b), (c), and (d) repeated 20 times
   (B) *At bedtime*
      1. Child drinks fluids
      2. Child repeats training instructions to trainer
      3. Child retires for the night
   (C) *Hourly awakenings*
      1. Minimal prompt used to awaken child
      2. Child walks to bathroom
      3. At bathroom door (*before* urination), child is asked to inhibit urination for one hour (omit for children under 6)
         (a) If child could not inhibit urination
            (i) Child urinates in toilet
            (ii) Trainer praises child for correct toileting
            (iii) Child returns to bed
         (b) If child indicated that he could inhibit urination for one hour
            (i) Trainer praises child for his urinary control
            (ii) Child returns to bed

    4.   At bedside, the child feels the bed sheets and comments on their dryness

    5.   Trainer praises child for having a dry bed

    6.   Child is given fluids to drink

    7.   Child returns to sleep

(D) *When an accident occurred*

    1.   Trainer disconnects alarm

    2.   Trainer awakens child and reprimands him for wetting

    3.   Trainer directs child to bathroom to finish urinating

    4.   Child is given Cleanliness Training

        (a) Child is required to change night clothes

        (b) Child is required to remove wet bed sheet and place it with dirty laundry

        (c) Trainer reactivates alarm

        (d) Child obtains clean sheets and remakes bed

    5.   Positive Practice in correct toileting (20 practice trials) performed immediately after the Cleanliness Training

    6.   Positive Practice in correct toileting (20 practice trials) performed the following evening *before* bedtime

II. Post Training Supervision (Begins the Night after Training)

(A) *Before bedtime*

    1.   Alarm is placed on bed

    2.   Positive Practice given (*if* an accident occurred the previous night)

    3.   Child is reminded of need to remain dry and of the need for Cleanliness Training and Positive Practice if wetting occurred

    4.   Child is asked to repeat the parent's instructions

(B) *Nighttime toileting*

    1.   At parents' bedtime, they awaken child and send him to toilet

    2.   After each dry night, parent awakens child 30 minutes earlier than on previous night

    3.   Awakenings discontinued when they are scheduled to occur within one hour of child's bedtime

(C) *When accidents occurred, child receives Cleanliness Training and Positive Practice immediately upon wetting and at bedtime the next day*

(D) *After a dry night*

    1.   Both parents praise child for not wetting his bed

    2.   Parents praise child at least 5 times during the day

    3.   Child's favorite relatives are encouraged to praise him

III. Normal Routine—Initiated after Seven Consecutive Dry Nights

(A) *Urine-alarm is no longer placed on bed*

(B) *Parents inspect child's bed each morning*

    1.   If bed is wet, child receives Cleanliness Training immediately and Positive Practice the following evening

2.   If bed is dry, child receives praise for keeping his bed dry
(C) *If two accidents occur within a week, the Post-Training Supervision is reinstated*

Table 13-2. Sequence of steps in the dry-bed procedure.

The Training Night

About an hour before bedtime, the parents and the child were given a complete description of the dry-bed procedure, and the rationale for each step, as well as a review of the advantages that would result from eliminating the bedwetting problem. In order to increase the frequency of urination, the child was then given a glass of his favorite drink, and the urine-alarm was placed on his bed. The child next performed the Positive Practice procedure, which was designed to establish in the child the habit of rousing and toileting himself. The child lay in bed with the lights off and slowly and silently counted to fifty (younger children counted to a lower number) at which time he arose, walked to the toilet, and attempted to urinate. Then he returned to bed where he began counting again, repeating the procedure until twenty such trips were made. The parent remained outside of the room and counted the trips.

Then the child again drank as much as he could of his favorite drink, and he stated his understanding of the procedures to be followed that night, namely that he would be awakened hourly to practice going to the toilet rapidly and that, if he had an accident, he would change his bed sheets and practice toileting several times. The child then went to sleep.

Hourly Awakenings

Every hour, the trainer awakened the child by using a minimal prompt needed for awakening. Occasionally the child could only be aroused by guiding him to a sitting position and gently shaking him. This guidance was faded out as soon as possible to a mere touch. Rarely, the bedroom light was turned on to assist in awakening the child. If, upon awakening, the child did not immediately walk to the bathroom, the trainer would first point toward the bathroom and then ask the child, "What did you promise to do when I woke you?" If the child still showed no signs of arising and walking to the bathroom, the trainer quickly guided him into the bathroom saying, "You have to *hurry* to the bathroom if you don't want to wet your bed!"

At the bathroom door, the trainer stopped the child and inquired whether he could inhibit urination for another hour. If the child replied that he could, the trainer praised him for his bladder control, and the child returned to bed. If the child answered that he could not inhibit urination for an hour, the trainer tried to persuade him to inhibit urination for just a few minutes, after which he praised the child for his control and allowed him to urinate. Immediately following urination, the child was praised for correct toileting and returned to bed.

When the child arrived at his bed, he was directed to feel his sheets and was asked if they were dry. He was then praised for having kept his sheets dry and encouraged to keep them dry during the next hour. Finally, the child was asked to repeat his instructions for the next hourly toileting, was given another drink, and then was allowed to return to sleep.

Accidents during Training

Whenever a bedwetting accident occurred, the urine-alarm sounded. The trainer immediately disconnected the alarm, awakened the child (if he was not already awake), and reprimanded him for having wet. The child was then directed to the bathroom to finish urination. When he returned to the bedroom, he was given Cleanliness Training which required him to change his pajamas, remove the wet sheets from the bed, wipe off the mattress, and deposit the soiled linen in the appropriate place. While the child transported the soiled linen, the trainer replaced the cloth material between the metal pads of the urine-alarm apparatus and reset the device. When the bedwetter returned, he was required to obtain clean sheets and to remake his bed. After the bed sheets were changed, the child was informed that his accident indicated that he needed more practice in correct toileting in order to stay dry in the future. He was then given the Positive Practice training in arising and toileting correctly until he had performed twenty practice trips to the bathroom. No reinforcement was given for correct urination during Positive Practice. The child then returned to bed.

On the evening *following* a bedwetting accident, the child was given twenty Positive Practice trials before he retired to bed.

Post-Training Supervision

Following the single evening of intensive training, the alarm was placed on the bed each night prior to the child's bedtime. If the child had had an accident during the previous night, he was given Positive

Practice before going to bed. Immediately before the parents' bedtime, usually about 11:00 to 12:00 P.M., the parents awakened their child and sent him to the bathroom. After each dry night, the parents awakened the child for toileting a half-hour earlier on the following evening. This nighttime awakening was discontinued when the time of awakening was scheduled to follow the child's bedtime by no more than one hour. If a bedwetting accident occurred, the child was given the same procedure as during the initial training; namely, he was awakened, reprimanded for wetting, and given Cleanliness Training and Positive Practice in toileting. Encouraging fluid intake and awakening the child hourly were discontinued during the Post-Training Supervision. The Post-Training Supervision continued until the child had been dry for seven consecutive days.

After a Dry Night

If no bedwetting occurred during a given night, the next day the child was praised for having kept his bed dry. The parents were instructed to continue praising the child at appropriate and convenient times during the day, for example at meals and before bedtime. Close relatives or other persons whom the child admired and respected were invited to call and congratulate the child for not wetting his bed and to encourage him to remain dry at night.

Normal Routine

After the Post-Training Supervision was discontinued, the urine-alarm was no longer used nor were the nighttime awakenings continued. The parents inspected the child's bed in the morning. If the bed was wet, they required the child to remake it immediately and, before bedtime that evening, the bedwetter was given Positive Practice in correct toileting. If bedwetting occurred on two nights within a week, the Post-Training Supervision procedure was reinstated until the child had no accidents on seven consecutive nights.

The rationale and general description of particular procedures such as Cleanliness Training, Positive Practice, fading prompts, encouraging fluid intake, and Graduated Guidance can be found in previous reports (Azrin and Foxx 1971, Azrin, Kaplan, and Foxx 1973, Azrin, Sneed, and Foxx 1973, Foxx and Azrin 1972, 1973a,b,c). These procedures, as used in both daytime and nighttime toilet training, are described in especially great detail for use with retarded persons in Foxx and Azrin (1973a) and for normal children in Azrin and Foxx (1974).

Results

Figure 13-1 shows the median number of accidents per week for the twenty-six enuretic children. Before training, bedwetting occurred every night. The standard urine-alarm procedure reduced the accidents slightly to six bedwettings during the first week of training and to five accidents per week during the second week. After the one night of intensive training by the dry-bed procedure, the median number of accidents was only one during the first week, one during the second week, and none after the third week for the six-month follow-up. A statistical comparison of the two procedures during the first two weeks by the t test for differences showed that the number of accidents was significantly less for the children trained by the dry-bed procedure than by the standard urine-alarm procedure ($p < 0.005$).

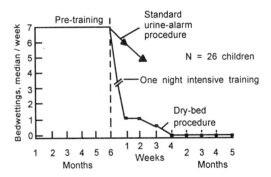

Figure 13-1. The median number of nights per week that the twenty-six enuretic children wet their bed. The pre-training data was the report of the parent of the average number of bedwettings during the previous six months. The data points are presented for each week for the first four weeks after training and for each month thereafter. The "break" in the curve represents the single evening during which the dry-bed training procedure was used. The "triangle" data points are for the thirteen matched-control children who were given the standard urine-alarm conditioning procedure. The "circle" data points are for the new dry-bed procedure and include the thirteen enuretic children in the treatment group as well as the eleven children in the control group who failed to remain dry after two weeks of the standard conditioning procedure.

Examination of the individual children trained by the standard urine-alarm procedure showed that only two of the thirteen children remained dry for more than six nights during the first two weeks of training. No attempt was made to retrain these two children by the dry-bed procedure. The other eleven children were retrained by the dry-bed procedure and are included in the data points of Figure 13-1.

Examination of the individual children trained by the dry-bed procedure, including the eleven children who had been given the standard urine-alarm training, showed that all twenty-four children were trained. Figure 13-2 shows that the slowest learner had nine accidents before achieving fourteen consecutive dry nights, whereas the average child (median) had only two accidents. The fastest learners had no accidents and included three of the twenty-four children (12 percent).

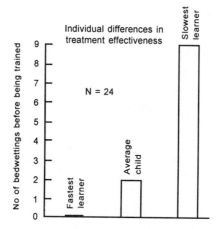

Figure 13-2. The range of individual differences in trainability by the new dry-bed procedure of the twenty-four enuretic children. Each vertical bar designates the number of nights that the child wet his bed after the one-night training session before he reached the criterion of fourteen consecutive dry nights. All children were trained, the slowest child having had nine bedwettings, the fastest children (three) having no bedwettings, and the average child (median) having two accidents before achieving the criterion of dryness.

The number of accidents was virtually the same during the parent-only-alarm procedure of Experiment II and the parent-and-child alarm procedure of Experiment I. The mean number of accidents during the first two weeks was 2.6 and 2.2, respectively, for the two procedures and was not significantly different.

None of the children relapsed to their pre-training level of bedwetting at any time during the six-month follow-up. The procedure had required the reinstatement of the urine-alarm apparatus should two accidents occur within a week. In only seven instances did two such accidents occur. In each instance, the child had no further accidents during the week after the urine-alarm was reinstated, and the apparatus was, therefore, again discontinued.

After the intensive night of training, the urine-alarm was no longer put on the bed once the child had seven consecutive dry nights. This criterion resulted in a median of nineteen days of alarm usage after training. The dry-bed procedure also called for a gradual discontinuation of the nighttime awakenings. A median of six days was required to eliminate these awakenings.

Discussion

The new procedure proved both effective and rapid in eliminating bedwetting. Enuresis was eliminated for all twenty-four children without exception including those under 6 years of age. No major relapses occurred and no intensive retraining was necessary during the six-month follow-up. Reinstatement of the urine-alarm apparatus for a brief one-week period was sufficient to maintain dryness in the few instances when accidents started to recur. The elimination of enuresis was almost immediate. The average child had only two bedwettings before achieving two consecutive weeks of dryness, and he wet his bed only once during the very first week after training. The training period itself was very brief: only one night of intensive training followed by about two to three weeks of the urine-alarm apparatus.

Compared with other methods of treating enuresis, the present method appears more effective and efficient. The urine-alarm conditioning procedure has been shown to be the most effective of the alternative treatments but requires months of training, permits many relapses, and does not arrest enuresis for some children (see reviews by Jones 1960, Lovibond 1964, and Yates 1970). A direct comparison between the urine-alarm conditioning procedure and the new method was made in the present study by the matched-control design. The results showed that the urine-alarm conditioning procedure produced only a slight reduction in bedwetting during the two-week period it was used. In contrast, the new method eliminated bedwetting almost entirely during that same period. All children who were not improved by the conditioning procedure did stop wetting when they were trained by the new dry-bed procedure. The new method appears to be far more rapid and effective than the urine-alarm conditioning procedure.

The present method was based on the conception of enuresis as a learning problem that involved such diverse and complex factors as motivation, degree of voluntary control over urination, parental concern, the strength of alternative responses, and the ease of arousability from sleep. The present method had used the urine-alarm apparatus for the purpose of arranging these social and motivational factors as a reaction to bedwetting. In contrast, the urine-alarm conditioning procedure has viewed enuresis as a simple problem of Pavlovian conditioning of the bladder sphincter and uses the apparatus for the purpose of associating the buzzer, as an unconditioned stimulus, with sphincter relaxation. To evaluate this conditioning function of the urine-alarm apparatus, the present method was modified (Experiment II) to omit the buzzer for the enuretic child. It was found that enuresis was eliminated just as effectively when the buzzer did not sound for the enuretic child, but only for the parent. These results demonstrate that Pavlovian conditioning did not contribute to the effectiveness of the present procedure.

One may speculate that Pavlovian-type conditioning is not the underlying process responsible for the effectiveness of the usual urine-alarm procedure. Rather, the buzzer may be merely the method of producing other and more important events such as annoyance by the child and parent at being awakened, the need to change the wet sheets, or the need to wash oneself. Other investigators also have recently challenged the role of Pavlovian conditioning in accounting for the effectiveness of the urine-alarm procedure (Lovibond 1964, Turner et al. 1970). Further support of this conclusion was obtained in a previous study (Azrin, Sneed, and Foxx 1973) that found no reduction of bedwetting by the urine-alarm apparatus unless social and motivational events were associated with the buzzer.

References

Azrin, N. H., and Foxx, R. M. (1971). A rapid method of toilet training the institutionalized retarded. *Journal of Applied Behavior Analysis* 4:89–99.
———— (1974). *Toilet Training in Less than a Day*. New York: Simon & Schuster.
Azrin, N. H., Kaplan, S. J., and Foxx, R. M. (1973). Autism reversal: eliminating stereotyped self-stimulation of the retarded. *American Journal of Mental Deficiency* 78:241–248.

Azrin, N. H., Sneed, T. J., and Foxx, R. M. (1973). Dry bed: a rapid method of eliminating bedwetting (enuresis) of the retarded. *Behaviour Research and Therapy* 11:427–434.

Foxx, R. M., and Azrin, N. H. (1972). Restitution: a method of eliminating aggressive-disruptive behavior of retarded and brain damaged patients. *Behaviour Research and Therapy* 10:15–27.

———— (1973a). *Toilet Training the Retarded: A Rapid Program for Day and Nighttime Independent Toileting*. Champaign, IL: Research Press.

———— (1973b). The elimination of autistic, self-stimulatory behavior by overcorrection. *Journal of Applied Behavior Analysis* 6:1–14.

———— (1973c). Dry pants: a rapid method of toilet training children. *Behaviour Research and Therapy* 11:435–442.

Kimmel, H. D., and Kimmel, E. (1970). An instrumental conditioning method for the treatment of enuresis. *Journal of Behavior Therapy and Experimental Psychiatry* 1:121–123.

Jones, G. H. (1960). The behavioral treatment of enuresis nocturna. In *Behavior Therapy and the Neuroses*, ed. H. J. Eysenck, pp. 377–403. Oxford, England: Pergamon Press.

Lovibond, S. H. (1964). *Conditioning and Enuresis*. New York: Macmillan.

Mowrer, O. H., and Mowrer, W. M. (1938). Enuresis—a method for its study and treatment. *American Journal of Orthopsychiatry* 8:436–447.

Turner, R. K., Young, G. C., and Rachman, S. (1970). The treatment of nocturnal enuresis by conditioning techniques. *Behaviour Research and Therapy* 8:367–381.

Yates, A. J. (1970). *Behavior Therapy*, pp. 77–106. New York: Wiley.

14

Retentive Encopresis

LAURA A. NABORS AND SAM B. MORGAN

The prevalence of functional childhood encopresis is between 1 percent and 2 percent (Thapar et al. 1992), with a male to female ratio of 4 or 5:1 (Howe and Walker 1992). The criteria presented in the *Diagnostic and Statistical Manual of Mental Disorders (DSM-III-R)* (American Psychiatric Association 1987) state that the child must be at least 4 years old and have a history of defecating in inappropriate places which is not caused by a physical problem and occurs at least once a month for a six-month period. Researchers (Doleys 1983, Fleisher 1976, Walker 1978) have described different categories of functional encopresis. Retentive encopresis, the most common category, is identified by (a) chronic constipation; (b) daily soiling accidents, with small stains of liquid stool; and (c) infrequent bowel movements (Doleys 1983, Howe and Walker 1992).

Before implementing behavioral treatments for encopresis, the clinician usually refers the child for a medical consultation to rule out physical causes for the disorder. Provided that there is no physical problem, a diagnosis of retentive encopresis is often made. Treatment usually consists of having parents regularly administer a purgative (e.g., enemas, laxatives, mineral oil, and/or suppositories). Also, parents typically learn to use one or more behavior modification techniques in order to help the child learn appropriate toileting behavior. These techniques include (a) correction for inappropriate toileting, which involves having the child clean his or her pants and body after soiling episodes; (b) stimulus-control training, which involves practicing appropriate toileting, often at times when the child is likely to defecate; and (c) reinforcement of appropriate toileting (Houts et al. 1988, Levine and Bakow 1976, Steege and Harper 1989, Thapar et al. 1992, Wright 1975). Thapar and colleagues (1992) provide a review of current treatments for childhood encopresis.

Other successful intervention techniques include educating parents about possible causes and treatments for encopresis, rewarding appropriate toileting, paying attention to "clean" days rather than days when the child has an accident, and reducing blame for accidents (Levine and Bakow 1976, Lowery et al. 1985, Steege and Harper 1989, Wigley et al. 1984). In their recent review, Thapar and colleagues (1992) suggest that multicomponent treatment packages including outpatient education and explanation, and rewards for appropriate toileting and clean days, with the use of oral laxatives, if necessary, are likely to be the most important elements of treatment for most children.

Behavioral techniques combined with regular doses of laxatives have also been successful in treating encopresis (Levine and Bakow 1976, Lowery et al. 1985); however, long-term use of laxatives has been associated with reductions in child-initiated toileting or passive defecation (Doleys 1983, Fleisher 1976, 1978, Houts et al. 1988). A pattern of passive defecation may increase the child's dependence on laxatives. Thus, use of laxatives has been criticized because they may interfere with the child's ability to learn to initiate appropriate bowel movements (Houts et al. 1988).

Thapar and colleagues (1992) recommend further evaluation of dietary modification as a treatment for encopresis. Dietary changes usually consist of increasing the child's daily intake of liquids and dietary fiber. The rationale for this treatment is based on the idea that increased fluid and fiber intake promote bowel movements (Graham et al. 1982, Houts et al. 1988). Houts and colleagues (Houts et al. 1988, Houts and Peterson 1986) have reported successfully treating males with retentive encopresis using dietary modification in combination with behavior modification techniques. For example, Houts and colleagues (1988) found that diet modification and stimulus-control training were effective in eliminating soiling and increasing appropriate bowel movements. In an earlier case study, Houts and Peterson (1986) showed that a program combining diet modification, stimulus control, correction for soiling episodes, and reinforcement of appropriate toileting was successful. In both treatment programs, changes occurred and then were maintained without using laxatives, eliminating potential problems related to passive defecation.

Dietary modification may be a substitute for treatment with laxatives, because relying on laxatives may cause the child to begin a pattern of passive defecation (Doleys 1983, Fleisher 1976, Houts et al. 1988). Also, diet modification is a less invasive and potentially less painful technique than using laxatives and therefore may be preferred by most parents and children. Consequently, researchers need to continue to investigate whether a high-fiber diet and increased fluid intake are effective components of treatment programs.

This case study describes a treatment program developed for a 4½-year-old male with retentive encopresis. Components of the treatment program included laxatives, diet modification, and behavior modification techniques. Behavioral techniques were (a) correction for soiling episodes; (b) stimulus control, which was practicing appropriate toileting; and (c) a positive reinforcement system, which included rewarding the child for dietary changes (increasing daily fiber and fluid intake) and appropriate toileting behaviors. This program was implemented by the child's parents in the home environment and successfully maintained with the help of monthly clinic visits and weekly phone contacts. Parents discontinued using laxatives and using the correction technique after one month. Thus, treatment consisted primarily of dietary modification, a stimulus-control procedure, and positive reinforcement.

Procedure

Background Information

The boy's parents participated in an intake session and provided a history of the child's encopresis. They described their son as having a history of constipation with large and painful bowel movements every five or more days. Each bowel movement was followed by several accidents as he "cleaned out his system." He had small stains in his pants on a daily basis, as if fecal fluid were "leaking." They said that the stains were worse a few days before he had a bowel movement. Soiling accidents usually occurred in the evening, after eating. When asked about his diet, they said that he did not eat much at meals and that his intake of dietary fiber was low. Also, he did not drink many fluids. They were referred to a pediatric gastroenterologist, who found no physical complications, and recommended treatment using behavior management techniques and daily doses of Milkinol (1 tablespoon), a mineral oil. Senokot (1 teaspoon), a stimulant laxative, was to be administered if the boy went three days without having a bowel movement.

Baseline

The boy's parents returned for further training in behavior management techniques and dietary modification. The therapist reviewed educational information about retentive encopresis and described different treatment techniques. They also signed a consent form for their son's treatment to be a case study for research purposes. During a four-week baseline, the boy's parents kept daily records of their child's daily fluid and dietary fiber intake and recorded the days they administered Milkinol or Senokot. They also kept a daily record of his soiling accidents by recording the time of day and type of soiling accident. There were three types of soiling accidents: "(a) small stain, (b) small, formed bowel movement, and (c) full, formed bowel movement" (Houts et al. 1988, p. 438).

Treatment Phase 1

Phase 1 began in Week 5 and ended in Week 8. The boy and his mother met with the therapist for fifty-minute sessions during Weeks 6 and 8. The therapist reviewed the boy's progress with his mother and then spent twenty minutes playing games with the boy as a reward for his efforts. Treatment included dietary modification and implementation of behavior management techniques.

Dietary modification involved increasing daily fiber intake and fluid consumption. Daily fiber points were increased by 4 points per day. The boy's daily fiber intake was monitored using the food and fiber point system developed by Houts and associates (Houts et al. 1988, Houts and Peterson 1986). Fiber points were assigned based on portion size; for example, one serving of food was about 8 ounces or 1 cup. The boy's mother used the information provided on food labels to assign fiber points to those foods not listed on the chart. His fluid intake was increased to 4 cups per day. He was encouraged to finish a cup of juice with each meal and 1 cup at snack time. Additionally, he was given Milkinol each morning. Senokot was administered about every 4.5 days. The boy's parents recorded his daily progress on a graph, depicting daily fiber intake, soiling accidents, staining episodes, and appropriate bowel movements.

During Phase 1, they also implemented three behavioral techniques. The first, correction for soiling, involved having the boy clean himself and his pants after accidents and staining episodes. The second was stimulus control, in which the parents required their son to practice going to the bathroom for ten minutes after dinner each evening (this was the time when most soiling accidents had occurred). While practicing, the child read a story or looked at his baseball cards in order to make the experience less aversive. The third was developing a system to administer positive reinforcement. The therapist and the boy's parents developed a reinforcement chart, with daily and weekly goals. The boy chose daily (candy) and weekly (two hours of playing games with his mother) rewards. The chart had four daily goals: clean underwear, eat 10 fiber points, practice having a bowel movement in the evening, and drink 4 cups of liquid. The child made a check mark on the chart for each goal he attained. He would win a piece of candy if he made at least two of his daily goals. If he made sixteen checks in a week, he could play games with his mother.

Treatment Phase 2

Phase 2 began in Week 9 and lasted for two months. As in Phase 1, the therapist met with the boy and his mother every two weeks. All goals had been achieved from Phase 1; therefore, treatment was modified. Daily doses of Milkinol and use of Senokot were discontinued. Also, correction techniques were discontinued and clean underwear was no longer a goal on the boy's reinforcement chart because there were no accidents or staining episodes. Hence, treatment in Phase 2 included increasing his intake of dietary fiber by 5 points per day, maintaining daily fluid intake (4 cups), stimulus control training, and the positive reinforcement system. The boy's parents continued to record his daily fiber intake, soiling accidents, staining episodes, and appropriate bowel movements.

Follow-Up

During the follow-up, Phase 2 treatment was discontinued. The boy's parents stopped using the reinforcement system and stimulus control training was discontinued. The boy's parents stopped formally recording daily fiber and fluid intake but continued to encourage the boy to eat high-fiber foods and drink juice at meals and snack times. The therapist contacted the boy's mother by phone each month and they discussed his progress. The mother did continue to record soiling accidents, staining episodes, and average number of bowel movements per week.

Results

Figure 14-1 depicts the results of the treatment program in terms of the frequency of accidents and appropriate bowel movements during baseline, treatment, and follow-up.

During the baseline period, the boy consumed an average of 6 to 7 daily fiber points and drank only about 2 cups of liquid per day. His parents inconsistently administered Milkinol. He averaged 2.25 soiling episodes per week.

During Treatment Phase 1, daily fiber intake increased to an average of 9 points and he drank 4 cups of liquids per day. His parents administered Milkinol daily. He successfully met behavior management goals, including correction for soiling episodes and stimulus-control training. He always earned his reinforcer at the end of each week. He had no accidents and five small staining episodes. He averaged three or four appropriate bowel movements each week.

During treatment Phase 2 (Weeks 9 to 16), daily fiber intake increased to an average of 14.5 points and he drank an average of 4 cups of liquids per day. However, during Week 14 his fiber points dropped to 8, and one soiling accident and two large stains in his pants were reported. During the rest of the two months, he had no accidents and only two staining episodes. He had an average of three appropriate bowel movements each week.

As shown in Figure 14-1, during the eight-month follow-up he had one soiling accident, no staining episode, and he averaged three bowel movements per week. One soiling accident occurred during Week 20 when he was eating less fiber, according to his mother's informal observations. She administered Senokot one time the day of his soiling accident. There were no other accidents or soiling episodes for the remainder of the follow-up period.

Discussion

In this case study, dietary modification and behavior modification techniques were used to treat a young boy with retentive encopresis. Treatment involved two phases. Phase 1 consisted of a month of intensive treatment including increasing daily fiber and fluid intake and daily administration of mineral oil (Milkinol). Senokot, a stimulant laxative, was administered every four or five days. The parents also used three behavioral techniques with the boy: (a) correction or self-clean-

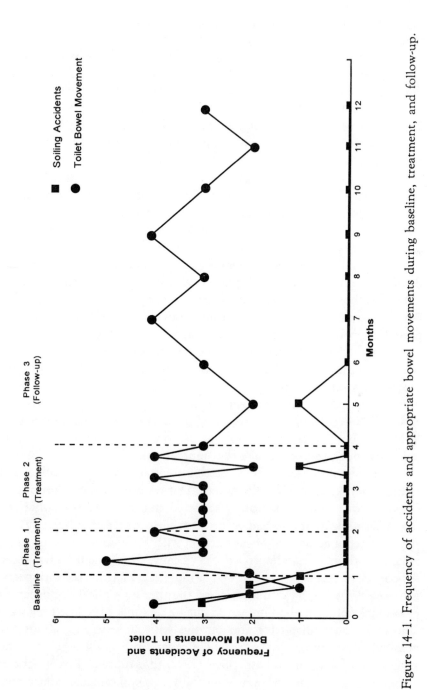

Figure 14-1. Frequency of accidents and appropriate bowel movements during baseline, treatment, and follow-up.

ing after soiling accidents and staining; (b) stimulus control, which required the boy to practice having bowel movements at the time when most accidents occurred; and (c) a reinforcement system, which included a chart where the boy recorded his progress each day. In Phase 2, they discontinued administering Milkinol and stopped using the correction technique but continued the rest of the treatment plan from Phase 1. The boy had only one accident during the three-month treatment period, which was a significant improvement compared to the daily staining episodes and weekly accidents that had occurred during the baseline period and the year prior to this intervention. Thus, as in the case studies presented by Houts and associates (Houts et al. 1988, Houts and Peterson 1986), we found that dietary modifications, including increasing daily fiber and fluid intake, and behavioral techniques, were successful treatments for retentive encopresis.

During Phase 2, daily fiber intake was increased (5.5 points per day). As mentioned, the boy's parents also stopped administering laxatives. The boy was able to learn appropriate toileting according to his body's natural patterns, without using mineral oil. This eliminated any potential problem with passive defecation (Doleys 1983, Fleisher 1976, Houts et al. 1988), in which he might have become dependent on daily doses of mineral oil to stimulate bowel movements. Also, the boy's mother reported that he felt pride in his ability to "eat what his body needed" and that he was relieved about ". . . not having to take Milkinol." According to his mother, on several occasions he reported feeling "happy" about being able to use the "bathroom on my own" (e.g., without needing to take the mineral oil).

The changes associated with this treatment program influenced lasting changes in the family system. During several follow-up phone conversations, the boy's mother reported that she and his father felt that a permanent change had occurred in their son's eating habits. Also, she reported a great deal of satisfaction with his emotional well-being, which she thought had improved. Specifically, she thought he was more self-confident and expressive as well as more eager to interact with peers. Moreover, the boy's mother reported that her own and her husband's emotional well-being had improved during treatment because they were able to go on family trips and outings without worrying about the possibility of soiling accidents. These reports are consistent with the suggestion of Thapar and associates (1992) that successful treatment of encopresis may result in improving the ". . . psychological adjustment of the child and carer(s)" (p. 344).

This case also shows that one dose of a laxative may be used to help a child return to a pattern of appropriate bowel movements after periods of time when a high-fiber diet is not followed. For example, the boy consumed less dietary fiber during Weeks 14 and 20, which was probably associated with his soiling accidents. The boy's mother administered one dose of Senokot the day after both accidents and he resumed eating recommended amounts of daily fiber. He immediately returned to appropriate toileting after both soiling accidents. This suggests that parents may need to administer a dose of laxatives to get a child "back on track" after periods of low fiber intake followed by soiling episodes. On the other hand, this child might have been able to resume appropriate toileting by increasing his intake of dietary fiber and liquids without taking laxatives. More controlled research is needed to investigate whether lapses in dietary fiber intake cause children with retentive encopresis to have soiling accidents. Also, researchers need to investigate whether returning to the high fiber diet without using laxatives is related to increasing appropriate bowel movements and decreasing soiling accidents after periods of time when the child has a lower fiber intake and a soiling episode occurs.

During the follow-up, all formal treatment procedures were discontinued; however, the boy's parents felt that they had successfully changed his eating habits. Therefore, he was still eating more daily fiber and drinking more fluids than during the baseline period. Houts and colleagues (1988) proposed that withdrawal of dietary modification may not be desirable if a successful lifestyle change occurs. In this case, withdrawal of dietary modification was not appropriate since the treatment was related to changes that had ameliorated a health risk problem.

This case study shows that a treatment plan including laxatives (Milkinol and Senokot), diet modification, and behavioral techniques including correction, stimulus control, and a positive reinforcement system, was successful in eliminating soiling accidents for a preschool age boy. Treatment consisted of two phases; in Phase 1 all treatment methods were applied for one month, and in Phase 2 dietary modification, stimulus control, and positive reinforcement were used but laxatives and correction after soiling accidents and staining episodes were discontinued. Results from this treatment case indicate that dietary modification, including increases in daily fiber and fluid intake, may be viable alternatives to using laxatives when developing treatment programs as interventions for children with retentive encopresis.

Several limitations should be considered when interpreting the present findings. First, because several treatment techniques were used, it is not possible to determine which contributed most to treatment success. Controlled experimentation is needed to isolate more precisely the effectiveness of different treatment techniques. One method would be to compare outcomes for waiting-list control cases to outcomes for several treatment cases, using multiple baseline periods to implement treatment techniques in isolation and different combinations. Researchers also need to continue to investigate whether dietary modification is an effective component of treatment plans for children with retentive encopresis (Thapar et al. 1992). Although present study results suggest that increasing dietary fiber and fluid intake may be an alternative to laxatives for treating encopresis, we do not know whether these treatment results would occur for other children (e.g., older and younger boys and girls at different ages) with similar presenting problems. Controlled investigations could provide a way to investigate the influences of laxatives, diet modification, and the interaction of these two factors in treating retentive encopresis.

References

American Psychiatric Association. (1987). *Diagnostic and Statistical Manual of Mental Disorders*, 3rd rev. ed. Washington, DC: American Psychiatric Association.

Doleys, D. M. (1983). Enuresis and encopresis. In *Handbook of Child Psychopathology*, ed. T. H. Ollendick and M. Hersen, pp. 201–226. New York: Plenum.

Fleisher, D. R. (1976). Diagnosis and treatment of disorders of defecation in children. *Pediatric Annals* 5:71–101.

———— (1978). Encopresis, enemas, and gold stars. *Pediatrics* 61:155.

Graham, D. Y., Moser, S. E., and Esters, M. K. (1982). The effect of bran on bowel function in constipation. *American Journal of Gastroenterology* 77:599–603.

Houts, A. C., Mellon, M. W., and Whelan, J. P. (1988). Use of dietary fiber and stimulus control to treat retentive encopresis: a multiple baseline investigation. *Journal of Pediatric Psychology* 13:435–445.

Houts, A. C., and Peterson, J. K. (1986). Treatment of a retentive encopretic child using contingency management and diet modification with stimulus control. *Journal of Pediatric Psychology* 11:375–383.

Howe, A. C., and Walker, C. E. (1992). Behavioral management of toilet training, enuresis, and encopresis. *Pediatric Clinics of North America* 39:413–432.

Levine, M. D., and Bakow, H. (1976). Children with encopresis. A study of treatment outcome. *Pediatrics* 58:845-852.

Lowery, S. P., Stour, J. W., Whitehead, W. E., and Shuster, M. M. (1985). Habit training as treatment of encopresis with chronic constipation. *Journal of Pediatric Gastroenterology and Nutrition* 4:397-401.

Steege, M. W., and Harper, D. (1989). Enhancing the management of secondary encopresis by assessing the acceptability of treatment: a case study. *Journal of Behavior Therapy and Experimental Psychiatry* 20:333-341.

Thapar, A., Davies, G., Jones, T., and Rivett, M. (1992). Treatment of childhood encopresis—a review. *Child: Care, Health, and Development* 18:343-353.

Walker, C. E. (1978). Toilet training, enuresis, encopresis. In *Psychological Management of Pediatric Problems*, vol. 1, ed. P. R. Magrab. Baltimore, MD: University Park Press.

Wigley, V., Yule, W., and Berger, M. (1984). A primary solution to soiling. *Special Education Forward Trends* 9:27-30.

Wright L. (1975). Outcome of a standardized program for treating psychogenic encopresis. *Professional Psychology* 6:453-456.

15

Parent-Administered Behavior Therapy for Inappropriate Urination and Encopresis

ROGER BACH AND JOSEPH J. MOYLAN

The subject of this study was a 6-year-old boy of normal intelligence who urinated inappropriately and had secondary reactive encopresis (that is, previously toilet trained, and subsequently incontinent of feces, with constipation [Silber 1969]). The child had been almost totally incontinent for two-and-a-half years, despite the efforts of two pediatricians and a psychiatrist whom the parents had consulted. The pediatricians diagnosed the problem as "functional megacolon" caused by the withholding of feces, and recommended a daily regime of laxatives, suppositories, and/or enemas. Unfortunately, the insertion rituals and mandatory trips to the toilet were a great source of aversion to both the parents and child. Thus, these programs were never consistently or successfully executed. The psychiatrist diagnosed "depressed child with encopresis and defective object relationships" and recommended long-term psychotherapy for the parents as a prerequisite for dealing with the encopresis.

The parents had many problems of their own. The child's mother, who carries the diagnostic label of chronic undifferentiated schizophrenic, had experienced several lengthy hospitalizations. The father was an active alcoholic. Both parents met while they were patients at the Hawaii State Hospital and the child's problem was brought to the attention of the senior author during marital counseling with the parents subsequent to the wife's most recent discharge.

Case reports in the literature describing successful elimination of encopresis through operant methods deal with cases treated within an institution (Gelber and Mayer 1965, Neale 1963), or the children were either the author's own (Tomlinson 1970), or they were children of fellow professionals or faculty members (Lal and Lindsley 1968, Peterson and London 1965). An exception to this was Edelman (1971), who successfully trained parents to effect a dramatic decrease in the encopretic behavior of a 12-year-old girl. Our initial hesitation about becoming involved in the treatment of this child stemmed from the fact that the parents would have to implement the program, both of them could be considered "marginally adjusted," and, of course, the treatment would take place in their own home. In the end, we felt compelled to intervene because the child's behavior was a constant source of disruption in an already precariously balanced home situation, and financial considerations precluded their obtaining help elsewhere.

Method

The first phase of this program involved establishing a baseline for daily bedwetting, pants wetting, soiling of pants, and appropriate use of the toilet. During this period principles of operant control were discussed with the parents and the reinforcer agreed upon was money. Late during the baseline period, however, the child so badgered the father for money in order to accompany his friends to the store, the father violated our instructions and said, "If you go to the toilet right now and do a 'kaka,' I'll give you a quarter." The boy trotted to the bathroom and expelled his feces into the toilet for the first time in two and a half years. This event was immediately communicated to us and we decided to begin the program which had been discussed.

We explained to the boy that he would receive 25 cents for every bowel movement in the toilet, 10 cents for every time he urinated appropriately in the commode, and 10 cents every morning that his bed was not wet. The parents were to give the reinforcers directly after the desired behaviors occurred and to praise the child. In addition they were told to ignore all inappropriate bowel and bladder movements, and to change their son's clothes as perfunctorily as possible. Both these instructions and others were frequently violated by the parents during the early phases of the program.

This program was carried out for twelve weeks, when it became apparent that while the boy's enuretic problem was responding satisfactorily, the same could not be said for the soiling. There were two possible reasons why the encopresis program was not moving along fast enough: (1) the boy might not have had the sensation of fullness, and, therefore, had no physiological cues which would tell him he could earn a quarter; and (2) the child might have experienced a fear of going to the bathroom and not being able to produce a bowel movement. We decided that the parents should begin to prompt the child and give him 5 cents and social praise for "just trying to go kaka." In this way we hoped to eliminate any fear about going into the bathroom and failing, and simultaneously to increase the number of trials so that he might catch himself with a full rectum.

Results

The 10-cent reward was immediately effective in curtailing bedwetting behavior for eleven weeks. He wet the bed three times in Week 12 and once in Week 19. The causal factors involved in the four instances were not clearly evident to the parents or the therapists and the program of ignoring the behaviors and withholding the reinforcer was followed.

A dramatic improvement in the rates of bladder movements in the toilet and a consequent decline in pants-wetting also occurred. From a baseline of zero for toilet use, the rate shot up to forty-five in Week 3 and thirty-five in Week 4. This behavior declined, however, and it was deemed unnecessary to institute a fixed-interval schedule. As treatment progressed, his rate of pants-wetting decreased until between Weeks 15 and 20 there was only one mishap. The total number of appropriate urinations varied widely from week to week, probably as a function of the boy's diet, his time spent at home, and his desire for money.

Figure 15–1 charts the course of treatment for encopresis. The first week produced seven occurrences of appropriate bowel movements, and a small but noticeable decrease in soiling. This rate of improvement did not maintain itself, however, and during Weeks 4 to 11 the boy soiled forty times and used the toilet on twenty-two occasions. Marked improvement began with the institution of friendly, prompt social praise, and a nickel reward for "trying to go kaka." Between Weeks 12 and 20 there were seventy-six appropriate bowel movements and only three incidents.

An interesting feature of the nickel reward for "trying to go kaka" was that the frequency of such rewards dropped to almost zero within five weeks. The child began to respond to his parents' prompting in one of two ways: (1) he told them he had no need to evacuate and refused to go into the bathroom; or (2) he went into the bathroom and successfully evacuated, thereby receiving the higher reinforcement for that behavior instead of the nickel for trying.

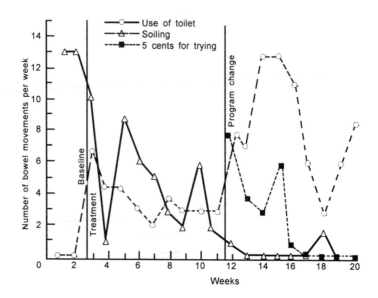

Figure 15-1. Course of treatment for encopresis.

Discussion

In summation, the results obtained from this program clearly indicate that a staightforward operant method can be administered successfully by otherwise disturbed parents to eliminate incontinence of urine and feces. The failure of the previous pediatric programs may lie in the fact that the parents could not administer them.

Additional problems beset this particular case. The parents found it very hard to refrain from punishing the child for soiling, and needed constant reminders to dispense the reinforcer immediately after the desired behaviors occurred. For a while, when the child seemed to be losing interest in the reinforcer, we discovered that the parents had been leaving their money lying openly about, and he had been helping himself.

At the time of writing, almost two years have elapsed since the period represented on the graphs. The child has developed regular bowel and bladder movements just prior to bedtime, and the monetary rewards have been faded into a weekly allowance. In the same time period there have been no instances of soiling. Finally, a word may be said about the more general benefits derived from this experience. For the parents there was a tremendous feeling of accomplishment after three years of frustration. More important, the number of praising interactions between parents and child multiplied considerably. It was very clear that they enjoyed one another more, even though there was no observed change in either of the parents' individual problems.

References

Edelman, R. I. (1971). Operant conditioning treatment of encopresis. *Journal of Behavior Therapy and Experimental Psychiatry* 2:71–73.

Gelber, H., and Mayer, V. (1965). Behavior therapy and encopresis: the complexities involved in treatment. *Behaviour Research and Therapy* 2:227–231.

Lal, H., and Lindsley, O. R. (1968). Therapy of chronic constipation in a young child by rearranging social contingencies. *Behaviour Research and Therapy* 6:484–485.

Neale, D. H. (1963). Behavior therapy and encopresis in children. *Behaviour Research and Therapy* 1:139–149.

Peterson, K. R., and London, P. (1965). A role for cognition in the behavioral treatment of a child's eliminative disturbance. In *Case Studies in Behavior Modification*, ed. L. P. Ullman and L. Krasner, pp. 289–294. New York: Holt, Rinehart & Winston.

Silber, D. L. (1969). Encopresis: discussion of etiology and management. *Clinical Pediatrics* 8:225–231.

Tomlinson, J. R. (1970). The treatment of bowel retention by operant procedures: a case study. *Journal of Behavior Therapy and Experimental Psychiatry* 1:83–85.

16

The Habit-Reversal
Method of Eliminating
Nervous Habits and Tics

NATHAN H. AZRIN AND ROBERT G. NUNN

Nervous habits and tics are psychological disorders which are highly resistant to general types of treatment. As concluded by Eriksson and Persson (1969), "some patients become permanently disabled and resistant to every form of treatment. Judging from the literature, no single form of treatment is universally effective" (p. 351). Similarly, Yates (1970) described tics as "notoriously resistant to almost any form of treatment" (p. 201).

Different theoretical explanations of nervous habits have been proposed, each of which has served as the basis for different types of treatment. The psychoanalytic view, as expressed by Mahler and Luke (1946), considers tics as "erotic and aggressive instinctual impulses . . . which are continually escaping through pathological discharge" (p. 441). The treatment derived from this view is to provide counseling that persuades the client that these impulses are the cause of his problem ("giving him insight") and to teach him to channel these impulses elsewhere. A second theoretical view is that nervous habits are caused by tension. Two types of treatment are based on this rationale; one is negative practice (Jones 1960, Rafi 1962, Yates 1958) in which the client is required to perform the tic rapidly, thereby preventing the tension reduction that otherwise would result. The second method of treatment that follows this tension-reduction rationale is treatment by tranquilizing relaxant drugs (Challas and Brauer 1963, Connell et al. 1967). A third theoretical account is that nervous habits are learned responses that are maintained by operant reinforcement. The treatment derived from this theory has been to arrange for aversive stimuli for the response in order to counteract the effect of these reinforcers (Brierly 1967, Bucher 1968).

Present Rationale

The present rationale is that a nervous habit originally starts as a normal reaction. The reaction may be to an extreme event such as a physical injury or psychological trauma (see also Yates 1970), or the symptom may have started as an infrequent, but normal, behavior that has increased in frequency and been altered in its form. The behavior becomes classified as a nervous habit when it persists after the original injury or trauma has passed and when it assumes an unusual form and unusually high frequency. Under normal circumstances the nervous habit would be inhibited by personal or social awareness of its peculiarity or by its inherent inconvenience. The movement may, however, have blended into normal movements so gradually as to escape personal and social awareness. Once having achieved this transformation, the movement is performed so often as to become a strongly established habit that further escapes personal awareness because of its automatic nature. For some tics, the continuing execution of the movement may even strengthen the specific muscles required for that movement and the opposing muscles become relatively unused, thereby causing difficulty for conscious inhibition of the tic and further contributing to the low level of awareness of the tic movement. Also, social reinforcement in the form of sympathy may result, especially for those movements that have had a medical origin.

This analysis of nervous habits suggests several methods of treatment. The client should learn to be aware of every occurrence of the habit. Each habit movement should be interrupted so that it no longer is part of a chain of normal movements. A physically competing response should be established to interfere with the habit. When atrophy has resulted from the disuse of the antagonistic muscles, those antagonistic muscles should be strengthened. Social reinforcement should be reversed or eliminated.

Method

The procedure was evaluated by a within-subjects comparison. A measure was obtained of the extent of the problem prior to counseling and was considered to be the baseline level. This baseline level was compared with the measures taken after counseling.

Clients

Twelve clients were treated. Five clients contacted the counselor in response to a newspaper advertisement, three were children who were referred by their parents at the suggestion of their teacher, one was referred by a psychologist who had unsuccessfully treated the client for two and a half years, and the other three by various types of word-of-mouth knowledge of the service. No client was excluded. Their clients' ages varied from 5 to 64 years; eight were female and four were male. Educational level varied from a preschool child to a client who had an M.A. degree. All clients had been previously treated for their habits by various professionals such as a psychiatrist, psychologist, physician, dentist, speech therapist, or, for the children, by their parents and teachers. All of the adult clients reported that their nervous habit seriously interfered with their functioning. Some of the habits caused medical problems; in the case of gum-sucking, by causing softness of the gum and mouth surfaces. Dental problems were caused by the thumbsucking. The student teacher who lisped was told her teaching duties were unsatisfactory because of the lisping. Interference with all normal physical activities was caused by the head and shoulder tics. Problems of social appearance were caused by the eyelash picking and by the nailbiting. For all clients, the habits had been a long-standing problem of at least three years' duration; for five clients the problem had existed continuously for at least seven years.

Types of Nervous Habits

Eleven of the clients had one habit; one client had two. Figure 16–1 (left-hand column) illustrates the appearance of the different types of habits. Two clients experienced a shoulder-jerking tic; for one of them the right shoulder jerked upward suddenly about five inches and then immediately fell. For the other client the right shoulder jerked upward and forward while his elbow simultaneously jerked against his ribcage. Two or three of the shoulder jerks usually occurred in rapid succession followed by an interlude preceding the next series of spasm-like movements. For one client, his head jerked violently upward such that he was facing almost directly upward and slightly turned to one side at the end of the movement. One client's head moved rapidly up and down and side to side in short, rapid movements with the neck stationary, resembling the tremor-like movements seen in Parkinson's disease. One client pressed her tongue firmly against the gum-line of her upper front

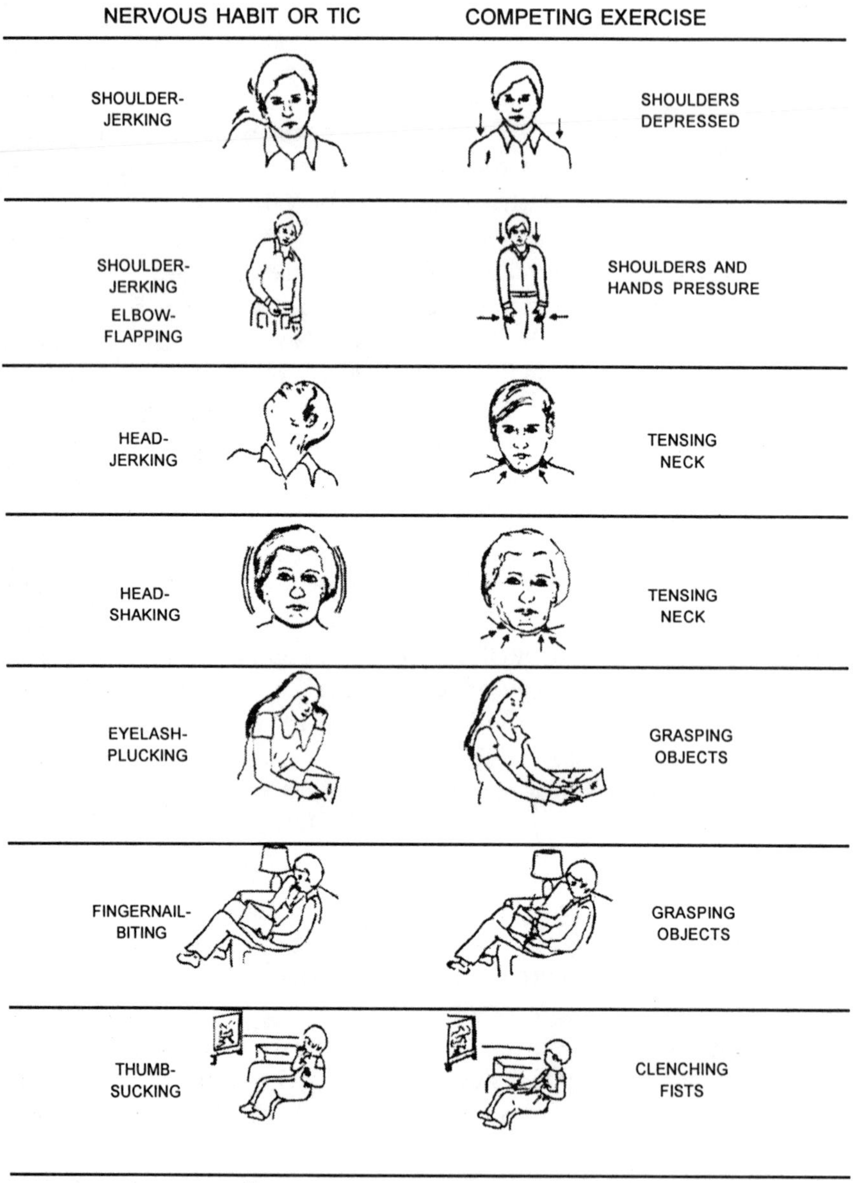

NERVOUS HABIT OR TIC			COMPETING EXERCISE
SHOULDER-JERKING			SHOULDERS DEPRESSED
SHOULDER-JERKING ELBOW-FLAPPING			SHOULDERS AND HANDS PRESSURE
HEAD-JERKING			TENSING NECK
HEAD-SHAKING			TENSING NECK
EYELASH-PLUCKING			GRASPING OBJECTS
FINGERNAIL-BITING			GRASPING OBJECTS
THUMB-SUCKING			CLENCHING FISTS

Figure 16–1. A pictorial representation of the various types of nervous tics or habits. The left-hand column illustrates the different tics or habits. The adjacent illustration in the right-hand column illustrates the type of competing exercise used for that nervous tic or habit. The arrows in each of the Competing Exercise illustrations show the direction of isometric muscle contraction being exerted by the client.

teeth while she sucked against the roof of her mouth. Also, she found herself pressing her tongue firmly into the spaces between her lower back molars in the manner one uses the tongue to dislodge particles of food. Another client stroked her eyelashes repeatedly, such that the upper and lower eyelashes of both eyes were entirely plucked out. Another client lisped on all "s" and "z" sounds. Although this problem is not ordinarily considered a nervous habit, but rather a speech problem, it was included here because of its apparent amenability to the present type of treatment. Four clients bit their fingernails, resulting in the absence of all projecting portions of all ten fingernails. Two clients (both children) sucked continually, one on her thumb, the other on her index and middle fingers.

Recording

The incidence of the nervous habit was recorded by the client. Each client stated about how often the habit was occurring during the previous week either in terms of the number of incidents per minute or day, or in terms of the percentage of their time each day that they experienced the habits. Each client selected the measure that was more meaningful to him in view of the nature of the habit. For the first two weeks after treatment, the client reported each day the incidence of the habit. After about two weeks, these measures were obtained at less frequent intervals of about twice per week. After several weeks elapsed, the measure was taken only about twice per month. For every client, a validating report was also obtained from individuals who were in a position to observe the client frequently, such as a spouse, parent, teacher, roommate, co-worker, or boyfriend. The counselor had face-to-face contact after counseling with all but two of the clients. Since the other two clients were at a great distance, the counselor relied heavily on detailed validating reports from their family members. For the young clients below 14 years of age, the primary measures were obtained from the parents and secondarily from the client or his teachers. The reports of the validating observer were generally in agreement with the primary observer. When the primary observer reported a large number of incidents on a given day, then the validating observer in virtually every case reported that the habit was a problem that day. Similarly, in virtually every instance in which the client reported zero incidents on a given day, the validating observer reported having seen no instances on that day.

Awareness Training

The client was made very much aware of the nervous habit by means of several procedures. In one procedure, the Response Description Procedure, the client was required to describe the details of the movement to the counselor, using a mirror if necessary, while he reenacted several instances of the typical movement. In the second procedure, the Response Detection Procedure, the counselor taught him to detect each instance of the movement by alerting the client when an instance of the tic occurred. A third procedure was the Early Warning Procedure wherein the client was given practice in detecting the earliest sign of the habit movement, such as when the hand of the nailbiters first approached the face. The fourth procedure was the Competing Response Practice (described below) in which the client maintained heightened awareness of the nervous habit by tensing for a few minutes the muscles that were incompatible with the movement. The fifth procedure, Situation Awareness Training, created awareness of the situations in which the habit occurred by having the client recall all situations, persons, and places where the habit was likely to occur and having him describe how the habit was performed in each of those situations.

Competing Response Practice

This part of the procedure was derived in part from the overcorrection rationale described elsewhere (Azrin et al. 1973, Foxx and Azrin 1972, 1973a,b) for treating other types of psychological disorders by having the client practice a behavioral pattern opposite to that of the problem behavior. A major departure from the overcorrection approach is the attempt to minimize any aversiveness of the required practice, since the objective was to have the client maximally motivated to carry out the practice.

Each client was taught a specific response pattern that would be incompatible with the nervous habits and would, therefore, prevent the habit from being continually intertwined in normal activities. In addition, the incompatible movement was designed to have the characteristics of (1) being opposite to the nervous movement, (2) capable of being maintained for several minutes, (3) producing heightened awareness by an isometric tensing of the muscles involved in the movement, (4) being socially inconspicuous and easily compatible with normal ongoing activities, but still incompatible with the habit, and (5) strengthening the muscles antagonistic to the tic movement for the muscle tics.

The clients were instructed to engage in the competing responses for about three minutes following either the temptation to perform a tic or the actual occurrence of a tic.

A different type of exercise was used for the different types of nervous habits. Figure 16–1 pictorially illustrates the exercise in the right-hand column; the left-hand column depicts the nervous habit. The exercises were as follows:

Head-Jerking

The competing response for the backward head-jerking tic consisted of isometric contraction of the neck flexors (sternocleidomastoid group) by pulling the chin in and down. For the first day, the client pushed his chin onto his sternum, but once having the necessary strength to control the jerking movement, isometric tension in the stationary eyes-forward position was substituted for the more conspicuous chin-on-sternum exercise.

Shoulder-Jerking

The same client also displayed an upward jerking of the right shoulder; the competing response of isometrically contracting the shoulder depressors was used to strengthen the muscles which work in opposition to this upward jerking movement.

Head-Shaking

The client who displayed the head-shaking tic was instructed to slowly contract isometrically her neck muscles until the head was perfectly still.

Forward Shoulder-jerking

The competing response for the client who displayed an upward and forward jerking of his right shoulder consisted of the client pushing his hands down and backward against some objects, such as the chair arms while sitting, or against his leg while standing.

Tongue-Pushing

For the client who constantly sucked against the roof of her mouth while poking against the gum line of her upper teeth, the competing response required that she press her tongue against the roof of her mouth (in a position different than that while performing the habit) and against the bottom of her mouth for each incident of the habit.

Lisping

For lisping, the client was instructed to jut her jaw slightly forward, placing her tongue against the gum line of her lower teeth and to press her tongue against the gum line for each incident of lisping. Whenever possible, she was also instructed to repeat the word she had lisped fifty times correctly (the lisper and gum-sucker are not depicted in Figure 16–1).

Eyelash-Picking, Thumbsucking, and Fingernail Biting

For the nervous habits of eyelash-picking, fingernail-biting, and thumbsucking, each client was instructed to place his hands down by his sides, and to clench his fists until he could feel tension in his arms and hands. In the case of the small thumbsucking children, the parents were asked to manually guide their child's hands through an open-close exercise twenty times, while gradually fading out their manual assistance for each uncorrected incident performed by the child. Whenever the clenching exercises for nail-biting and eyelash-picking interfered with the client's ongoing activities, they were instructed merely to grasp an object or objects appropriate to that situation and squeeze until they could feel a slight amount of tension.

Habit Control Motivation

Preliminary efforts with other clients had indicated that little success would result if the client was only casually interested in eliminating his habit. Sufficiently strong motivation was indicated if the adult client sought out the treatment himself, rather than being urged to do so by others. Several procedures were used to increase further the client's motivation to be rid of the nervous habit. The first procedure was the Habit Inconvenience Review, in which the counselor and client reviewed, in detail, the inconveniences, embarrassment, and suffering that resulted from the habit. This existing motivation for controlling the habit was supplemented by Social Support Procedures, introduced once the client had demonstrated he could control his habits during the counseling session. His family and close friends were instructed to strengthen his motivation by (1) commenting favorably on his efforts and improved appearance when they noted a habit-free period, (2) reminding him of the need to "practice your exercises," when they noted an instance of the habit overlooked by the client, and (3) the counselor telephoned the clients regularly after treatment praising the client for his efforts in inhibiting the habit. These calls also were used to obtain the data regarding the frequency of the habit. The frequency of the calls has been noted above under the "Recording" section.

A special motivational problem existed with children since the parents and not the child desired to be rid of the habit, the parents having presented the child for treatment. For these very young, often uncooperative children, the parents and teachers increased their child's motivation to control his habit by manually guiding the child's hands through the required exercises whenever the child failed to initiate the exercises himself. Similarly, the uncooperative older children were further motivated to control their habit by requiring them to perform their exercises in the bedroom whenever they failed to initiate the exercises themselves. In all other instances, the exercises were designed to be nonaversive and noninterfering with normal activities.

Another special motivational problem existed for those tics such as the head and shoulder jerks that seemed neurologically caused and therefore not subject to voluntary control. In such instances, the family and friends believed effort at self-control futile. For these clients a Public Display Procedure was used. The family was required to observe the demonstration of self-control during the counseling sessions, and the friends and teachers or fellow employees were notified of this ability by the client and counselor immediately after the counseling session.

Generalization Training

During the counseling sessions, the client was given practice and instructions as to how he should control his nervous habit in his everyday situations. First, the counselor had him practice his exercise until he was performing it correctly, this period usually requiring less than five minutes. To teach the client to be aware of the habit movement in many situations, the counselor used a Symbolic Rehearsal Procedure in which the client was to imagine common and habit-eliciting situations and to imagine that he detected a habit movement and was performing the required exercise. This symbolic rehearsal utilized the list of situations obtained previously from the client in the Situation Awareness Procedure described previously and required about fifteen minutes. To provide actual practice in detecting the habit movement and exercising for three minutes thereafter, the counselor engaged the client in casual conversation on a variety of habit-irrelevant topics for about half an hour. During that time, the client was to detect the movement himself, but if he failed to do so, the counselor reminded him using as minimal a suggestion as possible such as staring at the moving limb, or saying "hmm" or raising his eyebrows, at which time the client would assume the competing exercise for three minutes while the conversation continued uninterrupted.

Results

Table 16–1 shows the pre- and post-treatment (third week) frequency of the nervous habit for each of the clients individually. For every client the habit was reduced by at least 90 percent; for ten of the twelve clients, the habit was absent during the third week after treatment.

Client	Nature of tic or habit	Pretreatment occurrence of tic or habit	Post-treatment (third week) occurrence of tic or habit
14-year-old male	Head- and shoulder-jerking	8000/day	12/day
14-year-old male	Elbow-flopping, shoulder-jerking	250/day	0
64-year-old female	Head-shaking	75% of day	0
59-year-old female	Gum-sucking, tongue pressing	100% of day	8% of day
21-year-old female	Lisping on "s" or "z" sounds	100% of time	0
31-year-old female	Eyelash-picking	50% of day	0
6-year-old female	Thumbsucking	100% of day	0
5-year-old female	Finger-sucking	85% of day	0
28-year-old female	Fingernail-biting	50% of day	0
28-year-old female	Fingernail-biting	300/day	0
21-year-old female	Fingernail-biting	20/day	0
8-year-old male	Fingernail-biting	50% of day	0

Table 16–1. Description and frequency of occurrence of the nervous tics and habits for each of 12 clients pre-treatment and 3 weeks post-treatment by the habit-reversal method

Figure 16–2 shows the day-by-day changes for all clients averaged together. Each data point of Figure 16–2 is the percentage reduction in the rate of occurrence of the habit from the pretreatment level (see Table 16–1 for the pretreatment level). The data points are for each day for the first month and for monthly periods thereafter. All twelve clients are represented for the first three weeks; one client terminated her treatment efforts after three weeks. At the time of this writing, sufficient time had elapsed that data for seven clients were available for five months. The data show that the habit-reversal training reduced the nervous habits by an average of about 95 percent on the first day after training, about 97 percent after the first week, and about 99 percent after the third week. This average reduction of about 99 percent was evident for as long as data were available, which was a period of seven months for the earliest clients (not shown in Figure 16–2). The habit-reversal method was rapid, requiring only one counseling session for all the clients. Two clients were given a second session two months and five months, respectively, after the first one. One client, a 21-year-old female nail-biter, decided to abandon her successful efforts after three weeks; no further data could be obtained thereafter.

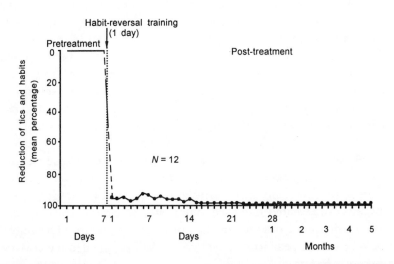

Figure 16–2. The mean percentage reduction of nervous habits following treatment by the habit-reversal method. The pretreatment level is designated as 0 percent reduction and was obtained for the seven-day period immediately preceding treatment. The habit-reversal training required about two hours on the day designated by the arrow and dotted line. The post-treatment data points are given daily for the first twenty-eight days and monthly thereafter. Each data point is the average reduction relative to the pretreatment level. The data points are for all twelve clients up to Day 21, for eleven clients for seven weeks, for nine clients for two months, and for seven clients for five months.

The eleven continuing clients were able to perform their exercises and continued to do so. When asked whether the exercises caused difficulties, all of the adult clients stated that the exercises seemed meaningful, were easy to perform, and did not interfere with their ongoing activities. In response to direct questioning, the clients and their validating observers stated that no new habit appeared when the treated habit was eliminated.

Discussion

The habit-reversal procedure appears to be an extremely effective method of eliminating nervous habits. The new method had a substantial effect, having eliminated, or virtually eliminated, the habits. The method was rapid, requiring only one or two counseling sessions. The treatment was durable in that the nervous habits remained absent after treatment and only one or two special telephone calls were usually needed to overcome the occasional relapses of some of the clients. (Preliminary results of a study in progress by Nunn and Azrin indicate that relapses can be eliminated almost entirely for the nail-biting habit by a modified procedure.) The method was a general treatment for many types of nervous habits, as seen by its effectiveness on such diverse habits as head-jerking, lisping, nail-biting, and thumbsucking. Given that the client was movitated, the method seemed to be effective for all types of individuals: very young children as well as adults, males as well as females, those with high-frequency or severe habits as well as those with lower-frequency or milder habits. A possible side effect of the treatment was that the competing response might itself become a nervous habit. As noted, however, no such "symptom substitution" occurred, possibly because the treated habit was eliminated so rapidly thereby requiring only infrequent practice of the competing response. The habit-reversal methods appear to be a general as well as an effective treatment for nervous habits.

Evaluation of the clinical value of the present method requires comparison with the clinical results obtained with other methods of treating nervous habits. Many procedures have produced some benefit in restricted office, laboratory, or hospital situations, such as self-monitoring of the tic (Thomas et al. 1971); TV feedback and light aversion (Bernhardt et al. 1972); and noise termination (Barrett 1962). We are concerned here only with methods that have produced clinical benefits that have occurred in the clients' everyday life. Four such methods are psychotherapy, drugs, shock-aversion, and negative practice. In the major clinical evaluation of psychotherapy (Mahler and Luke 1946, Paterson 1945), about one-quarter of the clients were cured with treatment lasting several months. Combining the findings of the two major studies of aversion therapy (Brierly 1967, Bucher 1968), about three-quarters of the clients were cured. Haloperidol, the most effective of the drug treatments, has been evaluated in a number of studies (Challas and Brauer 1963, Connell et al. 1967, Shapiro and Shapiro 1968, Stevens and Blachly 1966). A complicating factor of this drug is its serious side effects at high doses. At safe dosages that could be used continuously, the haloperidol eliminated the tics for about one-half of the clients (Connell et al. 1967, Ford and Gottlieb 1969). Negative practice has been evaluated in a large number of case studies (Clark 1966, Jones 1960, Rafi 1962, Walton 1961, 1964, Yates 1958) and in one large sample study (Smith 1957). Overall, negative practice has eliminated the tics for about one-third of the clients. The present method appears to be clinically more useful than any of the alternative treatments since it was effective for virtually all clients and required only one or two sessions.

References

Azrin, N. H., Kaplan, S. J., and Foxx, R. M. (1973). Autism reversal: a procedure for eliminating the self-stimulatory behaviors of the institutionalized retarded. *American Journal of Mental Deficiency.*

Barrett, B. H. (1962). Reduction in rate of multiple tics by free operant conditioning methods. *Journal of Nervous and Mental Disease* 135:187–195.

Bernhardt, A. J., Hersen, M., and Barlow, D. H. (1972). Measurement and modification of spasmodic torticollis: an experimental analysis. *Behavior Therapy* 3:294–297.

Brierly, H. (1967). The treatment of hysterical spasmodic torticollis by behavior therapy. *Behaviour Research and Therapy* 5:139–142.

Bucher, B. D. (1968). A pocket-portable shock device with application to nailbiting. *Behaviour Research and Therapy* 6:389–392.

Challas, G., and Brauer, W. (1963). Tourette's disease: relief of symptoms with R1625. *American Journal of Psychiatry* 120:283–284.

Clark, D. F. (1966). Behavior therapy of Gilles de la Tourette's syndrome. *British Journal of Psychiatry* 112:771–778.

Connell, P. H., Corbett, J. A., Horne, D. J., and Matthews, A. M. (1967). Drug treatment of adolescent tiqueurs: a double blind trial of diazepam and haloperidol. *British Journal of Psychiatry* 113:375–381.

Eriksson, B., and Persson, T. (1969). Gilles de la Tourette's syndrome: two cases with an organic brain injury. *British Journal of Psychiatry* 115:351–353.

Ford, C. V., and Gottlieb, F. (1969). An objective evaluation of haloperidol in Gilles de la Tourette's syndrome. *Disorders of the Nervous System* 30:328–332.

Foxx, R. M., and Azrin, N. H. (1972). Restitution: a method of eliminating aggressive-disruptive behavior of retarded and brain damaged patients. *Behaviour Research and Therapy* 10:15–27.

——— (1973a). The elimination of autistic self-stimulatory behavior by overcorrection. *Journal of Applied Behavior Analysis* 11:35–48.

——— (1973b). *Toilet Training the Retarded: A Rapid Program for Day and Nighttime Independent Toileting.* Champaign, IL: Research Press.

Jones, H. G. (1960). Continuation of Yates' treatment of a tiqueur. In *Behavior Therapy and the Neuroses*, ed. H. J. Eysenck, pp. 25–258. Oxford, England: Pergamon.

Mahler, M. S., and Luke, J. A. (1946). Outcome of the tic syndrome. *Journal of Nervous and Mental Disease* 103:433–445.

Paterson, M. T. (1945). Spasmodic torticollis: results of psychotherapy in 21 cases. *Lancet* 2:556–559.

Rafi, A. A. (1962). Learning theory and the treatment of tics. *Journal of Psychosomatic Research* 6:71–76.

Shapiro, A. K., and Shapiro, E. (1968). Treatment of Gilles de la Tourette's syndrome with haloperidol. *British Journal of Psychiatry* 114:345–350.

Smith, M. (1957). Effectiveness of symptomatic treatment of nail biting in college students. *Psychology Newsletter* 8:219–231.

Stevens, J. R., and Blachly, P. H. (1966). Successful treatment of the maladie des tics. *American Journal of the Disabled Child* 112:541–545.

Thomas, E. J., Abrams, K. S., and Johnson, J. B. (1971). Self-monitoring and reciprocal inhibition in the modification of multiple tics of Gilles de la Tourette's syndrome. *Journal of Behavior Therapy and Psychiatry* 2:159–171.

Walton, D. (1961). Experimental psychology and the treatment of a tiqueur. *Journal of Child Psychology and Psychiatry* 2:148–155.

——— (1964). Massed practice and simultaneous reduction in drive level—further evidence of the efficacy of this approach to the treatment of tics. In *Experiments in Behavior Therapy*, ed. H. J. Eysenck, pp. 398–400. Oxford, England: Pergamon.

Yates, A. J. (1958). The application of learning theory to the treatment of tics. *Journal of Abnormal Social Psychology* 56:175–182.

——— (1970). *Behavior Therapy.* New York: Wiley.

17

Self-Monitoring and Self-Administered Overcorrection for the Modification of Nervous Tics

THOMAS H. OLLENDICK

Nervous tics are compulsive, persistent muscle movements which are highly resistant to treatment (Yates 1970). Unlike organically caused conditions such as spasms and tremors, nervous tics are subject to voluntary control, do not result in muscular atrophy, and are not painful. The prevalence of nervous tics is estimated to be approximately 1 percent of the population (Azrin and Nunn 1977). Jerking of the shoulder, jerking of the head to the side, blinking of the eyes, and jerking of the mouth and cheek are examples of the many different types of nervous tics.

A variety of behavioral techniques has been employed in the treatment of nervous tics, including operant conditioning (Barrett 1962), negative practice (Yates 1958, 1970), self-monitoring (Maletzky 1974, Thomas et al. 1971), and habit reversal, which is based on the principles of overcorrection (Azrin and Nunn 1973, 1977, Beck and Fedoravicius 1977). While each of these methods results in a degree of effectiveness, recent attention has centered around self-monitoring and habit-reversal procedures. In two uncontrolled case studies (Maletzky 1974, Thomas et al. 1971), self-monitoring was observed to be tic inhibiting and was associated with long-lasting remission of symptoms. Self-monitoring is also employed as an awareness training device for the early detection of tic onset in the Azrin and Nunn (1973, 1977) habit-reversal procedure. In addition to self-monitoring, a specific muscle-response pattern that is incompatible with the nervous tic is practiced. Upon awareness of the onset of the tic (self-monitoring), the client contingently practices the competing response (habit reversal).

While the habit-reversal procedure has been found to be effective, the relative contribution of self-monitoring and competing response practice to its effectiveness has not been investigated. Recent research has clearly shown that self-monitoring results in reactive changes in behavior, usually in therapeutic directions (e.g., Kazdin 1974, Lipinski et al. 1975). Although not conclusive, the previously cited uncontrolled case studies by Maletzky (1974) and Thomas et al. (1971) suggest that self-monitoring alone might be sufficient in the treatment of tics.

The primary purpose of the present study was to systematically evaluate the contribution of self-monitoring and competing response practice to the effectiveness of the habit-reversal procedures. A secondary purpose was to examine the reliability of self-monitoring in children. Two male children, both exhibiting facial tics, served as subjects.

Method

Subjects

According to his parents, Marty, a 9-year-old white male, developed excessive eye-blinking when his maternal grandfather had a stroke which left him with numerous and diverse tremors and loss of sight in the right eye. Marty, an only child, was 6 years of age at the time and was "very close" to his grandfather. This excessive eye-blinking continued for three years and remained untreated, since the parents were informed that "it would likely go away." Upon referral, Marty had developed a more elaborate tic: simultaneous blinking of the right eye and "bunching up" of the right cheek. This more elaborate tic, along with refusal to sleep in his own room, developed following the death of his maternal grandfather one month earlier. School reports revealed that Marty was in the superior range of intelligence and was an "A" student, but was not well liked by his peers.

David, an 11-year-old white male, exhibited excessive eye-twitching since he was 5 years of age. Parents reported that the eye-twitching developed when David entered kindergarten and his mother was hospitalized for glaucoma treatments. In the summer preceding the mother's operation and David's entry into kindergarten, his mother had recurring visual problems which resulted in numerous examinations and brief hospitalizations. David, the second of three children, and described as "mommy's boy," was highly distraught by these happenings and was placed on medication. Like Marty, David's eye-twitching continued over the years and had begun to include the mouth and cheek. The only precipitating stress that was identified at the time of referral was David's entry into his first year of junior high school (seventh grade). It was hypothesized that his entry into the new school was sufficiently similar to entry into kindergarten to result in an intensification of the nervous tic. Reports from his elementary school revealed that he was of average intelligence, achieved at an average level, and was well liked by his peers.

Experimental Design

The present investigation employed single-subject multiple-baseline designs across settings (Hersen and Barlow 1976) to demonstrate functional control over the target (i.e., nervous tic) behaviors. For David, treatment consisting of baseline, self-monitoring, and self-monitoring plus competing response practice was sequentially applied in the school setting and then in the home. While it was intended to use the same design with Marty, treatment consisting of baseline and self-monitoring was sequentially employed, first in the school setting, and then in the home. Self-monitoring plus competing response practice was not employed with Marty.

Procedure

David and Marty were seen at different times but the procedures employed were similar. During the week preceding baseline conditions, the teachers in both schools and the mothers of both children were trained in behavior recording. Nervous tics for both David and Marty were operationally defined, and the importance of unobtrusive, accurate recording was stressed. Tics were tallied on index cards during a study period in school and following the evening meal at home. Twenty-minute sampling periods were employed. The children were unaware that their behavior was being recorded in these settings.

Following the collection of five days of baseline data by the teachers and mothers, the children were seen over the weekend (as they were throughout the study) and instructed in the importance of accurate self-monitoring of their nervous tics in school so that they and the therapist would know when the frequency of their nervous tics was decreased. Each child was provided an obtrusive wrist counter to enhance accuracy (Nelson et al. 1978). They were told to count each nervous tic and to record the frequency on an index card at periodic intervals. Specific intervals were later used for reliability checks. At the end of five days of self-monitoring, both children were again seen over the weekend to review their progress and to instruct them in competing response practice. For David, competing response practice consisted of extensive practice in tensing the muscles antagonistic to his tic. He was instructed to hold his head centered, keep his eyes forward, and to tense the opposing eye and cheek muscles until the tic abated. He was taught to hold this position for three minutes. During the last half of the session, he practiced this competing response whenever a nervous tic occurred. At the end of the session, he was told to continue to self-monitor his tics in school and to self-administer the competing response for three minutes contingent on the occurrence of the nervous tic. Following five days of self-monitoring plus self-administered competing response practice in school, David was instructed to begin self-monitoring his nervous tics at home and then to practice the competing response at home in the same manner as described above. David was seen for a total of eight treatment sessions and three follow-up sessions.

For Marty, following the first five days of self-monitoring in the school, it was not necessary to implement competing response practice since the number of nervous tics approached a near-zero level. Rather, he was instructed to continue his self-monitoring in school and to initiate self-monitoring in the home. Marty was seen for a total of four treatment sessions and three follow-up sessions.

Reliability of Self-Monitoring

To determine the reliability of self-monitoring for each child in each setting, separate Pearson product-moment correlations were computed between the daily frequency of nervous tics recorded by the child in that setting and the daily frequency recorded by the teacher (school) or mother (home). For David, reliability of self-monitoring was .88 (Days 6 to 40) in the school and .89 (Days 16 to 40) in the home; for Marty, reliability of self-monitoring was .88 (Days 6 to 20) in the school and .89 (Days 11 to 20) in the home. While the children self-monitored their tics throughout the school day and at home, only those periods during which the teachers and mothers also recorded the tics were used for estimates of reliability.

Inspection of Figure 17-1 reveals that the frequency of David's nervous tics in school was reduced by approximately 50 percent following initial self-monitoring in that setting. While the effects of self-monitoring were immediate, it failed to reduce the frequency further. With the introduction of self-monitoring plus self-administered overcorrection, however, the frequency was reduced to a near-zero level in five days and maintained at that level for the remainder of intervention and at one year follow-up. Further inspection of Figure 17–1 shows that the frequency of nervous tics at home was unaffected while treatment was conducted in the school setting. With the introduction of self-monitoring and then self-monitoring plus self-administered overcorrection in the home setting, the frequency of nervous tics decreased in a manner similar to that observed in the school.

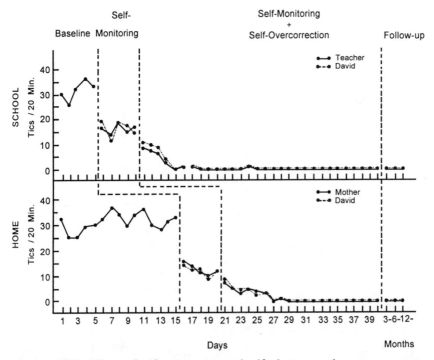

Figure 17–1. Effects of self-monitoring and self-administered overcorrection in the school and home: David.

For Marty (Figure 17–2), the frequency of nervous tics in school was reduced to a near-zero level following the introduction of self-monitoring. Hence, self-administered overcorrection was not employed. The frequency of nervous tics in the home was not affected by the results obtained in school. Upon contingent application of self-monitoring in the home, an immediate reduction in nervous tics occurred and was maintained at that level for the remainder of treatment and follow-up.

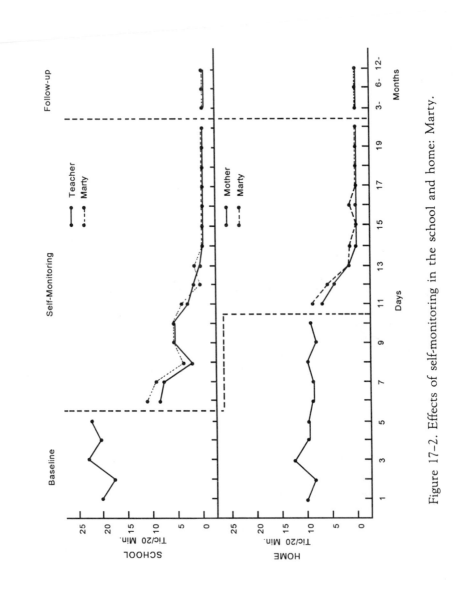

Figure 17–2. Effects of self-monitoring in the school and home: Marty.

Discussion

Both self-monitoring and the combination of self-monitoring plus self-administered overcorrection appear to be useful methods in eliminating nervous tics in children. While self-monitoring alone was effective for Marty, it was necessary to enhance self-monitoring with self-administered overcorrection for David. Several differences were evident between these subjects. Marty was younger, more intelligent, and, perhaps more important, the duration of his nervous tic was half that of David's and more clearly related to a specific antecedent event (death of grandfather). While it is only speculative at this point, it would appear that nervous tics of longer duration are more refractory to self-monitoring procedures and require more intensive treatment such as the self-administered overcorrection procedures. Nonetheless, the results clearly support the initial efficacy of self-monitoring alone and indicate that the dramatic results obtained with overcorrection are, at least in part, attributable to self-monitoring procedures.

Not only was the additive effect of self-monitoring and self-administered overcorrection determined in this study but, through the use of the multiple-baseline design across settings, clear functional control of the treatment procedure was also demonstrated. From a clinical standpoint, these results may appear discouraging. While functional control was established, generalization of control over nervous tics was not. These findings are not inconsistent with other findings obtained in the application of overcorrection procedures (Ollendick and Matson 1978) and reaffirm the necessity of including generalization strategies following effective treatment. By including the two settings in which the nervous tics occurred most frequently and by employing the self-control strategies of self-monitoring and self-administered overcorrection, a high degree of maintenance and generalization eventually occurred in the present study. At follow-up, both Marty and David and their mothers reported an absence of nervous tics in *all* settings.

Finally, results of the present study indicate that children are proficient in self-monitoring their behavior and self-administering treatment procedures. The children were observed by their teachers and mothers to follow the program closely and to be highly motivated to change their behavior. Such observations, combined with the present results, indicate that greater effort should be directed toward securing the child's active involvement in treatment and providing him with effective self-control strategies.

References

Azrin, N. H., and Nunn, R. G. (1973). Habit reversal: a method of eliminating nervous habits and tics. *Behaviour Research and Therapy* 11:619–628.
——— (1977). *Habit Control in a Day.* New York: Simon & Schuster.

Barrett, B. N. (1962). Reductions in the rate of multiple tics by free operant conditioning methods. *Journal of Nervous and Mental Disease* 135:187–195.

Beck, S., and Fedoravicius, A. S. (1977). Self-control treatment of an eye blink tic. *Behavior Therapy* 8:277–279.

Hersen, M., and Barlow, D. H. (1976). *Single Case Experimental Designs: Strategies for Studying Behavior Change.* New York: Pergamon.

Kazdin, A. E. (1974). Reactive self-monitoring: the effects of response desirability, goal setting, and feedback. *Journal of Consulting and Clinical Psychology* 42:704–716.

Lipinski, D. P., Black, J. L., Nelson, R. O., and Ciminero, A. R. (1975). Influence of motivational variables on the reactivity and reliability of self-recording. *Journal of Consulting and Clinical Psychology* 43:637–646.

Maletzky, B. M. (1974). Behavior recording as treatment: a brief note. *Behavior Therapy* 5:107–111.

Nelson, R. O., Lipinski, D. P., and Boykin, R. A. (1978). The effects of self-recorder's training and the obtrusiveness of the self-recording device on the accuracy and reactivity of self-monitoring. *Behavior Therapy* 9:200–208.

Ollendick, T. H., and Matson, J. L. (1978). Overcorrection: an overview. *Behavior Therapy* 9:830–842.

Thomas, E. J., Abrams, K. S., and Johnson, J. B. (1971). Self-monitoring and reciprocal inhibition in the modification of multiple tics of Gilles de la Tourette's syndrome. *Journal of Behavior Therapy and Experimental Psychiatry* 2:159–171.

Yates, A. J. (1958). The application of learning theory to the treatment of tics. *Journal of Abnormal and Social Psychology* 56:175–182.
——— (1970). *Behavior Therapy.* New York: Wiley.

18

Parent-Modified Thumbsucking

JOEL A. ROSS

Thumbsucking is a socially disapproved habit that persists among 10 percent of children 6 to 11 years of age (Roberts and Baird 1971) and has been shown to be related to malocclusion (Haryett et al. 1967, Longstreth 1968). Baer (1962) demonstrated that it could be manipulated in a laboratory setting by removing the re-presenting cartoons contingent upon thumbsucking and nonthumbsucking respectively. More recent attempts at control in the classroom also yielded positive results (Ross 1974, Ross and Levine 1972, Skiba et al. 1971). In the present study, reduction of a child's thumbsucking at home was attempted through parents administrating aversive consequences. An in vivo adaptation of Baer's (1962) procedure was employed in the daytime while a commercial product for inhibiting nailbiting and thumbsucking was systematically used during sleep.

Subject

Charlie, 9 years old, sucked his thumb at home during an average of two hours of daily television viewing and while asleep. Orthodontia for a very noticeable malocclusion of the front teeth could not begin until thumbsucking was discontinued. In addition, speech was marked by a severe lisp which may have been indirectly related to the thumbsucking. Neither frequent reminders in the daytime nor applying medication to the hand *before* bedtime were successful in reducing the habit.

Method

Daytime.

The mother made three observations per day at predesignated times during television viewing. A record was kept on whether, at first glance, Charlie's thumb was in or out of his mouth. Observations were made unobtrusively and without forewarning so that the mother's arrival could not be anticipated. She checked *only* during the three predetermined times, to preclude an increase in observations during treatment phases.

After two weeks of observation (Baseline 1, Figure 18-1), Charlie and his two sisters, who usually watched with him, were told that the TV would be turned off for five minutes each time he was seen thumbsucking. Siblings were asked to help by keeping after Charlie to stop whenever they saw him sucking his thumb. They were therefore made culpable if he were caught by the mother, thus justifying their loss of TV time too. After five weeks, the contingency (Treatment 1) was removed for three weeks (reversal) and then reinstated (Treatment 2) indefinitely, with data collected for six weeks.

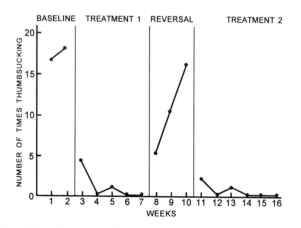

Figure 18-1. Thumbsucking frequency during television viewing (twenty-one observations per week).

Sleeptime.

During each of the four phases (Figure 18-2), three observations were made after Charlie had gone to bed: (1) approximately a half hour after he had fallen asleep; (2) approximately midway between the first and third observations; (3) just before the mother went to bed. If the thumb was in his mouth during any sleeptime observation, it was removed. Additionally, the father, who rose first in the morning, checked to see if Charlie's thumb was in his mouth at that time. In this way some inference could be made about his thumbsucking tendency during those six to seven hours when there were no observations. The number of days in each of the four sleeptime phases coincided with those of the daytime procedure. During the treatment periods Charlie's hand was coated twice with medication, soon after he had fallen asleep and just prior to the mother's retiring.

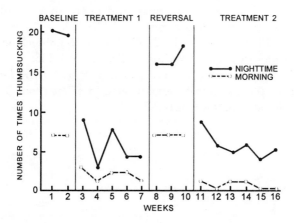

Figure 18–2. Thumbsucking frequency during sleep at night (twenty-one observations per week) and in the morning (seven observations per week)

Results and Discussion

From Figures 18–1 and 18–2, it is clear that both daytime and sleeptime procedures were significantly effective in reducing thumbsucking.

Gradual systematic reduction of amount and frequency of medication was suggested once the behavior was under control. However, the parents preferred maintaining both the daytime and sleeptime experimental procedures, which, six months after discontinuance of data collection, were still being used to prevent thumbsucking during TV viewing and sleep.

References

Baer, D. M. (1962). Laboratory control of thumbsucking in three young children by withdrawal and re-presentation of positive reinforcement. *Journal of the Experimental Analysis of Behavior* 5:525–528.

Haryett, R. D., Hansen, F. C., Davidson, P. O., and Sandilands, M. L. (1967). Chronic thumbsucking: the psychological effects and the relative effectiveness of various methods of treatment. *American Journal of Orthodontry* 53:569–585.

Longstreth, L. E. (1968). *Psychological Development of the Child.* New York: Ronald.

Roberts, J., and Baird, J. T. (1971). *Parent Ratings of Behavioral Patterns of Children.* Washington, DC: DHEW Publication No. (HSM) 72–1010.

Ross, J. A. (1974). Use of teacher and peers to control classroom thumbsucking. *Psychological Reports* 34:327–330.

Ross, J. A., and Levine, B. A. (1972). Control of thumbsucking in the classroom: case study. *Perceptual Motor Skills* 34:584–586.

Skiba, E. A., Pettigrew, L. E., and Alden, S. E. (1971). A behavioral approach to the control of thumbsucking in a classroom. *Journal of Applied Behavior Analysis* 4:121–125.

19

Habit-Reversal Treatment of Thumbsucking

NATHAN H. AZRIN, RICHARD G. NUNN, AND
S. FRANTZ-RENSHAW

Thumb- or finger-sucking has been found to occur among 42 percent of 2-year-olds, 46 percent of 3-year-olds, and 37 percent of 4-year-olds (Honzik and McKee 1962). Even at 12 years of age, 22 percent sucked their thumbs in a survey by Baalack and Frisk (1971). Thumbsucking is usually considered offensive aesthetically but also has been shown to be associated with dental problems, especially for children 4 years of age and older (Wright et al. 1979). Bitter-tasting substances on the thumbs have been commonly employed, but experimental evaluations of this procedure are rare (Flesher 1956) and have not included follow-up data permitting evaluation. The most common professional method of treatment has been the palatal arch or crib which may include spurs that discourage thumbsucking but causes considerable inconvenience. Haryett et al. (1967, 1970) found that the palatal arch had no effect, but that the palatal crib with spurs eliminated thumbsucking in almost all children if worn for several months, although also producing emotional problems and difficulties in speech as well as in eating. Counseling or psychotherapy has produced little or no benefit (Foster and Stebbins 1929, Haryett et al. 1967).

Operant procedures have been used in several small-scale applications, with less than four children, or in time-limited applications, with beneficial results that hold promise for larger-scale evaluations. These operant procedures have used reinforcement of nonthumbsucking as the principal method (Baer 1962, Bishop and Stumphauzer 1973, Feniger 1971, Kaufman and Scranton 1974, Knight and McKenzie 1974, Martin 1975, Ross 1974, 1975, Ross and Levine 1972, Shirbroun 1974).

A second type of operant approach to thumbsucking has been the habit-reversal method which consists of teaching competing reactions, identifying the habit-prone situation, arranging social support by the family, providing a response-contingent period of competing reactions, and identification of response precursors. Initially developed to treat the autistic behavior of retarded and autistic children who also may exhibit undesirable oral habits (Azrin et al. 1973, Foxx and Azrin 1973, Freeman et al. 1977), the method was found effective in eliminating thumbsucking of two normal children (Azrin and Nunn 1973). The present study attempted to evaluate the method more fully with normal children by using a larger number of subjects and also providing a comparison with the commonly used method of painting the thumb and fingers with a bitter-tasting substance.

Method

Subjects

Thirty-two children were enlisted as subjects by a newspaper advertisement. All respondents were included, except for three adults. Random assignment by a coin flip resulted in eighteen children being assigned to the habit-reversal method and fourteen children to the control method. Two of the controls were not used since their parents declined to participate in the control procedure to which they were assigned in that they had used that procedure previously without success. Of the thirty children, 20 percent were boys; the mean age was 8.3 years with a range of 2.5 to 14 years, 75 percent had consulted a dentist regarding the problem, and 25 percent had worn orthodontic appliances. For the habit-reversal children, the median number of thumbsucking episodes was twenty-five per day with a mean of 36 and S.D. of 28. The control children had a median of twenty-two, mean of 52, and S.D. of 58 episodes per day. Chi square or t tests, as appropriate, showed no significant differences between the treatment and control groups for any of the above dimensions. One of the children was reported as sucking only at night and scored as having one episode per day. Sucking of the thumb was the pattern for most children (72 percent), but some children sucked the index finger.

Recording

The parents provided an estimate at the initial contact of the frequency of thumbsucking. Standard recording sheets were used thereafter on which to record daily the number of thumbsucking episodes, which were reported by phone or mailed. Follow-up calls were made about every ten days during the first month, every two weeks during the next ten months, and once per month thereafter. Follow-up was not conducted after three months for the control children. Thumbsucking was recorded in terms of the frequency, rather than duration, since this measure appeared more meaningful to the parents who usually interrupted the behavior upon detecting it. Observer reliability measures were desired but did not seem feasible since the mother was usually the only adult in continuing contact with the child.

The counseling occurred in a single session of one to two hours' duration, the first portion of which was spent teaching the child what to do; in the latter portion, the child described the program, with the counselor's assistance, to the parent and requested the parent's assistance. In the "annoyance review" procedure, the child listed all of the problems created by the thumbsucking. In the "heightened awareness" procedure, the child acted out the usual response sequence, especially the precursors of the thumbsucking, so as to identify the stimulus antecedents of the behavior.

The child was taught competing reactions, such as making a fist in which the thumb gripped the fingers if the child was a fingersucker or the fingers gripped the thumb if a thumbsucker, or the child grasped some convenient object. This competing reaction was rehearsed until performed correctly. The grasping-clenching reaction was to endure for about one to three minutes. The children timed the duration by counting aloud slowly to one hundred, or, in the case of younger children they repeated a count to ten several times. The competing reaction served as a preventive measure in the identified habit-prone situations as well as a corrective measure when thumbsucking or any face touching occurred. For the first few children, this competing reaction consisted of holding the hands away from the body, but this was discontinued when children reacted unfavorably to it. Since nighttime sucking was especially likely, the children were told to keep their hands by their side with the fists clenched when they went to sleep at night.

Social support (social reinforcement) was encouraged by the parent praising the child when sucking was absent and by providing pleasant surprises, visits, and so on, when sucking was absent for an extended period. For all habit-reversal children, the parents were to turn off the television set or interrupt the suggested bedtime story whenever thumbsucking occurred. Also, concerned persons were identified, such as neighbor or grandparents, whom the child was to call to report progress.

The procedure was presented as a game involving "exercises" (clenching and grasping) that were the responsibility of the child, the parent serving to provide reminders and encouragement and enforcing the program only should the child fail to perform the exercises after a gentle reminder. The various procedures and probable problem situations were role-played.

Control Procedure (bitter tasting substance)

The children in the control group were not counseled directly by the counselor, but rather the counselor instructed the parents by phone on the use of a commercially available liquid containing cayenne pepper extract and citric acid and sold for the purpose of deterring thumbsucking. The liquid was to be applied every morning and evening. The parents were encouraged to be consistent in the application and to instruct babysitters and other caretakers to apply it in the parents' absence. The parents were instructed to keep daily records of the child's thumbsucking in the same manner as did the habit-reversal parents. Since these children and parents were advised only by phone, they constitute only a partial control to determine how well this commonly used procedure functioned with minimal professional contact.

Results

Figure 19-1 shows the changes in thumbsucking expressed as the mean percentage reduction from the pretreatment baseline level. The data are expressed in terms of percentage change rather than absolute frequency since the children varied greatly from one to two hundred episodes per day. Measure of control tendency based on absolute frequency would have given disproportionate weight to the small number of high-rate thumbsuckers. For the habit-reversal children, follow-up data were available for all clients up to the third week, for seventeen up to the fourth month, eleven up to six months, and nine clients at the twenty-month follow-up. The habit-reversal children had a mean reduction of 88 percent on the first day, and about 95 percent thereafter until the twentieth month when the reduction was 89 percent. In contrast, the mean percentage reduction of thumbsucking for the control children was 34 to 44 percent during the three months of follow-up. At the three-month follow-up, the difference between groups in the reduction of thumbsucking was statistically significant ($t = 4.79$: $p < 0.0001$).

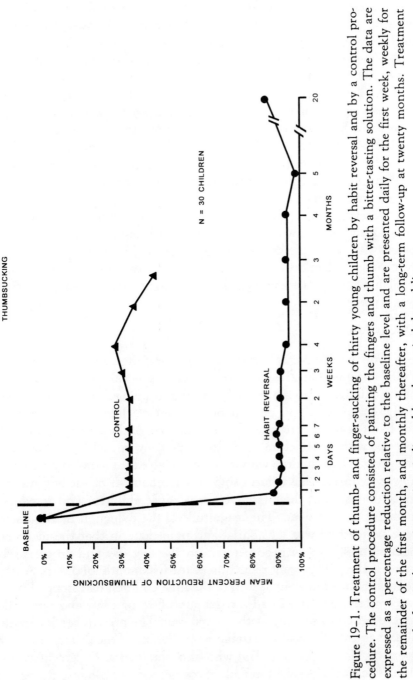

Figure 19-1. Treatment of thumb- and finger-sucking of thirty young children by habit reversal and by a control procedure. The control procedure consisted of painting the fingers and thumb with a bitter-tasting solution. The data are expressed as a percentage reduction relative to the baseline level and are presented daily for the first week, weekly for the remainder of the first month, and monthly thereafter, with a long-term follow-up at twenty months. Treatment consisted of a single training session, indicated by the vertical dotted line.

In terms of absolute frequency, the habit-reversal children had a mean of 1.8 episodes per day at the three-month follow-up compared to the pretreatment mean of 36 episodes per day. The control children had a mean of 21.2 episodes per day at the three-month follow-up compared to their pretreatment mean of 52 episodes per day.

Analysis of the individual data of the habit-reversal children at the three-month follow-up in terms of percentage reduction showed that 47 percent had stopped thumbsucking completely, and all of the others had a reduction of at least 50 percent. Of the control children at the same three-month follow-up, 10 percent had stopped completely; 60 percent of the children showed little or no change (less than a 50 percent reduction).

To evaluate the effect of the children whose data became unavailable during the follow-up, their scores at their last recording were compared with those of the remaining children. The mean difference in percentage reduction between those children whose data became unavailable during follow-up and the remaining children at the same time was 3 percent.

Discussion

The habit-reversal method was more effective in eliminating thumbsucking than the use of the bitter-tasting substance. About half of the children receiving the habit-reversal training stopped sucking entirely, compared to 10 percent of the control children. The effect of the habit-reversal continued for the duration of the twenty-month follow-up, with a reduction of 89 to 98 percent in sucking throughout the period. The children who were unavailable for follow-up were probably not unrecorded failures since their reduction of sucking was almost the same at their last record as those children who remained available for follow-up. The magnitude of the reduction by the habit-reversal method was substantial and immediate in that the mean reduction of sucking was 88 percent on the first day and progressively increased to a 98 percent reduction at the five-month follow-up. At the twenty-month follow-up, seven of the nine children had stopped sucking entirely, one child had a reduction of 98 percent, and one child had returned to sucking at the initial rate. The present results appear almost as favorable as those obtained by the use of the palatal crib with spurs by Haryett et al. (1970) who also obtained a 90 percent reduction. The habit-reversal method, of course, did not produce the eating and speaking problems which have been reported for the crib. Future evaluations of the present method might well use a control group which receives the same face-to-face contact as the treatment group. Also, future applications of the method might well omit the arm exercises which were used with some of the children, but discontinued for them and the subsequent children because of their effortfulness and negative emotional reaction.

References

Azrin, N. H., Kaplan, S. J., and Foxx, R. M. (1973). Autism reversal: eliminating stereotyped self-stimulation of retarded individuals. *American Journal of Mental Deficiency* 78:241–248.

Azrin, N. H., and Nunn, R. G. (1973). Habit reversal: a method of eliminating nervous habits and tics. *Behaviour Research and Therapy* 11:619–628.

Baalack, I.-B., and Frisk, A.-K. (1971). Finger-sucking in children: a study of incidence and occlusal conditions. *Acta Ondonta Scandinavica* 9:499–512.

Baer, D. M. (1962). Laboratory control of thumbsucking by withdrawal and representation of reinforcement. *Journal of the Experimental Analysis of Behavior* 5:525–528.

Bishop, B. R., and Stumphauzer, J. S. (1973). Behavior therapy of thumbsucking in children: a punishment (time-out) and generalization effect—what's a mother to do? *Psychological Reports* 33:939–944.

Feniger, T. M. (1971). Stimulus-seeking behavior as a symptom substitute for thumbsucking. *Dissertation Abstracts International* 32:1820–1821.

Flesher, W. N. (1956). Thumbsucking can be corrected. *Journal of the Oklahoma Dental Association* 45:11–12.

Foster, S., and Stebbins, D. (1929). Problems presented and results of treatment in 150 cases seen at the habit clinic for pre-school children in Boston. *Mental Hygiene* 13:529–541.

Foxx, R. M., and Azrin, N. H. (1973). The elimination of autistic self-stimulatory behavior by overcorrection. *Journal of Applied Behavior Analysis* 6:1–14.

Freeman, B. J., Moss, D., Somerset, T., and Ritvo, E. R. (1977). Thumbsucking in an autistic child overcome by overcorrection. *Journal of Behavior Therapy and Experimental Psychiatry* 8:211–212.

Haryett, R. D., Hansen, F. C., and Davidson, P. O. (1970). Chronic thumbsucking. A second report on treatment and its psychological effects. *American Journal of Orthodontry* 57:164–178.

Haryett, R. D., Hansen, F. C., Davidson, P. O., and Sandilands, M. L. (1967). Chronic thumb-sucking: the psychologic effects and the relative effectiveness of various methods of treatment. *American Journal of Orthodontry* 53:569–585.

Honzik, M. P., and McKee, J. P. (1962). The sex difference in thumb-sucking. *Journal of Pediatrics* 61:726–732.

Kaufman, J. M., and Scranton, T. R. (1974). Parent control of thumbsucking in the home. *Child Study Journal* 4:1–10.

Knight, M. F., and McKenzie, H. S. (1974). Elimination of bedtime thumbsucking in home settings through contingent reading. *Journal of Applied Behavior Analysis* 7:33–38.

Martin, D. (1975). A six year old "behaviorist" solves her sibling's chronic thumbsucking problem. *Corrective Social Psychiatry Journal of Behavioral Technology, Methods and Therapy* 21:19–21.

Ross, J. A. (1974). Use of teacher and peers to control classroom thumbsucking. *Psychological Reports* 34:327–330.

——— (1975). Parents modify thumbsucking: a case study. *Journal of Behavior Therapy and Experimental Psychiatry* 6:248–249.

Ross, J. A., and Levine, B. A. (1972). Control of thumbsucking in the classroom: case study. *Perceptual Motor Skills* 34:584–586.

Shirbroun, D. D. (1974). Generalization and maintenance of intervention effects across time and across settings for thumbsucking treatment in children. *Dissertation Abstracts International* 34:5691–5692.

Wright, L., Schaefer, A. B., and Solomons, G., eds. (1979). *Encyclopedia of Pediatric Psychology.* Baltimore, MD: University Park Press.

20

Chronic Nailbiting

KENNETH W. ALLEN

Introduction

Recent research has begun to suggest that it may be possible to refine the habit-reversal package first described by Azrin and Nunn (1973) by attempting to identify its essential components. As De Luca and Holborn (1984) argue: "isolation of powerful components of a treatment package [leads] to more cost-effective procedures."

In their study, self-monitoring, relaxation training, and competing response were used to eliminate nailbiting in a 17-year-old female to two-year follow-up. They go on to describe competing response training which required the patient to clench her fists for three minutes whenever nailbiting occurred or was likely to occur. They suggest that competing response was the effective component while acknowledging that relaxation training may have contributed to the outcome.

Miltenberger and Fuqua (1985) concentrated on five elements of the habit-reversal package as potentially powerful: these were relaxation training, competing response, social support, self-monitoring, and inconvenience review. They found that contingent practice of competing response was most effective in decreasing unwanted behavior in a range of habit disorders including nailbiting. Horne and Wilkinson (1980) suggest that competing response is the component essential for long-term maintenance of treatment efficacy. Bayes (1983), on the other hand, argues that learning a competing response is not essential for a favorable outcome and that incidental factors play an important part in this method.

Self-recording, in other words recording incidence of one's nailbiting behavior, alone has been claimed to reduce the frequency of nailbiting. Maletzky (1974) and Ollendick (1981) have reported improvement using self-monitoring as the sole treatment approach.

However, there are scant empirical data available on the efficacy of the competing response package though it would seem to be a potentially important treatment method. A different treatment modality employs mild aversion using bitter substances and has produced significant increases in nail length among nailbiters (Vargas and Adesso 1976). It also seems clear that self-monitoring should be included in any treatment program.

Silber and Haynes (1992) compared mild aversion against competing response along with self-monitoring; the study included a third group as a control who had self-monitoring alone. Twenty-one student volunteer subjects, seven per group, participated over four weeks with weekly therapist contact. Significant improvements in nail length were reported for both treatment methods, but not for the control group. Competing response showed the most beneficial effect as well as showing significant improvement in ratings of skin damage and the subjects' sense of control over their habit which were not seen for the other two conditions.

Subjects

Forty-five subjects of mixed sex and ages were recruited by local advertisements. They were allocated to one of three groups serially as subjects made themselves available. The competing response group had sixteen subjects, the mild aversion group had fourteen subjects, and the self-monitoring group had fifteen subjects. The mean age of the competing response group was 30.6 years, the mean age of the mild aversion group was 36.5 years, and the mean age of the self-monitoring group was 37.8 years. The mean number of years for which subjects had been biting their nails was 27.0, 33.3, and 34.8, respectively.

Materials

A bitter substance called "Stop 'n Grow," manufactured by the Mentholatum Company Ltd, England, was used in the mild aversion treatment group.

A questionnaire provided data concerning subjects' control over their nailbiting, including antecedents and consequences of their unwanted behavior.

Procedure

During the first session, pretreatment nail measurements were taken. Nail length was measured from the base of the nail where it separates from the cuticle to the center point of the top of the nail. Each nail was also rated on a scale of 0 to 3 for skin damage and severity of biting using Malone and Massler's (1952) classification.

All subjects were required to keep a daily record of the number of separate occasions each day in which they engaged in nailbiting or felt the urge to bite using a self-monitoring chart. Subjects were informed that this would help by promoting increased awareness of and attendance to the unwanted behavior as a crucial element in achieving control over the habit. Subjects were then instructed on their method of treatment.

The competing response treatment group was advised that each habit movement should be interrupted so that it no longer formed part of a chain of normal movements and that a physically competing response should be established to interfere with the habit. Subjects were asked to engage in a competing activity, with the "offending" hand to make a fist with the thumb against the palm until a slight tension was felt and to maintain that pressure for three minutes. This was to be done whenever they became aware that they were nailbiting or whenever the urge to nailbite took place.

The mild aversion treatment group received a slightly different rationale, that by administering an aversive stimulus to be paired with an unwanted response, this would increase awareness and so inhibit the habit and its strength would be diminished (Wolpe 1973). Nailbiters in this condition were instructed to apply the bitter substance twice a day to their nails and surrounding skin.

The self-monitoring treatment group was instructed to continue to record their nailbiting throughout and to bring their self-monitoring charts for scrutiny at each appointment.

At the second appointment, four weeks later, all measures were repeated, the nailbiting questionnaire was again completed, self-monitoring sheets collected, progress reviewed, and praise or encouragement given.

The final appointment was at twelve weeks from the first, measures were again repeated, nailbiting questionnaire completed, and self-monitoring sheets collected. Subjects were thanked for their participation and those who requested further help were offered behavioral treatment.

Results

Figure 20–1 shows the mean scores for the effect of time on nail length. There was a significant main effect of time [$F(2,54) = 26.84$, P $= 0.00$]. The mean for pre was 8.69 mm, the mean for post was 10.54, and the mean for follow-up was 11.01. There was also a significant main effect of digit on nail length scores, ANOVA (analysis of variance) results were [$F(4,108) = 53.03$, P $= 0.00$]. The means were: little finger $= 8.13$; ring finger $= 9.73$; middle finger $= 10.02$; index finger $= 9.83$; and thumb $= 11.50$. In addition there was an interaction between group and time for nail length [$F(4,54) = 3.12$, P < 0.05].

When analyzing further the interaction between group and time for nail length the following findings were obtained. There was a significant difference between pre- and follow-up scores for the mild aversion group (3.27). For competing response the pre- and follow-up scores just failed to reach significance (2.66), and for self-monitoring pre-to follow-up scores were not significant (0.83). For all groups there were no significant differences between pre-and post scores, or for post to follow-up scores.

In assessing whether the starting levels were different across the three groups the Tukey test revealed no significant differences between conditions at pretreatment. This is seen clearly in Figure 20–1.

Using therapist ratings of severity of skin damage on a simple visual rating scale, ANOVA results showed significant effects of time [$F(2,54) = 12.86$, P $= 0.00$], and of digit [$F(4,108) = 4.90$, P $= < 0.01$], where the means were: little finger $= 0.42$; ring finger $= 0.39$; middle finger $= 0.51$; index finger $= 0.57$; and thumb $= 0.6$. However the Tukey test showed no significant difference for paired comparisons.

There was also an interaction for time by digit in measures of skin damage [$F(8,216) = 2.48$, P $= 0.014$], and there were significant differences to the 0.01 level for all fingers at pre-post and pre-follow-up with the exception of the little finger where pre-post scores were significant to the 0.05 level. No significant differences were found at the post follow-up point for any finger. Pretreatment scores found a significant difference in skin damage ratings between the little and the index fingers only; at post and at follow-up no significant differences across digits was found.

Scores for degree of biting, using Malone and Massler's (1952) classification, also show a significant main effect of time [$F(2,54) = 14.81$, P $= 0.00$]. The mean pre score was 1.69, mean post score was 0.66, and mean follow-up score was 0.77.

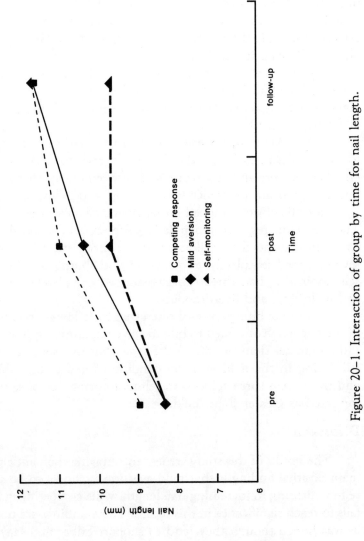

Figure 20-1. Interaction of group by time for nail length.

For the subjects' own ratings of the degree of control they had over their nailbiting, there was a significant effect of time [F(2,54) = 27.26, P = 0.00]. The means were, at pre 1.93, post 3.02, and at follow-up 2.56.

There was a significant main effect of time on the frequency of urges to nailbite [F(2,54) = 09.33, P = 0.00]. Ratings were measured in millimeters, with the left end of the visual analog scale being zero. At pretreatment, the mean was 65.82 mm, at post it was 44.82 mm, and at follow-up it was 40.1 mm.

Frequency of acts of nailbiting again showed a significant main effect of time [F(2,54) = 14.58, P = 0.00]. Using the same method of measurement as above, the means were at pre 62.75, at post 32.75, and at follow-up 32.30.

As can be seen, for every dependent variable there was a main effect of time. In each case the Tukey test revealed a significant difference between pre and post scores and between pre and follow-up scores, but no significant difference between post and follow-up scores.

Not all subjects stopped biting their nails over the twelve weeks. The competing response group had six subjects who stopped completely, five who continued to nailbite, and five dropouts; mild aversion had seven stopped completely, two continued nailbiting, and five dropouts; self-monitoring had three subjects stopped completely, seven continued nailbiting, and five dropouts.

Severity of biting scores showed that by follow-up two subjects out of the five who continued to bite in the competing response group had ratings greater than "mild"; by the same time one subject out of seven still biting in the mild aversion condition rated greater than "mild"; and there were three subjects in self-monitoring out of seven still biting rated as greater than "mild."

Discussion

The results of this study are less encouraging than anticipated. The main positive finding is that mild aversion is shown to be superior to self-monitoring in increasing nail length while competing response just fails to reach significance in this regard. These findings are not as strong as was hoped though they tend to support Silber and Haynes (1992) in that the direction of the findings is similar.

Figure 20–1 shows the trend of both mild aversion and competing response scores to be continuing to improve by follow-up, which is what was hoped for, while self-monitoring has not resulted in significant improvement and appears to have leveled off. This does not support the view of other researchers (Maletzky 1974) that self-monitoring could be used as a main treatment in itself.

Again, Figure 20-1 shows that for both competing response and mild aversion there is a similar rate of improvement until the means converge at about the 11.5 mm point. The competing response group began with a slightly higher score and it is open to question whether such a rate of improvement could have been maintained to a mean score so much higher than the mild aversion group at post treatment.

The effect of mild aversion in this study supports the findings of Vargas and Adesso (1976), who found that aversion therapy using mild shock, negative practice, or bitter substances has a beneficial effect on nail length. It should be noted that all subjects in this present study had tried a variety of aversive substances in order to try to break their habit, without long-term benefit.

Frequent therapist contact allows greater reinforcement of the rationale underpinning the treatment strategy and while most nailbiters are familiar with the use of aversive substances as a means of attempting to control the habit, the rationale of competing response is a more unusual and, arguably, difficult concept to absorb on the strength of a single brief session.

The other main finding of Silber and Haynes (1992) was that the competing response condition left subjects feeling they had significantly more control over their nailbiting. This effect was not found in the present study and it is possible to speculate that reduced therapist contact may have a role to play in this.

A feature of the results of the study is the consistent significant effect of time on all of the measures for all three treatment groups. The improvement shown for ratings of skin damage, degree of biting, control, urges to bite, and acts of biting fails to identify between-group differences.

The lack of between-group differences raises the issue identified by Davidson and Denney (1976), who concluded that in their study nonspecific treatment factors such as demand, expectancy, and attention were sufficient to bring about "substantial" increases in nail length.

The use of the measure of nail length by researchers is well established (Christmann and Sommer 1976, Horne and Wilkinson 1980, Silber and Haynes 1992), but the issue of using nail length as a measure itself raises questions of external factors which could have an effect on the nails themselves; subjects were advised to trim any rough or broken nails and file them smooth; weak, snapped, and broken nails had resulted in resumed biting and relapse. Other factors may be age, gender, health, and occupation of subjects. The pattern of biting was not recorded in this study; it is possible for the little finger to be bitten rarely and the thumb to be a favorite target for biting, which would influence their relative lengths.

The issue remains unclear. Mild aversion treatment requires financial outlay for the patient, whereas competing response treatment does not; however, both methods seem to require therapist contact to be really effective. This implies a demand on the time of the clinician which would need to be balanced against the resources available.

References

Azrin, N. H., and Nunn, R. G. (1973). Habit reversal: a method of eliminating nervous habits and tics. Behaviour Research and Therapy 11:619–628.

Bayes, R. (1983). Description, practical application and results of the Azrin and Nunn technique for modification of nervous habits. Quaderns Cuadernos de Psicologia 7:52–59.

Christmann, F., and Sommer, G. (1976). Behaviour therapy of fingernail biting: assertive training and self-control. Praxis der Kinderpsychologie und Kinderpsychiatrie 25:139–146.

Davidson, A. M., and Denney, D. R. (1976). Covert sensitization and information in the reduction of nailbiting. Behavior Therapy 7:512–518.

De Luca, R. V., and Holborn, S. W. (1984). A comparison of relaxation training and competing response training to eliminate hairpulling and nailbiting. Journal of Behavior Therapy and Experimental Psychiatry 15:67–70.

Horne, D. J., and Wilkinson, J. (1980). Habit reversal treatment for fingernail biting. Behaviour Research and Therapy 18:287–291.

Maletzky, B. M. (1974). Behaviour recording as a treatment: a brief note. Behavior Therapy 5:107–111.

Malone, A. J., and Massler, M. (1952). Index of nailbiting in children. Journal of Abnormal Social Psychology 47:193–202.

Miltenberger, R. G., and Fuqua, R. W. (1985). A comparison of contingent vs non-contingent competing response practice in the treatment of nervous habits. Journal of Behavior Therapy and Experimental Psychiatry 16:195–200.

Ollendick, T. H. (1981). Self-monitoring and self-administered overcorrection: the modification of nervous tics in children. Behavior Modification 5:75–84.

Silber, K. P., and Haynes, C. E. (1992). Treating nailbiting: a comparative analysis of mild aversion and competing response therapies. *Behaviour Research and Therapy* 30:15–22.

Vargas, J. M., and Adesso, V. J. (1976). A comparison of aversion therapies for nailbiting behavior. *Behavior Therapy* 7:322–329.

Wolpe, J. (1973). *The Practice of Behavior Therapy*. Oxford, England: Pergamon.

21

Hair Pulling

MICHAEL S. ROSENBAUM AND TEODORO AYLLON

Trichotillomania refers to high probability hair pulling in such areas as the scalp, eyebrows, eyelashes, moustache, beard, and pubic hair (Mehregan 1970). Since cases of hair pulling are treated by both dermatologists and psychologists, the incidence of this problem behavior is difficult to estimate (McLaughlin and Nay 1975). While bald spots typically appear in the areas in which hair pulling occurs, hair pulling and plucking can produce varying degrees of hair follicle damage, such as follicular atrophy (Mehregan 1970, Muller and Winkelmann 1972). Studies investigating the effectiveness of psychotherapeutic approaches to treating hair pulling, aimed at enabling clients to resolve hypothetical underlying conflicts, have produced mixed results (Mannino and Delgado 1969). Data on the effectiveness of dermatological approaches to treatment, consisting of an interview with the client to explain the cause of hair pulling combined with prescribing a topical medication to achieve a placebo effect (Mehregan 1970), have yet to be reported.

A review of the behavioral literature revealed several approaches to treating hair pulling, including thought stopping (Taylor 1963), consequating hair pulling with aversive stimuli (Bayer 1972, Horne 1977, MacNeil and Thomas 1976), behavioral contracting (Stabler and Warren 1974), reinforcement plus time-out (Evans 1976), relaxation plus self-reward (McLaughlin and Nay 1975), covert sensitization (Levine 1976), extinction (Wolff 1977), hypnosis (Gardner 1978, Horne 1977), and habit reversal (Azrin and Nunn 1973). Several drawbacks are associated with these studies, such as the inclusion of only one client, a lack of reporting data, and the inclusion of some form of self-recording in the absence of assessing the reliability of self-recorded data.

The present study focused on habit reversal in treating hair pulling and was designed to overcome the drawbacks described above by including four clients, providing ongoing assessment in the form of self-recorded data throughout six- and twelve-month follow-ups, and obtaining independent assessment of self-recorded data through measures by significant others in the client's environment and inspection of the areas affected by hair pulling.

Method

Clients

Linda

Linda was a 10-year-old female referred for treatment of hair pulling by a staff psychologist at a university medical center. Linda's mother reported that her daughter had been pulling single hairs out of her scalp for about three years, with the frequency of this behavior increasing during the previous six months. The frequency of this behavior was much greater at home than at school and had resulted in several areas of thin hair on Linda's scalp.

Bob

Bob was a 28-year-old male outpatient at a Veterans Administration Center. He had received the diagnosis of anxiety neurosis and had been treated by a staff psychiatrist for insomnia, tension headaches, tongue biting, and pulling hairs out of his moustache four months prior to the present study. Although this latter behavior decreased for a short time, its increase to pretreatment levels prompted the psychiatrist to refer Bob for treatment of hair pulling. This behavior had resulted in several areas of thin hair on Bob's moustache.

Steve

Steve was a 27-year-old male pharmacy extern who heard about the present research from a friend and sought treatment for pulling hairs out of his scalp and beard. He reported that hair pulling had begun when he entered pharmacy school and had become more severe when he began his externship three months earlier. Steve described the externship as anxiety producing because of the number of decisions concerning medications for patients he had to make. Hair pulling had resulted in areas of thin hair on his scalp and beard.

Vicki

Vicki was a 21-year-old female college student referred for treatment of hair pulling and excessive scratching by the dermatology clinic at a university medical center. Her six-year history of hair pulling had produced two well-defined bald spots on her scalp. Since she also scratched these areas excessively, the skin was irritated and no new hairs could grow. She reported that both of these behaviors increased markedly when she was studying, especially for an examination.

Setting and Recording

An explanation of the purpose of the research, description of the problem behavior by the client, and instruction in self-recording the frequency of this behavior was conducted during an initial interview with three of the clients. A 3 by 5 inch index card was divided into seven columns, and a slash mark was recorded each time a target response was detected throughout the entire day. The only exception to this procedure was that Linda's mother was instructed to record the frequency of her daughter's hair pulling at home. Additionally, each client was asked to save all hairs pulled on a daily basis and bring them to meetings with the researcher.

Self-recording was obtained daily during baseline and throughout the first month following treatment. Baseline data were reported at the treatment session. Two weeks following the treatment session, data were reported via phone. Data for the next two weeks were reported at the one-month follow-up session. Thereafter, Linda's mother and Bob recorded the frequency of hair pulling one week per month for the next eleven months. Following the daily recording period, Steve and Vicki recorded their frequencies of hair pulling one week per month for five months. These data were reported via phone on a monthly basis.

Response Definitions

Hair pulling for Linda and Vicki consisted of placing the hand on the head and pulling on hair. Vicki also recorded scratching, which consisted of placing her hand on either bald spot on her scalp and scratching for at least five seconds. Steve's hair pulling included his scalp and beard, whereas hair pulling for Bob included only his moustache. Hair pulling did not have to result in the actual loss of hair accompanying each instance of this behavior.

Reliability

Reliability was obtained in the form of validating reports from individuals in each client's environment who frequently interacted with him/her. When possible, one of these individuals (e.g., Linda's father) was asked to count the number of instances of hair pulling for purposes of providing reliability of this measure. On each of these occasions, reliability was calculated by dividing the smaller number recorded by the larger and multiplying the resulting quotient by 100. Additionally, growth of hair in bald spots or extremely thin areas of hair indicated changes in the frequency of hair pulling. This was based on judgments by the first author at the six-month follow-up sessions relative to the baseline appearance of these areas for Linda, Steve, and Bob, and at the six-month follow-up session for Vicki by the dermatologist who referred her for treatment of hair pulling.

Research Design

In assessing the effectiveness of treatment, separate comparison designs (AB) (A [baseline], B [treatment]) representing a group of direct replications were conducted.

Procedure

Baseline

This consisted of the period of time between the initial interview and the treatment session.

Treatment (Habit Reversal)

This technique has been described by Azrin and Nunn (1973, 1977). A verbal description while demonstrating hair pulling was provided in the response description procedure. Then, each client was taught to detect bringing the hand toward the area in which hair pulling occurred (e.g., scalp, beard, moustache) (early warning). Additionally, Vicki was taught to detect bringing her hand toward the two bald spots on her scalp that she scratched. The client listed and described those situations in which hair pulling usually occurred or increased in frequency (situation awareness training). To increase the motivation to cease hair pulling, unpleasant aspects of this behavior were described (habit inconvenience review).

The competing response practice procedure consisted of teaching the client an isometric exercise incompatible with hair pulling and characterized by: (a) being maintained for at least one minute, (b) involving the tensing of muscles used in hair pulling, (c) being as socially inconspicuous as possible, (d) being implemented easily with normal activities, and (e) preventing hair pulling from remaining a routine part of the client's normal activities. Each client was taught to place the hands in the lap or by the side of the body and clench the fists, until a comfortable amount of tension was produced in the hands and forearms. The client was instructed to perform this competing response for two minutes following the urge to pull hair, any antecedent to hair pulling, or any occurrence of hair pulling. Vicki was instructed to follow the same procedure for her scratching. Linda's mother was instructed to prompt her daughter to perform the competing response on any occasion when she failed to perform it on her own. Additionally, her mother was asked to praise Linda whenever she performed the competing response without being prompted.

To maximize the generalizability of the competing response outside the treatment session, the client chose one situation in which hair pulling increased in frequency (symbolic rehearsal). As an actual instance of hair pulling in that situation was recalled, the client performed the competing response. This procedure was repeated several times, followed by the client discussing the topics of interest with the researcher. To allow further practice of the competing response, the client was instructed to perform the competing response whenever an urge to pull hair, antecedent to hair pulling, or actual hair pulling occurred. Hair pulling that the client failed to detect was pointed out by the researcher, who instructed the client to perform the competing exercise. The entire treatment session lasted about sixty minutes.

Follow-up

Follow-up sessions were conducted one month and six months following treatment. On these occasions the researcher inspected the areas affected by hair pulling, praised the client for improvement noted (i.e., an increase in hair growth), and encouraged him/her to continue using the treatment procedures when needed. Additionally, on each occasion that data were reported via phone, the researcher praised the client for improvement (i.e., decrease in the frequency of hair pulling or maintenance of this response at a low level), and reminded him/her to continue following the treatment procedures.

Results

Linda

Linda's mean frequency of hair pulling was 6.9/day at home during baseline (Figure 21-1). Only two instances of this behavior occurred during the three-week period of daily recording following the treatment session (M = 0.09/day). Hair pulling had not recurred at any of the follow-ups. Additionally, Linda's teacher reported that the child ceased performing this behavior at school following the treatment session. On the two occasions that Linda's father recorded the frequency of his daughter's hair pulling (Days 5 and 20), his records matched those of her mother (100 percent agreement). Finally, at the six-month follow-up session, the previously thin areas of hair on Linda's scalp could not be differentiated from the remainder of hair on her scalp as judged by the first author.

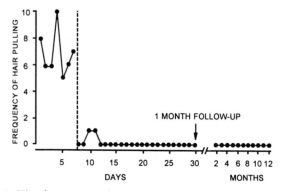

Figure 21-1. The frequency of hair pulling for Linda on a daily basis and averaged over one week per month.

Bob

During baseline, the mean frequency of Bob's hair pulling was 8.1/day (Figure 21-2). This frequency decreased following habit-reversal treatment (M = 0.6/day). The follow-up measures showed that hair pulling had not recurred. The two occasions that Bob's wife recorded the frequency of his hair pulling (Days 5 and 10) yielded 93 percent agreement between her records and those made by him. At the six-month follow-up session, there were no longer any thin areas of hair on Bob's moustache, based on the first author's judgment.

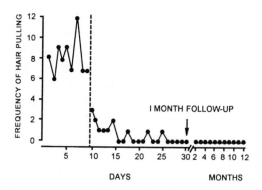

Figure 21-2. The frequency of hair pulling for Bob on a daily basis and averaged over one week per month.

Steve

Steve's mean frequency of hair pulling was 10.3/day during baseline (Figure 21-3). Following habit-reversal treatment, this behavior decreased markedly (M = 0.5/day). Hair pulling was eliminated nine days following baseline and was not noted at any of the follow-ups. Additionally, there were no thin areas of hair on Steve's scalp or beard at the six-month follow-up session, as judged by the first author. Since Steve lived alone, it was difficult to obtain reliability measures of his hair pulling.

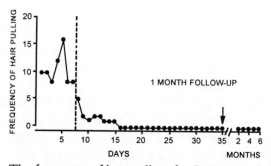

Figure 21-3. The frequency of hair pulling for Steve on a daily basis and averaged over one week per month.

Vicki

During baseline the mean frequency of Vicki's hair pulling was six/day (Figure 21-4). This behavior occurred once following treatment with habit reversal (M = 0.04/day). Hair pulling had not recurred at any of the follow-up measures. Her mean frequency of scratching bald spots on her scalp was 16.0/day during baseline. Habit-reversal treatment was associated with a decrease in this behavior (M = 6.8/day). At the six-month follow-up, the mean frequency of scratching was four day. At the one-month follow-up session, the bald spots on Vicki's scalp showed evidence of healing according to the referring dermatologist, although there were no signs of new hair growth. At the six-month follow-up session, healing continued and signs of new hair growth were visible, according to the same dermatologist. Unfortunately, there was no second party available to provide reliability measures of Vicki's hair pulling and scratching.

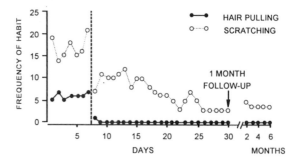

Figure 21-4. The frequency of hair pulling for Vicki on a daily basis and averaged over one week per month.

Discussion

The results indicate that the habit-reversal technique effectively eliminated relatively mild cases of hair pulling. The decreases obtained for the four clients were immediate and were maintained over long periods of time (i.e., six- and twelve-month follow-ups). The effectiveness of this treatment may have been related to the severity of the cases studied (i.e., the highest frequency of hair pulling was 10.3/day, and only one client had a bald spot), with the response of more severe cases to this form of treatment requiring further investigation.

Several factors appeared to be related to the effectiveness of the habit-reversal technique. Self-recording required three clients to focus on hair pulling, thereby increasing their awareness of its occurrence and providing them with immediate feedback concerning its frequency. This feedback, in turn, may have produced reactive effects, thereby resulting in an alteration in the frequency of hair pulling (e.g., Kazdin 1974, McFall 1977, Nelson 1977). The self-recording, response description, early warning, situation awareness training, and habit inconvenience review procedures may have contributed to the successful implementation of the competing response practice procedure by increasing the client's awareness of hair pulling, including its antecedents and consequences. An additional contributing factor for Linda may have been her mother's prompts to perform the competing response when Linda failed to do so on her own.

The competing response practice procedure interrupted the typical chain of events terminating in hair pulling and provided a time period (two minutes) for the client to remain aware that either an urge to pull hair, an antecedent to hair pulling, or hair pulling itself had occurred. By incurring minimal response cost to the client, the competing response could be practiced easily in the client's daily routine.

One limitation associated with the present study was the lack of objective ratings of the relative hairiness of the target areas for each client. One method of obtaining these ratings would have been to take pictures on a pretreatment basis and at the six-month follow-up session and have them blindly rated by a dermatologist as to the presence or absence of hair or evidence of hair pulling. Future research in this area should include methods for the objective quantification of hair pulling.

The most commonly used and successful forms of treatment for hair pulling have involved reinforcing consequences for appropriate behavior and aversive consequences contingent on hair pulling, used alone and in combination. Azrin and Nunn's (1973) application of habit reversal, however, represented the most cost-efficient treatment procedure, in terms of maximum therapeutic benefit from minimal therapeutic intervention. By replicating this finding, the results of the present research serve to extend the generality of the habit-reversal technique as a cost-efficient method for treating hair pulling, at least with mild cases of this problem behavior.

References

Azrin, N. H., and Nunn, R. G. (1973). Habit-reversal: a method of eliminating nervous habits and tics. *Behaviour Research and Therapy* 11:619–628.
—— (1977). *Habit Control in a Day.* New York: Simon & Schuster.
Bayer, C. A. (1972). Self-monitoring and mild aversion treatment of

trichotillomania. *Journal of Behavior Therapy and Experimental Psychiatry* 3:139–141.

Evans, B. (1976). A case of trichotillomania in a child treated in a home token program. *Journal of Behavior Therapy and Experimental Psychiatry* 7:197–198.

Gardner, G. G. (1978). Hypnotherapy in the management of childhood habit disorders. *Journal of Pediatrics* 92:838–840.

Horne, D. J. de L. (1977). Behavior therapy for trichotillomania. *Behaviour Research and Therapy* 15:192–196.

Kazdin, A. E. (1974). Reactive self-monitoring: the effects of response desirability, goal setting, and feedback. *Journal of Consulting and Clinical Psychology* 42:704–716.

Levine, B. A. (1976). Treatment of trichotillomania by covert sensitization. *Journal of Behavior Therapy and Experimental Psychiatry* 7:75–76.

MacNeil, J., and Thomas, M. R. (1976). Treatment of obsessive-compulsive hair pulling (trichotillomania) by behavioral and cognitive contingency manipulation. *Journal of Behavior Therapy and Experimental Psychiatry* 7:391–392.

Mannino, F. V., and Delgado, R. A. (1969). Trichotillomania in children: a review. *American Journal of Psychiatry* 126:505–511.

McFall, R. M. (1977). Parameters of self-monitoring. In *Behavioral Self-Management*, ed. R. B. Stuart. New York: Brunner/Mazel.

McLaughlin, J. G., and Nay, W. R. (1975). Treatment of trichotillomania using positive coverants and response cost: a case report. *Behavior Therapy* 6:87–91.

Mehregan, A. H. (1970). Trichotillomania: a clinicopathologic study. *Archives of Dermatology* 102:129–133.

Muller, S. A., and Winkelmann, R. K. (1972). Trichotillomania: a clinicopathologic study of 24 cases *Archives of Dermatology* 105:535–539.

Nelson, R. O. (1977). Methodological issues in assessment via self-monitoring. In *Behavioral Assessment: New Directions in Clinical Psychology*, ed. J. D. Cone and R. P. Hawkins. New York: Brunner/Mazel.

Stabler, B., and Warren, A. A. (1974). Behavioral contracting in treating trichotillomania: case note. *Psychological Reports* 34:401–402.

Taylor, J. G. (1963). A behavioral interpretation of obsessive-compulsive neurosis. *Behaviour Research and Therapy* 1:237–244.

Wolff, R. (1977). Trichotillomania: Harriet's treatment. *Psychological Reports* 40:50.

22

Excessive Scratching

K. EILEEN ALLEN AND FLORENCE R. HARRIS

Introduction

From 1963 to 1965, the staff of the Laboratory Preschool studied the effects of adult attention on problem behavior in normal children. Results have indicated that the behavior was controlled by its immediate consequence, the attention of adults. Behavior which was immediately followed by teacher attention tended to be maintained or to increase in rate; behavior following which teacher attention was withheld (or was immediately withdrawn) tended to diminish rapidly or to drop out altogether. The problem behavior modified in accordance with the above adult social reinforcement contingencies included regressed crawling (Harris et al. 1964a,b), socially isolate behavior (Allen et al. 1964), excessive crying and whining (Hart et al. 1964), and deficits in motor skills (Johnston et al. 1966). Similar results have been reported in studies of modification of pathological behavior through the use of operant techniques (Ayllon and Haughton 1962, Wolf et al. 1964, 1965).

The staff of the Developmental Psychology Laboratory receives many requests from parents for help with the problem behavior of their preschool children. A very limited number of these children can be worked with directly by staff members. Parents, however, give several hours of attention to their children each day. The laboratory staff therefore decided to explore methods for teaching parents to modify their own attending behavior in ways that might help them resolve their child's problem. Development of such a methodology could decrease the staff time required per child and thus increase the number of children and parents who might be helped.

The exploratory study reported here delineates the procedures used in helping a parent eliminate self-scratching behavior in her child through the application of operant conditioning techniques. Although self-scratching might be considered as respondent behavior elicited by a preceding stimulus (skin irritation) rather than operant behavior responsive largely to its immediate consequences, there is some evidence that dermatitis may be under operant control (Walton 1960). Likewise, behavior such as vomiting (Wolf et al. 1965) and crying (Hart et al. 1964) has been shown to be responsive to its social consequences. In the present study it was hypothesized that the self-scratching behavior of the child was a function of the mother's attending behavior and that the behavior could be reduced or eliminated to the extent that the mother could be helped to modify her own attending behavior.

Case History

Fay, an alert, friendly, well-mannered child nearly 5 years old, was brought to the Developmental Psychology Laboratory by her mother. Consultation was sought because Fay, for almost a year, had been scratching herself until she bled. The scratching behavior had resulted in large sores and scabs on her forehead, nose, cheeks, chin, and one arm and leg. Neither pediatric nor psychiatric consultation had eliminated the scratching, although examinations had indicated that there was no basic medical problem. The last recommendation made to the mother was that Fay be fitted with expensive pneumatic arm splints in order to restrain her scratching activity. Though the mother was reluctant to do this, she saw little alternative if Fay were not to be permanently disfigured.

According to the mother, the parents had tried every disciplinary approach to stopping the scratching. The father spanked the child, sometimes severely, when she scratched. He berated the mother for her verbal but equally ineffectual techniques. The mother declared that she had come to dislike the child so intensely and to be so repelled by her appearance that she felt it might be better if Fay were placed outside the home to live. The marriage itself was threatened, according to the mother, due in large part to constant quarrels over disciplinary procedures.

At the time of the initial contact, the mother was expecting another child in three months. This situation, together with what appeared to be the desperate state of both mother and daughter,

prompted the staff to attempt an investigation of whether immediate help could be given through work with the mother. The duration of the study was necessarily limited.

Procedures and Results

In the initial interview with the mother, the above information
was secured. The mother was told that, although the investigators did
not know whether or not they could help her resolve such a problem
as scratching, they would be willing to try if she wished to cooperate
in a program that would require her to follow specific procedures at
home and to come weekly for a limited number of weeks with her
daughter to the laboratory. When the mother expressed eagerness to
cooperate, an appointment was made for her to bring Fay to the Laboratory Preschool the following week, after laboratory school hours.

Session 1

The first session began with a fifteen-minute introductory period
in the school playroom. While one investigator discussed tentative plans
with the mother at one end of the large room, Fay became engrossed
in the doll corner at the opposite end of the room. The other investigator attended and observed her. Following this brief introductory
period, Fay and her mother were taken to a clinic playroom equipped
with a one-way viewing screen. The mother had been instructed to
behave as normally as possible during a fifteen-minute observation
period, which would be followed by a conference. The investigators then
left the mother and child alone and went to the adjacent observation
room. Two significant behavioral conditions were evident to the observers. One, Fay was a highly capable and competent little girl with a
large repertoire of well-developed social, intellectual, and physical skills.
Two, the mother spoke to the child only to criticize, direct, or explain
why the child should behave in a different fashion.

At the close of the observation period, while Fay again played with
an investigator in the school playroom, the mother was asked to keep
a one-week record of the child's behavior as well as her own behavior
in response to the child. She was to note such things as how often Fay
scratched; how often she engaged in other behavior that mother disapproved of; how often she was spanked, isolated, scolded severely; how
often she engaged in behavior that the mother considered appropriate, and what this appropriate behavior was.

Subsequent sessions followed this pattern: one investigator worked with the mother while the other attended Fay's play indoors and out. The results of the mother's work during each week were in this way observable by the investigators, and they could give weekly recognition and approval to any progress by the mother as it was evidenced in the child's appearance and the mother's behavior.

Session 2

When the mother returned the following week, her records, though kept inconsistently, yielded significant information. First, there were periods in the day when the child did not scratch herself. These periods usually coincided with the times Fay was engaging in some constructive play activity. Secondly, the mother was berating and punishing the child for a wide range of so-called misdeeds: sauciness, dawdling, poor table manners, playing with certain neighborhood children of whom the mother disapproved, and many minor misdemeanors. Thirdly, even though the father punished Fay severely when she scratched herself to a bloody state, she and the father also had mutually enjoyable times together, both at home and on outings. By contrast, the mother, who was with the child a large portion of the day, never struck her, but verbally punished and criticized her continuously, perpetuating between herself and the child a constant state of friction. The mother stated again that she could hardly bear to look at Fay because of the angry state aroused by her daughter's unsightly appearance.

On the basis of the home observation records, two recommendations were made. One, the mother was not to attempt to change the father's behavior. It was pointed out that fathers differ from mothers in their methods of discipline. As long as the father and Fay had a good relationship in spite of the spankings, little would be accomplished by mother's direct attacks on father's disciplinary action. Mother agreed that this had already been demonstrated.

The second recommendation was that the mother discontinue her efforts to correct all instances of Fay's misbehavior and concentrate her efforts first on eliminating the one type of behavior that troubled the mother most: scratching. A carefully structured program was suggested. First, all scratching was to be ignored, no matter how bloody the results. Mother said that they had already tried this procedure for a whole month and it had not worked. When asked for details, she said that she and the father had informed Fay that they were no longer going to discuss the scratching. During this period Fay came to them frequently to show them that she had not scratched herself for a whole morning or a whole afternoon. Mother cited her own response to Fay on these occasions: "I told you, we're not going to talk about it. We don't care whether you scratch or not. You're a big girl and it's up to you. I don't want to hear any more about it." It was pointed out to the mother that she had ignored or even punished the appropriate behavior of not scratching, thereby missing an opportunity to strengthen the *desired* behavior. Ignoring the scratching, it was explained, meant giving absolutely no attention, positive or negative, to the child when she was actually scratching or had fresh evidence on her face and limbs of recent scratching. At all other times, Fay was to be given approval and attention for whatever commendable behavior was ongoing, such as play with dolls, helping set the table, looking at a book, and *not* scratching.

Although the previously cited studies in the laboratory preschool indicated that the approving attention of significant adults is a potent factor in shaping the behavior of young children, it seemed very difficult for this mother to attend to her child in a positive fashion. It was therefore decided to employ token reinforcements in addition to whatever social approval the mother could muster. For most young children gold stars are highly reinforcing; therefore, a system of token reinforcement was worked out as follows. Every twenty or thirty minutes, if Fay had not scratched during that interval, the mother was to go to Fay and approve her play in as warm a fashion as she was able, at the same time giving her a gold star to paste in a special little booklet. During the early days of the program every second or third gold star was to be accompanied by a primary reinforcer Fay liked, such as a cookie, a bit of candy, or a small glass of the child's favorite beverage. At midday and suppertime, if no scratching had occurred, the accumulated gold stars were to be counted, approved as an achievement, and reinforced by giving inexpensive trinkets which were pleasing to the child. The mother was to try this program for one week and report results at the weekly conference.

Session 3

In the third session, one week after the inception of reinforcement procedures, the mother reported that there had been some lessening of the scratching, but whatever progress had been made during the day seemed nullified at night, since Fay was still arriving at the breakfast

table with evidence of freshly scratched sores. The mother was discouraged.

In consideration of time limitations on the total program, it seemed
mandatory to find more powerful reinforcers at this point. A careful
inquiry into the sorts of playthings which were most pleasing to Fay
revealed that she frequently asked for items for her Barbie doll. Fortu-
nately these items are manufactured in endless variety. Furthermore,
the mother said that she was willing and able to pay for whatever Fay
might select. Therefore, it was planned that each afternoon of a scratch-
free day the mother and Fay would go shopping for the next morning's
reinforcer: a new Barbie doll item. Fay was to be allowed to choose
what she wanted. Then the mother was to put the item out of reach
but in plain view until the next morning. If there was no evidence of
fresh scratching in the morning, Fay was to be given the item. The
previous program of approving attention and gold stars, backed up by
trinkets, was also to be continued. On the fifth day of this week, the
mother spontaneously telephoned to report exuberantly that they had
had four scratch-free days and nights.

Session 4

When mother and child came in for the fourth session, two weeks
after beginning the reinforcement program, the mother pointed out that
some of the sores had begun to heal. For the first time, the mother
volunteered a description of newly discovered desirable behavior on
Fay's part. The mother was given much social reinforcement by the
investigator for her careful maintenance of the program. In addition,
of course, she was already being highly reinforced by Fay's improved
appearance and by Fay's evident efforts to please her.

The program continued for the next week with steady diminution
of the sores.

Near the end of this third week of reinforcement procedures, the
mother telephoned one of the investigators to report with despair that
the whole program had fallen apart. Fay had scratched herself during
the night and drawn blood in several places. The father had flown into
a frenzy in the morning and had spanked Fay until he left red marks.
Both parents were ready to abandon the program as futile. The mother
was asked to review the preceding day step by step. The reason for Fay's
"backsliding" soon became evident.

When the mother and Fay had gone to the store to buy a Barbie
accessory, the item Fay selected cost more money than the mother had

with her. Five-year-olds, of course, have scant knowledge of the importance of various amounts of money. Fay insisted on the item she had chosen. Mother became irritated at what seemed to her highly unreasonable behavior and told Fay she would take what mother bought and like it. Fay did not like it and began to sulk. The mother bought the item anyway and put it on the customary shelf while Fay silently watched. That night Fay scratched open all of the nearly healed areas on her face. As the whole complex of interacting behavior on the part of both mother and Fay was sorted out, the mother of her own accord volunteered the probable explanation for reinstatement of the nearly extinguished scratching behavior. The mother was asked to take Fay the next day to buy the desired item and also to be sure to go adequately prepared on future buying expeditions.

Session 5

According to the mother's report in Session 5, a high point for her came shortly after the above episode, when the father said that he wanted her to help him refrain from beating Fay when he was angry. He said that he had known all along that beatings had not been effective. Yet when nothing else worked, he beat the child because he felt impelled to take some kind of action. The mother was advised to arrange with the father, in some calm moment, a cue she might give him when she saw him on the verge of losing control with Fay; for example, "Dear, will you please get a loaf of bread from the corner store?"

The next two weeks (fourth and fifth weeks of reinforcement procedures) went smoothly with no really low periods occurring. The parents could now, the mother reported, sit down together and discuss Fay without each accusing the other of employing faulty discipline. Fay's lesions continued to heal and to diminish in size.

Session 6

In the sixth session, when Fay's skin was practically clear of scabs, it seemed advisable to start a gradual reduction of extrinsic reinforcers. First, the mother was instructed to omit one by one the mid-morning and mid-afternoon trinkets, at the same time maintaining a high level of social approval of all desirable behavior. Then the daily trips for Barbie doll accessories were to be made every other day; then bi-weekly, weekly, and finally only occasionally, when a whole page of stars would be exchanged for one item. The gold stars were retained largely because they seemed to be effective in reminding the mother to take overt notice of the many examples of desirable behavior shown by her little girl. Fay, too, was reported to be highly reinforced by filling the pages of her book with stars. However, the pleasure of her parents' approval of her many skills and her pretty appearance, coupled with the reduction of punishment by both mother and father, may have been sufficiently instrumental in maintaining Fay's nonscratching behavior.

Session 7

At the end of six weeks of the mother's using reinforcement procedures, every sore was healed completely, although there remained vividly red scars, especially on the one cheek and chin. Session 7 was the terminal session of the training program. Had circumstances permitted, the experimenters thought it would have been advisable to continue the sessions until the mother had completed her reduction of extrinsic reinforcement. Four months later, however, when Fay and her mother were seen at home in order to secure a post-check on the guidance procedures, the scars had faded to a pale pink barely discernible without close scrutiny.

Results of the study suggest that a young child's problem behavior may be treated through helping the mother to modify her own behavior, that is, through direct action guidance. Moreover, the behavior of self-scratching proved to be under the control of its immediate social consequences. Further investigation of direct action approaches seems to offer a promising extension of the treatment methods available to child guidance specialists.

References

Allen, K. E., Hart B., Buell, J. S., et al. (1964). Effects of social reinforcement on isolate behavior of a nursery school child. *Child Development* 35:511–518.

Ayllon, T., and Haughton, E. (1962). Control of the behavior of schizophrenic patients by food. *Journal of the Experimental Analysis of Behavior* 5:343–352.

Harris, F. R., Johnston, M. K., Kelley, C. S., and Wolf, M. M. (1964a). Effects of positive social reinforcement on regressed crawling of a nursery school child. *Journal of Educational Psychology* 55:35–41.

Harris, F. R., Wolf, M. M., and Baer, D. M. (1964b). Effects of adult social reinforcement on child behavior. *Young Child* 20:8–17.

Hart, B. M., Allen, K. E., Buell, J. S., et al. (1964). Effects of social reinforcement on operant crying. *Journal of Experimental Child Psychology*
1:145-153.

Johnston, M. K., Kelley, C. S., Harris, F. R., and Wolf, M. M. (1966). An
application of reinforcement principles to development of motor skills of
a young child. *Child Development.*

Walton, D. (1960). The application of learning theory to the treatment of a
case of neurodermatitis. In *Behaviour Therapy and the Neuroses*, ed. H. J.
Eysenck, pp. 272-274. Oxford, England: Pergamon.

Wolf, M. M., Birnbrauer, J. S., Williams, T., and Lander, J. (1965). A note on
apparent extinction of the vomiting behavior of a retarded child. In *Case
Studies in Behavior Modification*, ed. L. P. Ullmann and L. Krasner, pp.
364-366. New York: Holt, Rinehart & Winston.

Wolf, M. M., Risley, T., and Mees, H. (1964). Application of operant conditioning procedures to the behavior problems of an autistic child.
Behaviour Research and Therapy 1:305-312.

PART IV
Immature Behaviors

23

Crying and Colic

T. BERRY BRAZELTON

Different adaptive purposes for the cry of the human infant are apparent soon after birth. The physiologic and neurologic reorganization of extrauterine existence may be speeded by the cry-startle-cry response in the neonate. Crying is likely to test and to speed up extrauterine cardiopulmonary function. As a response to physiologic needs—hunger, discomfort, and the need for temperature change—it serves different purposes. A parent will be likely to respond to each of these cries, learning very early to differentiate their etiology in the infant (Boukydis and Burgess 1982, Bowlby 1969). As these demands are met by the parent, a conditioning element is added. The infant soon learns to "expect" a response from the environment that will relieve his[1] need. The parent in turn expects that her intervention will relieve the infant's crying (Brazelton 1962).

Because the "paroxysmal fussing" that was first described by Wessel and colleagues (1954) begins in a majority of infants soon after arrival at home, new parents are likely to feel responsible for alleviating it. This crying is likely to occur at discrete periods during the day and is relieved briefly by picking up, comforting, feeding, and carrying. The cry characteristics of this fussing are different from cries of pain and other forms of distress (Lester 1976). Barr and his colleagues have demonstrated that a significant proportion of this kind of fussing can be reduced by maternal carrying for part of the day (Hunziker and Barr

---

[1] In general, I shall use the masculine pronoun for the infant, the feminine for the parent.

1986). This same "paroxysmal fussing" can be compounded by environmental tension (Stewart 1954). When parents are unable to quiet their crying baby, their tension is bound to build. For understandable reasons, the cycle of fussy crying is likely to build into more prolonged and insistent crying. Crying in the infant represents a failure in appropriate nurturing to most new, young parents. Their anxious efforts to compensate create extra stimuli for the newborn, and the resulting tension is added to his innate reason for crying. An ever increasing cycle leads to excessive crying or "infantile colic." The etiology of the original crying is superseded by the tense, overloaded nervous system of an immature baby. The intestinal tract becomes hypersensitive and hyperactive, as do the rest of the autonomic and central nervous systems, as this tension in the infant and the environment builds up (Brazelton 1985).

This cycle has led to a need for definition of paroxysmal fussing as it is differentiated from "colic" or excessive crying. Barr and colleagues (1989) have demonstrated that the amount and duration of crying bouts are susceptible to manipulation by the environment. In 1962, having been impressed with the importance of the regular cyclical crying at the end of each day that occurs in most infants, I studied a group of eighty "normal" infants. Their parents kept three months of detailed records for me (see Figure 23-1) of their infants' crying (Brazelton 1962).

In the second week (the first week at home) there was a median of one and three-quarter hours of crying, with a spread of half an hour in the upper quartile and twenty minutes in the lower quartile. There was a gradual increase to a peak median of two and three-quarter hours at 6 weeks, with a decrease in quantity of crying thereafter.

At 3 weeks of age, a spread of fussing is recorded throughout the day, with major concentration from 6:00 to 11:00 P.M. This is the period when the father is at home, the mother is physically more exhausted, and other siblings are making more demands. Other humps occur in the early morning (4:00 to 7:00 A.M.) and later morning (9:00 to 11:00 A.M.).

At 6 weeks of age, the concentration of crying is more marked at the end of the day, with a small hump in the early morning. The period from 3:00 P.M. to midnight is now seen as the interval in which the long periods of crying and fussing occur in over half the infants. This would seem to emphasize the environmental influence on the timing of these "fussy" periods. Many parents consciously attempted to manipulate the timing of these periods so that they occurred at a time when the rest of the family could tolerate the crying.

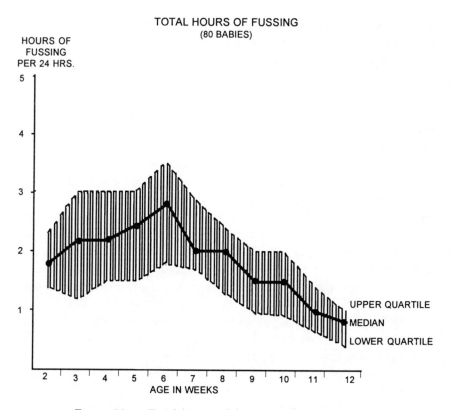

Figure 23-1. Total hours of fussing in normal infants.

At 10 weeks of age, the infants were quieting down to a marked extent, and there were two intervals—6:00 A.M. to noon and 5:00 to 11:00 P.M.—when the much reduced crying occurred.

In summarizing the total amount of crying in two extreme groups (the heavy and the light fussers) it became apparent that their other activity also markedly differed. In particular, their extranutritional sucking activity deviated greatly from the averages reported previously for the same ages. The total amount of sucking in these two groups seemed to bear a reliable inverse relationship to the total amount of crying.

Mothers commented that their infants seemed to substitute finger-sucking for fussing at certain times and that a pacifier could reduce the total amount of crying (cf. Levine and Bell 1950). On observation, this substitute sucking pertained only to moderate crying, and sucking would not become a substitute for more intense fussing. This observation seemed pertinent to the inverse correlation that seemed to exist between the total amount of crying in these infants and their ability to discharge this energy in other activity (such as sucking) in the early weeks.

Coincident with the decrease in crying, which started by 8 weeks, was an increase in other activity, such as sucking, cooing, watching hands, turning over, and so on. Extranutritional sucking was below average for the first 7 weeks, but by 10 weeks had increased to two and a half hours a day. The average for this age group was two hours. Whether these new activities represent an improvement in the neuromuscular organization and in the ability of the infant to satisfy his needs in other ways than by crying, or whether there is a decrease in the gross tension accumulated and less need for such a total kind of discharge as crying, is not answerable by these data. The cumulative time spent in these two types of oral activity (crying and sucking) increases over the twelve-week period and does not suggest a decrease in total activity output. That the overall organization of the babies in this group may be proceeding rapidly in other ways is suggested by the fact that night feedings were given up by these babies one and a half weeks before they were given up by the quieter babies.

The amount of total oral activity in these fussier babies, as evidenced by the sum of crying plus sucking, is reliably different and averages one hour more than the total in the quieter babies. This suggests a more vigorous congenital activity type, or one that is more sensitive to accumulated tension in the former group.

This study led me to reconsider the importance of this fussy, irritable period at the end of the day. Because it was so common in our culture, and seemed to be present in other carrying cultures as well (Barr et al. 1989, Brazelton 1972), it deserved a more physiological explanation. The combination of a sensitive organism and a tense parent could certainly heighten and prolong the crying at the end of the day. The inevitability of this cyclical crying seemed to deserve a more normative explanation.

The fact that this irritable crying period began between 2 and 3 weeks, and seemed to disappear by 12 weeks, was of significant interest. The cyclical evening aspect seemed to point to its purpose as a discharge phenomenon. Parents reported that the baby was better organized after this period was over—sleeping better, eating more effectively, and so on. The organization of state behavior seems to be paralleled by this use of a crying period at the end of the day. The cycling of feeding, sleep, and wakefulness improves at 3 weeks. By the end of the regular fussy period at 10 to 12 weeks, the baby's nervous system has matured more effectively and other behaviors can be substituted for the crying period.

That an immature newborn would make efforts to maintain responsive periods during a twenty-four-hour period seemed obvious as one observed the infant. Even as a newborn, a well-organized baby made efforts to hold down his or her interfering motor responses in order to pay prolonged attention to one's face and voice. In a twenty-four-hour day, there were many such periods of attention, but they seemed to be at some physiological cost to the small babies. The cost to a baby of overloading his receptive and motor central nervous system seemed obvious. The harder a baby worked, the more he seemed to need to disintegrate afterward. Crying at the end of the day began to look to me as if it were a regulatory mechanism that allowed a developing infant to balance the costly but vital mechanisms he was mastering as he learned to control his states of attention (Brazelton 1962). The babies learned to master their reflex motor activities in order to pay prolonged attention to information from the environment, but it was at some cost to them. After a period of discharge by crying, an infant would sleep more deeply and effectively, and he was again available with more prolonged and effective periods of interaction with the environment. Many parents made the association that the fussy period turned into a socially interactive period as the infants developed more and more social competence from the age of 10 to 12 weeks. The reason these crying periods appeared limited to three months seemed to coincide with increasing competence of an infant's central nervous system (CNS) to respond to and handle sensorimotor responses in other ways. In a period of social interaction, a baby was now able to pay prolonged attention. A baby could smile and gurgle, in long trains of responsive behavior, without overloading his systems.

However, we do feel that there is a group of hypersensitive, hyperreactive newborns who can be predicted to do more crying than might be expected, to cry more easily, and to be more difficult to console. These babies (approximately 10 percent) show a combination of the following:

(1) Hypersensitivity or overreactivity to stimuli:
   (a) Their ability to habituate to stimuli in semi-sleep states is poor;

    (b) Their reactivity to stimuli throughout the exam shows evi-
        dence of overreactivity, such as repeated startling and avert-
        ing of the eyes, exhaustion after stimulation, and attempt-
        ing to sleep or cry in order to shut out stimuli;
(2) Poor state control:
    (a) An inability to maintain quiet alertness for any relatively
        long period;
    (b) Shooting from quiet states to crying and back again to an
        exhausted state, with either a very short latency or a lag and
        prolonged latency, or maintenance of insulated crying states
        in the face of social stimulation;
(3) Poor consolability when upset either by themselves or by the
    examiner;
(4) Increased amount of irritability over the total twenty- to thirty-
    minute exam.

A combination of any two or all of these findings in the neonate
exam seems likely to predict a baby who could become colicky.

Intervention in the neonatal period can involve sharing the preceding findings with the parents before discharge. When a baby over-
shoots or cannot maintain an alert, steady state, he may start crying
more quickly than one would expect. A baby ends up by demonstrating a kind of overreactivity to all social stimuli, as well as lability of
state behavior. This defines him as a labile, hard-to-control baby, and
it can be predicted that he will cry often, especially at the end of the
day. As I demonstrate the hypersensitivity and the labile state behavior, I describe it to the parents without using pejorative language. A
description of this behavior might be, "He certainly shoots from sleeping to crying in a hurry." The mother will then say, "I've found that,
too. What do I do about it?" Because I do not know what to do about
it at that point, I reply, "I'm not sure yet, but you and I will need to
keep in communication so we can help him work it out. As he gets
older, he may well learn how to control it himself; if he doesn't, we
may have to work to teach him." In this way, I am trying to ally myself with the mother in "our" work with the baby to help him learn
smoother state control.

The other symptoms of hypersensitivity are handled similarly, in
order to help the parents see that these are a part of the baby himself,
and to set the goals for our work helping him mature toward a
smoother, more comfortable organization. If the parents can see that
these mechanisms reside in their baby, they will not be at the mercy of

the inevitable feeling that an infant's crying and irritability are symptoms of their own failure as parents. After sharing the baby's behavior during the behaviors elicited by the neonatal assessment, I urge the parents to communicate with me about the progress they are making toward handling their infant. I discuss the daily crying that may occur in the second or third week. We speak of it as if it may well become part of a baby's daily cycle and as serving an organizing purpose. I assure them that this kind of crying need not be representative of any other pathology, such as neurological or gastrointestinal pain, or else they will worry about these later, and I shall need to remind them of my having accounted for them in my exam. We discuss other kinds of crying at this time. I anticipate with them the quality of the cries an infant may have that will represent pain, hunger, discomfort, and sleepiness, and we talk briefly about what their own parental responses should be to each of these.

As the regular crying period develops at 2 to 3 weeks, I expect a phone call from the parents. We discuss the way in which to differentiate this predictable crying from one that needs attention. We attempt to rule out a cry of pain and distress. Our differentiating criteria become:

1. If the crying period appears at a regular time of day;
2. If the crying stops when the baby is picked up or played with;
3. If it starts as an irritable whimper and only gradually builds up to an intense cry;
4. If it can be interrupted easily.

When I make recommendations about how to handle the type of crying that may be occurring, they are based on the kind of baby we have shared initially, and the parents know that I know their baby. If I am assured by their description that this crying does not represent real pain or discomfort and that there is no real pathology behind it, I suggest instituting a routine to help allay their fears and to help the baby with his or her crying period. This routine will consist of

1. Trying to find a reason for a baby's cry;
2. If this is unsuccessful, allowing him to fuss for ten to fifteen minutes at a time;
3. Picking the infant up to soothe him; afterward,
4. Feeding him water or sweetened water to give him a chance at extra sucking; and
5. Trying to bring up a bubble.

Then I suggest reducing stimuli at this time of the day. Carrying him during the day; soft, low-keyed music; swaddling the infant, coupled with other attempts to teach the infant how to calm himself, including a pacifier or thumbsucking, may be of real help. I accompany these suggestions with a repetition of our original observation of the hypersensitivity and state lability of a baby and an understanding of the activity cycle to include the fussing period at the end of the day.

Crying in an infant can be a reflection of an unreachable baby. We (Als et al. 1976) found a group of babies who were small for gestational age by ponderal index (a relationship of length to weight) (Miller and Hassanein 1971). In these babies, the placenta had been inadequate in nurturing the baby at the end of the pregnancy. They were skinny, lean, and worried looking. Their fat and subcutaneous tissue stores were depleted, and they had loose, peeling skin. As neonates, these infants had poor motor tone and low activity levels. They showed poor responsiveness to social stimuli—to the face and voice and to being cuddled—and showed poor responses to being consoled. In the first two weeks, they preferred to be left alone. We felt that they were already overwhelmed by any stimulation from the environment. Their frowns in response to social stimuli indicated how easily they were overstimulated by usual social cues. They looked exhausted after a short period of interaction. We felt that, as a group, they were hypersensitive babies and were more easily overloaded and exhausted by social interaction. As newborns, their mothers claimed they were quiet, "good, and preferred to be left alone." If their mothers played with them too much, they would frown or go to sleep. If they played with them at feeding time, these babies would spit up. Therefore, their mothers left them alone, and they rarely cried in the first three weeks.

Beginning at 3 weeks of age and lasting to 16 weeks, the mothers reported long, unreachable crying periods. We felt that the costly hypersensitivity that accompanied their undernourished state at birth resulted in hypersensitive, crying babies later on. As they became stronger, their "shutting out" of stimuli took the form of crying rather than quiet sleeping. This group of babies may represent one end of a spectrum of normal infants who have a neurophysiological hypersensitivity at birth. Crying may be one of their few ways of dealing with this problem. We have since recognized other groups of such infants in our clinical work, and there are probably many etiological reasons, in addition to poor nutrition, for hypersensitivity and the crying that results from it.

Intractable crying or colic may be a reflection of pathology in the parents, as well. A depressed or an anxious mother may certainly contribute to a breakdown in parenting in which the baby begins to cry for long, inconsolable periods. The emotional state of the parents needs to be a serious consideration in the treatment of "colic."

We have found clinically that using the concept of prevention, rather than therapy after intractable colic or crying periods are in place, can reduce significantly the duration of the crying periods at the end of the day for most parent–infant triads.

References

Als, H., Tronick, E., Adamson, L., and Brazelton, T. B. (1976). The behavior of the full term yet underweight newborn. *Developmental Medicine and Child Neurology* 18:590.

Barr, R. G., Spiess, H., McMullan, S. J., et al. (1989). *Carrying as Colic Therapy: A Randomized Controlled Trial.* Paper presented at the meeting of the Society for Behavioral Pediatrics, November.

Boukydis, C. F. Z., and Burgess, R. (1982). Adult physiologic response to infant cries: effects of temperament of infant, parental status and gender. *Child Development* 53:1291–1298.

Bowlby, J. (1969). *Attachment and Loss*, vol. I, *Attachment*. New York: Basic Books.

Brazelton, T. B. (1962). Crying in infancy. *Pediatrics* 29:579–588.

——— (1972). Implications of infant development among the Mayan indians of Mexico. *Human Development* 15:90–111.

——— (1985). Application of cry research to clinical perspectives. In *Infant Crying*, ed. B. M. Lester and C. F. Z. Boukydis, pp. 325–340. New York: Plenum.

Hunziker, U. A., and Barr, R. G. (1986). Increased carrying reduces infant crying: randomized control trial. *Pediatrics* 77:641–648.

Lester, B. M. (1976). Spectrum analysis of the cry sounds of well nourished and malnourished infants. *Child Development* 47:237.

Levine, M. I., and Bell, A. I. (1950). Treatment of colic in infants by the use of a pacifier. *Journal of Pediatrics* 37:750.

Miller, H. C., and Hassanein, K. (1971). Diagnosis of impaired fetal growth in newborn infants. *Pediatrics* 48:4.

Stewart, A. (1954). Excessive Infant crying (colic) in relation to parent behavior. *American Journal of Psychiatry* 110:687–693.

Wessel, M. A., Cobb, J. C., Jackson, E. B., et al. (1954). Paroxysmal fussing in infancy: sometimes called "colic." *Pediatrics* 14:421–434.

24

Operant Crying

BETTY M. HART, K. EILEEN ALLEN, JOAN S. BUELL,
FLORENCE R. HARRIS, AND MONTROSE M. WOLF

The application of reinforcement principles as a preschool guidance technique under field conditions has recently come under study (Allen et al. 1964, Harris et al. 1964, Johnston et al. 1963). Other applications made under field conditions in hospital situations include Wolf's treatment of autism in a child (Wolf et al. 1964) and Ayllon's work with psychotic patients (Ayllon and Haughton 1962). The present chapter deals with the application of reinforcement principles to two cases of "operant crying."

Two classes of crying behavior seem readily discriminable on an "intuitive" basis by almost every teacher and parent: *respondent crying* and *operant crying*. Criteria for each class can be defined in terms of its dependent variables. Respondent crying occurs in response to a sudden unexpected and/or painful stimulus event. In general, preschool teachers assume crying to be respondent if the child has a hard or sudden fall; if he falls in an awkward position or is caught in equipment; if he is forced down and pummeled by a larger child; or if he has just faced a dire, unexpected event, such as a near accident. Teachers attend at once to respondent crying. Operant crying, on the other hand, is emitted and/or maintained depending upon its effects on the social environment. In general, the most clear-cut indication that a crying episode is operant rather than respondent is that the child looks around momentarily and makes eye contact with an adult before he begins to cry. An increase in the volume and intensity of the child's cry when an adult fails to attend immediately, together with the child's neither calling nor coming for help, provides other criteria for operant crying. Crying that is initially respondent may readily become operant.

Since by 3 years of age children vary widely in their patterns of response to pain/fear situations, any reasonably exact discrimination between respondent and operant crying of an individual child can be made only on the basis of close daily observation of his crying behavior.

This chapter presents two studies of the systematic use of positive social reinforcement to help children showing a high rate of operant crying to acquire more effective behavior in mildly distressful situations. Although the studies were conducted at different times, procedures and recording methods were the same in each.

Method

Subjects

Both subjects were enrolled in the Laboratory Preschool at the University of Washington. Both were in the same group, which included eight boys and eight girls of similar age (4 to 4½), socioeconomic level (upper middle class), and intelligence (above average). All children attended school five mornings a week for approximately two and a half hours.

Subject 1

The first subject, Bill, was 4 years and 1 month old when he entered school. He was a tall, healthy, handsome child with well-developed verbal, social, and motor skills. Outdoors he ran, climbed, and rode a tricycle with energy and agility; indoors he made use of all the available materials, though he appeared to prefer construction materials such as blocks, or imaginative play in the housekeeping corner, to activities such as painting or working with clay. His verbalizations to both teachers and children were characterized by persuasive and accurate use of vocabulary, and frequently demonstrated unusually sophisticated conceptualizations. He and many of the other children who entered nursery school at the same time had been together in a group situation the previous year and were thus fairly well acquainted. His former teachers had described Bill as a child eagerly sought by other children as a playmate. His capability and desirability as a playmate were immediately evident at the beginning of the second year. He moved almost directly into play with two other boys, and with his many good ideas structured one play situation after another with them, situations which often lasted an entire morning. Bill was frequently observed arbitrating differences of opinion between his playmates, insisting on his own way of doing things, or defending his own rights and ideas; nearly always, he did so verbally rather than physically.

In the first few days of school, teachers noted that in spite of Bill's sophisticated techniques for dealing with children, he cried more often during the morning than any other child in school. If he stubbed his toe while running or bumped his elbow on a piece of furniture, he cried until a teacher went to him. If he fell down, or if he was frustrated or threatened with any kind of physical attack by another child, he screamed and cried; all play, his and his companions', stopped until Bill had had several minutes of comfort from a teacher. In view of his advanced verbal and social skills, teachers questioned whether his crying was due to actual injury or maintained by adult attention.

Subject 2

The second subject, Alan, lacked two weeks of being 4 years old when he entered the Preschool. He was enrolled in the same 4-year-old group as Bill. Unlike Bill, however, Alan was new to the group and therefore had had no previous acquaintance with any of the children. He spent most of the first month of school exploring with vigor all the equipment, materials, and social situations the school had to offer. He climbed, rode trikes, swung and dug, with skill and application. His use of creative materials was free and imaginative; his block-buildings were complex, intricately balanced structures. With children and adults he spoke confidently and assertively, often demanding that they listen to a lengthy story or fulfill his requests immediately. He defended himself both verbally and physically, holding on tenaciously to a possession or saying, "Don't!" over and over. Sometimes he forcibly appropriated an object from another child, calling names when the child resisted; but though he was the physical equal or superior of most of the others, he rarely attacked another child. He was attractive and vivacious as well as skillful. By the end of the first six weeks of school he was playing as an integral member of one or more groups of children every morning.

Though he did not cry quite as often as Bill, Alan cried equally as hard over much the same kinds of bumps and falls. Like Bill, he screamed and cried whenever another child succeeded in appropriating an object in his possession. He was observed to endure shoving and even hitting by a child smaller than he but to cry vociferously at a push by a child equal to him in size and strength. Though Alan's crying was noted from the beginning of school, the staff thought that Alan should fully adapt to the school situation and develop in play skills before any procedures were undertaken to deal directly with his crying behavior.

In dealing with both Alan and Bill, a distinction was made between respondent and operant crying. Teachers had observed that neither was unjustifiably aggressive; both could defend themselves, were physically strong and large relative to the group, and had better than average physical, verbal, and social skills. Neither had injured himself or been injured by another child in the group. Both were often observed to make momentary eye contact with a teacher before beginning to cry, and the cries of both rapidly increased in volume until a teacher attended to them. Teachers agreed that both children would benefit if the frequency of crying episodes could be decreased and if more appropriate responses to mild pain and frustration could be developed.

Recording of Crying Episodes

In both cases the operant crying behavior was recorded by a teacher using a pocket counter. She depressed the lever on the counter once for each crying episode. A crying episode was defined as a cry (a) loud enough to be heard at least 50 feet away and (b) of 5 seconds or more duration. At the end of the day the total number of crying episodes was recorded and plotted on a cumulative graph.

Procedures for Presenting and Withdrawing Reinforcers

For ten days before initiating reinforcement–extinction procedures, the number of Bill's operant crying episodes per morning was to be recorded in order to obtain a baseline record of the operant level of the behavior. This was done at the end of his first month of school. A baseline record of Alan's daily crying episodes was similarly planned several months later, after Alan had attended school for three months.

For each child, extinction of operant crying was to be instituted immediately after these data had been secured. Teachers were to ignore each child's operant cries, neither going to him, speaking to him, nor looking at him while he was crying, except for an initial glance in order to assess the situation. If he was in close proximity to a teacher when he began to cry, she was to turn her back or walk away to be busy with another child. However, every time that either child responded in a more appropriate manner after a fall, scrape, push, or dispossession, however minor, he was immediately to be given much teacher attention and approval.

In order to substantiate the hypothesis that the operant crying of these children was truly a function of adult reinforcement, it was judged necessary, if the extinction process was successful, to reinstate the behavior. At first teachers were to give attention to every approximation to a cry, such as whimpering and sulking; then, if and when the behavior was reestablished in strength, they were to go to the child immediately every time he began to cry and give him solicitous attention for several minutes.

If and when operant crying had again reached a level similar to that of the baseline period, it was again to be extinguished. The procedures of the first extinction period were to be reinstituted, teachers ignoring all operant cries by turning away or focusing their attention elsewhere. At the same time, they were to reinforce the boys for all verbal responses emitted during mild pain or frustration. As the second extinction progressed, teachers were gradually to refine the criteria for reinforcement to "appropriate" verbal responses, and differentially reinforce more socially acceptable verbal behavior evoked by minor injuries and frustrations. Threats and name-calling were to be ignored, and attention given only for such verbalizations as "Stop that," "That hurts," "Ouch!" or explanation of prior possession.

Results

Subject 1

As can be seen in the baseline period for Bill (see Figure 24-1), at the beginning of the study he was crying five to ten times every morning at school. Within five days after introduction of extinction procedures his operant crying decreased to between zero and two episodes per day. When continuous adult attention was again given to all operant cries and approximations to cries, the baseline rate of crying episodes was soon reestablished. Then, four days after reintroduction of extinction for operant crying, the behavior was practically eliminated.

Subject 2

Alan's rate of operant crying during the baseline period (see Figure 24-2) averaged about five episodes per morning. As with Bill, Alan's crying episodes decreased to two or fewer per day within five days after the introduction of extinction procedures. The behavior again

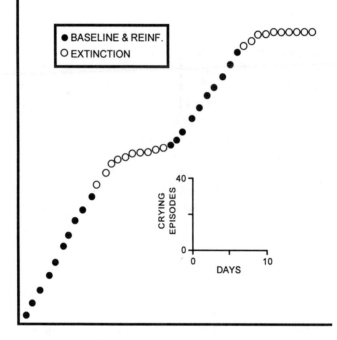

Figure 24–1. Cumulative record of daily operant crying episodes of Subject 1, Bill.

reached a level nearly as high as baseline four days after reinforcement of operant crying was reinstituted, and maintained approximately this level for six days. On the eleventh day of reinstatement of operant crying, the behavior suddenly decreased to one or fewer episodes per day (Day 28, Figure 24–2). After continuing reinforcement procedures for seven more days, teachers decided that, though their attention may have initially reinstated the behavior, other uncontrolled factors in the environment had apparently led to its cessation. Therefore, systematic reinforcement techniques were discontinued (after Day 35 on Figure 24–2). However, very soon the behavior reappeared and gradually increased in frequency until on the fiftieth day it had reached a frequency almost double that of the baseline period. Extinction procedures were again introduced (on Day 51, Figure 24–2). The rate of operant crying dropped much more gradually this time than had Bill's: there was a burst on the fifty-sixth day, and it was not until ten days later that operant crying episodes stabilized at one or fewer per day.

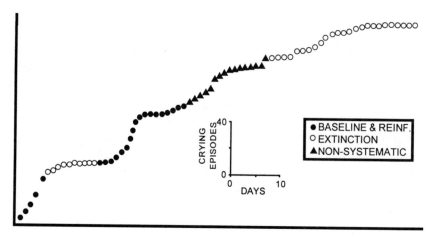

Figure 24-2. Cumulative record of daily operant crying episodes of Subject 2, Alan.

Discussion

During the extinction periods for both Bill and Alan, teachers noticed no unexpected side effects. They had anticipated that play would become more rewarding to both children once the frequent interruptions for crying episodes were eliminated. Each of the children, during the extinction periods, sustained a cooperative, sometimes directing, role in play. Each appeared to become more constructively absorbed in such play, often to the point of appearing oblivious to persons outside the realm of the imaginative play situation.

Subject 1

After Bill's operant crying was reinstated and his play was again being interrupted six or seven times a morning for operant crying episodes, teachers began to notice occasional signs of impatience on his part. Even as teachers comforted him and he continued to shriek, he sometimes turned away from their comfort, though he did not leave. Also, the extent of the interruption of his play seemed more noticeable than it had during the baseline period. At that time his companions had often ignored, or retreated from, his crying episodes. During the reinstatement period they usually remained near Bill, watching him throughout the episode. Teachers thought that the powerful reinforcement that Bill obtained from play with his companions greatly contributed to the rapidity of the second extinction process.

Subject 2

After Alan's operant crying had risen during the reinstatement period to a rate equal to that of the baseline period, the sudden disappearance of the behavior was completely unexpected. Teachers continued to reinforce all cries and approximations to cries for seven more days before deciding that some other factor in the environment had apparently decreased Alan's operant crying. Only after reinforcement procedures had been discontinued and the behavior had begun to reappear did teachers reflect on the possible significance of particular behaviors they had observed during the reinstatement period. At that time they had noticed that Alan often screwed up his face as though about to emit a loud cry when he was in close proximity to them. In accordance with the reinforcement procedures in effect, they immediately offered him comfort, and frequently he did not actually cry (only audible cries were counted in the data). One day, for example, Alan was climbing on an iron frame, a teacher watching him. As he climbed down from the frame he screwed up his face and clutched his ankle. The teacher approached at once, asked what had happened and comforted him. Alan explained that he had bumped his ankle, and then said, "I'm going to do that [climb the frame] again." As he descended the frame a second time, Alan bumped his leg and, looking at the teacher, emitted a low whimper. The teacher immediately comforted him, whereupon he again climbed the frame, and again bumped himself descending. On none of these occasions did Alan actually cry. It appeared, upon subsequent reflection, that Alan did not need to cry: he had apparently effectively "shaped up" a teacher to give him comfort and attention whenever he merely looked as if he were about to cry.

When systematic reinforcement procedures were discontinued and Alan's "looking as if he were about to cry" was no longer given immediate adult attention and comfort, full-scale operant crying reappeared and was apparently reinforced in the period that followed, on some sort of unsystematic intermittent schedule. The rate of operant crying increased irregularly; the decline in rate after several days of a rise in rate might possibly be correlated with (a) teachers' having inadvertently put the behavior on extinction for a time after it became aversive to them, and (b) such frequent interruptions in Alan's play that his playmates moved away from him and into other activities. These intervals of extinction, if such they were, were not, however, planned procedures.

After systematic extinction procedures were reinstated, Alan's operant crying behavior extinguished much more gradually than had

Bill's. A possible cause was the preceding unsystematic intermittent schedule of reinforcement in Alan's case. In the literature (e.g., Ferster and Skinner 1957), it has been well demonstrated that extinction after a continuous schedule of reinforcement is more rapid than after an intermittent schedule.

Though many of the findings concerning Alan's operant crying are still conjectural, the data from the studies seem to demonstrate that frequent crying may be largely a function of social reinforcement. The implications for parents and teachers in helping children to behave more appropriately appear evident.

References

Allen, K. E., Hart, B. M., Harris, F. R., and Wolf, M. M. (1964). Effects of social reinforcement on isolate behavior of a preschool child. *Child Development.*

Ayllon, T., and Haughton, E. (1962). Control of the behavior of schizophrenic patients by food. *Journal of the Experimental Analysis of Behavior* 5:343–352.

Ferster, C. B., and Skinner, B. F. (1957). *Schedules of Reinforcement.* New York: Appleton Century Crofts.

Harris, F. R., Johnston, M. S., Kelley, C. S., and Wolf, M. M. (1964). Effects of positive social reinforcement on regressed crawling in a preschool child. *Journal of Educational Psychology* 55:35–41.

Johnston, M. S., Kelley, C. S., Buell, J. S., et al. (1963). Effects of positive social reinforcement on isolate behavior of a nursery school child. Unpublished manuscript.

Wolf, M., Mees, H., and Risley, T. (1964). Application of operant conditioning procedures to the behavior problems of an autistic child. *Behaviour Research and Therapy* 2:305–312.

25

Multiple Childhood Sleep Disorders

V. MARK DURAND AND JODI A. MINDELL

Sleep disturbances commonly observed among young children include difficulty in falling asleep and persistent night waking. These disorders appear to represent chronic problems for a large number of children and their families. For example, Salzarulo and Chevalier (1983) found that, among clinic-referred children between the ages of 2 and 15, 23 percent experienced difficulty falling asleep and 28 percent exhibited frequent night wakings. Other studies of young children indicate that problems in falling asleep occur in 12.5 percent of 3-year-olds and 5 percent of 4-year-olds. Persistent night waking occurs in approximately 20 percent of 1- to 2-year-olds, 14 percent of 3-year-olds, and 8 percent of 4-year-olds (Jenkins et al. 1980, Richman 1981, Richman et al. 1975). These investigations indicate that a significant proportion of otherwise healthy children appear to exhibit serious sleep disruption.

Medical intervention appears to be a highly prevalent treatment of childhood sleep disturbances. Ounsted and Hendrick (1977) report that by 18 months of age, 25 percent of the first-born children in their study had been given sedatives for sleep problems. Yet, despite the prevalence of medical intervention for these problems, little empirical evidence is available demonstrating its effectiveness. Russo and colleagues (1976), for example, examined the effectiveness of diphenhydramine over a one-week period in fifty children aged 2 to 12. The drug was found to be more effective than a placebo in reducing sleep-onset latency and number of night wakings, but total time asleep was not affected. A more recent study (Richman 1985) investigated the use of trimeprazine tartrate (Vallergan Forte) in twenty-two children with chronic nighttime waking problems. Although the medication appeared initially to produce moderate improvements in night wakings, these gains were lost at a six-month follow-up. In general, use of medication as a treatment for nighttime sleep disturbances seems to be contraindicated.

Behavioral treatment of sleep problems among children has taken a variety of forms. Treatment for children who have difficulty falling asleep or who wake frequently during the night has involved procedures such as scheduled awakenings (e.g., Johnson et al. 1981, Johnson and Lerner 1985, Rickert and Johnson 1988) or extinction (e.g., Wolf et al. 1964, Yen et al. 1972). In a classic study, Williams (1959) described one 4-year-old boy who frequently had tantrums at bedtime. Treatment involved the withdrawal of parental attention for these nighttime tantrums. Although this intervention was initially successful, tantrums returned when the boy's grandmother attended to his disruptive behavior. Reinstatement of the contingencies again resulted in reduced tantrums at bedtime. Although extinction may effectively reduce nighttime disruption for some children, the study by Williams and research by others (see Rolider and Van Houten 1984) illustrates the difficulty parents and other guardians experience when asked to ignore the cries of a young child.

Although the effect of these sleep disorders on family life has not been extensively investigated, their disruptive influence has been described in clinical writings. For example, Ferber (1985) characterizes parents of children with chronic sleep problems as being "at the end of their rope" (p. 15) because of their own disturbed sleep patterns (due to their children's night wakings) and because of failed attempts to remedy their child's nighttime problems. Despite the obvious conclusion that nightly interruption of parental sleep would negatively affect family life, there currently are no experimental data on the effect of children's sleep disorders on family satisfaction.

Although group comparison studies of individual sleep disorders exist (e.g., Richman et al. 1985, Rickert and Johnson 1988), the present study is unique because it sought to evaluate the effectiveness of a simple behavioral intervention on the *multiple* sleep disorders (i.e., bedtime disturbance and night waking) of one young child. In addition, an evaluation was carried out on the effects of these sleep disturbances on the parents and subsequent changes following successful treatment of the child's sleep problems. Anticipated was an improvement in parental satisfaction measures (i.e., depression, marital satisfaction) following improvement in their child's sleep disturbances.

Method

Participants

The participants were a 14-month-old girl (Beth) and her natural parents. They were solicited for inclusion in this study through an advertisement in a local newspaper. Baseline measures indicated that Beth was going to sleep between 10:15 P.M. and 12:30 A.M. each night and was sleeping on the average of 7.8 hours per evening. Additionally, Beth was waking up from one to three times each evening. Her parents reported that she exhibited no other behavior problems at home or in her day-care setting. Beth was this intact couple's first child. Both parents had completed some college, and resided in a small city in upstate New York.

Procedure

The intervention was introduced sequentially, corresponding to a multiple baseline across sleep problems (i.e., bedtime disturbance and night waking) (Barlow and Hersen 1984).

Preassessment

Prior to the start of the treatment program, a ninety-minute interview was conducted with Beth's parents. Information was collected on the extent of her sleeping difficulties, possible initiating and maintaining variables, parental history of sleeping difficulties, parents' present sleeping behavior, and the impact of the child's sleep problems on the family. At this time the parents also completed the Beck Depression Inventory and the Dyadic Adjustment Scale. Prior to the start of treatment, a medical waiver was obtained from the child's pediatrician to rule out any possible medical cause for Beth's sleeping problems.

Baseline

During this and all subsequent phases, the parents were required to complete daily diaries of their own and their child's sleep habits. Additionally, on a weekly basis, the child's bedtime routine was videotaped. No instructions were given to the parents on how to handle their child's sleeping difficulties.

Treatment for Night Waking

Following the initial interview and three-week baseline period, possible maintaining factors for Beth's sleeping difficulties were identified. These factors included the parents' presence when Beth fell asleep and the parents attending to Beth following her required bedtime and during middle-of-the-night wakings. The first treatment phase targeted night wakings, because this was reported by the parents to be the most disruptive of Beth's sleep problems. A one-hour parent-training session was conducted during which Beth's parents were instructed on how to respond to her when she awoke at night. A modified version of Ferber's (1985) recommendations for intervention was used for this family. The treatment plan included having one of Beth's parents enter her room for a brief period when she woke (e.g., approximately fifteen to thirty seconds), at which time the parent was to provide reassurance (e.g., saying, "It's okay, go to sleep now," in a neutral tone of voice), check for any problems, then leave the room. This shorter visit for Beth's parents was suggested over that of Ferber's recommendations (two to three minutes) because it was felt that her parents could discriminate the briefer visit better than the longer visit. The parents were then told to wait progressively longer periods of time before reentering the child's room (i.e., in five-minute increments). On subsequent nights, the length of time was extended, with the longest period being twenty minutes before they should go into the room. The goal of this routine was to reduce the amount of attention given to Beth and to allow her to experience falling back to sleep by herself.

Treatment for Bedtime Disturbances

Two weeks after beginning treatment for night waking, treatment was implemented for Beth's bedtime problems. Typically, Beth would have a tantrum (e.g., loud screams, hitting furniture) for up to an hour prior to going to bed. Beth required a parent present in bed with her before falling asleep. Intervention for this problem was identical to the treatment for night waking. Her parents were instructed to put her to bed and to wait successively longer periods of time before going into her room if she were having a tantrum, only providing brief and neutral reassurance.

Dependent Measures

Child's Sleep

Several measures of Beth's sleep were collected. Her parents were asked to keep a daily diary including Beth's bedtime, the number of minutes between the time she was put to bed and the time she fell asleep, the time and length of all night wakings, and the total amount of sleep (including naps). Beth's bedtime routine was videotaped weekly to obtain information regarding maintaining factors of the sleep problems and problems with treatment implementation, as well as to monitor treatment progress. The integrity of treatment implementation was also assessed through these tapes for the bedtime treatment program.

The videotapes were also used to assess reliability of the diary data, and were scored by independent observers for the time Beth was put to bed and the time she fell asleep (a night-light was on in her room, permitting taping). It was found that the parents reported Beth's bedtime to be, on the average, ninety-three minutes later than the recordings indicated. In addition, they reported the time Beth fell asleep to be 24.5 minutes later than observed. However, there was no systematic bias across phases of treatment. In other words, the parents consistently noted that Beth went to bed and fell asleep later than actually occurred during the baseline period and all treatment phases.

Parental Measures

A number of measures of parental behavior were also obtained. Diaries of the parents' sleep were kept in a manner identical to the diaries kept on Beth's sleep. Additionally, measures of parental depression (Beck Depression Inventory: Beck et al. 1961) and marital satisfaction (Dyadic Adjustment Scale: Spanier 1976) were obtained from Beth's mother and father. All measures were administered during baseline, after treatment for night waking, after treatment for bedtime disturbances, and at one-, two-, and nine-month follow-ups.

Child's Sleep

Figure 25–1 illustrates the effects of treatment on Beth's night waking and bedtime. She averaged 71.1 minutes of night waking during baseline (range, 62 to 81), which was reduced to a mean of 16.5 minutes following treatment (range, 0 to 38). Follow-up observations revealed maintenance of these effects at one month (mean, 26.2 minutes, range 19 to 36), two months (mean, 2.0 minutes, range, 0 to 4), and nine months (mean, 19.4 minutes, range 2 to 69). In addition, the number of night wakings also was reduced from an average of 1.47 times per night during baseline (range, 0.86 to 2.4) to 0.69 times per night following treatment (range, 0.33 to 0.88). This reduction continued to be maintained at one-month (mean, 0.79, range, 0.57 to 1.29), two-month (mean, 0.15, range 0 to 0.29), and nine-month follow-ups (mean, 0.72, range, 0.14 to 2.3).

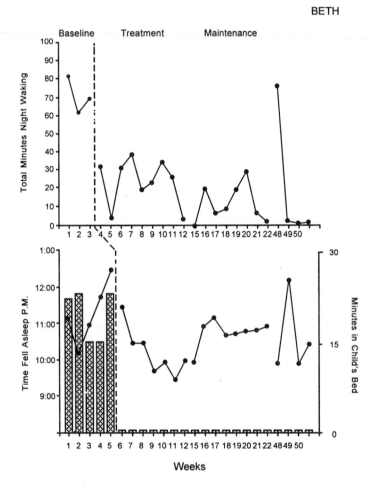

Figure 25-1. The filled circles in the top graph represent the mean number of minutes of night waking each week. The filled circles on the bottom graph represent the average time Beth fell asleep each night, and the hatched histograms are the mean number of minutes one of Beth's parents was in her bed at bedtime.

Prior to treatment for bedtime tantrums, Beth fell asleep anywhere between 10:15 P.M. and 12:30 A.M. Following intervention, her bedtime was earlier, typically at 10:00 P.M. It should be noted that this was the goal set by Beth's parents (i.e., 10:00 P.M. bedtime), because they wanted to spend time with her in the evening (both parents worked and/or attended school during the day). Again, this bedtime was generally maintained at the one-month, two-month, and nine-month follow-ups.

A second change that was instituted at bedtime was the elimination of the parent lying down with Beth when she fell asleep. During baseline a parent was typically in the bed with Beth for an average of twenty minutes. Following the start of treatment for bedtime problems, her parents did not spend any time lying down with Beth. This was maintained through all follow-up observations.

Parental Measures

The apparent impact of Beth's sleep problems on her parents and subsequent changes following successful treatment of these disturbances can be found in Figures 25-2 and 25-3. At the time of the initial assessment, both parents reported being dissatisfied with certain aspects of their marriage. Following treatment, however, an improvement was observed in both the mother's and the father's satisfaction with their marriage. It appears that with an improvement in Beth's sleep, a positive change in marital satisfaction was also observed. Ratings of depression were also completed by the parents, and a positive change in maternal depression was reported. A slight improvement was also noted in the depression ratings reported by the father.

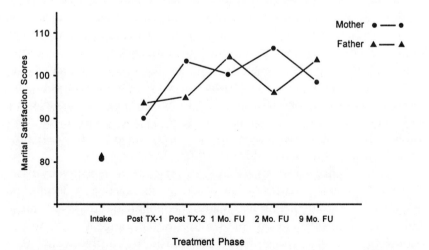

Figure 25-2. Scores from the Dyadic Adjustment Scale for both of Beth's parents are displayed during each phase of the study.

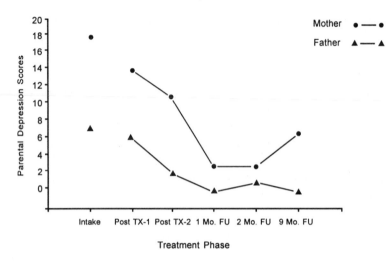

Figure 25–3. Scores from the Beck Depression Inventory for both of Beth's parents are displayed during each phase of the study.

Little change was found in the parents' sleep reports except for a decrease in the number of night wakings experienced by the mother. This change in night wakings, however, did not occur until the one-month follow-up. During baseline, Beth's mother experienced, on the average, 1.1 night wakings per night (range, 0.43 to 2.2). This was similar to her rate initially following treatment (mean, 1.2, range, 1.0 to 1.3). At the one-month follow-up a reduction was observed (mean, 0.6, range, 0.22 to 1.0), which was maintained at two months (mean, 0.37, range 0.14 to 0.57). This rate increased, however, at the nine-month follow-up (mean, 1.63, range, 1.0 to 3.3). The mean number of minutes of night wakings for the mother paralleled the data on frequency of night wakings (baseline mean, 30.8 minutes, range 23.6 to 39.0; initial treatment mean, 29.3, range 22.5 to 45.0; one-month mean, 22.7, range 12.9 to 30.0; two-month mean, 11.9, range 2.1 to 21.4; nine-month mean, 38.2, range, 15.0 to 100.7).

Little change was observed in the sleep patterns reported by Beth's father. At baseline, Beth's father woke, on the average, 0.3 times per night (range, 0 to 0.5). This was maintained following treatment (mean, 0.4, range, 0 to 0.86), at one month (mean, 0.2, range, 0 to 0.29), two months (mean, 0.1, range, 0 to 0.2), and nine months (mean, 0.23, range, 0 to 0.3). No change in the mean number of minutes of night waking was reported across treatment phases (baseline mean, 7.9 minutes, range, 0 to 17.1; initial treatment mean, 6.5, range, 0 to 12.9; one-month mean, 4.9, range, 0 to 10.0; two-month mean, 3.4, range, 0 to 4.9; nine-month mean, 3.4, range, 0 to 5.0).

Discussion

We were successful in treating the multiple sleep problems exhibited by one 14-month-old girl using a graduated extinction procedure (Ferber 1985). Both night wakings and bedtime disturbances were significantly reduced as a function of this intervention. A brief regression at Weeks 48 and 49 (when Beth stayed with her grandmother) was reversed by the parents who, without additional consultation, reimplemented treatment. Concurrent with the improvements in this child's sleep patterns, her parents reported improvements in marital satisfaction and maternal depression. The present study illustrates that a behavioral intervention for a child's sleep problems can have wide-ranging effects on family life.

It is not immediately obvious how the graduated extinction procedure was able to reduce bedtime problems and night waking. Waiting successively longer periods of time while Beth was crying before going into the room resembles intermittent reinforcement of crying. If going into the room is a reinforcer, and we essentially instruct the parents to wait until Beth cries for longer and longer periods of time before entering the room, then we might expect Beth to learn to cry for extended lengths of time. However, as we observed, Beth quickly stopped crying both at bedtime and during night wakings. One explanation for this result is that having the parents go into the room, but not allowing them to pick her up, sing to her, or engage in any extended conversations, did not serve as a potent reinforcer. Thus, over successive nights, Beth had to cry for extended periods of time for a relatively neutral interchange with her parents. Her choice, then, became one of either crying or going to sleep on her own, and it appeared that Beth quickly chose to go to sleep without her parents in the room. The success of graduated extinction, therefore, can be attributed to the gradual withdrawal of parental attention for nighttime disturbances.

The observed improvements in marital satisfaction and maternal depression as an apparent result of Beth's improved sleeping patterns were also encouraging. This effect confirms our frequent clinical observation that normally intact families can be seriously disrupted by children's sleep disturbances. We caution that not all marital dissatisfaction or parental depression that occurs concurrently with child sleep disorders is a result of such child problems. However, this phenomenon (i.e., parental distress as a consequence of child sleep problems) seems to occur in a significant number of families and warrants our attention when dealing with families and marriages in distress.

Not only did Beth's sleep problems appear to affect marital satisfaction and parental depression, they also seemed to affect her parents' sleep. In this family, the child's sleep problems appear to have affected only her mother's sleep. This was probably due to her mother having major responsibility for caring for Beth at bedtime and throughout the night. Interestingly, changes in the mother's sleep did not completely mirror Beth's sleep pattern. It took longer for her mother's sleep to return to normal following improvements in Beth's sleep. It is possible that continuing concern over her child's sleep contributed to this delay in returning to normal sleep, or it may be that adult sleep patterns are not as malleable as are children's.

This study, although involving only one family, suggests that chronic sleep problems in children may be amenable to behavioral intervention. In the present case, a graduated extinction approach was not only successful in reducing sleep problems but was an acceptable treatment to the child's parents. And, as we observed in this study, improvements in the child's sleep patterns may have resulted in generalized positive effects on family satisfaction and parents' sleep.

References

Barlow, D. H., and Hersen, M. (1984). *Single Case Experimental Designs: Strategies for Studying Behavior Change*, 2nd ed. New York: Pergamon.

Beck, A. T., Ward, C. H., Mendelson, M., et al. (1961). An inventory for measuring depression. *Archives of General Psychiatry* 4:561–571.

Ferber, R. (1985). *Solve Your Child's Sleep Problems*. New York: Simon & Schuster.

Jenkins, S., Bax, M., and Hart, H. (1980). Behavior problems in preschool children. *Journal of Child Psychology and Psychiatry* 21:5–17.

Johnson, C. M., Bradley-Johnson, S., and Stack, J. M. (1981). Decreasing the frequency of infants' nocturnal crying with the use of scheduled awakenings. *Family Practice Research Journal* 1:98–104.

Johnson, C. M., and Lerner, M. (1985). Amelioration of infant sleep disturbances. II: Effects of scheduled awakenings by compliant parents. *Infant Mental Health Journal* 6:21–30.

Ounsted, M. K., and Hendrick, A. M. (1977). The first-born child: patterns of development. *Developmental Medicine and Child Neurology* 19:446–453.

Richman, N. (1981). A community survey of the characteristics of 1- and 2-year-olds with sleep disruptions. *Journal of the American Academy of Child Psychiatry* 20:281–291.

—— (1985). A double-blind drug trial of treatment in young children with waking problems. *Journal of Child Psychology and Psychiatry* 26:591–598.

Richman, N., Douglas, J., Hunt, H., et al. (1985). Behavioral methods in the treatment of sleep disorders—a pilot study. *Journal of Child Psychology and Psychiatry* 26:581–590.

Richman, N., Stevenson, J. E., and Graham, P. J. (1975). Prevalence of behavior problems in three-year-old children: an epidemiological study in a London borough. *Journal of Child Psychology and Psychiatry* 16:277–287.

Rickert, V. I., and Johnson, C. M. (1988). Reducing nocturnal awakening and crying episodes in infants and young children: a comparison between scheduled awakenings and systematic ignoring. *Pediatrics* 81:203–212.

Rolider, A., and Van Houten, R. (1984). Training parents to use extinction to eliminate nighttime crying by gradually increasing the criteria for ignoring crying. *Education and Treatment of Children* 7:119–124.

Russo, R., Gururaj, V., and Allen, J. (1976). The effectiveness of diphenhydramine HCL in paediatric sleep disorders. *Journal of Clinical Pharmacology* 16:284–288.

Salzarulo, P., and Chevalier, A. (1983). Sleep problems in children and their relationship with early disturbances of the waking-sleeping rhythms. *Sleep* 6:47–51.

Spanier, G. B. (1976). Measuring dyadic adjustment: new scales for assessing the quality of marriage and similar dyads. *Journal of Marriage and Family* 38:15–28.

Williams, C. D. (1959). The elimination of tantrum behavior by extinction procedures. *Journal of Abnormal Social Psychology* 59:269–273.

Wolf, M., Risley, T., and Mees, H. (1964). Application of operant conditioning procedures to the behavior problems of an autistic child. *Behaviour Research and Therapy* 4:305–312.

Yen, S., McIntire, R. W., and Berkowitz, S. (1972). Extinction of inappropriate sleeping behavior: multiple assessment. *Psychological Reports* 30:375–378.

26

Pediatric Insomnia

CATHLEEN C. PIAZZA AND WAYNE W. FISHER

A variety of procedures for the treatment of childhood sleep disorders has been recommended in the literature. In this chapter we present outcome data from two cases of pediatric insomnia successfully treated using a simple bedtime fading procedure. The procedure is similar to that of Adams and Rickert (1989). However, Adams and Rickert combined bedtime routines (positive routines), repeated returns to bed, and a fading procedure for treatment of bedtime tantrums, and did not present systematic data on the actual sleep of their subjects. The present procedure involves gradually fading the bedtime (i.e., making it earlier) with the goal of increasing durations of appropriate nighttime sleep.

Case Histories

TC was a 6-year-old female of normal intelligence with attention deficit-hyperactivity disorder (AD-HD), nocturnal enuresis, and insomnia. Her grandmother reported that she slept four to six hours per night. Previous attempts to resolve TC's sleep disorder were unsuccessful and included the establishment of a bedtime routine, the establishment of a regular bedtime, diphenhydramine, and chloral hydrate. Despite these treatments, TC routinely refused to go to bed at her scheduled bedtime (9:00 P.M.) and got out of bed after being escorted there. The grandmother would argue with the child at bedtime, but would frequently "give in" and allow her to get out of bed and play with toys or watch television. She would generally fall asleep out of bed between 10:30 P.M. and 1:00 A.M. The grandmother reported being awakened during the night by TC and being unable to go back to sleep while the child was awake.

SI was a 4-year-old profoundly mentally retarded female with tu-
berous sclerosis. According to her mother, SI was difficult to keep awake
during the day and typically fell asleep several times throughout the
day. At night, mother would put SI to bed at 8:30 P.M., but she would
not fall asleep. SI would get out of bed, run around the house, and
was disruptive (e.g., bang on walls) and destructive (e.g., break objects).
Mother would stay up with the child until she (SI) fell asleep sometime
between 10:30 P.M. and 2:00 A.M.

Treatment of the Case

For SI, sleep treatment was initiated during an inpatient stay in a
pediatric hospital for the developmentally disabled. For TC, sleep treatment was conducted by her grandmother on an outpatient basis.

Baseline

During baseline, daytime sleep was interrupted for meals, medical
procedures, therapy sessions, and necessary daily care. At other times
sleep was neither encouraged nor discouraged. A consistent bedtime
routine was implemented each night prior to the scheduled bedtime. If
early or night wakings occurred, the child was monitored by an adult
and prompted to go back to bed at half-hour intervals.

Data Collection

On the inpatient unit, a momentary time sampling procedure was
utilized twenty-four hours a day in which the child was scored as in
bed or out of bed and awake or asleep at each half-hour interval by
trained observers. If there was a question whether the child was awake
or asleep, the observer would stand within one foot of the child and
whisper the child's name. Observers also noted behavior such as the
absence of verbal or motor responses (e.g., opening eyes) as indications
of sleep.

The same half-hour momentary time sampling procedure was used
for TC until the grandmother went to bed (at approximately midnight).
After the grandmother's bedtime, she made two scheduled checks, one
at 2:00 A.M. and one at 4:00 A.M. According to the grandmother's report, she always woke when the child did, and thus each night waking
was recorded.

Reliability

Interobserver agreement was assessed for SI by having two independent observers score the child as awake or asleep during both assessment and treatment on 83 percent of intervals for SI. Mean interobserver occurrence agreement was 95 percent (range, 78 to 100); nonoccurrence agreement was 97 percent (range, 79 to 100); and total reliability was 98 percent (range, 91 to 100).

Operational Definitions

Scheduled sleep and wake times were based on developmental norms (Weissbluth et al. 1981) in conjunction with the parental goals for ideal sleep and wake times for their child. To illustrate, 3-year-olds average eleven hours of sleep per night and have a one-hour nap during the day (i.e., twelve hours of waking time). If a 3-year-old child was expected to sleep from 8:00 P.M. to 7:00 A.M., and from 1:00 P.M. to 2:00 P.M., and she averaged eight hours of sleep per night from 11:00 P.M. to 7:00 A.M. and two hours of sleep per day from 1:00 P.M. to 3:00 P.M., then her: (1) percent appropriate sleep would equal 75 percent (nine hours occurring during the target time, divided by 12, multiplied by 100); and percent inappropriate sleep would equal 8 percent (one hour of sleep occurring during the defined wake time, divided by 12, multiplied by 100).

Treatment

The first step in treatment involved utilizing baseline data to determine a bedtime at which rapid sleep onset (i.e., within fifteen minutes) was highly probable. This initial bedtime (from which fading occurred) was determined by calculating the average bedtime during baseline and then adding one-half hour (e.g., if the average time of sleep onset was 10:30 P.M. during baseline, then the initial bedtime was set at 11:00 P.M.). The child was not allowed to go to bed or fall asleep before this time, or to sleep past the scheduled wake time.

Fading consisted of adjusting the child's bedtime based on latency to sleep onset for the previous night. If the child fell asleep within fifteen minutes of bedtime for two consecutive nights, the bedtime was made fifteen minutes earlier on the third night. If the child did not initiate sleep within fifteen minutes of bedtime for two consecutive nights, the bedtime was made fifteen minutes later on the third night. The child's bedtime was not changed until one of the two criteria was met.

Results

The percentage of appropriate sleep for each child is depicted in Figure 26–1. Both children showed improvements in the percentage of appropriate sleep. TC's sleep increased from an average of 34 percent (range, 27 to 41) in baseline to 100 percent after treatment; SI averaged 75.3 percent (range, 59 to 86) appropriate sleep in baseline, 81.9 percent (range, 68 to 91) after treatment.

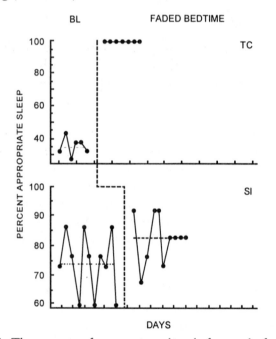

Figure 26–1. The percent of appropriate sleep before and after treatment for two girls with insomnia.

The percent of inappropriate sleep for SI is depicted in Figure 26–2. Her inappropriate (daytime) sleep decreased from an average of 16.5 percent in baseline to 0.6 percent after treatment. TC did not have any inappropriate sleep before or after treatment.

For both children, their durations of sleep were increased, and their sleep became less variable. For TC, the procedure also eliminated the problems of refusal to go to bed and night waking. Interestingly, when interviewed at the completion of the treatment protocol, the grand-mother reported that TC actually began *requesting* to go to bed prior to the target bedtime on many nights, and that nocturnal enuresis had ceased.

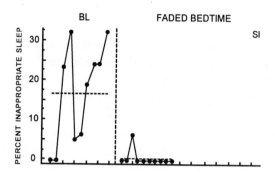

Figure 26-2. The percent of inappropriate sleep for SI before and after treatment.

Discussion

Utilization of a faded bedtime protocol with two school-aged girls resulted in regulation in the timing and amount of sleep of both. There are several factors that may have contributed to the treatment effects observed in these cases. First, selecting an initial target bedtime which was later than the time the child generally fell asleep during baseline probably contributed to the child's rapid sleep onset during the initial days of treatment. Thus, classical conditioning may be a factor in this procedure, in that maximizing the likelihood that the child falls asleep quickly after being placed in bed probably conditions the act of lying in bed as a cue for initiating sleep.

Establishment of a regular sleep initiation and wake time increased the likelihood that treatment effects would be maintained after the bedtime was faded to earlier in the night, when our manipulation of sleepiness was no longer a significant factor. Thus we were able to use a fading procedure to change the bedtime, while sleep continued to be initiated within fifteen minutes each night.

There are several advantages of this procedure over other recommended procedures for treating pediatric insomnia. First, the treatment involves manipulations at bedtime rather than in the middle of the night, when a parent is likely to be fatigued and may make implementation errors. Second, power struggles between parent and child over going to bed are generally eliminated because the child is not instructed to go to bed until a time when the probability of compliance is very high. Finally, the procedure may regulate sleep in such a way that multiple sleep-related problems are eliminated (e.g., night wakings, nocturnal enuresis).

References

Adams, L., and Rickert, V. (1989). Reducing bedtime tantrums: comparison between positive routines and graduated extinction. *Pediatrics* 84:756–761.

Weissbluth, M., Poncher, J., Given, G., et al. (1981). Sleep duration and television viewing. *Journal of Pediatrics* 99:486–488.

27

Morning Dawdling

CHRISTINA D. ADAMS AND RONALD S. DRABMAN

Children's dawdling and noncompliance with morning routines can often lead to parent–child conflict and tardiness in going to school. "Beat-the-Buzzer" is a contingency method which has been successfully used with many families of elementary school age children (Drabman and Creedon 1979, Drabman and Rosenbaum 1980). The procedure has been used most often in the home setting for morning dawdling; however, it has also been employed for classroom dawdling (Wurtele and Drabman 1984). "Beat-the-Buzzer" involves the manipulation of both antecedent events (e.g., setting a time limit for getting ready in the morning) and consequent events (e.g., television viewing time, staying up late) to reduce dawdling. When dawdling is significantly reduced, parent–child interactions are more likely to become more positive and enjoyable (McGrath et al. 1987).

Drabman and Creedon (1979) outlined the steps for using "Beat-the-Buzzer": (1) parents explain the child's responsibilities for the morning routine (e.g., washing face, brushing teeth) on the night before the program begins; (2) a list of these responsibilities is displayed in an obvious locale such as the bathroom mirror; (3) child is awakened as usual and the parent informs the child of a specific time to be ready (usually ten minutes prior to leaving time); (4) parent sets a timer for this time limit; (5) parent is permitted to remind the child only *once* of any one duty each morning; (6) if the child is on time or early (beats the buzzer), he or she receives a reward such as being allowed to stay up one-half hour later that evening; (7) if the child is late, he or she loses one-half hour of television viewing time for *each* one minute late past the buzzer, and cannot engage in pleasurable activities during the lost time. Anecdotally, Drabman and Creedon (1979) reported that the child typically does very well for a few days, is late one morning and contingencies are enforced, and then continues to do well thereafter. The authors argue that most children are rarely late after the procedure has been in effect for about three weeks.

Since initially presented, several case studies and single-case design experiments have been conducted utilizing variants of the procedure. For example, Hudson and Hudson (1981) expressed concern over the demands of the aforementioned procedure (e.g., measuring exact degree of lateness, having to closely monitor permitted television viewing time). They simplified the procedure by requiring a total loss of television viewing privileges on days when any instance of lateness occurred. This modification was successful at reducing dawdling in a 9-year-old girl who had been habitually late for school. The authors reported that, even when she was late, the subject typically was ready shortly after the buzzer. However, these results may not generalize to other children. For example, some children may recognize that privileges are already lost and subsequent noncompliance can not be punished further.

"Beat-the-Buzzer" has also been used with a family with a history of child abuse (Wolfe et al. 1981). Again, procedures were somewhat modified from that of the original article (Drabman and Creedon 1979). Given the family's history of aversive interactions, the focus of consequences shifted from a response cost procedure to a positive reinforcement procedure. Specifically, the two target children selected a reward whenever they beat the buzzer. Using a multiple-baseline procedure across subjects, mean preparation time decreased from eighty to thirty-eight minutes and from fifty-five to twenty-nine minutes for each child, respectively. Their preparation time was well within limits set (forty-five minutes). In addition, using "Beat-the-Buzzer" gave the parents an opportunity to manage their children's undesirable behavior through positive contingencies.

Especially with young children, one potential hazard to the success of the "Beat-the-Buzzer" procedure is the delay in providing consequences. Hudson and colleagues (1985) modified the "Beat-the-Buzzer" procedure to provide more immediate consequences to on-time or dawdling behavior. Two subjects, ages 6 and 7 years, were required to self-monitor completion of each morning task by placing a smiley face or star on a chart. Whenever the child was ready on time, he or she received an immediate reward (either money or watch cartoons until time to leave). Failure to complete all tasks on time resulted in no reward that day. The program was immediately successful for both children and treatment gains were maintained at follow-up.

In addition to measuring the impact of "Beat-the-Buzzer" with on-time behavior, McGrath and colleagues (1987) measured its concomitant effect on parent–child interactions in the morning. This was the first study to evaluate treatment acceptability of the procedure. Using a multiple-baseline design across two subjects and a single-case replication, data were gathered through parents' report of number of noncompliant behaviors, number of reminders required, whether the child was ready on time or not, and time it took the child to get ready. Additionally, the children were asked to rate their interaction with their parents daily. The effectiveness of the program was demonstrated by increases in on-time behavior and compliance and decreases in the amount of time required to get ready and the number of noncompliant behaviors and reminders. Finally, parents rated the procedure as being effective and easy to use and children rated their daily interactions as more positive.

"Beat-the-Buzzer" has been successfully used with various families, including one with an abusive history, and with different types of modifications in the procedure. However, to date [1994], all research using "Beat-the-Buzzer" has been conducted with intellectually average children. Hudson and colleagues (1985) noted that further research was needed to evaluate the need to adjust the procedure to children at different developmental levels. Since the concept of time is difficult and the "Beat-the-Buzzer" program involves delayed consequences, there was some question as to whether individuals with significant developmental disabilities could understand and successfully operate under the contingencies of the program. Therefore, the current study investigates the use of the "Beat-the-Buzzer" procedure with a boy who had a consistent history of dawdling and parent–child conflict in the morning. Despite his significant developmental delays (both cognitive and motor) and multiple handicaps (e.g., cerebral palsy), relatively minor modifications were made in the "Beat-the-Buzzer" procedure.

Method

Subject

James, a 12-year-old Caucasian male from a lower middle class family, was of moderate level of mental retardation (Full Scale IQ =

46 as measured with the Wechsler Intelligence Scale for Children-III). He has also been diagnosed with cerebral palsy, psychomotor seizures, and significant speech deficits. James was born premature to an adolescent mother who had various difficulties with her pregnancy. At birth, James suffered an intraventricular hemorrhage, respiratory distress, cardiac problems, and kidney difficulties. His maternal grandmother became the legal guardian of James as an infant; therefore, he only knows her and we will refer to her as his mother. Reportedly, James has exhibited significant cognitive and motor delays since a very young age. He received numerous orthopedic surgeries between the ages of 18 months and 11 years and was in a body cast for the majority of the time until age 5.

At the time of this study, James exhibited problematic behaviors such as morning dawdling, noncompliance, and hyperactivity. James was enrolled in a self-contained special education class as a result of both significant cognitive and motor delays. Prior to the current school year, James had been inappropriately placed in an educational setting at which he met few demands for learning and behavior. The situation was rectified and he began the current school year at a new school with a new teacher. Reportedly, his new teacher had a more structured routine, required more pre-academic work, and provided more consistent consequences than did his previous teacher. As a result, James's behavior and knowledge had substantially improved and this pleased his mother. Despite the increased demands of his new educational setting, James did not complain and actually reported that he enjoyed school more. Yet, at first, James exhibited morning dawdling and noncompliance with his morning routine at the onset of the current school year. His morning dawdling on school days persisted consistently for two months prior to the study. His mother reported that the frequency and intensity of the morning conflicts had progressively increased.

A functional analysis of James's morning dawdling was conducted via interviews with James and his mother. This assessment revealed that the antecedent condition for James's dawdling was having to get ready for school. Indeed, he usually did not have difficulty getting up and dressed on weekend mornings. On school mornings, James typically would refuse to get out of bed, argue with his mother, make excuses, refuse to get dressed when made to get out of bed, cry, whine, and go back to bed. Reportedly, James did not gain access to preferred play items (e.g., television) and was not attempting to avoid school because he apparently enjoyed his class. When James dawdled, his mother indicated that she often argued with him or yelled at him, criticized him, repeated instructions, and threatened him. Additionally, she felt that she would have to resort to spanking despite her dislike for that punishment procedure. It appeared clear that frequent negative parental attention was the consequence for dawdling and noncompliance to morning routine. The increase in maternal attention seemed to be serving as reinforcement for James's dawdling. Additionally, James's mother reported that prior use of rewards other than her attention (e.g., eat breakfast at a favorite restaurant) and removal of privileges (e.g., cannot go to a preferred activity) had not improved his behavior. Based on the functional analysis of James's morning dawdling, a treatment procedure which would decrease parental attention to inappropriate behavior (e.g., dawdling, arguing against being awakened) and increase attention to appropriate behavior (e.g., being ready on time) was sought.

Data Collection

Since the target behaviors included both dawdling and parent–child conflict, data collection procedures were modeled after those of McGrath and colleagues (1987). The subject's mother was interviewed and a checklist of fifteen negative parent–child interaction behaviors developed. This checklist was incorporated into a daily monitoring form which also included the following variables: (1) time the child was awakened, (2) time limit set on the buzzer, (3) time the child was ready, and (4) scheduled bedtime (based on compliance/noncompliance with buzzer limit). Treatment integrity variables were also monitored: (1) total time of television viewing, (2) actual bedtime, and (3) number of times out of room after bedtime.

James's mother was required to monitor and record the aforementioned variables each school morning. Reliability data were not collected. James's father could not be used as a reliability observer since his occupation required him to be away all week and return home only for weekends. Additionally, James's mother felt that an observer would be intrusive and, given his attention-seeking nature, would alter the child's behavior. Further practicality issues, such as the family living over 150 miles away, precluded sending an independent observer. However, given the objective nature of gathering time data (e.g., time buzzer set, time child was ready), reliability of such data should be enhanced over that of more subjective data (e.g., Likert-type ratings). Data were not collected on school holidays and over three days when James's mother was hospitalized and he was in respite care.

Procedure

Baseline

During baseline, James's mother recorded all variables on a daily monitoring form, without setting the buzzer, each school day. The buzzer time limit was recorded as the time that the child was required to be ready in order to leave for school on time. James was not aware that his behavior was being monitored. James's mother was encouraged to continue to respond to James's behavior as she typically had done prior to data collection. The baseline phase lasted seven school days.

Treatment

The treatment procedure was utilized for forty-four school days. The "Beat-the-Buzzer" procedure has been outlined in McGrath and colleagues (1987) and Wolfe and colleagues (1981). The treatment consisted of manipulating antecedents (e.g., setting a time limit) and consequences (e.g., rewards, early bedtime) to reduce dawdling and parent–child conflict on school-day mornings. First, his mother explained the entire procedure to James. Second, a list of steps required to get ready and magazine pictures depicting each step were posted on James's bedroom door (to aid James's memory given that he could not read). Third, James was awakened at a consistent time and the buzzer (timer) set for a specific time (typically fifteen minutes before the child had to leave the house) each school day morning. Typically, James was given approximately fifty-five minutes to get ready each morning. Fourth, the child was encouraged to refer to the posted steps when necessary and to try to "Beat-the-Buzzer" (be ready before the timer sounded). Given James's ability to complete the steps independently, his mother was instructed to leave the area and reduce her attention to inappropriate behavior. If he was ready on time, he was always given praise and often received various rewards (e.g., later bedtime, candy, special activity). When James was late, he had to go to bed thirty minutes early for each one minute past the buzzer. If he was not sleepy, James was required to get ready for bed, put on his pajamas, and get into bed with the lights turned off. He was not allowed to enjoy other activities (e.g., television viewing) after his bedtime.

Follow-up

The follow-up period was conducted thirteen weeks after the end of treatment for a duration of fifteen consecutive school days. Between treatment and follow-up, "Beat-the-Buzzer" was used for two weeks and then gradually faded. After the program had been faded, James's on-time behavior was maintained with praise only and his mother did not reimplement the program until follow-up. During follow-up, the treatment procedure was utilized, except that rewards for on-time behavior were given less frequently than in the treatment phase. After follow-up, the treatment procedure was discontinued.

Measures

The dependent measures were gathered by the mother on all school days. James's mother was given a daily monitoring sheet to record the following dependent measures.

On Time

During baseline, James's mother provided the clock time that James was required to be ready (e.g., washed, dressed, eaten breakfast, gathered school supplies) (when the buzzer would have rung during treatment) and what time he was actually ready. During treatment, *on time* was indicated by whether the child's preparation time to get ready was within the buzzer time limit indicated. In other words, on time was being ready before the buzzer rang.

Preparation Time

James's mother recorded the time that James was awakened and the time at which he was ready to leave the house for school. From these data, the amount of preparation time required to get ready was calculated by subtracting the wake-up time from the time ready.

Negative Behavior Checklist

A checklist of fifteen negative parent and/or child behaviors was provided on the data sheet. James's mother was required to check the frequency with which each of these behaviors occurred each school-day morning. The behaviors listed included: parent yelled at child, child yelled at parent, child cried, child whined, child refused to eat breakfast, parent gave instructions/reminders repeatedly, child said that he did not have to go to school today, parent criticized child, child went back to bed, child took off his shoes or leg braces, child refused to get dressed, parent and child argued, child refused to get out of bed, child made excuses (e.g., could not find something), and parent threatened child.

Treatment Integrity Variables

To check on treatment manipulation, James's mother was asked to record the amount of time that James spent viewing television each night, his actual bedtime, and the number of times that he left his room after bedtime. This information was used to determine whether the parent followed through with consequences for morning behavior as outlined in the treatment protocol.

Consumer Satisfaction Data

Prior to baseline data collection, James's mother was asked to rate the quality of her morning interactions with James on a 6-point Likert scale, with zero indicating the worst possible interaction and 5 indicating the best possible interaction. After follow-up data were collected, his mother was asked to rate her morning interactions with James using the same Likert scale. Additionally, she was asked to evaluate: (1) the ease of implementing the "Beat-the-Buzzer" treatment procedure (0 = extremely difficult; 5 = extremely easy); (2) the improvement of James's compliance with the morning routine while using "Beat-the-Buzzer" (0 = extremely worse; 5 = extremely improved); and, (3) the overall effectiveness of the treatment in reducing morning dawdling and parent–child conflicts (0 = extremely ineffective; 5 = extremely effective).

Results

In reviewing data records, it was apparent that James's mother consistently and satisfactorily monitored variables across all baseline, treatment, and follow-up days. Furthermore, interviews as well as review of treatment integrity variables suggested consistent adherence to treatment procedures.

On Time

During baseline, James was ready for school on time 0 percent of the days. For treatment and follow-up, his on-time behavior increased as indicated when he "Beat-the-Buzzer" 84 percent and 93 percent of the days, respectively.

Preparation Time

Typically, James was given 55 minutes (range = 45 to 60) to get ready each morning. The daily mean preparation time for James at baseline was 92.9 minutes. The daily mean preparation time decreased from baseline to 51.8 and 50.1 minutes for treatment and follow-up phases, respectively. Results for preparation time are displayed in Figure 27–1.

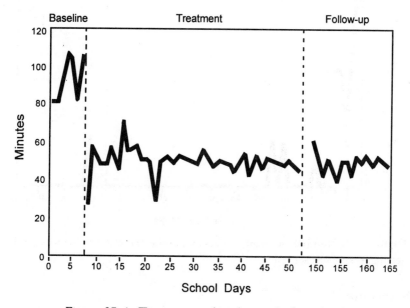

Figure 27–1. Time required to be ready for school.

Negative Behaviors

During baseline, James's mother reported a daily average frequency of 5.6 negative behaviors on school day mornings. At treatment, the daily average decreased to 0.1 negative behaviors. These results were maintained at follow-up (daily mean = 0.1 negative behaviors). Results of negative parent–child behaviors are shown in Figure 27–2.

Consumer Satisfaction Data

Prior to baseline data collection, James's mother rated the quality of her morning interactions with James as a zero (worst possible rating). After follow-up data were collected, her rating increased to a 5 (best possible rating). Subsequent to follow-up, she evaluated "Beat-the-Buzzer" as "moderately easy" (rating = 4) to use and "extremely effective" (rating = 5) in reducing morning dawdling and parent–child conflicts. Additionally, she rated James's behavior as "extremely improved" (rating = 5) after having used "Beat-the Buzzer."

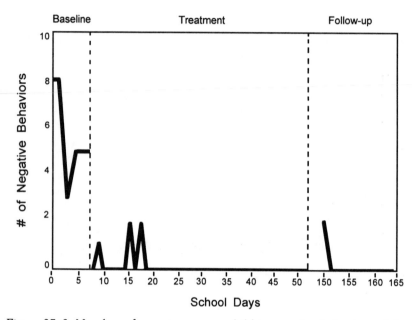

Figure 27-2. Number of negative parent–child interaction behaviors while getting ready for school.

Discussion

The current case study reinforces the utility and efficacy of the "Beat-the-Buzzer" technique for reducing morning dawdling and parent–child conflict as found in previous literature (e.g., Hudson et al. 1985, McGrath et al. 1987). By manipulating antecedent events (e.g., setting a time limit) and consequences (e.g., praise, rewards, early bedtime), James's compliance with morning routine substantially improved. Given the nature and severity of the child's multiple handicapping conditions (e.g., moderate mental retardation, cerebral palsy, speech deficits), results suggest that the procedure can be effective with a variety of populations, including children with developmental disabilities.

James's mother indicated that the procedure was initially somewhat difficult to implement; however, it quickly became easy to use and effective at reducing dawdling and parent–child conflict. Indeed, even on treatment days in which James was not ready on time, the preparation time and frequency of negative behaviors closely approximated that of days in which he successfully "Beat-the-Buzzer."

James's mother indicated that "Beat-the-Buzzer" was effective in areas other than simply decreasing dawdling. First, his mother indicated that the procedure led to more pleasant mornings for both of them. When the family initially presented with James's problem behavior, his mother indicated that she feared losing control of her anger. Since all previous efforts (e.g., rewards) had failed, she was considering the use of spanking as a consequence despite her disapproval of physical punishment. When using "Beat-the-Buzzer," James's mother reported that she was able to stop "nagging" and to provide James with consistent praise. Second, James's mother reported that promoting James's independent behavior was very important to her. "Beat-the-Buzzer" helped James to be more independent in getting ready for school. Except for assistance in putting on his leg braces, James's mother was able to allow James to get ready independently on school mornings while she attended to necessary tasks.

In addition to treatment efficacy using the standard treatment protocol, several anecdotal issues regarding variants in treatment appeared. First, treatment effects were found to generalize to another setting (respite care in a hospital) seven days after treatment was initiated. Although the treatment protocol was not followed in the respite care program since it was during a weekend, James's compliance and on-time behavior in getting ready in the morning was reported to have been substantially improved over previous stays when it had been described as problematic. Second, on four of the forty-four treatment days, the usual routine was varied (e.g., the time awakened and time required to be ready) due to external demands (e.g., relative in the hospital). James did not successfully "Beat-the-Buzzer" on the first of these days; however, he was ready on time for the remaining three. These results suggest that the treatment program effects may have generalized to other settings and situations. Finally, treatment effects were found to have been maintained over three months since the end of treatment despite fading the program prior to follow-up. After follow-up, the procedure was discontinued. James's mother informally reported that he was not late getting ready for school and her morning interactions with him were without conflict for the remainder of the school year.

In summary, "Beat-the-Buzzer" effectively modified target behaviors, improved the overall home atmosphere on school mornings, and required very little involvement from the child's mother. The "Beat-the-Buzzer" program was developed to be easy to use and relatively cost-free (families may need only to purchase a timer). However, there was some question as to whether the procedure would be easy to use and effective with someone with low cognitive abilities and physical handicaps. Indeed, the procedure was readily understood by James, was effective quickly, and his mother reported that it was not difficult to use. This finding is interesting given James's inability to identify numbers and to tell time. Still, his mother reported that James understood at which point the timer would ring and independently checked the timer between morning tasks to monitor his time limits. Being able to see the timer as it moved closer to zero was very helpful to James in understanding the procedure.

Clinicians and researchers in this area should consider utilizing this procedure for morning dawdling with children who have developmental disabilities. The use of a larger, heterogeneous sample of children with developmental disabilities in an experimental design could extend the generalization of results beyond that of a single case study. Moreover, research on various parameters (e.g., type of negative and positive consequences, changes in routines, generalization to other settings) of the "Beat-the-Buzzer" procedure needs to be systematically evaluated. In fact, Hudson and associates (1985) noted that some children may not need the consequences because they find the procedure to be intrinsically motivating. More research is also needed on how to fade the procedure. Wolfe and colleagues (1981) successfully included a maintenance period with social reinforcement only. Finally, it would be instructive to compare the relative efficacy and treatment acceptability of "Beat-the-Buzzer" with other potential parenting practices for dawdling.

References

Drabman, R. S., and Creedon, D. L. (1979). Beat the buzzer. *Child Behavior Therapy* 1:295–296.

Drabman, R. S., and Rosenbaum, M. (1980). Pediatric counseling with parents regarding childhood behavior problems: misbehavior away from home and early morning dawdling. *Journal of Developmental and Behavioral Pediatrics* 1:86–88.

Hudson, A., and Hudson, T. (1981). Beat the buzzer: an early morning game for tardy children. *Australian Behaviour Therapist* 8:1–3.

Hudson, A., Vincent, J., Wilks, R., and Drabman, R. (1985). "Beat the Buzzer" for early morning dawdling: two case illustrations. *Behaviour Change* 2:136–142.

McGrath, M. L., Dorsett, P. G., Calhoun, M. E., and Drabman, R. S. (1987). "Beat-the-Buzzer": a method for decreasing parent–child morning conflicts. *Child and Family Behavior Therapy* 9:35–48.

Wolfe, D. A., Kelly, J. A., and Drabman, R. S. (1981). "Beat the Buzzer": a method for training an abusive mother to decrease recurrent child conflicts. *Journal of Clinical Child Psychology* 10:114–116.

Wurtele, S. K., and Drabman, R. S. (1984). "Beat the Buzzer" for classroom dawdling: a one year trial. *Behavior Therapy* 15:403–409.

PART V
Disruptive Behaviors

28

Enhancing Children's Ability to Cope with Anger

MICHAEL L. BLOOMQUIST

Children with behavior disorders often have difficulty controlling their anger. These children may not know how to control strong emotions. If these children don't learn how to cope with this problem, it can lead to many future personal and social problems. This chapter will provide you with some ideas to help your child learn to control anger.

Blowing a Cork

Miles is a 14-year-old male who, according to his parents, Frank and Beverly, often "blows his cork." It takes very little to get him angry. Whenever things don't go his way or he gets frustrated, he is sure to explode in rage or anger. He seems to have this problem at home, at school, with his parents, and with his friends. It doesn't matter where he is or who he's with; he is prone to getting extremely angry. Recently, because he could not find his jeans, he yelled at his mother. Another time he tried to fix a lawn mower in the garage, became frustrated, and threw a wrench, damaging the garage door. If his parents confront him about his behavior, he often becomes more angry. Although he has never been violent, his parents are concerned that his anger problem is getting serious and might get worse.

What Is an Anger Problem?

When a child has habitual anger outbursts that seem out of proportion to the situation at hand, it is a problem that needs to be addressed. There is a real anger problem when a child becomes too angry too often and in many settings such as at home, in school, in the neighborhood, and so forth.

It is important and necessary to consider *when and where* the child displays his anger problem. If your child only displays this problem when interacting with parents or family members, it may not be an anger problem. Instead, this may be a problem related to noncompliance, not following the rules, and/or family conflict.

Helping Children Learn to Cope with Anger

All children will experience anger or frustration at various points in their lives. Some children are able to cope with these feelings better than others. The following section describes how you can help your child develop skills important for coping with this very strong and usually negative feeling.

Step 1. Determine If Your Child Is Ready to Learn How to Cope with Anger

Some children will not be able to benefit from many of the procedures discussed in this chapter. Many children are too young to learn the skills necessary to manage their anger. Young children (below the age of 8 to 10 years) may not be able to learn how to cope with anger on their own. Also, some children are too defensive to learn how to cope with anger. They deny that they have problems with their feelings. Sometimes their defenses are so strong that they are not able to benefit from learning to control anger.

If you have determined that your child is too young or too defensive, you may wish to reconsider whether or not he will be able to benefit from instruction on coping with anger. An alternative strategy might be simply to teach your child how to understand and better express his feelings. Many children become angry, frustrated, sad, anxious, and so forth because they cannot articulate and express their feelings very well. A parent may be wise to start with any child who has a problem managing anger by helping him learn to understand and express feelings first.

An alternative would be to avoid using anger management with a defensive child. Instead, emphasizing family conflict management may be more productive. Your child may be less resistant if "everyone" is working on one issue instead of just him. By participating in family conflict management training, your child would still be learning many skills that relate to anger management.

Step 2. Define Anger

You may be surprised to find out that many kids with anger problems aren't very good at defining anger. Ask your child to give a definition of "anger." Help your child understand that anger is a negative emotion, a feeling of displeasure that occurs in response to a real or perceived situation that doesn't go as one would like it to. Help your child understand that anger feelings can range from frustrated (mild) to mad (moderate) to rageful (severe). Ask your child to describe times or situations when he felt frustrated, mad, or rageful forms of anger. Be sure to help your child define different levels of anger in later discussions of anger with him.

Step 3. Teach Your Child to Recognize Anger Signals

Learning to recognize when one is angry involves understanding the "signals" that are often indicators that emotions are high. This can be accomplished through a discussion with your child about signals. First explain that everyone feels anger, but it is how one handles it that determines whether or not it is a problem. Explain further that most strong feelings have three parts, including a "body part," a "thought part," and an "action part." Work with your child to develop a list on a piece of paper of all the "body signals," "thought signals," and "action signals" that you and he can generate.

Common body, thought, and action signals for anger are as follows:

Body Signals	Thought Signals	Action Signals
• Breathing rate increased	• "I hate myself."	• Punch/hit
• Heart rate increased	• "I feel like hurting myself."	• Yell
• Sweating increased	• "I hate her."	• Cry
• Red face color	• "I'm going to hit him."	• Threaten
• Tense muscles	• "I hate doing homework."	• Faint
• Body feels "hot"	• "I want to break something."	• Fidget
	• "I am dumb."	• Tremble
	• "I can't do anything right."	• Run
	• "I give up."	• Withdraw

After all of the signals have been listed, take some time to discuss and role-play what these signals are all about. Ask your child to think about times when he was very upset and what signals he thinks may have applied during those situations. After some discussion has taken place, role-play what the signals might look like. For example, you might model and then have your child role-play what tense muscles look like when one is angry. The modeling and role-plays can be taken further where the parent might act out being very angry and frustrated. Ask your child to identify the signals that were present during your demonstration. This could be repeated several times. Later you could ask your child to demonstrate anger, and you could identify signals in him.

Step 4. Teach Your Child to Relax

Once your child has learned how to identify when he is experiencing anger, he then can learn to use skills to cope with or reduce the anger. Learning to reduce body tension through relaxation is an important first step. This can be accomplished in a number of different ways, depending on your child's age and level of sophistication.

The following is a list of possible methods you could use to instruct your child to relax:

1. Deep breathing

Instruct, model, and have your child demonstrate how to do deep breathing exercises. The basic idea is to have him inhale deeply and exhale very slowly.

2. Visualization

Have your child visualize a very relaxing scene in his mind. For example, he might visualize himself floating on a raft on a lake. He would continue to visualize floating on the lake, going up and down gently with the waves, with the sun beating down, and so forth. You can combine deep breathing with visualization. For example, ask your child to visualize a candle in front of him. As he exhales, he makes the candle flicker but not go out. You can help a younger child by discussing the visualization process and helping him construct the visual scene. Older children probably can construct their own visual scenes.

3. Robot/Rag Doll Technique

The robot/rag doll technique is a useful muscle tension/release relaxation approach used with younger children (age 10 years and below). At first, ask your child to tense up all muscles in the body and visualize himself as a robot. Have him hold this tense state for approximately fifteen seconds. Then ask your child to release all the tension and visualize himself as a rag doll with all muscles very loose. He should hold this relaxed state for fifteen seconds. Have him continue to practice the robot/rag doll technique until he appears to know how to relax.

4. Systematic Muscle Tension/Release Relaxation Procedure

The systematic muscle tension/release procedure is better suited for older children and adolescents (age 11 and above). There are professionally constructed audiotapes that are available in many bookstores and other specialty shops that would aid in this regard. The basic idea is to have your child or adolescent tense up small muscle groups one at a time, starting at the lower end of the body and working up. For example, your child would tense up his feet, holding them tense for five to ten seconds and then relaxing them for five to ten seconds. This would be followed by going up to the lower legs, upper legs, abdomen, chest, shoulders, neck, and, finally, the face. During each of these steps while he progressively goes up the body, he practices holding that particular area tense for five to ten seconds, releasing and maintaining a relaxed state for five to ten seconds. Eventually, his entire body will be relaxed. Once a person gets good at this, he can learn to relax all muscle groups simultaneously and quickly.

Try one or two of these methods over several meetings to teach your child to relax. Make sure he knows this skill before proceeding to the next skill.

Step 5. Teach Your Child to Use Coping Self-Talk

The next area of coping with anger involves utilizing "coping self-talk." This involves talking to oneself in a helpful manner. First explain to your child that if he talks to himself in a helpful manner, he will be able to control anger better.

Explain to your child that self-talk involves saying things to oneself (thoughts) to calm down. Tell him this goal can be met by talking to himself in a manner such as the following:

- "Take it easy."
- "Stay cool."
- "Chill out."
- "Take some deep breaths."

- "It's okay if I'm not good at this."
- "I'm sad Tanya doesn't want to play with me, but many other kids like to play with me."
- "I'm getting tense. Relax!"
- "Don't let him bug me."
- "I'm gonna be okay."
- "I'll just try my hardest."
- "Try not to give up."

After your child seems to understand the purpose of coping self-talk, then you can move on to modeling and role-play exercises. You could model how to use coping self-talk when you are angry. For example, you could demonstrate getting frustrated with trying to fix some plumbing under a kitchen sink. First, you could demonstrate how not to cope with this particular situation (e.g., throwing tools, swearing, yelling, etc.). Next you could model how to cope with this same situation utilizing coping self-talk such as, "I need to relax," "I'm going to cool down," "I won't let this get to me," and so forth. After you have modeled this skill several times, ask your child to do similar role-plays.

Step 6. Teach Your Child to Take Effective Action

The final step in learning how to cope effectively with anger is to take action and/or solve the problem that originally made the person angry. Taking action might involve expressing feelings, asking for a hug, going for a walk, relaxing, being assertive with someone, and so forth. Problem-solving skills can also be used to take action. It is important to tell your child that he still needs to solve the problem that made him feel upset. Review all the procedures with your child so that he understands what taking action and problem solving are all about.

Step 7. Model Coping with Anger

It is extremely important for you to model anger-control skills. This can be done on an ongoing basis while you cope with normal situations at home that cause anger and frustration. You should try to cope effectively with your own feelings and to be a good example for your child. This can be done by informing your child that you are going to try to cope with anger, and then model relaxing, using coping self-talk, and taking effective action. Try to fill out an anger coping worksheet (see Step 8a, below) occasionally and share it with your child.

Step 8a. Implement a Formal Anger-Coping Procedure

The ultimate goal is to help your child apply the anger management skills in real-life situations. The formal manner of helping your child use the skills involves completing the Coping with Anger Worksheet at the end of this chapter. Ask your child to complete this worksheet when he gets angry. The worksheet instructs your child to go through a step-by-step procedure of coping with anger. The first step involves your child writing down what event or problem made him feel angry. The second step entails your child writing down the body, thought, and action signals that told him he was experiencing anger. The third, fourth, and fifth steps are about describing how he is going to cope with the anger (relaxing, using coping self-talk, taking action, etc.). Finally, he would rate himself on a 4-point rating scale as to whether or not he has effectively coped with his anger. It's tough to learn anger management. So occasionally your child may explode, but could still complete the worksheet afterward.

Your child can fill out this chart either independently or with your guidance, depending on what you think is best for him. It's not that important who actually completes the form, but that it be used to structure the anger-coping process.

It is important to use reinforcement to promote your child's use of anger management skills. The formal method of reinforcement would involve using the Tally for Using Coping with Anger Worksheet chart that is found at the end of this chapter. This chart is used with the Coping with Anger Worksheet. At the end of a specified time period, total up the 1 and 2 ratings, and 3 and 4 ratings, from the Coping with Anger Worksheet, and transfer that information to the Tally chart. If there are more 3 and 4 ratings, your child gets a reinforcement.

Step 8b. Implement an Informal Anger-Coping Procedure

The informal method of helping a child incorporate these new skills in everyday situations would be simply to ask him to use the skills when needed. If your child becomes angry or frustrated, you might say something such as, "This might be a good time to try to practice coping with anger." The Cool Down chart, found at the end of this chapter, can be used as a visual cue to guide your child through the steps of anger management. You might want to remind your child to look at this chart as he is trying to cool down. Try to use directed-discovery questions to guide your child to use anger management skills.

Informal reinforcement involves you noticing, commenting on, and praising your child for using the skills. Try to reinforce your child regularly and often enough to promote his use of the skills.

Summary Points

1. A child with a significant anger problem is prone to numerous personal and social problems.
2. A child may not have a true anger problem if he displays the anger only while interacting with parents or other family members. This more likely indicates a parent–child or family problem.
3. Young (below age 8 to 10 years) and/or resistant children may not benefit from learning to cope with anger.
4. Teach your child to recognize the body, thought, and action signals associated with anger.
5. Teach your child relaxation skills to cope with anger.
6. Teach your child to use coping self-talk to cope with anger.
7. Teach your child to take effective action and problem-solve to cope with anger.

Capping the Cork

Back to Miles, Frank, and Beverly: Frank and Beverly decide that they are going to try to take some action with young Miles. They sit down with him and explain how he might be able to learn how to control his anger by utilizing some coping with anger skills. At first Miles is resistant, but through a friendly and supportive discussion, they get him to acknowledge that he may benefit from working on anger control skills. They go through all the steps and procedures involving learning to recognize when one is angry, as well as learning how to cope with the feelings of anger through relaxing, using coping self-talk, and taking effective action. Miles and his parents have worked out an agreement so that when he is able to utilize the Coping with Anger Worksheet successfully five times, he will have earned the privilege of going to a concert of his choice. At first Miles stumbles and has difficulty. At one point his mother asked him to use anger management, and that made him even more angry. Gradually, over time, however, Miles begins to incorporate the anger management strategies. At this point he still gets angry occasionally, but his anger outbursts have become less frequent, and he is aware of his anger problem.

EXAMPLE:
COPING WITH ANGER WORKSHEET

Name: *Miles*

Date: *Sunday*

Directions: A child and/or parent can complete this worksheet. It's best to fill out the worksheet while you are angry, but it's also OK to fill it out after you have coped with anger.

1. **What event or problem is making me feel angry?**
   The kid next door keeps bugging me and my friends. He won't leave us alone.

2. **What are the signals that tell me I am angry?**

   a. **Body signals** *My muscles are tense. My heart is pounding.*

   b. **Thought signals** *I wish he would go away. He's gonna steal my friends.*

   c. **Action signals** *I yelled at him.*

3. **What can I do to relax my body?**
   I will take some deep breaths and try to relax my body.

4. **What "coping self-talk" can I use to control my thoughts?**
   "Don't let him bug me." "Keep cool." "Relax."

5. **What effective action can I take to deal with the situation or solve the problem?**
   I'll talk to him. I'll ask him to let me play with my friends alone. If that doesn't work, I'll ask Dad for help.

Coping with Anger Rating (circle one)

1. Didn't try to cope with anger at all.
2. Sort of tried to cope with anger, but it didn't really work.
3. Tried hard to cope with anger, but it didn't really work.
4. Tried hard to cope with anger, and it worked.

From *Skills Training for Children with Behavior Disorders: A Parent and Therapist Guidebook* by Michael L. Bloomquist. © 1996 The Guilford Press: New York. Used with permission.

EXAMPLE:
TALLY FOR USING COPING WITH ANGER WORKSHEET

Name: *Miles*

Date: *Monday*

Direction: At the end of a designated time period, add up all the ratings from the Coping with Anger Worksheets. Add up all the 1 and 2 ratings, and then add up all the 3 and 4 ratings. If there are more 3 and 4 ratings, then your child gets to select a reward. ____

Total ratings of 1 and 2   3   **Total ratings of 3 and 4**   5

Reward = *Have a friend stay overnight on Friday.*

COOL DOWN

1. Am I angry?

2. Cool down my body.

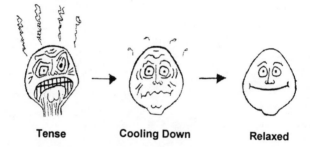

| Tense | Cooling Down | Relaxed |

3. Use cool-down thoughts.

4. Do something to solve the problem.

29

Treatment of Temper Tantrums

RACHEL T. HARE-MUSTIN

The use of paradoxical tasks in therapy can often produce striking and rapid changes in behavior. Frankl (1966) has developed the technique of paradoxical intention, which involves replacing the usual restrictions on undesired behavior with intentional and even exaggerated effort by the patient. He has found that this enables patients to develop detachment and gain distance from their own behavior and leads to behavior change. Haley (1973) has described the effectiveness of paradoxical procedures as used by Milton Erickson in terms of the power relationship between patient and therapist. Resistance to the task by the patient opposing the therapist's direction produces change in the desired direction. Paradoxical interventions have been explained by Nelson (1968) as a reversal of the usual figure and ground, with the therapist taking over the patient's position so the patient is left with the opposite position. Paradoxical tasks have been used in family therapy (Hare-Mustin 1975), in the treatment of physical symptoms such as headaches, insomnia, and nervous mannerisms (Weakland et al. 1974), and in treating obsessive thoughts (Solyom et al. 1972). The present study concerns the use of a paradoxical intervention in the treatment of temper tantrums.

Temper tantrums in children are often explained in terms of reinforcement principles with the attention the child receives for tantrums being considered the positive reinforcer. Reports on the extinction of tantrum behavior reveal that a number of tantrum incidents occur before the behavior is extinguished, and a second series of extinction trials may be required following spontaneous recovery (Kakkar 1972, Williams 1959). The use of a paradoxical intervention as described in the case below seems to be a more effective method for the treatment of temper tantrums.

History of the Problem

When he was brought for treatment, Tommy, age 4, was a rather small, immature child. His 7-year-old sister was also immature and dependent. A brother had died shortly before Tommy's birth, and his parents had had some counseling at that time. The parents were over-protective and given to using a "reasoning" approach with their children, which they had learned in a child study group. The mother frequently stayed with Tommy at nursery school "to help out." Both parents admitted they felt helpless and frantic over Tommy's temper tantrums, which could occur anywhere and might be as frequent as ten a week but were usually of daily occurrence.

Treatment

The family was seen for eight consecutive weekly sessions with the children being present for all or part of each session. The first three sessions involved the treatment of Tommy's temper tantrums. In the first session, after I had acquainted myself with the family, I inquired in some detail about when and where the tantrums occurred and what seemed to prompt them. I asked the family to describe the most recent tantrum. I then pointed out that what was disturbing about tantrums was that they were not predictable, in fact they could occur anywhere. I said that I wanted Tommy to *continue* to have his tantrums but only in a chosen "tantrum place" at home. The family and Tommy decided together in the session where the place should be. I participated by encouraging them to pick a place that was safe and not in the middle of things, but it need not be an isolated place such as is used by some families for time-out. We spent some time in this discussion, reviewing the possible places in the house with care. The family decided the up-stairs hall was the best place. I then very carefully explained to Tommy and his family that if Tommy should start to have a tantrum at any other place, he was to go to or be taken to the "tantrum place." We discussed other places he might be, and I pointed out that if he were away from home, such as at the store when he started to have a tantrum, he should be told he would have to wait until he got home to go to the "tantrum place."

At the second session a week later, the family reported that there had only been one occurrence of tantrum behavior, and on that occasion Tommy was taken to the "tantrum place." On another occasion he stopped the behavior when his mother started to take him there. There were no occasions outside the home.

I said that it was now necessary to agree at what time of day the tantrums were to take place. As different times were suggested and considered in detail, I mentioned a two-hour period that had been the most frequent time of occurrence. The family agreed that the 5:00 P.M. to 7:00 P.M. period was a good choice. I carefully pointed out to all of them that if Tommy should start to have a tantrum at another time he was to be reminded by his mother or father that he had to wait until 5:00 P.M. because it was not time to have a tantrum until then. I reminded them that the tantrums should still occur only in the "tantrum place."

By the third week Tommy's tantrums had diminished so markedly that the family could not remember if he had had any; they thought not. I expressed my puzzlement and concern that the rate of change had been too rapid and suggested in an offhand way that Tommy might want to have a tantrum the following week. I said he should still have it in the "tantrum place" and at the "tantrum time," but he could choose the day by himself during the week. No further tantrums were reported.

Results

The first session's assignment of having tantrums only in a "tantrum place" was accomplished in one week with a reduction in tantrums from the six or seven reported before treatment began to one. Following the second session's additional assignment of having tantrums only between 5:00 P.M. and 7:00 P.M., there were no tantrums. Despite the therapist's concern about the rate of change, during the remaining five weeks of treatment no further tantrums were reported.

The parents were clearly surprised and proud of their effectiveness, and Tommy was also rather pleased. Tommy's control of his tantrums under the paradoxical task assignments enabled the parents to recognize that they could be more relaxed about giving their children responsibility for managing their own behavior. The remaining sessions dealt with some shifts in responsibilities and expectations for their daughter as well as Tommy.

Follow-up

Nine months later the mother returned to treatment for herself.

At that time she reported that Tommy had had no further temper tantrums. His improved behavior was also evident at nursery school where it had been commented on by his teachers. She no longer accompanied him to nursery school.

Discussion

The dramatic disappearance of tantrum behavior that occurred in the present case is not unusual. In the use of paradoxical interventions, I have found that behaviors can often be terminated merely by the assignment of the paradoxical task without a single further occurrence, a change that Wolpe (1974) agreed cannot be accounted for by the usual learning principles involved in behavior modification, systematic desensitization, negative practice, or implosion. The therapist's detailed and matter-of-fact approach reduces anxiety in the patient and communicates the expectation that this is no different from other behaviors that can change. In Gestalt perceptual terms, the figure now recedes into the ground.

Some colleagues find it hard to believe that patients will accept such outlandish prescriptions, but my experience has been similar to that of Weakland and colleagues (1974), who report that patients usually do accept them. The question has been raised as to whether the presenting complaint is a real problem or rather exaggerated to satisfy the initial interest of the therapist. My experience has been that a careful inquiry can establish clearly the frequency and intensity of a behavior complaint.

Obviously, what is happening is that the presenting symptom is being brought under control as the therapist specifies the time and place of its occurrence. My expressing concern about the rapid rate of improvement is a further paradoxical intervention that I have found often increases the rate of improvement. Also, the behavior is now "taken over" by the therapist, so instead of telling Tommy to stop having tantrums, as everyone else has done, I tell him to continue to have them but to do it my way. In the final discussion of his tantrums, he was told that he could be the one to choose the day, but as expected, no more tantrums occurred.

One of the advantages of using a paradoxical intervention in the treatment of temper tantrums is that it engages the parent in the "cure process." Temper tantrums are very distressing to parents because they render them peculiarly helpless and incompetent in their own view and that of others. Children often select very awkward public places for tantrums. The paradoxical intervention is presented in such a reasonable way as to restore parents' confidence in themselves as well as respect for their child as the behavior problem disappears. For children, it is an important and enhancing experience to discover they can control their own behavior.

References

Frankl, V. E. (1966). Paradoxical intention: a logotherapeutic technique. *American Journal of Psychotherapy* 40:520–535.

Haley, J. (1973). *Uncommon Therapy*. New York: Norton.

Hare-Mustin, R. (1975). Paradoxical tasks in family therapy: Who can resist? *Psychotherapy: Theory, Research, and Practice*.

Kakkar, S. B. (1972). Experimental extinction of tantrum behavior. *Indian Journal of Experimental Psychology* 6:76–77.

Nelson, M. C., ed. (1968). *Roles and Paradigms in Psychotherapy*. New York: Grune & Stratton.

Solyom, L., Garza-Perez, J., Ledwidge, B. J., and Solyom, O. (1972). Paradoxical intention in the treatment of obsessive thoughts: a pilot study. *Comprehensive Psychiatry* 13:291–297.

Weakland, J. H., Fisch, R., Watzlawick, P., and Bodin, A. M. (1974). Brief therapy: focused problem resolution. *Family Process* 13:141–168.

Williams, C. D. (1959). The elimination of tantrum behavior by extinction procedures. *Journal of Abnormal Social Psychology* 59:269.

Wolpe, J. (1974). Personal communication, November.

30

Modifying Parent Responses to Their Children's Noncompliance

GINA S. RICHMAN, KELLEY A. HARRISON, AND
JANE A. SUMMERS

Researchers in the field of behavioral parent training have recognized that the focus of inquiry must be expanded beyond child-related variables to incorporate indices of parent behavior change (O'Dell 1974, Rickert et al. 1988, Rogers-Wiese 1990). The rationale for this shift in perspective is that children's behavior problems need to be evaluated within the context of the dynamic and reciprocal nature of parent–child interactions (Dumas 1984), as parent responses play a role in shaping, reinforcing, and maintaining both desirable and maladaptive child behavior patterns (Wahl et al. 1974).

Given that the interactions within a particular parent–child dyad are idiosyncratic, it is important to examine individual differences in parents' use of behavior management strategies (Houlihan et al. 1992). This is necessary because distinctive parenting styles or approaches may emerge even though the presenting problems are similar in nature. For instance, one parent may have a tendency to ignore his or her child's appropriate behavior while a different parent may reinforce his or her child's inappropriate behavior. In either case, the focus of intervention would differ even though the children may exhibit similar response topographies.

It is important for parents of children with behavior problems to be able to identify causal relationships within the parent–child interaction and program alternative antecedents and consequences. Child noncompliance with adult directives and requests is a relatively common occurrence in both clinic (Charlop et al. 1987) and nonreferred populations (Quay 1986). The importance of modifying this behavior is increased when considering that child noncompliance may occur in conjunction with other problems of an "antisocial" nature, such as verbal opposition, aggression, and tantrums (Bernal et al. 1980), which themselves are predictive of poor adjustment and outcome. Noncompliance is associated with increased levels of maladaptive behavior and is inversely related to more appropriate, prosocial forms of behavior (Parrish et al. 1986, Russo et al. 1981). Moreover, child noncompliance has been found to be associated with higher levels of stress and disharmony within the family unit (Campbell et al. 1986, Richman 1977). The result may be a cyclic pattern of interaction whereby stressed parents become more negative in response to child noncompliance, thus contributing to the maintenance of the problem (McMahon and Wells 1989).

The previous issues take on greater relevance when applied to children with developmental disabilities. These children often display a variety of behavior problems (Koller et al. 1982), one of which is noncompliance (Bates and Wehman 1977, Parrish et al. 1986, Russo et al. 1981). Children's behavioral excesses, in combination with their deficits in adaptive functioning, often interact to exacerbate parents' level of stress, and negatively influence their attitudes toward dealing with a child who has a handicap.

A recent study (Richman et al. 1994) evaluated specific parent and child responses within the context of a compliance training program. Parents' proficiency in providing appropriate consequences for child compliance and noncompliance was evaluated and subsequently increased during direct-instruction training sessions that focused primarily on remediating skill deficits. The current study offers an extension of these results by conducting a microanalysis of parent consequences for child compliance and noncompliance to identify specific error-response patterns. This assessment information formed the basis for individualized instruction to remediate areas of weakness. Measures of generalization and maintenance of treatment gains were obtained in order to evaluate the effectiveness of the training approach. Finally, the target population was expanded to include children both with and without developmental delays.

Method

Participants and Setting

Four boys and one girl participated in this study along with their primary caregivers. Three of the children (Bryan, age 7; Craig, age 4;

and Amy, age 4) were of average intelligence and attended regular education classes. The other two children carried diagnoses of developmental delay (Donny, age 5, Mild Mental Retardation; Randy, age 4, Communication Delay, functioning at 2-year level). The chief referring complaint was noncompliance. Also observed were temper tantrums, aggression, disruption, and verbal abuse. The behavior problems were identified during an intake evaluation via a departmental behavior problem checklist and the Child Behavior Checklist (Achenbach 1991). In each case, child noncompliance and/or oppositional behavior was rated as the most significant behavior problem. Parents resided in both inner city and suburban areas. All caregivers had a high school education or equivalent. The study was conducted in the outpatient behavioral psychology department of a pediatric hospital serving children with a wide range of behavior and medical problems.

Target Behaviors

Parent and child responses were broken down into specific categories to identify interactional patterns within each dyad.

Parent Behaviors

Parental instructions were defined as requests to the child to initiate and complete one specific task. During all phases of the study, requests involving multiple commands or instructing the child to terminate an activity were not counted. Parental responding to child compliance was defined as correct if the parent immediately responded with praise, physical affection, and/or access to a preferred activity. Correct parent responding to noncompliance for children without developmental delays was defined as the parent restating the instruction (e.g., "Susie, pick up your toys or you will have a time-out") and providing a specific consequence if the child continued to engage in noncompliance. Correct parent responding to child noncompliance for children with developmental delays was defined as the parent using a three-step guided compliance procedure (i.e., verbal, gestural, and physical prompts). Parents were told to issue instructions that were appropriate for the child's level of functioning, and included tasks previously identified by the clinician or the child's classroom teacher.

Parental errors in responding to child compliance and noncompliance were classified as: (a) parent ignored child's response (i.e., did not provide a consequence for correct or incorrect responding); (b) parent completed the task for the child; (c) parent repeated an instruction without a prompt or warning of the consequence for noncompliance; or (d) parent made a negative statement/reprimand in response to compliance or noncompliance (e.g., "You never do anything right!").

Child Behaviors

Child compliance was defined as the child initiating the task within ten seconds of the instruction and completing the entire task within five minutes without exhibiting any inappropriate behaviors (e.g., whining, complaining, tantruming, aggression, disruption, or verbal abuse).

Reliability

Interobserver agreement was calculated for each of the parent responses and child compliance and noncompliance on at least 40 percent of the sessions across all phases of the study. Using the kappa reliability coefficient transformed to a percentage, each parent behavior was recorded as follows: ignores noncompliance 99.6 percent; completes task 99.4 percent; repeats demand 91.4 percent; verbal reprimand 99.4 percent; ignores compliance 97.6 percent; and negative statement to compliance 100 percent. Average kappa values (expressed as percentages) for child compliance and noncompliance were 97.8 percent and 98.2 percent, respectively.

Procedure

Baseline

Each parent–child pair interacted in a clinic room with an adjoining one-way observation room. Parents were encouraged to bring siblings to the sessions if they were typically present when behavior problems occurred with the target child. Before the initial session commenced, parents identified instructions or activities that were very likely to result in noncompliant behavior. Parents typically stated that their child was most noncompliant when asked to comply to an instruction while engaging in a play activity. These situations were then incorporated into the therapy sessions to simulate as closely as possible typical parent–child interactions. Treatment rooms were arranged to include both play and instructional materials (e.g., books). Parents were told to begin issuing instructions after the child had started to engage in play activities. Each time the parent issued an instruction, a child behavior was scored as either compliant or noncompliant and the parent response was scored as either correct or incorrect. Both the child noncompliant behaviors and the parent incorrect behaviors were scored according to the specific response categories outlined previously under Parent behaviors and Child behaviors. Each parent was requested to issue at least ten instructions to her child; however, the type and timing of each instruction was individually determined. Each clinic session typically lasted one hour and was conducted one time per week.

Parent-Instruction Training Procedure

This procedure involved several components. First, the parents were given definitions of child compliance and noncompliance, along with a description of the specific components of a compliant response and the different ways in which a child could exhibit a noncompliant response. The definitions were intended to serve as both a guide to parents to discriminate compliance from noncompliance and to assist them in being consistent in the delivery of consequences. The therapist discussed the definitions with each parent, gave examples, and encouraged parents to ask questions if further clarification was needed.

The second component of treatment involved didactic instruction with parents in the use of appropriate consequences for child compliance and noncompliance. If necessary, parents were instructed to gain their children's attention before issuing instructions. Parents were taught to provide praise and/or physical affection for compliant behaviors. Parents of children without developmental delays were taught to use time-out or privilege removal (e.g., loss of a toy or preferred activity during the clinic session) for noncompliant behaviors. Explanations of the two procedures were discussed with each parent, and a determination was made based on the acceptability of the procedure to the parent. Two of the three parents chose to implement a time-out procedure, while the third parent implemented a privilege removal procedure.

Parents of children with developmental delays were taught to provide a verbal prompt as the initial consequence for noncompliance. Following the second noncompliant response, parents were trained to repeat the instruction along with a gestural prompt. In cases in which the child did not comply with the verbal or gestural prompt, parents were taught to provide a physical prompt to accompany the instruction. Parents were currently using this prompting procedure for other behaviors and found it very acceptable as an effective consequence for noncompliance.

The third component involved behavioral rehearsal, whereby the therapist worked directly with the parent and child to provide feedback each time compliance was requested. Parents were told to issue instructions exactly as they had during baseline while the therapist remained in the room. The focus of these training sessions was to target individual areas of deficiency in parental responding. For example, if a particular parent had difficulties reinforcing child compliance, the therapist concentrated primarily on this area of weakness.

The therapist's role was twofold. If a parent delivered an appropriate consequence, the therapist praised the parent and also had the parent discuss why the particular consequence was given (e.g., "Katie picked up the toys like I asked her"). If the parent gave an inappropriate consequence, the therapist immediately corrected the parent, gave a short explanation according to the definitions discussed previously, and had the parent provide the correct response. This procedure, therefore, allowed the therapist and parent to concentrate more time and effort working on areas of individual difficulty while spending relatively less time on areas of proficiency. Feedback was provided until the parent reached an 80 percent accuracy criterion for two consecutive tentrial blocks.

Post-Training Sessions

Clinic observations of the parent–child dyads were conducted after the parent met the training criteria. These sessions were conducted to assess the effects of the direct instruction procedure on parents' correct responding to compliance and noncompliance in the absence of the trainer and corrective feedback (i.e., under the same conditions described in baseline). If the parent scored below the 80 percent criterion, direct instruction was again implemented. Once the 80 percent criterion was attained, another post-training session was conducted. This process enabled the parent to receive additional training and feedback in areas of weakness before another post-training session took place.

Generalization Probes

During both baseline and treatment conditions, data were collected in a second setting for each child in the same manner described during post-training sessions. These data were collected in public places where noncompliance had a high probability of occurring (e.g., restaurant, waiting room) to assess the frequency of the target behavior in a setting in which training did not occur.

Follow-up

To assess the long-term effectiveness of the treatment procedure, follow-up was conducted in the child's home environment where the behavior problem was initially identified. Data were collected for four of the five families (Randy's family moved after treatment was completed) in the same manner described during baseline and probe conditions. These data were obtained from one month to five months post-treatment, depending on the availability of the family.

Experimental Design

A multiple-probes design (Horner and Baer 1978) was used to evaluate the effectiveness of the direct instruction training procedure for increasing parents' use of appropriate consequences.

Results

As shown in Table 30–1, during baseline, parents showed different patterns of incorrect responding to their children's compliant and noncompliant behaviors. For example, Bryan's mother tended to respond to both compliance and noncompliance by ignoring the behavior. However, she also responded to noncompliance by repeating the request without following through with a consequence. Following treatment, all parents showed a decrease in the percent of responses to both compliance and noncompliance that were classified as errors. This decrease was maintained at follow-up with the exception of Bryan's mother, who responded to his two noncompliant responses by repeating the request without a warning. However, it is noteworthy that Bryan complied with the requests when they were repeated.

Figure 30–1 depicts parental responding to child compliance and noncompliance before and after treatment, in and outside the treatment setting, as well as during follow-up sessions. During the baseline phase, parents' use of correct consequences for compliance and noncompliance was low and variable. The baseline data also show no consistent differences between data collected in the clinic and generalization settings. Following implementation of the parent-instruction treatment procedure, all parents showed substantial improvement in their use of correct consequences for both compliance and noncompliance in both the clinic and generalization settings. The number of training sessions conducted ranged from one to eleven (Donny, one; Amy and Randy, two; Bryan, six; and Craig, eleven).

| | Parent Responses | | | | | |
| | Noncompliance | | | | Compliance | |
Phase	Ignores	Completes Task	Repeats Demand	Verbal Reprimand	Ignores	Negative Statement
Bryan						
Baseline	54.5	0	40.9	4.5	97	0
Post training	0	0	0	0	14	0
Follow-up	0	0	100	0	24	0
Craig						
Baseline	3.6	10.7	67.9	10.7	78.8	8.7
Post training	9.5	9.5	4.8	0	21.8	0
Follow-up	0	0	0	0	50	0
Amy						
Baseline	15.4	23	46	15.4	50	15.2
Post training	0	0	0	0	18.5	0
Follow-up	*	*	*	*	20	*
Randy						
Baseline	71.4	0	0	0	81	0
Post training	0	0	0	0	0	11.1
Donny						
Baseline	61.5	7.7	23	0	78.8	3
Post training	0	0	0	0	11	0
Follow-up	0	0	0	0	0	0

Note. * = Noncompliance did not occur

Table 30-1. Percent of parental responses to noncompliance/compliance.

Follow-up data demonstrated that maintenance of treatment gains varied across parent–child dyads. Bryan's mother continued to respond correctly to her child's compliant responses but failed to respond appropriately to noncompliance (Bryan exhibited noncompliance following only two of his mother's requests.) Craig's mother, in contrast, continued to demonstrate appropriate responding to 100 percent of her child's noncompliant responses while correct responding to compliance decreased to 50 percent. Amy's mother demonstrated correct responding to compliance; however, because Amy was compliant to 100 percent of her mother's requests, parental responding to noncompliance

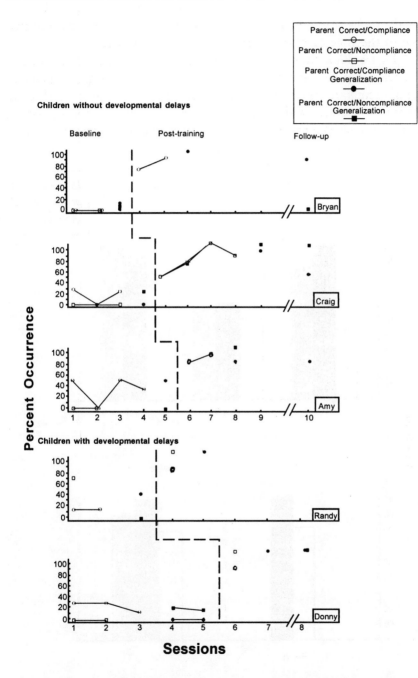

Figure 30–1. Correct parental responding to child compliance and non-compliance for children with and without developmental delays.

could not be assessed. Donny's mother responded correctly 100 percent of the time to both compliance and noncompliance.

Figure 30–2 shows child compliance during baseline, treatment, and follow-up. On average, all five children showed a higher percentage of compliant responses following treatment. The most notable improvement was seen with Bryan (43.5 percent compliance during baseline sessions versus 95.8 percent compliance during post-treatment sessions).

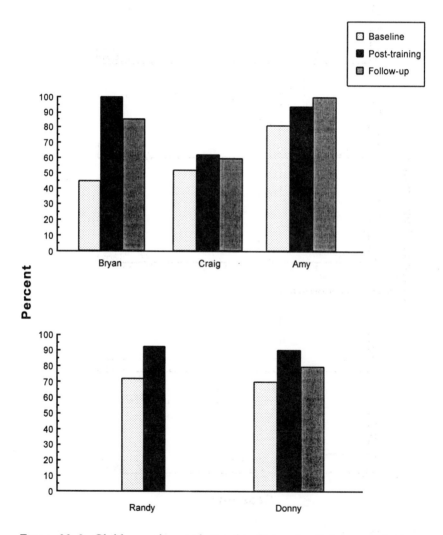

Figure 30–2. Child compliance during baseline, post-training, and follow-up.

Discussion

The results of this investigation demonstrated that parents display different response patterns to their children's noncompliant behavior. Prior to treatment, parents' error response patterns to child noncompliance were classified. This assessment information was used to tailor an intervention program that concentrated on each parent–child interaction pattern, thus ensuring that training was addressing the individual strengths and weaknesses of each dyad. Selecting parental behaviors as the primary dependent measure avoided the necessity to wait for child noncompliance to occur in the clinic before initiating treatment. It is interesting to note that parents delivered a sufficient number of appropriate instructions prior to treatment such that instruction-giving did not need to be a focus of the intervention.

Following the implementation of the treatment program, each parent showed improvement in correctly responding to her child's compliant and noncompliant behaviors. Positive changes were evidenced by each parent–child dyad regardless of the specific pretreatment patterns of responding. There was a concomitant increase in child compliance as well, albeit not as substantial as parent behaviors given the initial baseline levels. It was noteworthy that child compliance was not an accurate indicator of how well parents were delivering consequences for appropriate and inappropriate behavior during baseline. The children's behavior may have been affected by factors other than the parents' use of consequences, such as the demand characteristics of the clinic situation. Future studies should utilize procedures to increase the opportunities to observe noncompliance in the clinical setting. For instance, parents and teachers may complete a compliance probability checklist to identify instructions that reliably elicit high rates of noncompliance.

The gains demonstrated by each dyad during treatment generalized to a second setting where treatment was never implemented. Furthermore, follow-up conducted up to six months post-treatment in the children's homes showed that for most of the dyads, treatment gains were maintained over time. The most frequent mistakes displayed by parents to their children's noncompliant behavior were ignoring the behavior or repeating the request without a warning or a prompt. It is interesting to note that parents never needed to implement consequences for noncompliant behavior. After noncompliance occurred and a warning of a consequence followed, all children responded appropriately to the instruction.

Both the generalization and the follow-up data attest to the robustness of the procedure across settings and over time. Although this program was effective for the parents of children with and without developmental delays, the procedure required more steps for the families of the former group. For example, these parents were taught prompting procedures in the event that their children did not respond to verbal instructions, potentially minimizing problems with attention and motivation. In addition, it is noteworthy that the way in which parents delivered instructions was not modified by the therapists in any way since this was not the focus of treatment. In all phases of the study, only the instructions that required the child to complete a task (versus stopping an activity) were scored. Parents delivered a sufficient number of appropriate requests in each condition to preclude the inclusion of this component.

The present study emphasizes the importance of assessing patterns of parental responding to child noncompliance. By doing this, the clinician can focus more or less attention on specific treatment components with each family. Although it may be standard practice in the parent-training literature to evaluate parental skill deficits in order to individualize treatment approaches (e.g., McMahon and Forehand 1983), there is a lack of empirical data regarding this issue. Future research should evaluate the role of the parent(s) in assessing a host of childhood behavior problems to more fully understand the dynamic relationship that exists between parents and their children. Before implementing a treatment program based on a parents' assumptions regarding their children's problematic behavior, clinicians should be cautioned to more fully evaluate and understand the parents' role in maintaining child behaviors.

References

Achenbach, T. M. (1991). *Integrative Guide for the 1991 CBCL/4–18, YSR, and TRF Profiles.* Burlington, VT: University of Vermont, Department of Psychiatry.

Bates, P., and Wehman, P. (1977). Behavior management with the mentally retarded: an empirical analysis of the research. *Mental Retardation* 15(6):9–12.

Bernal, M. E., Klinnert, M. D., and Schultz, L. A. (1980). Outcome evaluation of behavioral parent training and client-centered parent counseling for children with conduct problems. *Journal of Applied Behavior Analysis* 13:677–691.

Campbell, S. B., Breauz, A. M., Ewing, L. J., and Szumowski, E. K. (1986). Correlates and predictors of hyperactivity and aggression: a longitudinal study of parent-referred problem preschoolers. *Journal of Abnormal Child Psychology* 14:217–234.

Charlop, M. H., Parrish, J. M., Fenton, L. R., and Cataldo, M. F. (1987). Evaluation of hospital-based outpatient pediatric psychology services. *Journal of Pediatric Psychology* 12:485–503.

Dumas, J. E. (1984). Interactional correlates of treatment outcome in behavioral parent training. *Journal of Consulting and Clinical Psychology* 52:946–954.

Horner, R. D., and Baer, D. M. (1978). Multiple-probe technique: a variation of multiple baseline. *Journal of Applied Behavior Analysis* 11:189–196.

Houlihan, D. D., Sloane, H. N., Jones, R. N., and Patten, C. (1992). A review of behavioral conceptualizations and treatments of child noncompliance. *Education and Treatment of Children* 15:56–77.

Koller, H., Richardson, S. A., Katz, M., and McLaren, J. (1982). Behavior disturbance in childhood and the early adult years in populations who were and were not mentally retarded. *Journal of Preventive Psychiatry* 1:453–468.

McMahon, R. J., and Forehand, R. (1983). Consumer satisfaction in behavioral treatment of children: types, issues and recommendations. *Behavior Therapy* 14:209–225.

McMahon, R. J., and Wells, K. C. (1989). Conduct disorders. In *Treatment of Childhood Disorders* ed. E. J. Mash and R. A. Barkley, pp. 73–132. New York: Guilford.

O'Dell, S. (1974). Training parents in behavior modification: a review. *Psychological Bulletin* 81:418–433.

Parrish, J. M., Cataldo, M. F., Kolko, D. J., et al. (1986). Experimental analysis of response covariation among compliant and inappropriate behaviors. *Journal of Applied Behavior Analysis* 19:241–254.

Quay, H. C. (1986). Conduct disorders. In *Psychopathological Disorders of Childhood*, 3rd ed., ed. H. C. Quay and J. S. Werry, pp. 35–72. New York: Wiley.

Richman, G. S., Hagopian, L. P., Harrison, K., et al. (1994). Assessing parental response patterns in the treatment of noncompliance in children. *Child and Family Behavior Therapy* 16:29–42.

Richman, N. (1977). Behaviour problems in pre-school children: family and social factors. *British Journal of Psychiatry* 131:523–527.

Rickert, V. I., Sottolano, D. C., Parrish, J. M., et al. (1988). Training parents to become better behavior managers: the need for a competency-based approach. *Behavior Modification* 12:475–496.

Rogers-Wiese, M. R. A *critical review of parent training research*. Poster presented at the 98th Annual Convention of the American Psychological Association, Boston, MA, 1990.

Russo, D. C., Cataldo, M. F., and Cushing, P. J. (1981). Compliance training and behavioral covariation in the treatment of multiple behavior problems. *Journal of Applied Behavior Analysis* 14:209–222.

Wahl, G., Johnson, S. M., Johansson, S., and Martin, S. (1974). An operant analysis of child–family interaction. *Behavior Therapy* 5:64–78.

31

The Marking Time-out Procedure for Disruptive Behavior

RONALD S. DRABMAN AND DEBRA L. CREEDON

Various techniques have been found effective in decreasing undesirable, disruptive, and inappropriate behavior of children. However, time-out or social isolation is fast becoming the most popular punishment procedure (Drabman 1976). Parents using time-out in the home as a means of controlling children's disruptive behavior are encouraged to isolate the child briefly in a nonstimulating, sensory-restricting environment contingent upon inappropriate behavior. But the problem arises: What to do when the target behavior occurs *outside* the home? Ideally, time-out programs must be immediate, but children are disruptive in the car, at the store, in church, and so on, so away-from-home alternative procedures must be developed. Additionally, children learn to discriminate situations in which punishment is not feasible. Thus, they often misbehave in public.

One solution we have found clinically effective with young children for discipline in public places can be termed "Marking Time-out." The Marking Time-out procedure is suggested for use by parents as an alternative to verbal and physical punishment usually employed.

Marking time is defined as "to keep time . . . by moving . . . without advancing" (Webster 1974). In Marking Time-out, the child virtually "marks time" until able to "serve time" in the regular time-out setting. This is done by the use of a water-based felt-tipped marking pen. The procedure is as follows:

Step 1: Time-out is established as a reliable punisher in the home.

Step 2: The child is told that, when a specific behavior occurs outside the home, he/she will receive one mark on the back of the hand. This mark represents a predetermined amount of time in the time-out area at home (five minutes if under 5 years old, ten minutes if older). When a disruption occurs, the parent informs the child that he/she has done something wrong (mentioning the exact disruptive behavior) and puts one mark on the child's hand, to be exchanged at home for time-out time. For example, "John, you teased your sister, so you get a mark and will go to the time-out room as soon as we get home."

Step 3: The rewarding of good behavior is an integral part of this procedure. This should be discussed with the child in advance. For example (in the grocery store), "If you behave and stay with me and receive no marks you may pick out a pack of gum when we reach the checkout counter."

Step 4: After explaining the new time-out system to the child, it is extremely important to plan a few practice trips. At this time, parents are to concentrate on implementing the Marking Time-out procedure. Before a practice trip, the parent explains to the child the behavior rules for the place they are to visit, what the reward for good behavior will be, and that at the second mark the child will be taken immediately home and placed in time-out. For example, the child is taken to the grocery store. He is not told that this is a practice trip. The parent proceeds as normal through the store, putting only nonperishables in the cart. This way, if the child misbehaves the shopping cart can be left and the child immediately taken home. When the child misbehaves, he/she is briefly informed of the misbehavior, the back of the hand is marked, and the child is assured of time-out upon arrival home. The second time the child misbehaves, he/she is briefly told the problem, marked on the hand, and abruptly taken home. When home, the child is immediately placed into the time-out area for two periods of time-out. Several practice trips are taken during the first weeks of the new program. In this way, the child will not learn to discriminate the practice trips from the real trips, and effective learning of the Marking Time-out system is possible. Practice trips should be taken to as many as possible of the places where the child tends to be disruptive. When the child has a successful practice trip, he/she receives the reward plus copious praise. After a few successful practice trips, real trips can be gradually introduced.

This method has been found successful with many families. Reward or punishment alone has not been nearly as effective as the Marking Time-out procedure. Although it is theoretically possible for the child to use misbehaving as a way of controlling the parents' visits, we have found that with judicious use of reinforcement this rarely occurs.

References

Drabman, R. (1976). Behavior modification in the classroom. In *Behavior Modification: Principles, Issues, and Application*, ed. E. Craighead, M. Mahoney, and A. Kazdin. New York: Houghton Mifflin.

Webster's New Collegiate Dictionary, 8th ed. (1974). Springfield, MA: G. & C. Merriam.

32

How to Deal with Manipulative Children

KAREN L. BECKSTRAND AND CHRIS E. STOUT

When working with parents of problematic youth, the practitioner often sees the parents being manipulated. Regardless of the mode of treatment (e.g., individual, family, or group), therapy context (e.g., inpatient, outpatient, school, pediatric), or orientation (e.g., systemic, dynamic, cognitive/behavioral, contextual, communications), issues of manipulation may exist.

It has been the authors' experience that manipulated parents are often blind to the manipulation. In some instances, they may see some situations for what they are, but this does not generalize to all or enough situations to be therapeutically appropriate. In response to this common phenomenon, the authors developed the parent handout which follows.

Parents seem more willing to grasp general printed material that relates to their specific situation than to rely solely on the comments of a professional they may not yet trust. The resistance some practitioners experience from patients may be mitigated by using materials such as this handout. The clinical impact can be manifold. In addition to decreasing resistance to change, parents also start to recognize their child's dysfunctional patterns for what they are and may then be more open to interventions and alterations of the dysfunctional pattern, system, or dynamic. There is also merit to the perspective of therapeutic family change without "blame placing" on parents. Often in seeking therapeutic help, parents may feel as if they are failures if their child is presenting with problematic behaviors. This handout focuses on the children's manipulations or patterns of behavior, which may then be systemically dealt with by the clinician without the parents feeling blamed or guilty. Parents also may be angry at their problematic child when they feel out of control or recognize that they are being somehow manipulated without recognizing the manipulation. This handout aids in clarifying the manipulation (thus highlighting ways the therapist can assist with intervention strategies) while decreasing parental anger by depathologizing manipulations that are common to many youth and parents.

The handout is written in a format that purports to train children in ways to manipulate their parents; the authors have found that this is an efficient and humorous (thus destigmatizing/normalizing) format that most parents quickly grasp.

Some parents have asked if it is appropriate for their children to see the handout. In most cases doing so does not create any problems. In all cases, good clinical judgment should be used in determining the potential risks and benefits of any intervention. It is hoped that this handout will provide child, adolescent, family, pediatric, and school practitioners with a helpful new adjunctive clinical tool to better deal with a common challenge in dealing with children who manipulate.

TECHNIQUES TO MANIPULATE PARENTS:
A USER'S GUIDE

MANIPULATING: An easy and fun way to change rules, limits, and expectations that you don't like.

SPLITTING: Ask Mom and Dad separately for something (or to do something) that they don't agree on; see if you can get them to argue, and thus deflect the issue away from your request.

MISQUOTING (very effective when used with *splitting*): Quote your parent as having said "next week" when he or she actually said "*maybe* next week."

DEFIANCE: Just do what you want to anyway and see if your parents get so disgusted with you that they just give up reinforcing the rules and let you do what you want.

PROMISES: "I promise to clean my room *after* I get back." It doesn't matter if the promise is kept or not.

BEGGING: "Please? Please? Pleeeeeeeeease?"

REPEATING: Make the same request over and over to see if you can get a different answer than "No." You've got nothing to lose!

BARGAINING (explicit or implied): An implied bargain is similar to a bribe, for example, cleaning the house first and then asking to do something.

GUILT TRIPPING: Give your parents the message: "If you really loved me you would let me _____," or "If you were good parents, you would _____." Don't forget the ever popular variation: "So-and-so's parents let him or her _____." It helps to imply that you will be emotionally shattered or socially scarred for the rest of eternity unless your parents give in. (**Parents are suckers for this one!**)

THREATENING: Either explicit or implied. Could be a threat to get even, to show them, to hurt yourself, or just to defy your parents. Remember: You're in control.

TIMING/CORNERING: Ask Mom or Dad for permission for something when they are busy, on the phone, or stressed out, and unable to process the information.

CRYING/ACTING PATHETIC: Give parents the message that only *they* can make it all better if they just do, buy, or give permission for _____. Use lots of whining, too. Works like a charm!

PUNISHING FAMILY BY ACTIONS: A "pay back"—for example, "accidentally" track in mud, play music too loud, or stay in bathroom too long. (A sullen face, sulking, and silent pouting is helpful.)

"YOU'RE BAD PARENTS": (a) Complain, (b) say "Don't you think I deserve it?" (c) laugh at your parents, (d) point out that your parents are *so* stupid, and/or (e) point out when parents are inconsistent.

IRRITATION: Bug your parents enough so that it feels like an ancient Chinese torture, and your parents will give right in just to shut you up. This works really well in stores, church, other people's homes, and other public places.

DEMANDING JUSTIFICATION: Demand reasons and answers and proof. Try: "Why? Why not? Don't you trust me?"

LYING (either by commission or by omission, simple and easy): For example, not telling your parents that so-and-so's parents are out of town, and asking to spend the night at so-and-so's house.

HURTING THEM: Rarely tell them, or show them, that you love them, respect them, or will, in adulthood, appreciate what they have done for you. Remember, actions speak louder than words.

33

Compulsive Stealing

RALPH WETZEL

Several investigators have demonstrated the effectiveness of behavioral techniques in the modification of so-called deviant behaviors. These demonstrations have involved settings varying from the hospital (Ayllon and Michael 1959, Wolf et al. 1964) and the nursery school (Harris et al. 1964) to the clinician's office (Wolpe 1958) and the home (Boardman 1962). Likewise, the modifications have varied from the establishment of new behavioral repertoires to the elimination of whole classes of behavior.

An important feature of many demonstrations is that the change in behavior is often accomplished by relatively untrained, nonprofessional individuals. Hospital attendants, nursery school teachers, parents, and others have all been effective in the modification of deviant behaviors heretofore considered the domain of highly skilled and usually highly paid professional individuals. Usually these nonprofessionals have received very little special training. The implications for the efficient use of consultant time, the reduction of treatment costs, and the dispersion of therapeutic effectiveness are obvious. Bandura (1962) has pointed out that the professional individual can best spend his time instructing others in the application of behavioral principles and the work of several authors has suggested some very practical and ingenious consulting procedures (Phillips 1960, Williams 1959, Wolf 1965).

The efficiency of behavioral techniques usually depends upon the control of specific response contingencies and has been most successfully applied in controlled environments. Outside of the laboratory, hospitals appear to provide the best control although the nursery school studies of Harris and colleagues (1964) demonstrate the achievement of control in a relatively free environment. Boardman (1962), in spite of the relative lack of control in the "natural" environment of a young boy, was able to significantly modify aggressive acting-out behavior using behavioral techniques, and Wolf (1965) has shown that parental cooperation can provide excellent control of specific behavior in the home.

In his discussion of Boardman's demonstration, Bandura (1962) is critical of the use of punishment for several very valid reasons and suggests that it is more desirable to remove reinforcers maintaining the target behavior and reinforce alternative behaviors. His suggestion, however, becomes more difficult to implement as the environment becomes more natural. In these situations there are probably multiple reinforcers controlling a behavior, many of which cannot be identified, much less controlled. On the school ground, for example, behavior which is under the control of other children is often difficult to handle because the situation requires modifying the behavior of several other individuals. Further, the natural environment frequently prohibits the use of potentially effective reinforcement contingencies. Although there are certain behaviors upon which parents and teachers may make meals contingent (such as handwashing), the use of food as a reinforcer is generally restricted. Thus, the general use of behavior principles in the more open, natural situation is often hampered by the existence of these multiple reinforcers and by a restriction in the range of reinforcers available for modifying the target behavior.

The present study further demonstrates the use of behavior principles in the modification of a deviant behavior. The "compulsive" stealing of a 10-year-old resident of a home for mildly disturbed children was successfully eliminated over a three-and-a-half-month period. Records indicate that the behavior had been a source of difficulty for at least five years. The behavior "therapy" was carried out in a field situation and made minimal use of professional time. The study demonstrates the use of nonprofessional individuals in the modification, observations, and recording of behavior, and indicates some of the hazards involved in so doing. Hopefully it also suggests some solutions to the problems involved.

Subject and History

The subject, who will be called Mike, was a Mexican-American boy, age 10 at the beginning of this study. He first came to the attention of professional individuals when school authorities expelled him from the first grade and referred his mother to a child guidance clinic. He had already long been a disciplinary problem to his mother who found him "impossible." She had had many complaints of stealing and destructive behavior from neighbors but was unable to exert any control over Mike. She most frequently resorted to locking Mike in his bedroom, but he usually tore open the screen and escaped through the window. On one occasion he left after setting fire to his bed. The father was hospitalized for a chronic condition resulting from a war injury and the family was considered by caseworkers as "marginal." The mother had four children, little money, and was described by the psychiatrist at the guidance clinic as "inadequate."

In the first grade Mike continued to steal, was destructive of school property, disturbed other children, and made no academic progress. At the child guidance clinic, at age 7, he was given a psychiatric and psychological examination. He was described as a nonpsychotic, anxious, "slow learner" with "poor impulse control." His Stanford-Binet IQ was 78. He was diagnosed "passive-aggressive personality, aggressive type, severe." A special education class was recommended from which Mike was expelled one month later because the teacher was unable to handle him. He was placed in a foster home by the public welfare agency.

In the first half of his eighth year, Mike alternately lived in foster homes or under juvenile detention. The complaints from the foster homes were consistently about his stealing and destruction (in one home he chopped up a dining room chair with an ax). Due to his inability to adjust to foster homes and the undesirable effects of his long-term detention residence, Mike was made a ward of the court at age 8½ and was placed in the Children's Home, a residential treatment center for midly disturbed children. The records of Mike's first few weeks at the Children's Home indicate the absence of destructive behavior but a high rate of tantrum behavior, bedwetting, and stealing. In his first interview with the consulting psychiatrist he complained of being picked on by the other children and accused of stealing. He admitted that he just could not stay out of their lockers. The psychiatrist felt that he had "many qualities of a full-blown psychopath" but that he was essentially workable and looking for controls. He was described by the staff as "charming," with little conscience and a tendency to "project his faults to others."

During the ensuing nine months, Mike was described as making some adjustment to the home. He saw a caseworker once or twice a week, entered special classes of a nearby public school, and gradually established some relationships with the staff. The latter were almost exclusively with the women child-care workers, with whom he made himself ingratiating and useful. He was variously described by them as "a charmer," "adorable," and "a manipulator." At the same time there was a noticeable reduction in the staff reports of tantrums and day-wetting.

His relationships with the other children at the home remained poor, apparently because he continued to steal. More and more the discussions with his caseworker took up the topic of stealing. The casework notes record Mike saying such things as, "I know I shouldn't steal people's things. I know it's wrong, so I am not going to do it." He complained about his inability to get along with "Englisher kids" because they picked on him for stealing. In spite of his complaints and promises, however, the incidence of stealing increased and spread to the school. He frequently brought home from the school toys, books, and assorted objects from the teacher's desk and the school bulletin board.

Various attempts were made to curb the stealing. It was noted, for example, that he frequently gave the objects he stole to another person. Suspecting that he was buying affections, his caseworker spent several sessions discussing Mike's need for affection with him and suggesting to Mike that his stealing enabled him to win affection from others. Mike usually replied by saying he was sorry and that he would not do it again. Another time a child-care worker suggested that Mike might derive some satisfaction from the attention his stealing brought and thought they should "simply see that he returns what he takes." This plan was never put into effect although it had merit.

At the end of his first nine months in the home, Mike showed definite improvement in all behaviors except stealing and bedwetting. His stealing was by far the most serious since it had prohibited his establishing rewarding relationships with his peers and had alienated most of the staff. At this time, his behavior was described as "kleptomania" in his records. The case work notes of this period reflect the general pessimism over his stealing:

> Mike has come to me almost every day saying, "I didn't steal at school"; sometimes he has and sometimes he hasn't. I feel our sessions are a "front." He simply wants me to feel he is trying even though he isn't.

The optimism expressed in the last summary in regard to Mike's "sticky fingers" was apparently premature since soon after the end of October he started stealing both from school and again from the home (whenever a closet was left open) and from the other children.

After nine months in the Children's Home, Mike was recommended for foster home placement. It was the general consensus that his behavior had improved considerably and that his stealing represented a bid for affection. It was hoped that the latter would improve in a home atmosphere with a "loving maternal figure." He was described as "a chronic bedwetter with occasional wet pants . . . seeking out women and relating to them in an immature way. . . . Lovable but often like a little pack rat." He was placed with a Mexican-American family described as "exceptionally warm," living on the Arizona desert with three boys and horses.

One can only speculate what happened in the foster home. Five months later the Children's Home received a letter from welfare stating that "Mike's behavior in his foster home suggests further deterioration in his capacity to adjust" and requesting that he be readmitted. He entered for the second time at the age of 9 years, 10 months.

After readmission, the frequency of stealing appeared to be greater than ever before. It was reported at staff conferences that he was stealing nearly every day and on each shopping trip. The other children had begun to blame him for every missing article and, according to staff notes, "the articles are invariably found in his locker, on his person, or located with another individual who states that they are gifts from Mike."

At one staff conference the rationale for the present study was suggested by the author. Though there was not complete agreement about the method, the nearly five-year history of previous failure and the shortage of staff for casework and interview therapy contributed, perhaps, to its acceptance.

Method

Training the Staff

Since the individuals in constant contact with Mike, the child-care workers, were relatively untrained and unsophisticated in psychological theory and technique, it was first necessary to acquaint them with a few behavior principles. This was done in a series of four one-and-a-half-hour conferences. These covered the nature of reinforcement, the effects of behavior consequences, and the recording of behavior.

In addition, the film *Reinforcement in Learning and Extinction* (McGraw-Hill 1956) was shown. Discussion was focused on the possible application of these principles to Mike's stealing behavior. The reactions of the staff were varied. Some were enthusiastic, others stated that behavior principles are just "common sense," while others stated that the approach was "too scientific," meaning apparently, that it was too remote and "disregarded feelings." The intention was to convey in these sessions three essential points: (a) the consequences of behavior can control the behavior; (b) recording of the behavior is essential to the success of the study; (c) the study is experimental and there may be a period of trial and error. It will be seen that these points were not completely conveyed.

Selecting the Reinforcer

The staff argued that punishment of the stealing was not desirable. Mike had shown himself resistant to the usual consequences of stealing. Scoldings and disapproval by the child-care workers, the anger of peers, the return of the objects all had no effect on the stealing rate. The history indicates that assorted punishments (including spanking and isolation) prior to his admission to the home had been ineffective. The general policies of the home, moreover, encouraged only the most minimal and judicious use of punishment. Extinction by removal of the consequences thought to maintain the stealing was also ruled out. There was no question but that a great deal of attention was paid to Mike's stealing. He had developed an extensive repertoire of excuses and explanations which could hold the attention of a child-care worker often for an hour. However, the removal of these consequences was difficult. Much of the attention came from peers, school children, and teachers, and was difficult to control. An attempt by the supervisor of the child-care workers to reduce the attention paid to the stealing had no effect. It was thus decided to withdraw positive reinforcement contingent on stealing.

The initial task was to find a positive reinforcer that could be conveniently and effectively removed. The child-care workers agreed that there was nothing Mike cared enough about that he would stop stealing to maintain. An examination of his personal relations indicated that he had no particular rapport with the child-care workers but that he did occasionally talk to one of the cooks, a Spanish-speaking Mexican-American woman who seemed fond of Mike. The decision was made to make the relationship with the cook the positive reinforcer.

Establishing the Reinforcer

Since Mike's relationship with the cook, Maria, was casual and tenuous at best, it was necessary to intensify it to give it effective reinforcing value. It was explained to Maria, through a translator, that she seemed to play an important role in Mike's life at the Children's Home and that it would be helpful if she could become even more important to him. It was also explained that she would eventually be asked to help Mike with his principal difficulty, stealing. Maria was very willing and a plan was devised whereby she saw Mike daily. He was invited into the kitchen, prepared Mexican foods, and taken to Maria's home for visits. Maria mended his clothes, took him shopping and to church. In a few days, Mike apparently was looking forward to his visits and Maria, in turn, became especially fond of him.

The Contingency

Maria was told that it was possible she could help Mike with his stealing. It was explained that whenever Mike stole she would be informed and that as soon as possible she was to say to him in Spanish: "I'm sorry that you took *so-and-so's blank* because now I can't let you come home with me tonight." It was emphasized that she should say nothing else, should listen to no explanations or excuses but should turn and walk away. The following day she was to resume her usual warm relationship with Mike and maintain it until the next stealing incident.

Recording Behavior

The child-care workers were told that whenever the property of another person, the school, or the home was found on Mike's person, in his locker, or in his room, and it was determined that the property had not been legitimately given to him, they were to (a) record a stealing incident on a daily chart and (b) when the time came, report the incident to Maria. Maria was instructed to keep a record of sessions she missed with Mike because of his stealing.

Results

Once a week the charts were collected and transferred to the cumulative record shown in Figure 33-1. Each step up represents *one or more* stealing incidents for a given day. The period of observation covers approximately five months and one week. The four days around Christ-

mas which Mike spent out of the home are not recorded since observation was impossible.

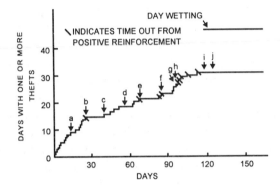

Figure 33-1. A cumulative record showing the effects of withdrawal of a
positive reinforcer on the stealing behavior of a 10-year-old boy. The
upper right line indicates the absence of day wetting as a substitute acting-out behavior.

It was planned to allow four weeks for the relationship with Maria
to develop. The child-care workers were instructed to continue the recording they had begun in the training sessions during this time. They
were told, also, to handle the stealing in whatever way they were ac-
customed.

The Baseline

The beginning of the record to *b* constitutes the baseline recording. At *c* Mike began his visits with Maria and the supervisor of the
child-care staff began to keep daily records of the interactions between
Mike and Maria as well as others. Some quotations from these records
will clarify the nature of the relationship between Mike and Maria.

11/10 Began daily hour with Maria—very pleased.

11/11 Went for five hours (in the) afternoon—brought me some
homemade tortilla from Maria's.

11/12 Clothes shopping with Maria. Pleased and made certain I
marked (them) properly in big letters, happy Maria bought him
shirts and took home and shortened sleeves before return—impressed on me what a good mother Maria is. I agreed.

11/13 Related he is teaching Maria English—he really likes to go with her because she has tortillas every day. Liked warm jacket Maria gave him. It was her boy's that he outgrew.

Although there was a reduction in stealing behavior immediately following the beginning of the visits with Maria, the rate soon returned to its original level. Since the record only indicates *one or more* stealing incidents per day, it does not accurately reflect the amount of stealing within days. The following lists the objects stolen in the five incidents between *a* and *b*: (a) a ten-cent-store ring, a ball, a pin, five pencils, all belonging to other children; (b) three rolls of toilet paper, three sweaters, and twelve pairs of socks belonging to other children; (c) some underwear, three bars of soap, and a model airplane; (d) a quarter; (e) a child-care worker's keys.

The First Contingency

At *b*, twelve days after the beginning of his sessions with Maria, Mike gave the supervisor such a difficult time that she decided to deny him his visit with Maria even though it was premature according to the general program. Her notes are explanatory:

> I left linen closet door open in process of getting towels to boys who went to shower without. Next thing I knew, Mike was having a toothpaste-squirting game all over the room. (He said) he took from closet—I had him clean up. After shower, rash of bandaids appeared all over. Mike admitted taking at same time as toothpaste. Said didn't have p.j.'s. At this point, I went to drawer and pulled (them) out wherein I found a pearl-handled pocket knife which belonged to George, and *Playboy* magazine. Said he took these from (child-care worker's) room when I went into relief room to answer telephone. I recognized with him I was very tired and really should know better than to ever leave a door open. . . . told him I considered this deliberate stealing four times within a half-hour and I would tell Maria and he would not go with her Monday.

Since this occurred late one evening, Maria was not informed until the next day nearly twenty hours after the behavior. Hence, the first contingency was hardly contingent, though the supervisor's threat certainly was.

The next day at dinner time Mike went into the kitchen as usual. He was followed by several child-care workers who were anxious to see what would happen. They reported that Maria looked "stern" as she spoke to Mike in Spanish. Mike, however, remained in the kitchen and seemed so unaffected that one of the child-care workers urged Maria to tell Mike again. Accordingly, Maria repeated the routine, turned, and went about her work in the kitchen. Mike wandered into a nearby sitting room where he had been allowed to wait. About five minutes later, a child-care worker told him he would have to return to his cottage. He was described as "pouty" the rest of the evening and throughout the next day. In the evening, he met Maria in the kitchen as usual. For the next thirteen days, no stealing was reported. It was apparently the longest he had gone without stealing at the home.

Removal of the Contingency

A new problem arose in the period represented by the interval c to e in Figure 33–1. Mike began to appear with assorted articles which seemed so minor to the child-care staff that they were not reported to Maria. Some matches which he said he found, some cookies which "a nice lady had given him," a little Christmas tree from the infirmary all seemed too innocent to report. The child-care staff offered two reasons for feeling lenient: (a) Mike already seemed better; (b) it was so close to Christmas that they hated to deny him his visit. d marks Christmas, and it can be seen that, like most children, Mike was especially good the few days on either side of this date.

The Second Contingency

At e several articles belonging to other children were found in Mike's locker and he was denied his visit. This was followed by ten days of nonstealing. At f, the supervisor, disturbed at the increasing rate in the previous days in spite of the contingency, urged the child-care staff to continue reporting and showed Mike the charts they were keeping, explaining how stealing eliminated his visit for that day.

At g the author was called in to consult. Mike had taken his roommate's jacket on one day and his hairbrush, the next. The child-care workers were concerned about reporting these incidents since it was not uncommon behavior in the home and they did not wish to penalize Mike unfairly. The author discovered at this time that the staff had recently changed, and there were some child-care workers who knew little about the program. The next day, Mike stole a pass key, a serious offense, but was not reported. At h the final meeting with the child-care staff was held at which it was stressed that the contingency must be used consistently and that the recent alternation might make Maria less effective. It was agreed to report the possession of anything not belonging to him. Although this seemed unfair in view of the borrowing behavior of the other children, it was felt that Mike had more to gain by nonborrowing. Beginning at h he was denied Maria for possessing someone's clothing and for the two subsequent incidents involving his roommate's hairbrush and some pictures from the school bulletin board. The last incident involved some toys belonging to another child at the home. Although he promised to return them and not "steal again," Maria was denied.

Nonstealing Behavior

In the consulting sessions, stress had been laid on the positive reinforcement of appropriate alternative behaviors. The staff was urged to praise and otherwise reinforce all of Mike's socially appropriate behavior. This proved difficult for nonstealing, however, and the only solution seemed to be to reinforce at certain intervals as long as he did not steal. The problem was resolved on "bank day" when the children bank part of the money they have earned for chores or otherwise accumulated. At i, instead of banking, Mike divided his money between two boys, stating that it was to replace some articles he had previously taken and lost and announced that he was "not stealing anymore." It was the first instance of denotable "nonstealing" behavior and was heavily reinforced by the supervisor and child-care staff with praise throughout the day.

At j a similar incident occurred. Mike took a textbook he owned to the public school where the teacher questioned him about it. Mike stated that he had not stolen it but bought it. The teacher, aware of the efforts to help him, verified the story, took Mike to the principal and explained the incident. The principal praised Mike for not stealing and being honest and gave him a set of bird pictures for being a "good boy." The display of these brought praise from the child-care staff.

Periodically over the last recorded month, Mike reminded the staff that he had not stolen or lied. Toward the middle of the last recorded month, he asked the child-care supervisor to tell Maria he was going to the carnival with the other boys and would not be able to visit with her. His times with Maria have since dropped to two to three times a week. Anecdotal evidence indicates that his relationships with peers have been improving.

Pants Wetting

At a staffing shortly after it became apparent that Mike had improved, it was suggested that he might have begun to wet his pants. A child-care worker thought he detected dampness. Many staff members agreed that pants wetting might be a substitute acting-out behavior to replace the stealing. Recording was begun to determine the increase. As Figure 33-1 shows, there have been no wet pants since the date of the first record.

Discussion

If, as suggested, the professional individual is to spend increasing amounts of time instructing others in the application of behavior principles, effective methods of consultation must first be developed. Most often, the individual who is to mediate the change in behavior is unsophisticated in behavioral techniques. In some cases (Boardman 1962, Wolf 1965), the "mediator" is simply given a set of specific instructions by the consultant who maintains frequent contact, often by phone, to insure that the instructions are carried out. This can be effective when the number of mediators involved is small (e.g., parents), but is inefficient if the number of individuals involved is large as in the study above, which involved sixteen people. It seemed desirable in this case to give the group enough of a foundation in behavior techniques to allow it to function at least semiautonomously. For this reason, the brief training session was instituted.

The training presented several difficulties. The time available and the educational backgrounds of most of the individuals prohibited anything but a rather superficial review of behavior principles. As such, the principles sounded deceptively simple and commonsensical and the systematic characteristic of the techniques tended to be missed. It was difficult, for example, for the child-care workers to understand the necessity of reinforcing immediately and consistently. Reinforcement was anything but systematic at the beginning of the program. The study points up the need for long-range staff-improvement programs in behavior principles and techniques if these are to be applied at the institutional level. The development of these can be an important part of the consultant's role.

The training of mediators in the observation and recording of behavior is essential. Accurate records can detect changes in behavior which otherwise might be missed and provide daily feedback on program effectiveness. The use of behavior records presented difficulties for the staff in this study, initially. First of all, recordkeeping disrupted ongoing routines and was viewed as bothersome. Further, some tended to regard them as a "criminal record" and were hesitant to report stealing incidents for fear of getting Mike into trouble. Eventually, however, the record came to be the principal source of reinforcement to the child-care workers since it provided feedback on their effectiveness. Thus, training mediators in recordkeeping not only provides the consultant necessary information but also provides a source of reinforcement for the mediator himself. The consultant can make his praise contingent on a good record or approximations to it.

Maintaining a systematic program involving several people is made considerably easier if the consultant can find an individual to act as coordinator. For example, in this case the supervisor of the child-care workers was invaluable. It is particularly important to be advised of important changes in the environment, illnesses, changes in personnel, and the like. Also, a coordinator can do much toward insuring that records are kept and the contingencies applied. This relieves the consultant from a great deal of legwork.

If the behavior is to be modified by reinforcement contingencies, the choice of the reinforcer is crucial. The consultant must evaluate the availability of effective reinforcers in the environment and his ability to make them contingent on specific behavior. In situations where the target behavior is maintained by recognizable and controllable reinforcers, extinction coupled with reinforcement of alternate behavior is probably most desirable, as Bandura (1962) suggests. Punishment of the behavior tends to be used more when the consequences maintaining the behaviors are unknown or uncontrollable. Punishment, however, is not only not permissible in many settings but also has several undesirable side effects (Bandura 1962). Removal of a positive reinforcer, as in this study, is usually not so aversive, often more natural, and within the permissible range. It can also be used when the maintaining consequences are unknown. In all cases special care should be taken to encourage mediators to reinforce desirable alternate behaviors.

The use of relationships as a source of reinforcement has long been a part of behavior modification. "Building rapport" is one way of establishing a reinforcer, as in this study. The consultant should be on the lookout for naturally existing reinforcers in the environment of the target individual. Maria, the reinforcer used in this example, was a "natural." She required no training in how to become reinforcing to

Mike. Her usual warmth and interest were entirely sufficient and the training of Maria, upon whom the success of the program rested, took no more than twenty minutes. The important factor was to make the relationship contingent on Mike's nonstealing. Just providing Mike with a warm mother figure, as suggested in his earlier therapy, was not sufficient. Even though his stealing rate dropped immediately after he began his visits with Maria, it quickly rose again. As a mother of a hospitalized patient known to the author recently remarked, "It's not just loving; it's what you love them for."

It is probably desirable to keep generalizability in mind when selecting reinforcers. Mike's nonstealing behavior appears to be coming under the control of the child-care worker and peer relationships which may be effective enough to maintain it. Whether or not his nonstealing can be maintained outside of the Children's Home is questionable. However, it can be now stated with some degree of assurance that Mike's stealing is sensitive to its consequences and at least one effective consequence can be specified. Such information should prove useful when future placement is considered for Mike, so that, whatever environment is eventually selected, socially appropriate behaviors leading toward a more rewarding life for Mike can be developed and maintained.

Finally, it should be pointed out that the successful application of behavioral techniques to the modification of deviant behavior probably depends on several conditions not specified by principles of reinforcement. For example, in the middle of this study Mike was shown the charts and informed of how his stealing eliminated a visit with Maria for the day. Although this event was not dictated by reinforcement principles, it very well might have influenced the effectiveness of the contingency. James and Rotter (1958), in fact, have demonstrated that the reinforcing value of a stimulus may be a function of whether or not the subject perceives the reinforcement to depend on his own behavior (skill) or the whims of the environment (chance). Likewise, contingencies imposed in a natural setting tend to generate several changes in the articulation of an individual and his environment well beyond the scope defined by the target behavior. The nature of these changes and their contribution to the outcome are seldom described or evaluated in most studies of environmental manipulation. Thus, though the technique of intervention may be the establishment of a particular reinforcement contingency, several other factors must be considered if the success of the technique is to be evaluated. So far, these additional conditions have been "played by ear" or handled through "clinical intuition." The James and Rotter study and others (Phares 1957, 1962, Rotter et al. 1961) indicate that conditions which augment or limit the effectiveness of environmental manipulation can be specified and suggest that behavioral principles can be extended eventually into a technology of intervention.

References

Ayllon, I., and Michael, J. (1959). The psychiatric nurse as a behavioral engineer. *Journal of Experimental Analysis of Behavior* 2:323-334.

Bandura, A. (1962). Punishment revisited. *Journal of Consulting Psychology* 26:298-301.

Boardman, W. K. (1962). Rusty: a brief behavior disorder. *Journal of Consulting Psychology* 26:293-297.

Harris, F. R., Wolf, M. M., and Baer, D. M. (1964). Effects of adult social reinforcement on child behavior. *Young Children* 20:8-17.

James, W. H., and Rotter, J. B. (1958). Partial and 100% reinforcement under chance and skill conditions. *Journal of Experimental Psychology* 55:397-403.

Phares, E. J. (1957). Expectancy changes in skill and chance situations. *Journal of Abnormal and Social Psychology* 54:339-342.

—— (1962). Perceptual threshold decrements as a function of skill and chance expectancies. *Journal of Psychology* 53:339-407.

Phillips, E. L. (1960). Parent–child psychotherapy: a follow-up study comparing two techniques. *Journal of Psychology* 49:195-202.

Reinforcement in Learning and Extinction. (1956). (film). New York: McGraw-Hill.

Rotter, J. B., Liverant, S., and Crowne, D. P. (1961). The growth and extinction of expectancies in chance-controlled and skilled tasks. *Journal of Psychology* 52:161-177.

Williams, C. D. (1959). The elimination of tantrum behaviors by extinction procedures. *Journal of Abnormal and Social Psychology* 59:269.

Wolf, M. (1965). Reinforcement procedures and the modification of deviant child behavior. Paper presented at Council on Exceptional Children, Portland, OR.

Wolf, M., Risley, T., and Mees, H. (1964). Application of operant conditioning procedures to the behavior problems of an autistic child. *Behaviour Research and Therapy* 1:305-312.

Wolpe, J. (1958). *Psychotherapy by Reciprocal Inhibition*. Stanford, CA: Stanford University Press.

34

Swearing

JOEL FISCHER AND ROBERT NEHS

One of the major concerns of behavior clinicians is to find naturally occurring and readily available reinforcers to use in their attempts to increase adaptive and decrease unadaptive behaviors. This concern is particularly evident when positive reinforcers are not available and aversive stimuli are used. A wide range of aversive stimuli has been reported in the literature, from spanking and "aversive tickling" to electric shock (Conway and Bucher 1974, Gardner 1969, Greene and Hoats 1971, Hamilton et al. 1967, Kircher et al. 1971, Lovaas et al. 1965, Moore and Barley 1973, Nordquist and Wahler 1973, Risley 1968, Saposnek and Watson 1974).

Unfortunately, many of the aversive stimuli used in these studies are so esoteric, complicated, or expensive as to be unavailable to most therapists working in the natural environment (e.g., the equipment necessary to use faradic stimulation). Furthermore, such stimuli present problems when attempting to teach their use to nonprofessionals, such as parents or teachers. And, of course, such stimuli often have ethical drawbacks or questions that limit their use. Hence, especially for problems that are not so severely maladaptive and difficult to diminish that they require extraordinary measures, there is a continuing search for aversive stimuli that do not present any of these problems, that is, which are readily available, easily taught, and contain few ethical questions as to their use. This study describes the use of one such aversive stimulus—the assignment of a disliked chore contingent on the performance of undesired behavior.

Method

Subject and Problem

The subject of this study was Mark, an 11-year-old boy, who attended the Salvation Army facilities for children in Honolulu, Hawaii. Mark could swear profusely at the dinner table. This behavior was particularly unnerving to the cottage parents, and no amount of coaxing or persuasive argument by them had any appreciable effect on Mark's swearing. The second author was then consulted for help in decreasing Mark's swearing.

Behavior Measure

Mark spent weekends at home and arrived on campus Monday mornings, leaving again on Friday evenings. Thus, the reporting periods cover those five-day blocks of time. The cottage parent in charge simply counted the number of times Mark swore during the thirty-minute dinner period for several five-day periods during this study. A second cottage parent also recorded the number of times Mark swore during the same period. Five reliability checks were conducted during this study yielding a rate of 100 percent agreement between the raters.

Treatment and Experimental Procedure

Baseline (A)

The number of times Mark swore during each dinner period was recorded each day for five days before intervention.

Intervention (B)

On the sixth day, Mark was informed that he would have to wash the windows in the cottage for ten minutes for each time he swore. (Washing windows was normally done by housekeeping personnel.) A punishment hierarchy was established and Mark was informed that his privileges would be curtailed if he were not to complete the window-washing assignment.

Baseline 2 (A)

After two weeks on the window-washing contingency, the cottage parents informed Mark that because he had done such a good job in cutting down on his swearing, the window-washing contingency would be removed.

Intervention 2 (B)

At the start of the fifth week (Day 21) of the study, the cottage parents informed Mark that washing windows was once again contingent upon swearing during the dinner period.

Post Check

The cottage parents recorded the number of times Mark swore on six of the fifteen days following termination of the program.

Results

Figure 34-1 summarizes changes in Mark's swearing behavior over the course of the study. During Baseline 1, Mark swore an average of 10.8 times during each dinner period. During the ten days of Intervention 1, Mark swore a total of thirteen times, or an average of less than once (0.76) per day. However, most of these occurrences (nine of thirteen) took place on the first day of the program, and were likely a function either of Mark's "getting acquainted" with or testing the program. During Baseline 2, Mark's swearing increased to an average of 4.5 times per dinner period. During the final intervention period, Mark's swearing dropped immediately to zero and remained there. In neither of the intervention periods was curtailment of privileges necessary. Post check on six of the fifteen days following termination of the program revealed only four swearing incidents. Informal discussion with the

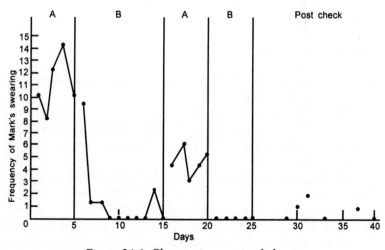

Figure 34-1. Changes in swearing behavior

cottage parents verified that this pattern of little or no swearing was maintained for the rest of the year.

Discussion

This study shows that Mark's swearing behavior could be rapidly and considerably decreased if that behavior resulted in his having to wash windows. It appears that washing windows, combined with the threat of loss of privileges if the window-washing was not completed, was indeed a sufficiently potent aversive stimulus for Mark to learn quickly to avoid it by decreasing his swearing behavior. However, future research is needed to examine the effects of these two procedures separately and in combination. Furthermore, informal discussion with the cottage parents revealed a "natural" increase in the amount of social reinforcement in the form of praise for Mark for making it through a dinner period without swearing. This condition was continued after termination of the formal program and was likely a factor in helping maintain the low rate of swearing.

The use of chores or other aversive tasks can serve as at least one source of aversive stimuli for use in the natural environment, and can be more readily acceptable to nonprofessionals than artificial or potentially harmful stimuli. It should be noted, however, that this was a chore to which Mark ordinarily would not be assigned. In order to avoid unnecessary pairing of everyday chores with possible negative reactions it would seem unwise to assign as punishment tasks or activities in which the individuals would be expected to engage in the ordinary course of events.

References

Conway, J., and Bucher, B. (1974). Soap in the mouth as an aversive consequence. *Behavior Therapy* 5:154–156.

Gardner, W. I. (1969). Use of punishment procedures with the severely retarded: a review. *American Journal of Mental Deficiency* 74:86–103.

Greene, R. J., and Hoats, D. (1971). Aversive tickling: a simple conditioning procedure. *Behavior Therapy* 2:389–393.

Hamilton, J., Stephens, L., and Allen, P. (1967). Controlling aggressive and destructive behavior in severely retarded institutionalized residents. *American Journal of Mental Deficiency* 7:825–856.

Kirchner, A. S., Pear, J. J., and Martin, G. L. (1971). Shock as a punishment in a picture-naming task with retarded children. *Journal of Applied Behavior Analysis* 4:227–233.

Lovaas, O. I., Schaffer, B., and Simmons, J. Q. (1965). Experimental studies in childhood schizophrenia: building social behaviors using electric shock. *Journal of Experimental Research in Personality* 1:99–109.

Moore, B. L., and Barley, J. S. (1973). Social punishment in the modification of a pre-school child's "autistic-like" behavior with a mother as therapist. *Journal of Applied Behavior Analysis* 6:497, 507.

Nordquist, M. V., and Wahler, R. G. (1973). Naturalistic treatment of an autistic child. *Journal of Applied Behavior Analysis* 6:79–87.

Risley, T. R. (1968). The effects and side effects of punishing autistic behaviors of a deviant child. *Journal of Applied Behavior Analysis* 1:21–34.

Saposnek, D. T., and Watson, L. S. (1974). The elimination of the self-destructive behavior of a psychotic child: a case study. *Behavior Therapy* 5:79–89.

35

Firesetting

CORNELIUS J. HOLLAND

Case Report

Robert was a 7-year-old boy, the oldest of three children, whose parents were referred to a psychiatric clinic by a private physician in order to receive counseling for family difficulties, the most distressing of which was Robert's habit of setting fires in the home. Since no child therapists were available at the time, Robert was placed on a waiting list, but his parents, both high school graduates, were placed in a married-couples group for the discussion of marital and family difficulties. The author was the group therapist and saw the couple for approximately a year, once weekly. The child was not seen by the author.

It soon became apparent that the firesetting problem was reaching increasingly serious proportions in terms of frequency and possibility of disaster for the family. Three months after the parents started the group, Robert was setting fires once or twice weekly. Usually the opportunities occurred on mornings of weekends whenever matches were available and the parents were still in bed or out of the house. Matches were either carelessly left around the home or Robert would find them in the street and hide them until an opportunity arose. Punishments such as being slapped, locked in his room, or touched with a smoldering object were successful for only short periods. Both parents, but the mother especially, by this time felt helpless and enraged, so that she and Robert exchanged very little affection, and apparently avoided each other as much as possible. The mother saw the child as an oppressive duty and her feelings of impotence and anger made it difficult for her to express anything positive toward him. Her attempts to control his behavior were almost exclusively through aversion. The father was able to be affectionate but his feelings of helplessness in coping with the problem often erupted into anger and physical punishment. The author at this time decided to attempt a more active intervention and saw the parents five times alone following the group session.

The problem was conceptualized as follows:

1. Some reinforcer obviously was maintaining the behavior. The reinforcer was never determined although many possibilities came to mind, some through the psychological and social history reports, and were available for speculation.
2. The behavior occurred only under discriminative conditions of presence of matches and absence of parents.
3. One goal was to make firesetting behavior a discriminative situation for effective punishment, thus suppressing the behavior.
4. A second goal was to strengthen the operant of bringing matches into the presence of the parents when the parents were available. This of course would prevent firesetting.
5. A third goal was to strengthen non-striking behavior when matches were available but the parents were not present to dispense reinforcers. This goal was designed to control Robert's firesetting behavior in the neighborhood, or in the home when the parents were away.

Procedures

Since the mother saw little hope in changing Robert and was not willing to participate initially, the following program was carried out by the father.

1. Robert had just been given a new baseball glove which he valued highly. The father told Robert that if he set any more fires he would lose the glove irrevocably. The father said he would either give it away or destroy it in Robert's presence. It was hoped that this rather drastic threat, to Robert, would induce a strong suppression of the behavior long enough for adaptive behavior to be instituted. This hope was realized. The tactic was also used to help make firesetting a discriminative situation for a significant loss.

2. At the same time, the father told Robert that if matches or match covers were found around the house they were to be brought to the father immediately. That same evening the father conspicuously

placed on a table an empty packet. It was assumed this was of little value to Robert, so that compliance with the father's commands would be readily emitted. When Robert brought the empty packet he was immediately given 5 cents and told he could now go to the store and spend it if he wished, which he did. These instructions were given to enhance the reinforcing properties of any money Robert was to receive during the program. During the same evening and for the next few evenings the father placed around the house packets containing matches which Robert promptly brought to him. Robert was put on a continuous reinforcement schedule for about eight trials with varying magnitudes of reinforcers, from 1 to 10 cents. He was also told during this phase of the program that he was not to expect money every time. Very shortly the desired behavior was occurring at a high frequency, so that matches or covers found outside during the day were saved and brought to the father when he returned from work. By this time the mother became interested in the program and began to reinforce Robert when he brought matches to her, although she said she found it somewhat difficult to reward the child for behavior incompatible with what "he should not have been doing in the first place."

3. The possibility remained that Robert would find matches outside the home when neither parent was available for dispensing reinforcers. A procedure to strengthen non-striking behavior (or anything but striking) was started after the match-bringing behavior was believed to be strongly established. The procedure used was an approach-approach conflict. One evening about a week after the start of the program the father told Robert he could strike a full packet of matches if he wished, under the father's supervision. The father also placed twenty pennies beside the pack and told Robert that for every match unstruck he would receive one penny. Conversely one penny was removed for every match used. The first trial resulted in Robert striking ten matches and receiving ten pennies. The second trial the following evening earned Robert seventeen pennies, and the third trial, twenty pennies. Thereafter Robert systematically refrained from striking matches. The father then told Robert he was not going to know what he would receive if he did not strike a match and varied the reward for the next few trials from no money to 10 cents.

4. Throughout this program the father was instructed (it is likely he would have done so nevertheless) to give social reinforcers with the monetary rewards, so that desired behavior was brought under control of a more relevant reinforcer.

Results

The first three weeks of the program were spent in developing the procedures, while the remaining two were spent in making minor modifications and discussing progress. The program was begun by the father at the end of the second week, and by the fifth week the habit was eliminated. The parents remained in the group until the author left the city eight months later. During this period the behavior did not recur, neither in the home nor from all evidence in the neighborhood. It was observed during the remaining months that without further guidance the father applied a variable ratio schedule for the money reinforcer.

Secondary results developed which were unexpected but gratifying. The mother was surprised with the changes she was observing and participated to some extent in the procedures described above. In addition, she began to apply some of the principles on her own to some problems involving Robert's disobedience. Although a program was not developed for this problem, the mother proved to be effective in applying the principles with desired results. Also by this time the procedures were a topic for group discussion, and created much interest and support for the mother. With her increased sense of adequacy in dealing with problem behavior, she began to relax her aversive control and was able to express affection for Robert, something which rarely occurred prior to this time.

Discussion

The growing evidence of the possibility of replicating the results obtained in this case history is too impressive to dismiss lightly (see Russo 1964, Wahler et al. 1965). Shortly after the above case, for example, the author had an opportunity to work with another group of parents (four couples) all of whom had come to the clinic for problems involving their children, such as "pathological" lying, disobedience, hyperactivity, and aggression against siblings. Following the success with Robert and other cases, the author defined the latter group as one employing directive parental counseling, applied operant principles systematically to analyses of the problems, taught the parents procedures for remediation, and achieved similar success. At times it was embarrassing to discuss with the rest of the staff changes in a child brought about by the parents. After much preliminary preparation by social workers, the psychological workup, the psychiatric evaluation, the ensuing staffings, the speculations and interpretations, and the often immense resulting gap between diagnosis and treatment, the problem was amenable to control within a relatively short period of time, within weeks or a few months. Although much research is needed in this area, such as a study of those personality variables of the parents which best predict success with this method, it promises to contribute at least to the amelioration of the manpower shortage in an important treatment area.

References

Russo, S. (1964). Adaptations in behavioral therapy with children. *Behaviour Research and Therapy* 2:43–47.

Wahler, R. G., Winkel, G. H., Peterson, R. F., and Morrison, D. C. (1965). Mothers as behaviour therapists for their own children. *Behaviour Research and Therapy* 3:113–124.

PART VI
Peer Problems

36

Sibling Rivalry

CAROLE E. CALLADINE

After fourteen years of leading parent education groups, it became apparent to the author that two child-rearing topics usually dominate the agenda. Parents are universally concerned about how to discipline children effectively, and how to manage sibling rivalry among brothers and sisters.

The popular parenting literature abounds with books on discipline. Little is written for parents, however, on sibling rivalry, behavior so labeled by psychoanalyst Dr. Alfred Adler in the early 1920s (Sutton-Smith and Rosenberg 1970). Therefore, the development of a theoretical framework to define and manage sibling rivalry in the family group for use for parent education became a professional challenge. The following framework, grounded in social groupwork principles combined with the application of child development knowledge, resulted from attempts to meet that challenge. The framework is based on the belief that sibling rivalry is inevitable but manageable in the family group.

Rivalry Styles

Sibling rivalry can take three different forms depending on how siblings learn to share the parent relationship, for at the heart of all sibling rivalries is the difficulty children have in sharing their parents. The parent–children relationship determines the predominant tone of the sibling relationship.

The three forms of sibling rivalry are identified and labeled as follows:

Heir/Heiress

The siblings perceive that one child is the parent's favorite. The heir apparent constantly receives the most parental attention, as the siblings see it.

Competitors

The siblings perceive that the parent-favored child changes depending on current behavior. The children constantly compete to get the most parental attention.

Peers

The siblings perceive that each is recognized as special to the parent and that they, the siblings, are important to each other as family members.

Naturally, peer sibling rivalry is the recommended form for families. Leadership styles, the family judicial system, contracting, and group discipline techniques are teachable skills to enable parents to make peer sibling rivalry the predominant sibling relationship.

Leadership Styles

Parents are the leaders of their families. Styles of leadership vary from parent to parent, but they can be divided into three categories: laissez-faire, autocratic, and democratic. Leadership studies by Lippitt and White (quoted in Krech and Crutchfield 1948) demonstrate the effects of differing leadership styles on group participants. These related leadership studies are particularly useful because the studied population was children.

Laissez-Faire

The laissez-faire leader offers no direction. The children are to manage their relationships and club projects as best they can on their own. Lippitt and White (1943) concluded that an aura of hopelessness and frustration marked laissez-faire groups. The children's projects were never completed and the work space was always marred by confusion. The children themselves gave a low rating to this leadership style.

Autocratic

The autocratic leader is in complete charge. He or she makes all the group decisions and has absolute control over the children's roles. The autocratic leadership groups were the most efficient groups; the children finished the most projects. However, Lippitt and White (1943) noted that when the children were given their projects to take home, they often tossed them around and broke them. It was observed that the children became silly and often aggressive with one another when the leader left the room; work on projects stopped. These were also the only groups in which some children were scapegoated and actually left the group. In spite of the scapegoating, the majority of the children rated autocratic leadership high; they felt secure.

Democratic

The democratic leader involves the children in the decision-making process. The children discuss and vote on the projects to be made and their role assignments. This involvement of the children in decision making produced positive group behavior. For instance, when a democratic leader left a room, a spirit of cooperation among the children remained; work on projects continued smoothly. Productivity was not as high as in the autocratic leadership groups, but the projects were the most creative. When given their projects to take home, the children spoke of using them as gifts or putting them on display.

These studies of children's groups enhance parents' understanding of different forms and values of leadership. Correlating leadership styles with the three defined forms of sibling rivalry focuses parents' understanding (Table 36–1).

	Leadership Styles		
	Laissez-faire	*Autocratic*	*Democratic*
Sibling rivalries	The Heir Apparent's wishes rule. Adult leadership is absent.	The Competitors compete for roles and attention.	The Peers learn to work together as each has an impact on the decision-making process.

Table 36–1. Leadership effects on sibling rivalry.

The varying leadership needs of the family group are stressed. For instance, in the many situations in which preschoolers have little judgment and few coping skills, they will need autocratic leadership. However, democratic leadership principles can help preschoolers mature when they are offered appropriate and limited choices. As parents' awareness of leadership styles increases, they can choose the form needed by the children in different situations.

The Family Judicial System

After helping parents become aware of sibling and leadership styles, a discussion of how family disputes are handled can be initiated. In an autocratic leadership role, for example, the parent becomes either the judge or referee when there is a sibling dispute. The parent listens to all sides and makes a reasonable decision. In this judge or referee climate, the competitive form of sibling rivalry is increased as the children clamor to be heard and get their way. One sibling usually feels he or she has won. Sometimes, each child feels that the other sibling(s) got the better deal.

To foster the peer sibling relationship, the *mediator parent* judicial role is recommended. The mediator parent becomes the facilitator of communication in the problem-solving process by moderating the children's discussion. When two or more siblings are in a dispute, the mediator parent emphasizes problem solving as an accomplishment for the sibling group. The first task of the mediator is to clearly state the problem in one sentence. Sibling solutions to the problem are then requested. The mediator should not allow the discussion to get sidetracked by name-calling, unrelated issues, or personality traits of the participants. The mediator keeps the discussion focused on problem solving.

For instance, if two sisters are fighting over the choice of music to be played on the family stereo, the parent mediator stabilizes the discussion by not taking sides and by encouraging the sisters to discuss their differences and needs until they arrive at a compromise solution. If they cannot work out an agreement, the privilege of using the stereo can be lost to both until a later discussion can resolve the issue.

Contracting

When there is a repetitive sibling dispute, the mediator parent can be taught to use contracting skills. For instance, if the sisters were arguing daily over the use of the stereo, a contract over the shared use of the stereo could be helpful. The contract emphasizes to the siblings that the decision-making process is their responsibility and that each sib is important to the other.

Steps to writing a family contract are:

1. Be clear on the purpose of the contract. A contract should be limited to one specific request, one definable piece of behavior, or use of one shared time.
2. Gather the concerned parties, choosing a convenient time for all involved. Tempers should be in check.
3. The mediator should define the goal(s) of the contract.
4. Allow for and encourage discussion by all participants. If a heated disagreement occurs, without resolution, set up another meeting date and adjourn.
5. The settling of the bargain is the next step. An agreed-upon plan should emerge. Not only should an agreement be reached, but the consequences of not honoring the contract should be included.
6. The contract should be put in writing as a memory aid.
7. Date the contract and set a renewal date.
8. The actual signing of the contract by all participants is important. Their signatures signify their commitment.
9. Post the contract as a visual reminder.

The mediator parent teaches children how to solve problems in groups and allows them the privilege and responsibility of finding solutions. The children's ownership of the decisions reached encourages a cooperative spirit among the siblings. In this process, children are taught the importance of being aware of varying viewpoints and the power of the spoken and written word in solving problems.

A further correlation can now be made between the three definitions of sibling rivalry, leadership styles, and the parent's role in resolving sibling disputes (Table 36-2).

Parent role in family judicial system	Declines responsibility	Judge/referee	Mediator contracting
Leadership style	Laissez-faire	Autocratic	Democratic
Sibling rivalry results	Heir/heiress	Competitors	Peers

Table 36-2. Correlation between sibling rivalries, leadership, and family judicial system.

Group Discipline Techniques

Group discipline techniques also encourage the growth of peer sibling rivalry. These techniques emphasize the group members' interactions rather than focusing on individual behavior. Every child present has a responsibility to help family members get along.

The following are examples of group discipline techniques for parents:

1. Take away a relevant privilege from the siblings when family rules are abused. For instance, if there is constant bickering while watching television, the privilege of watching television is taken away for a specific time period.
2. Role-play a sibling scene. Have the children change places to discover how the other sib feels.
3. Fistfighting between siblings to resolve an issue is taboo in establishing peer sibling rivalry. If a sib loses self-control and tries to physically abuse a sibling, one of the following measures is recommended. Securely hold from behind the out-of-control child to assure every sibling that no one is allowed to hurt or get hurt in the family. Isolate the siblings from each other until everyone is calm. Or give suitable work assignments to angry siblings to channel this aggression and get constructive use from powerful drives. Teach children the power of words to work out agreements, compromises, and contracts. Expect them to resolve their differences.
4. Disciplining siblings works best when parents' feelings are under control. A calm, reasonable approach and voice are needed in changing an undesirable sibling interaction.
5. Descriptive praise is useful in reinforcing admirable sibling behavior. Story hour, individualized car rides, a walk, or bedtime provide natural opportunities for a parent to reflect on specific, positive sibling behavior that was noticed that day. It is not recommended that the children's positive behavior be interrupted by praise. The children may feel that since they have just done so well, they cannot do better. Their cooperative interaction can then disintegrate.

Summary

Through parent leadership based on democratic principles, the development of the mediator role and use of contracting in resolving sibling disputes, and the use of group discipline techniques, peer sibling rivalry can predominate and flourish in families. The theoretical framework of peer sibling rivalry has been evaluated as extremely helpful by parents enrolled in family education discussion groups. It fosters the supportive sibling bonding process that parents want to promote to enhance lifelong, caring sibling relationships.

References

Krech, D., and Crutchfield, R. S. (1948). *Theory and Problems of Social Psychology*. New York: McGraw-Hill.

Lippitt, R., and White, R. K. (1943). The "social climate" of children's groups. In *Child Behavior and Development*, ed. R. Barker, J. Kounin, and H. Wright. New York: McGraw-Hill.

Sutton-Smith, B., and Rosenberg, B. G. (1970). *The Sibling*. New York: Holt, Rinehart & Winston.

37

Modification of Deviant Sibling Interactions

K. DANIEL O'LEARY, SUSAN O'LEARY, AND
WESLEY C. BECKER

Introduction

There have been many demonstrations in clinic settings of the application of a functional analysis of behavior to children's disorders (Ferster 1967a,b, Lovaas et al. 1965, Wahler et al. 1965, Wolf et al. 1964). However, applications of behavioral principles in the home have been limited (Hawkins et al. 1966, Williams 1959). With the increasing emphasis on the diagnosis and modification of behavior in situ, it is probable that in the future, behavior therapists will concentrate on the stimulus situations in which the problem behavior is most likely to be emitted. Ultimately it is the parental environment which must maintain the child's behavior, and behavior reinforced in the clinic will be extinguished if parents do not provide the contingencies to maintain it. On the other hand, if behavior extinguished in the clinic receives parental attention, it is likely that the problem behavior will be quickly reinstated. Therefore, direct modification of children's behavior by parents under a clinician's guidance would seem to be a very useful approach.

This case study demonstrates the application of a set of procedures selected to produce efficiently behavior change in two deviant siblings. The procedures combined prompting, shaping, and instructions to increase cooperative behavior. This behavior was reinforced initially by M & M candies and later by points which could be exchanged for small toys. In the latter half of the study, time-out from positive reinforcement (TO) was used to weaken some deviant behavior which was not reduced by the reinforcement of the incompatible cooperative behavior. TO was in the form of an isolation period (Hawkins et al. 1966, Wolf et al. 1964). Because of the exploratory nature of the application of these procedures in the home, the interactive behavior of two boys was first brought under control by the experimenter. Later this control was transferred to the boys' mother.

Subjects

A 6-year-old boy, Barry A., and his 3-year-old brother, Jeff, were the two subjects in this study. Both parents are university faculty members, and they have a third son who is 2 years old.

Psychiatric History

Barry had been under psychiatric treatment for two years and was described by his psychiatrist as "seriously disturbed." He was reported to be extremely hyperactive, aggressive, and destructive. His EEG was symmetric and within normal limits. Although it was not possible to give him an intelligence test, the psychiatrist felt that his intelligence was within normal limits. He was diagnosed as an "immature, brain-damaged child with a superimposed neurosis," although the nature and cause of his brain damage could not be specified.

Parental Report

According to Mr. and Mrs. A., Barry fought with his brother whenever they were alone. He damaged toys and furniture. He had temper tantrums and failed to follow parental instructions. Shortly before Barry was referred to our research unit, he had thrown a rock through a neighbor's window. He roamed away from home, and he would occasionally enter strangers' houses.

Mrs. A. reported that the boys angered her by screaming, yelling, and hurting each other when they were alone in the basement playroom. Consequently, an observer and the experimenter watched the interaction of the two boys when they played in the basement. From these observations it was quickly learned that there was a great deal of commanding behavior by Barry. If Jeff did not follow these commands, he would be coerced physically and often thrown on the floor. They would break each other's toys or constructions, and this would lead to further fighting. From the experimenter's observations in the home, it appeared that parental attention was largely contingent upon high-intensity undesirable responses. Since Mrs. A. usually remained upstairs while the boys were in the basement playroom, only the screaming, yelling, and fighting which could be heard easily received any attention.

On the basis of initial impressions made from the home observations it was decided to focus on the frequency of three general classes of behavior: deviant, cooperative, and isolate. The deviant behavior consisted of kicking, hitting, pushing, name-calling, and throwing objects at each other. The cooperative behavior was asking for a toy, requesting the other's help, conversation, and playing within three feet of one another. Isolate behavior was designated as the absence of verbal, physical, or visual interaction between the boys.

Procedures and Results

The treatment was divided into four stages: the first baseline period, the first experimental period, the second baseline period, and a second experimental period. Observation and treatment occurred approximately three times per week extending from November to March (sickness and vacations precluded some observations).

Base Period I

In order to assess interobserver reliability, the observer and the experimenter made observations on five occasions during the baseline period. The observer and the experimenter sat three feet apart so that it was not possible for one observer to detect the symbols recorded by the other. Observations were made on a twenty-second rate, ten-second-rest basis. Total observation time was approximately thirty minutes each day. The reliabilities were calculated by dividing the number of perfect agreements by the number of different responses observed. A perfect agreement was the presence of the same observed behavior for both raters in a twenty-second interval. The average reliability calculated thus was 0.78. Using two raters, the proportion of agreement in the three general classes of behavior can also be calculated by dividing the smaller score by the larger (Hawkins et al. 1966). Calculated thus, agreement on deviant responses ranged from 0.92 to 1.00 with a mean of 0.95. Agreement on cooperative responses ranged from 0.85 to 1.00 with a mean of 0.92. Agreement on isolate behavior was 1.00.

The experimental arrangement and the absence of a third trained observer made it difficult to obtain reliability checks after the first baseline period. While the failure to obtain reliability checks somewhat weakens the value of these data, the high level of initial reliabilities clearly demonstrates that the coding system could be objectively applied. The reported data are all based on the observations of the same observer.

Base period observations were made only when Mrs. A. was not in the playroom. She was, however, allowed to come down to the playroom to discipline the children as she saw fit, since the observers did not talk or interact with the children. Such times were simply excluded from the observations.

During the first baseline period (Figure 37–1), the frequency of cooperative behavior divided by the total frequency of cooperative and deviant behavior yielded percentages ranging from 39 to 57 percent with a mean of 46 percent. Although the percentage of cooperative behavior on the graph shows a slight rise, the percentage of cooperative behavior calculated on the basis of cooperative, deviant, and isolate behavior was actually declining. However, it was decided to graph only cooperative behavior as a percentage of cooperative behavior plus deviant behavior because our experimental operations were aimed at changing the topography of whatever interaction occurred, and isolate behavior is not an interaction.

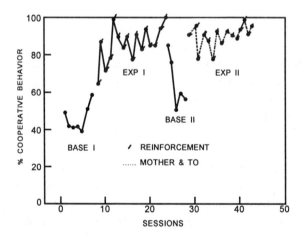

Figure 37–1. Percentage of cooperative behavior divided by the percentage of deviant and cooperative behavior.

Experimental Period I

During the first two days of the experimental period, cooperative responses emitted by either child were continually reinforced by the experimenter who put an M & M candy in the child's mouth and si-multaneously said "Good." The cooperative responses which were re-inforced were any instance of verbal utterances such as asking for a toy, requesting the other's help, and saying "Please" and "Thank you." On the third and fourth day the experimenter alternately reinforced approximately every second or fourth cooperative response. On the fifth day the boys were instructed that they would receive an M & M if they asked each other for things, if they said "Please" and "Thank you," if they answered each other's questions, and if they played nicely to-gether, for example, building things together, pulling each other in the wagon, taking turns, and carrying out a request. These instructions were repeated on all succeeding days of the experimental periods, and the children were prompted by the experimenter as he felt necessary throughout the study.

The token reinforcement system was also introduced on the fifth day. The boys were told that in addition to getting M & Ms, checks would be put on the blackboard for cooperative behavior and removed for deviant behavior. The blackboard was divided in half by a chalk line to designate separately the checks for Barry and Jeff. When a check was received for one or both boys the experimenter would tell them who was receiving a check. Checks could be exchanged for back-up reinforcers, which consisted of candy bars, bubble gum, caps, kites, comic books, puzzles, and other small toys. Frequent discussions were held with the boys' parents in order to ensure that the toys would indeed serve as reinforcers. The total cost of the token system through-out the treatment procedure was $10.67.

A procedure was used for each child in which the number of checks needed to receive the reinforcer was continually increased. On the twelfth day of the token system the use of M & Ms was discontin-ued, but a back-up reinforcer was always present. However, there were same days when one or the other of the boys did not receive enough checks to obtain a back-up reinforcer. Initially, when the boys did not receive a reinforcer, they cried, screamed, and had violent temper tan-trums. The experimenter simply ignored this behavior and instructed Mrs. A. to do likewise. The purpose of increasing the number of checks to receive a reinforcer was to permit transition to greater delay of rein-forcement without disruption and in order to maintain the high per-centage of cooperative behavior.

The amount of cooperative play was greatly increased during this period (Figure 37-1). As contrasted with the mean percentage of cooperative play during the first baseline of 46 percent, the mean percentage of cooperative play during the first experimental period was 85 percent.

Base Period II

During the second base period, in which the experimenter was absent and only the observer present, the amount of cooperative play gradually declined to a level similar to that of the first baseline (50 percent). This drop in the percentage of cooperative responses demonstrates that the experimenter could utilize instructions, prompts, and a token reinforcement system to control the children's behavior. As in the first base period, mother could intervene as she thought necessary.

Experimental Period II

With the reinstatement of the experimental procedures the amount of cooperative behavior increased markedly. Two days after the second experimental period started, when the boys had resumed their prior percentage of cooperative responding, Mrs. A. was instructed to run the token system exactly as the experimenter had done with two additional features. On the second day, a punishment procedure TO was made contingent upon kicking, hitting, pushing, name-calling, and throwing objects at each other. On the sixth day, a stretch-out of the token system was begun, requiring points to be earned over several days for payoff. As can be seen in Figure 37-1, when the second experimental period was terminated the delay of reinforcement was three days.

To assist Mrs. A. in learning what to do, two hand signals were used by the experimenter to indicate when Mrs. A. was to administer token reinforcers or the punishment procedure. During the second experimental period, the experimenter gradually faded into the background so that Mrs. A. was able to execute the procedures without signals from the experimenter.

Although the percentage of deviant behavior was relatively low during the first experimental period, occasional fights which ended in yelling and screaming occurred and were very disruptive. Since giving and removing checks was not powerful enough to eliminate all of the deviant behavior, a punishment procedure called *time-out from positive reinforcement* (TO) was instituted (Ferster and Appel 1961). The TO procedure consisted of isolating either of the children in the bathroom for the deviant behavior listed above. Everything which could easily be

removed was taken from the bathroom so that the boys had little opportunity to amuse themselves. After some initial resistance upon being taken to the bathroom, both boys accepted the TO without much
argument. They had to remain in the bathroom for at least five minutes. In addition, they had to be quiet for a period of three minutes
before they were allowed to come out. This latter requirement ensured
that termination of TO was contingent upon behavior which the
mother wished to strengthen (being quiet on request) and permitted
TO to function both as a punisher for behavior which led to TO and
a negative reinforcer for behavior which terminated TO.

During the first three days of the TO procedure, TO was used
approximately once a day for each child. It was used at most four times
a day, and during the last four days of the experimental period it was
used only once for Jeff. The decreasing frequency of the need for TO
is indicated in the cumulative record of Figure 37-2.

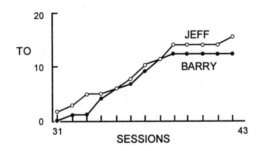

Figure 37-2. Cumulative frequency of TO.

As can be seen in Figure 37-1, this combination of procedures
under mother's control produced high cooperative behavior (90 percent) during the second experimental period.

The application of the TO procedure was restricted to the experimental hour initially, but following the ninth session of the second experimental period (Session 40) when the percentage of cooperative play
seemed relatively stable, Mrs. A. was allowed to use TO at other times.
In addition, following Session 40 the minimum amount of time the
children had to stay in the bathroom was increased to eight minutes.
The number of times TO was used outside the experimental session
fell from three times per day to less than one time every other day over
approximately one month. As can be seen in Figure 37-2, TO was not
needed in the experimental session after Day 40.

Discussion

As mentioned previously, cooperative behavior was represented as a percentage of deviant plus cooperative since our manipulations were aimed at changing the topography of whatever interactions occurred. From a graph of isolate behavior as a percentage of isolate, cooperative, and deviant behavior (Figure 37–3), it can be seen that the changes produced during the first experimental period were not due to a change in the amount of isolate play. That is, the experimental manipulations did not greatly reduce all interactions at the same time that cooperative interactions were made stronger.

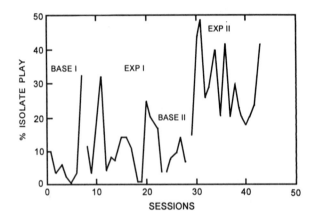

Figure 37–3. Percentage of isolate behavior divided by the percentage of deviant, cooperative, and isolate behavior.

The rise in isolate play during the second experimental period was probably the result of fewer prompts being used by Mrs. A. than by the experimenter. This increase in isolate play was not interpreted as a particularly undesirable outcome because the topography of their interactions had changed markedly. Our aim was to reduce the frequency of the hitting, kicking, pushing, name-calling, and throwing objects, and to increase cooperative interactions. Had we been concerned about a decrease in the frequency of interactions as such, we could have manipulated the contingencies in order to maintain a high level of interaction.

The drop in cooperative play during the second baseline could be attributed to the discontinuance of the token reinforcement system, the instructions, or the prompts. The physical absence of the experimenter during the second baseline period may also have been related to the changes in the behavior observed. Because of the severity of the boys' problems and parental concerns, it was impossible to introduce the experimenter, instructions, prompts, token and back-up reinforcers systematically. Consequently, the relative contributions of each aspect of the treatment cannot be here assessed. Furthermore, Jeff's increasing verbal repertoire probably helped maintain cooperative play as the study progressed. Other equally unknown factors may have accounted for the behavioral changes observed. Thus, this study represents a demonstration rather than an experimental analysis.

It should be made clear that the application of the set of procedures used in this study did not eliminate all deviant behavior. Barry sporadically emitted rough behavior at school and, because of his disruptive outbursts at school, he will be placed in a behavior modification class. Nonetheless, Barry's parents and teacher reported that he progressed markedly during the year. The incidents of hitting and kicking were greatly reduced. He will now ask for things rather than grab them and an anecdotal report indicates that he plays well with a neighbor's child.

The experimental phase of this study was not designed to reprogram the boys' entire environment, but reprogramming could be accomplished in many ways. Following the experimental phase of our work, Mr. and Mrs. A. were instructed to continue the use of TO for hitting, kicking, and pushing. Some of Barry's other behavior, such as his infrequent but repetitive head turning and occasional wild arm swinging, were simply to be ignored. Formerly, Barry had been under a great deal of aversive control and the parents were strongly advised to stop spanking Barry.

As mentioned previously, it was evident from parental report and home observation that many of Barry's low-intensity responses had been extinguished by his parents. However, disruptive behavior of high intensity received attention from both parents and this attention likely reinforced such behavior. In order to reverse this condition, both parents were advised to respond to the children when they were behaving appropriately, not only when they were misbehaving. The importance of praise and affection in maintaining appropriate behavior was repeatedly emphasized. In order to establish and reinforce more appropriate behaviors, Barry now receives a penny each time he makes his bed, and he has been saving this money for small toys.

Barry's enuretic problem was eliminated with the use of a commercially produced alarm device. The alarm is connected to a bed pad, and the alarm rings whenever the child urinates on the pad. Barry had worn diapers every night prior to the use of the alarm device, and he had a long history of failures in attempting to arrest the bedwetting. Consequently, both Barry and his mother were given as much understanding of the treatment process as possible, a realistic appreciation of the possibility of cure and of the demands which the treatment procedures would place upon them. Following Lovibond's account (1964), it was emphasized that about one-third of children whose bedwetting is arrested start wetting again and have to use the device a second time. Thus complete treatment was thought of as requiring the use of the device on two occasions. Records of the treatment were kept, and within seven weeks of starting the treatment Barry was completely dry. A three-month follow-up indicated that there was no relapse.

The fact that this boy, who had been diagnosed "brain damaged," could behave as well as he did astonished his parents. Such evidence should make one very hesitant to use such labels as "brain damaged." Like autism and mental retardation, the label "brain damaged" implies concepts and assumptions which generate attitudes of futility. Bijou's (1965) comment with regard to autism and retardation seems equally important concerning brain damage: "These disturbances, like other forms of psychological behaviors, are undoubtedly determined by multiple conditions—social, physical, and organismic—and, as such, call for not a dismissing label but a challenge for analysis."

The need for further exploration of behavior therapy techniques with children is great. It has been demonstrated that reinforcement techniques are effective in shaping cooperative responses in both normal and schizophrenic children (Azrin and Lindsley 1956, Hingten et al. 1965). However, the study reported here is one of the few demonstrations of behavior modification in the home, and our techniques were devised to meet clinical and research needs as the study progressed. It is evident, however, that the principles of behavior modification can be utilized readily by a parent to change a child's behavior.

References

Azrin, H. H., and Lindsley, O. R. (1956). The reinforcement of cooperation between children. *Journal of Abnormal Social Psychology* 52:100–102.
Bijou, S. W. (1965). Experimental studies of child behavior, normal and de-

viant. In *Research in Behavior Modification*, ed. L. Krasner and L. P. Ullman. New York: Holt. Rinehart & Winston.

Ferster, C. B. (1967a). An operant reinforcement analysis of infantile autism. *American Journal of Psychotherapy.*

———— (1967b). Operant reinforcement in the natural milieu. *Exceptional Children.*

Ferster, C. B., and Appel, J. B. (1961). Punishment of Ss responding in matching to sample by time out from positive reinforcement. *Journal of the Experimental Analysis of Behavior* 4:45, 56.

Hawkins, R. P., Peterson, R. F., Schweid, E., and Bijou, S. W. (1966). Behavior therapy in the home: amelioration of problem parent–child relations with the parent in a therapeutic role. *Journal of Experimental Child Psychology* 4:99–107.

Hingten, J. N., Saunders, B. J., and Demeyer, M. K. (1965). Shaping cooperative responses in early childhood schizophrenics. In *Case Studies in Behavior Modification*, ed. L. P. Ullman and L. Krasner. New York: Holt, Rinehart & Winston.

Lovaas, L., Schaeffer, B., and Simmons, J. (1965). Experimental studies in childhood schizophrenia: building social behaviors in autistic children using electric shock. *Journal of the Experimental Study of Personality* 1:99–109.

Lovibond, S. H. (1964). *Conditioning and Enuresis.* New York: Macmillan.

Wahler, R. G., Winkel, G. H., Peterson, R. F., and Morrison, D. C. (1965). Mothers as behavior therapists for their own children. *Behaviour Research and Therapy* 3:113–124.

Williams, C. D. (1959). The elimination of tantrum behavior by extinction procedures. *Journal of Abnormal Social Psychology* 59:269.

Wolf, M. M., Risley, T., and Mees, H. (1964). Application of operant conditioning procedures to the behavior problems of an autistic child. *Behaviour Research and Therapy* 1:305–312.

38

Social Behavior Problems

MICHAEL L. BLOOMQUIST

The ability to make and keep new friends is absolutely critical for all children. Children with chronic social difficulties are at high risk for social and emotional difficulties that continue into adolescence and adulthood. Your child's ability to form friendships depends in large part on how skilled he is at using social behavior skills. Promoting social behavior skill development may be a good place to start with younger and/or very socially delayed older children. This chapter will give you a few suggestions to improve your child's social skills.

Nobody Likes Me

Tony is a 10-year-old boy who has few friends. His parents, Debbie and Bruce, have received much feedback from school officials about Tony's social behavior. Apparently, he bugs other children and is sometimes aggressive toward them at school. In turn, he seems to be picked on and teased.

At home, Debbie and Bruce notice similar kinds of social interactions with Tony in the neighborhood and with his 8-year-old sister, Kathy. They observe that Tony is frequently bugging other children and Kathy and, again, is rejected, picked on, and teased. Although Tony goes out and plays with children frequently and does okay at first, after a little while it's not uncommon for Tony to come home crying, "Nobody likes me."

What Are Social Behavior Problems?

Many children who have difficulties in the social arena simply do not know how to behave in social situations. These children often exhibit many negative social behaviors, such as hitting, interrupting, bugging, and so forth, and few positive social behaviors, such as making eye contact, expressing feelings, sharing, or cooperating. In order for children to develop friendships, they need to reduce negative social behaviors and increase positive social behaviors. Children typically learn social behavior skills in the toddler, preschool, and early elementary school age years of development. If your child does not possess these skills, he will need to have the skills taught to him.

Teaching Children Social Behavior Skills

The following section describes how parents can help children develop social behavior skills. Social behavior skills training is a good first step toward promoting friendships for younger elementary school age children or for older children who are socially delayed. These procedures can be used to improve children's relationships with parents, siblings, or peers.

Step 1. Identify Social Behaviors to Target with Your Child

There are a variety of social behavior skills you could try to focus on to help your child learn. The first task is to figure out which negative social behaviors your child uses too often and which positive social behaviors your child does not use often enough.

Examples of negative social behaviors include the following:

- Physical aggression (hitting, kicking, etc.)
- Playing unfair
- Arguing
- Interrupting
- Name calling
- Bossing others
- Whining, complaining, and so forth
- Taking others' possessions
- Dominating the activity
- Making poor eye contact
- Being a poor sport
- Being too loud
- Showing off
- Teasing
- Butting in
- Bugging others
- Getting into others' space
- Withdrawing and isolating self
- Being passive
- Listening poorly
- Hoarding food, toys, and so forth
- Keeping feelings inside
- Talking too much
- Disobeying rules of play
- Being too rough in play
- Not handling peer pressure well (i.e., peers influence child to do things he shouldn't)

Examples of positive social behaviors include the following:

- Taking turns
- Sharing
- Expressing feelings
- Cooperating
- Making eye contact
- Starting conversations
- Being assertive
- Listening to others
- Complimenting others
- Accepting compliments
- Following rules of play
- Refusing to cooperate with peers' negative behavior

- Apologizing to others
- Asking questions
- Telling others about self
- Playing fair
- Ignoring when appropriate
- Inquiring about others' interests or desires
- Talking in a brief manner
- Asking for what one wants/needs
- Helping others
- Refusing to do negative things asked by peers

To figure out which behaviors to work on with your child you will need to take some time to observe him in social situations with peers and/or siblings. To get the information you need, it may be necessary to watch your child for several days or weeks in various social situations. You should observe your child in situations in which there is high structure (e.g., boy/girl scouting, sports, church activity, etc.) and low structure (e.g., playing with peers/siblings in the front yard or at the park, etc.). Try to notice how your child is accepted by his peers/siblings. Note whether your child seems to be rejected, neglected, or aggressive with other children. Furthermore, try to note which negative social behaviors your child uses too often and which positive social behaviors your child doesn't use enough (see previous examples of negative and positive social behaviors).

The Parent Observation of Child Social Behavior chart found at the end of this chapter may assist in identifying social behavior targets. This chart simply structures your observations to help you pinpoint negative and positive social behaviors in your child.

Step 2. Collaborate to Help Your Child Understand Social Behavior Problems and Select Target Social Behavior

It is very important to *work with your child* in selecting and working on specific positive social behaviors. It is often a very delicate situation because many children are nervous or defensive about working on social behaviors. At first, you should try to discuss the problem with your child in a supportive manner. Begin by pointing out that he seems to have some difficulty getting along with other children. Don't judge your child, but communicate to him that you would like to help. Explain that you have a plan on how he might be able to get along better with other children and that you would like to work with him to put the plan into action. Don't bother trying to work with your child regarding social behavior skills until this collaborative relationship has been achieved.

It's absolutely critical that your child understand his social behavior difficulties and have input about what to work on. The next step is to pinpoint which specific positive social behaviors your child would like to target. It can be helpful to review a list of possible behaviors (such as in the previous section). Ask for your child's input about which negative social behaviors he thinks he should do less and which positive social behaviors he thinks he should do more. If you think it helpful, share your observations regarding his interactions with other children. Together, select several target positive social behaviors to work on. Ideally the positive behavior selected is the opposite of the negative behavior (e.g., sharing vs. hoarding).

Step 3. Teach Your Child Social Behavior Skills

The next step is to teach your child specific positive social behavior skills. First, explain the targeted positive social behaviors and describe the behaviors in a way he will understand. The next step is to model or demonstrate what the positive social behaviors look like. This involves actual demonstration of the behaviors with your child observing. The next step is to role-play the targeted positive behaviors. Take turns "acting" until your child can demonstrate what the behaviors look like. Usually, after explaining, modeling, and role-playing, most children will have a good understanding of the targeted behaviors.

The following example pertains to teaching a child the positive social behavior of sharing toys. First the parent verbally explains the behavior by saying, for example, "Sharing toys means you let others play with you or you allow others to have some of the toys you have." Modeling in this case would be actual parent demonstrations of sharing behaviors. Finally, the parent would engage the child in role-playing whereby the child demonstrates to the parent what sharing behaviors look like.

Similar explaining, modeling, and role-playing procedures would be used for other social behaviors. Make sure your child understands completely and is able to perform the targeted social behavior before going on to the next step.

Step 4. Coach and Reinforce Desirable Social Behaviors in Real Social Situations

Coaching is critical in actually helping children use their newly acquired social behavior skills in real-life situations. Ideally, you would coach your child when he is in real-life situations. Coaching involves prompting or reminding your child to be aware of, and to perform, more positive social behaviors. The goal is to notice when your child might be having social interaction difficulties and encourage him to utilize the skills he has just learned. You could coach your child to practice the social skills in ongoing parent–child, sibling–child, or peer–child interactions. All of these social interactions provide good opportunities to practice the skills.

It might also be helpful to plan ahead about how your child could work on social behavior skills in future social situations. For example, if a parent knows that a child will be going to a boy or girl scout meeting, the parent and child might plan ways for the child to work on social behavior skills during the meeting.

Reinforcing social behavior can be done in a formal or informal manner. The formal reinforcement could be to give your child a tangible reinforcer for practicing the desired social behavior. The informal reinforcement procedure would involve simply praising your child when he engages in the desired social behaviors.

Step 5a. Implement a Formal Social Behavior Skills Practice Program

The Practicing Social Behavior Skills chart found at the end of this chapter can be used to help your child practice social behavior skills at a specified time during a specified event. This chart has five steps. The first one is to designate which social behavior your child will try to improve during a particular social event. The second step is to note when and where your child will try to engage in this specific social behavior. The third step is for the child to evaluate himself on the 5-point rating scale after the event has occurred. Note that the scale ranges from 1 (Not at all) to 5 (Great). The fourth step requires your child to reflect back and write down what he did to support the rating. The fifth step involves you rating your child and reinforcing him if he did well in practicing the specific social behavior during the event.

The Daily Social Behavior Goals chart at the end of this chapter can be used to help your child practice social skills on an ongoing basis. The chart requires your child to specify one or more social behaviors he will work on each day. At the end of the day, your child rates himself using the 5-point rating system found on the chart to evaluate how well he met his goals. You also rate your child on how he met the social goal and provide reinforcement if he did well.

The Practicing Social Behavior Skills and Daily Social Behavior Goals charts can be used to improve social behaviors in parent–child, sibling–child, and peer–child interactions. You can use either chart depending on what you think will work best for your child. If your child receives ratings of 3 or more on either of the charts, he could earn reinforcement.

Step 5b. Implement an Informal Social Behavior Skills Practice Program

If you prefer, you could use more informal procedures to promote social skill development. Steps 1 to 4 should still be utilized. You could then informally prompt your child to use certain social behaviors. This could be followed by praise as a reinforcement if your child does the desired social behavior.

Teaching Peer Pressure "Refusal" Skills

Many children are negatively influenced by peers. To fit in or be accepted by peers, children will do things such as violate rules or exhibit other problem behaviors. These behaviors could range from showing off to using drugs in response to peer pressure. Indeed, peer influences have much to do with children using drugs, engaging in sex, skipping school, vandalizing, committing crimes, and so forth. Consequently, it is very important for children to learn to refuse peer pressure.

Refusal skills involve a child behaving assertively when pressured by peers to do something he doesn't really want to do. To assist a child in refusal skills, it is important to collaborate with, educate, and train your child how to respond assertively to peers.

Collaborating means you and your child discuss peer pressure and agree to work together to deal with the problem. Identify the areas where your child feels pressure. With younger children, the pressure might be to throw rocks on the playground, goof off in class, tease other children, and so forth. With teens, the pressure might be to use drugs, skip school, break curfew, and so forth. If your child wants to work with you on these pressures, proceed further with education and assertiveness training. If your child does not cooperate, but has problems with peer pressure, then forget refusal skills, and try another procedure in this book or consult with a mental health professional. You may need to set up special rules and/or monitor your child more closely.

Educating involves discussing the potential consequences of submitting to peer pressure with your child. With a younger child, this may involve talking about how certain actions will get him in trouble and maybe could lead to physical harm of others. With an older child or teen, you may be able to take it further, and discuss how certain actions might make someone else feel.

Assertiveness training entails helping the child develop social behaviors to cope with peer pressure. This is best accomplished by *planning, rehearsing, and doing refusal behaviors*. It will help to plan how the child will respond when peer pressure situations come up. Ask your child to "think ahead" and plan what to do next time. This may involve thinking what to say to peers and what to do. For example, a child may plan to say, "No, thanks, I have to go home," and to walk home when peers pressure him to go into a convenience store to steal candy. Roleplaying is a good way to rehearse the refusal skills. You and your child act out various peer-pressure scenarios and the plan your child came up with to deal with the pressure. The role-playing offers a chance to modify the plan if the plan doesn't seem to work. The final, and hardest, step is to do the refusing. Your child is alone on this one. But you can check in with your child and discuss how it's going after each episode. This may present opportunities to modify plans and rehearse new plans.

You may want to use the Daily Social Behavior Goals chart found at the end of this chapter to promote refusal skills in your child. You could list "refusing peer pressure" as the target social behavior on the chart. See the previous section for instructions on how to use the Daily Social Behavior Goals chart.

Other Helpful Social Behavior Skills Training Ideas

Teach Siblings Similar Social Behavior Skills

Although siblings may not display social behavior difficulties with most children, they may do so with their behavior problem sibling. Therefore, it might be beneficial to train siblings to use social behavior skills too. It may also have more of an impact on your child if his siblings are involved.

Orchestrate Situations to Practice Social Behavior Skills

It may be helpful for you to arrange and plan specific activities in which your child can practice social behavior skills. For example, you could plan situations in which your child will be interacting with only one other child (e.g., sleep-over, dinner, trip to the fair, etc.). Once your child has achieved some success in one-to-one situations, you might arrange structured small group activities (e.g., invite several children for a sleep-over, invite a small group of children for a birthday party, etc.). Finally, once your child has achieved success in structured small group activities, you might want to orchestrate larger social situations for your child to practice the social skills behaviors (e.g., larger parties, larger group outings to events, etc.). During all of these activities, you should be involved in coaching and reinforcing your child according to the procedures discussed above.

Enroll Your Child in Specialized Groups

There are certain structured group activities that can help your child develop social behavior skills. Usually group activities without an intensive competitive atmosphere work best, for example, scouting, 4-H, church youth groups, arts and crafts groups, and so forth. Emphasize cooperation and typically have structure, rules, and adult supervision. Look for opportunities to enroll your child in such groups. It may help for you to be actively involved as well.

Some children have a very difficult time with social behavior skills and may not really improve solely from the ideas in this chapter. It may be helpful to enroll some children in a social behavior skills therapy group. These therapy groups provide children with an opportunity to learn and practice these difficult skills in a controlled setting. Consult a mental health professional about social behavior skills groups in your child's school and/or community.

Find Peer Helpers

Many schools have peer helper programs where older children are paired up with younger children so the older one can tutor the younger one in academic areas. This experience also provides a good opportunity to learn and practice social behavior skills. You might inquire at your child's school to see if your child could participate in a peer helper program.

Collaborate with School Officials

Many of the procedures described in this chapter could be used by school personnel who work with your child. If possible, set up a meeting and discuss ways in which you and school officials can work together using a similar system at home and school.

Work with Other Parents

Children who have social behavior problems are often teased and picked on by others. Sometimes a child with a behavior problem is the one doing the teasing. Occasionally, this teasing can get so out of hand that a child or group of children continue to have prolonged and chronic problems interacting with each other.

In these instances, it may be helpful to work with other children's parents. To accomplish this, it is obviously necessary that the other parent be willing to do so. One strategy is for only the parents to meet on their own and discuss ways to help their children get along better. Another strategy is for all parents to meet with all the involved children and work something out. The ultimate solution may be that your children agree to try harder to get along, that parents actively monitor social interactions, and that parents communicate periodically with each other.

Hang in There

Social problems in children are often extremely difficult to change. It can take weeks, months, or even years for a child to use a new skill regularly. Even if your child changes his behavior, others still may not change their opinion of your child due to previous "labeling." For these reasons, you need to work very hard and long. It's going to take time to help your child develop social behavior skills and to be accepted by other children.

Summary Points

1. Poor social relationships are related to children's behavioral and emotional problems.
2. It is critical to collaborate and work with your child in selecting target social behaviors.

3. Teach your child specific social behaviors by explaining, modeling, and role-playing.
4. Coach and reinforce social behavior skills in real-life social situations with your child.
5. Utilize formal practice procedures to help your child really learn social behavior skills.

Somebody Likes Me

Back to Tony and his parents, Debbie and Bruce. The parents decide that drastic measures need to be taken to help Tony develop some social behavior skills. At first, they simply observe Tony at play in the neighborhood, at his Little League baseball practice, and with his sister, Kathy. They observe that Tony seems isolated and by himself at first, and then he starts interacting negatively with other children. He does a lot of interrupting, bossing others, and bugging others, and very little taking turns and sharing. Later, they enlist Tony's cooperation through several discussions, and he agrees to work on social behavior skills. They explain, model, and role-play the targeted behaviors with Tony until he really understands them. Then they utilize the Practicing Social Behavior Skills chart as a formal method of implementing and reinforcing the social behavior skills training. At first they focus on sibling–child interactions, and then on peer–child interactions, using these methods. Tony earns rewards for his efforts. Finally, Debbie and Bruce also talk to the parents of the next-door neighbor's child. All of the parents and their children have a meeting and make some agreements about acceptable and unacceptable social interactions. The parents agree to work together cooperatively to monitor and help the children get along better.

EXAMPLE:
PARENT OBSERVATION OF CHILD SOCIAL BEHAVIOR

Name: *Tony*

Date: *Friday*

Directions: Set aside some time to observe your child interacting with peers and/or siblings. Answer each question below.

1. **What is the social setting of this observation?**

   Playing with children in the park

2. **What kinds of social problems did my child have?**

   At first, he was ignored by other children. Later he interfered in some children's game of baseball.

3. **What negative social behaviors did my child do too much?**

   Physical aggression, butting in, bugging others.

4. **What positive social behaviors did my child not do enough?**

   Taking turns, cooperating, asking questions, inquiring about others' interests and desires.

EXAMPLE:
PRACTICING SOCIAL BEHAVIOR SKILLS

Name: *Tony*

Date: *Saturday*

Directions: The parent and/or child can complete the form, but all involved should discuss it. Complete Steps 1 and 2 before the social event and Steps 3, 4, and 5 after the social event.

Before Social Event

1. **I will work on these social behavior goals:**
   Speaking to other children and making eye contact.

2. **When and where I will work on the social behavior goals** (designate time and place):
   Saturday morning at baseball practice.

After Social Event

3. **How well did I accomplish my social behavior goals?** (circle one)

1	2	3	(4)	5
Not at all	A little	OK	Pretty good	Great
☹		☺		☺

4. **What did I do that tells me how to rate myself?** (Write down how you know you deserve the above rating.)
   I talked to Chris and Steve about the next game. I looked into their eyes when I talked to them. I asked Mr. Jackson to throw some balls to me. I looked into his eyes, too.

5. **If my parent agrees with my rating and it is a 3, 4, or 5, I get this reward:**
   Pizza for supper.

From *Skills Training for Children with Behavior Disorders: A Parent and Therapist Guidebook* by Michael L. Bloomquist. © 1996 The Guilford Press: New York. Used with permission.

EXAMPLE:
DAILY SOCIAL BEHAVIOR GOALS

Name: *Tony*

Date: *Saturday*

Directions: Indicate below which negative and positive social behavior goals you will be working on. At the end of the day, rate how well you accomplished your goals. It may be helpful to get feedback from parents as to how well they think you are accomplishing your goals.

Child Evaluation

1. **I am working on these social behavior goals:**
   Sharing and expressing feelings.

2. **How well did I accomplish my goal?** (circle one)

1	2	3	④	5
Not at all	A little	OK	Pretty good	Great
☹		☺		☺

Parent Evaluation

3. **How well parent thinks child accomplished social behavior goal:** (circle one)

1	2	3	④	5
Not at all	A little	OK	Pretty good	Great
☹		☺		☺

Reward

4. **If my parent rates me as a 3, 4, or 5, I get this reward:**
   Select from reinforcement menu.

Credits

The editors gratefully acknowledge permission to quote material from the following sources:

"An Interview Guide for Counseling Parents," by Cornelius J. Holland, formerly titled "An Interview Guide for Behavioral Counseling with Parents," in *Behavior Therapy* 1:70–79. Copyright © 1970 by the Association for the Advancement of Behavior Therapy.

"A Single Interview," by Esther L. Cava, formerly titled "Training Parents in Behavior Modification during a Single Interview," in *The Behavior Therapist* 14:11–12. Copyright © 1991 by the Association for the Advancement of Behavior Therapy.

"Night Terrors," by Bryan Lask, in *Clinical Handbook of Sleep Disorders in Children*, edited by Charles E. Schaefer, pp. 125–134. Copyright © 1995 by Jason Aronson Inc.

"Night Fears," by Jonathan Kellerman, formerly titled "Rapid Treatment of Nocturnal Anxiety in Children," in *Journal of Behavior Therapy and Experimental Psychiatry* 11:9–11. Copyright © 1980 by Elsevier Science Ltd, Oxford, England.

"General Fears," by Peter J. D'Amico and Alice G. Friedman, formerly titled "Parents as Behavior Change Agents in the Reduction of Children's Fears," in *Innovations in Clinical Practice: A Source Book* 15:323–339, ed. L. Vandecreek, S. Knapp, and T. L. Jackson. Copyright © 1997 by Professional Resource Press.

Index